Kamichama Karin Chu

Koge-Donbo

Translated and adapted by Alethea Nibley and Athena Ni

Lettered by Foltz Design

DEL
REY

Ballantine Books ★ New York

A Del Rey Manga/Kodansha Trade Paperback Original

Kamichama Karin Chu volume 7 copyright © 2008 Koge-Donbo
English translation copyright © 2010 Koge-Donbo

Published in the United States by Del Rey, an imprint of The Random House Publishing Group,
a division of Random House, Inc., New York.

DEL REY is a registered trademark and the Del Rey colophon is a trademark of Random House, Inc.

Publication rights arranged through Kodansha Ltd.

First published in Japan in 2008 by Kodansha Ltd., Tokyo

ISBN 978-0-345-51035-8

Printed in the United States of America

www.delreymanga.com

1 2 3 4 5 6 7 8 9

Translators/adapters: Alethea Nibley and Athena Nibley
Lettering: Foltz Design

CONTENTS

A Word from the Creator

Hello! I'm Koge-Donbo. *Kamichama Karin chu* has reached its climax at last! The Three Noble Gods get mixed up in a terrible fate; can Karin-chan really save the future? And how!? Please, take a look to see how she'll resolve things!

Honorifics Explained

Throughout the Del Rey Manga books, you will find Japanese honorifics left intact in the translations. For those not familiar with how the Japanese use honorifics and, more important, how they differ from American honorifics, we present this brief overview.

Politeness has always been a critical facet of Japanese culture. Ever since the feudal era, when Japan was a highly stratified society, use of honorifics—which can be defined as polite speech that indicates relationship or status—has played an essential role in the Japanese language. When addressing someone in Japanese, an honorific usually takes the form of a suffix attached to one's name (example: "Asuna-san"), is used as a title at the end of one's name, or appears in place of the name itself (example: "Negi-sensei," or simply "Sensei!").

Honorifics can be expressions of respect or endearment. In the context of manga and anime, honorifics give insight into the nature of the relationship between characters. Many English translations leave out these important honorifics and therefore distort the feel of the original Japanese. Because Japanese honorifics contain nuances that English honorifics lack, it is our policy at Del Rey not to translate them. Here, instead, is a guide to some of the honorifics you may encounter in Del Rey Manga.

-san: This is the most common honorific and is equivalent to Mr., Miss, Ms., or Mrs. It is the all-purpose honorific and can be used in any situation where politeness is required.

-sama: This is one level higher than "-san" and is used to confer great respect.

-dono: This comes from the word "tono," which means "lord." It is an even higher level than "-sama" and confers utmost respect.

-kun: This suffix is used at the end of boys' names to express familiarity or endearment. It is also sometimes used by men among friends, or when addressing someone younger or of a lower station.

-chan: This is used to express endearment, mostly toward girls. It is also used for little boys, pets, and even among lovers. It gives a sense of childish cuteness.

Bozu: This is an informal way to refer to a boy, similar to the English terms "kid" and "squirt."

Sempai/
Senpai: This title suggests that the addressee is one's senior in a group or organization. It is most often used in a school setting, where underclassmen refer to their upperclassmen as "sempai." It can also be used in the workplace, such as when a newer employee addresses an employee who has seniority in the company.

Kohai: This is the opposite of "sempai" and is used toward under-classmen in school or newcomers in the workplace. It connotes that the addressee is of a lower station.

Sensei: Literally meaning "one who has come before," this title is used for teachers, doctors, or masters of any profession or art.

-[blank]: This is usually forgotten in these lists, but it is perhaps the most significant difference between Japanese and English. The lack of honorific means that the speaker has permission to address the person in a very intimate way. Usually, only family, spouses, or very close friends have this kind of per-mission. Known as *yobisute*, it can be gratifying when some-one who has earned the intimacy starts to call one by one's name without an honorific. But when that intimacy hasn't been earned, it can be very insulting.

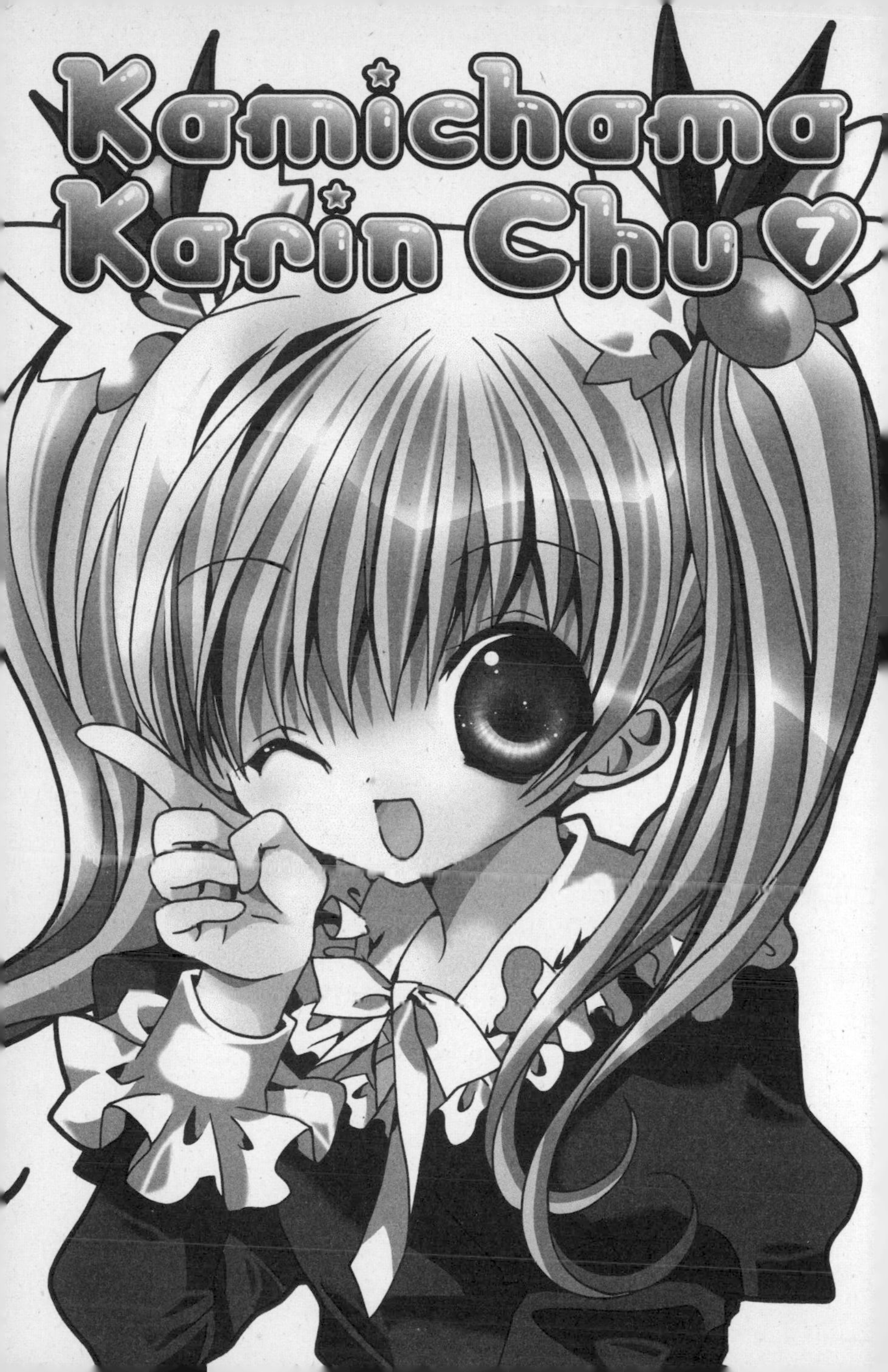
Kamichama
Karin Chu
7

KAMICHAMA CHU WORLD GUIDE

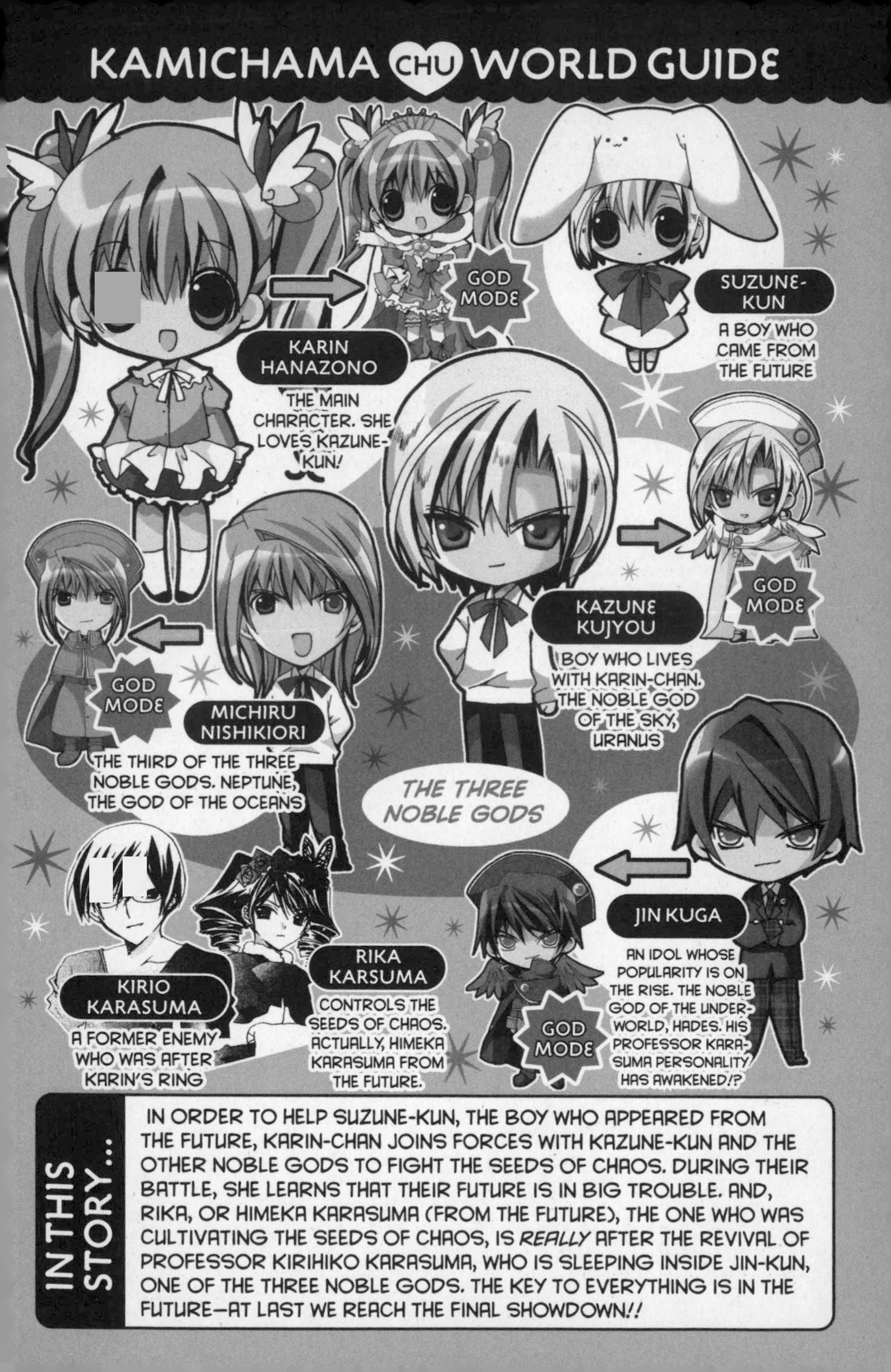
GOD MODE
SUZUNE-KUN
A BOY WHO CAME FROM THE FUTURE
KARIN HANAZONO
THE MAIN CHARACTER. SHE LOVES KAZUNE-KUN!
GOD MODE
KAZUNE KUJYOU
BOY WHO LIVES WITH KARIN-CHAN. THE NOBLE GOD OF THE SKY, URANUS
GOD MODE
MICHIRU NISHIKIORI
THE THIRD OF THE THREE NOBLE GODS. NEPTUNE, THE GOD OF THE OCEANS
THE THREE NOBLE GODS
JIN KUGA
AN IDOL WHOSE POPULARITY IS ON THE RISE. THE NOBLE GOD OF THE UNDERWORLD, HADES. HIS PROFESSOR KARASUMA PERSONALITY HAS AWAKENED!?
GOD MODE
RIKA KARSUMA
CONTROLS THE SEEDS OF CHAOS. ACTUALLY, HIMEKA KARASUMA FROM THE FUTURE.
KIRIO KARASUMA
A FORMER ENEMY WHO WAS AFTER KARIN'S RING

IN THIS STORY...

IN ORDER TO HELP SUZUNE-KUN, THE BOY WHO APPEARED FROM THE FUTURE, KARIN-CHAN JOINS FORCES WITH KAZUNE-KUN AND THE OTHER NOBLE GODS TO FIGHT THE SEEDS OF CHAOS. DURING THEIR BATTLE, SHE LEARNS THAT THEIR FUTURE IS IN BIG TROUBLE. AND, RIKA, OR HIMEKA KARASUMA (FROM THE FUTURE), THE ONE WHO WAS CULTIVATING THE SEEDS OF CHAOS, IS *REALLY* AFTER THE REVIVAL OF PROFESSOR KIRIHIKO KARASUMA, WHO IS SLEEPING INSIDE JIN-KUN, ONE OF THE THREE NOBLE GODS. THE KEY TO EVERYTHING IS IN THE FUTURE—AT LAST WE REACH THE FINAL SHOWDOWN!!

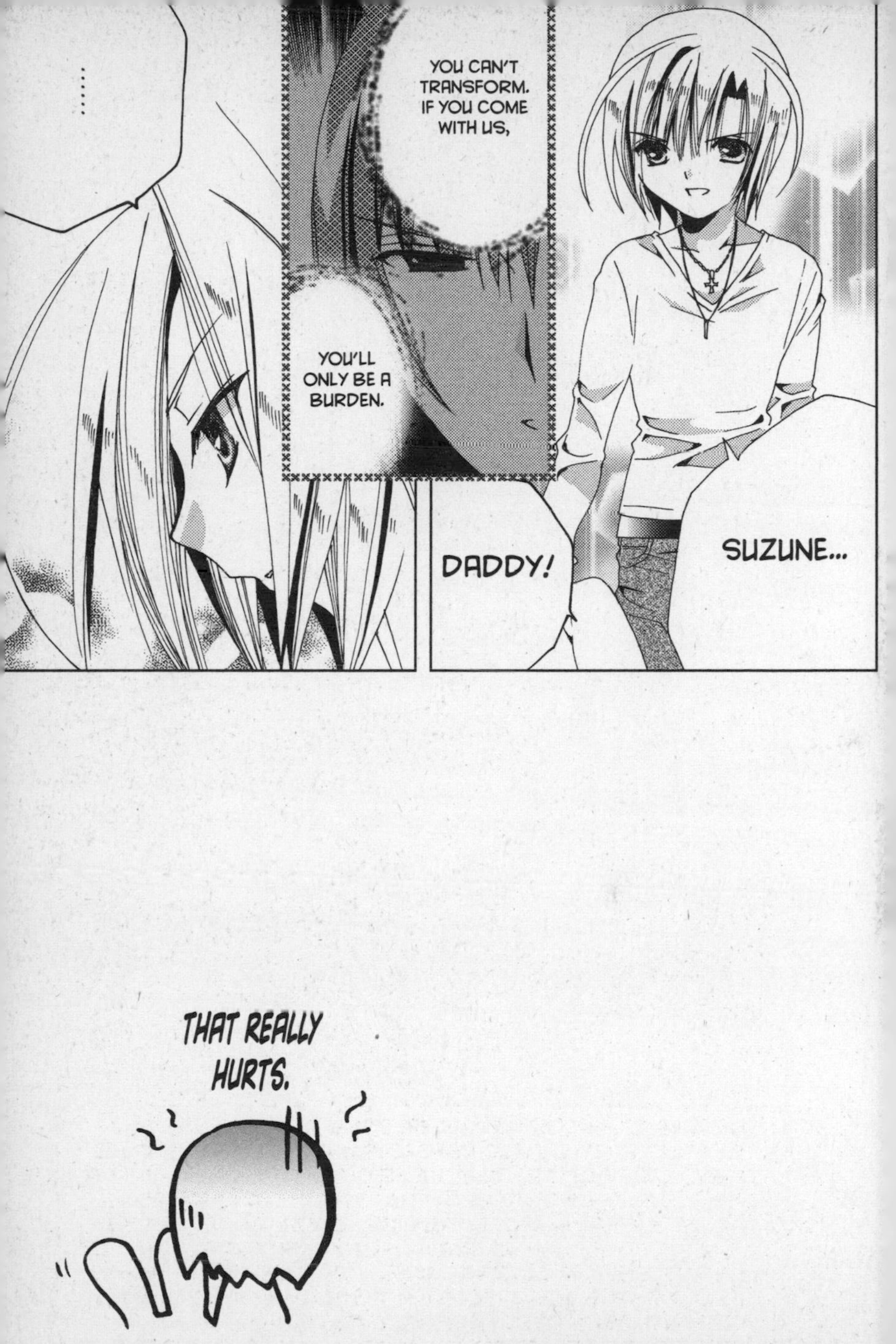
SUZUNE...
DADDY!
YOU CAN'T TRANSFORM. IF YOU COME WITH US,
YOU'LL ONLY BE A BURDEN.
......
THAT REALLY HURTS.

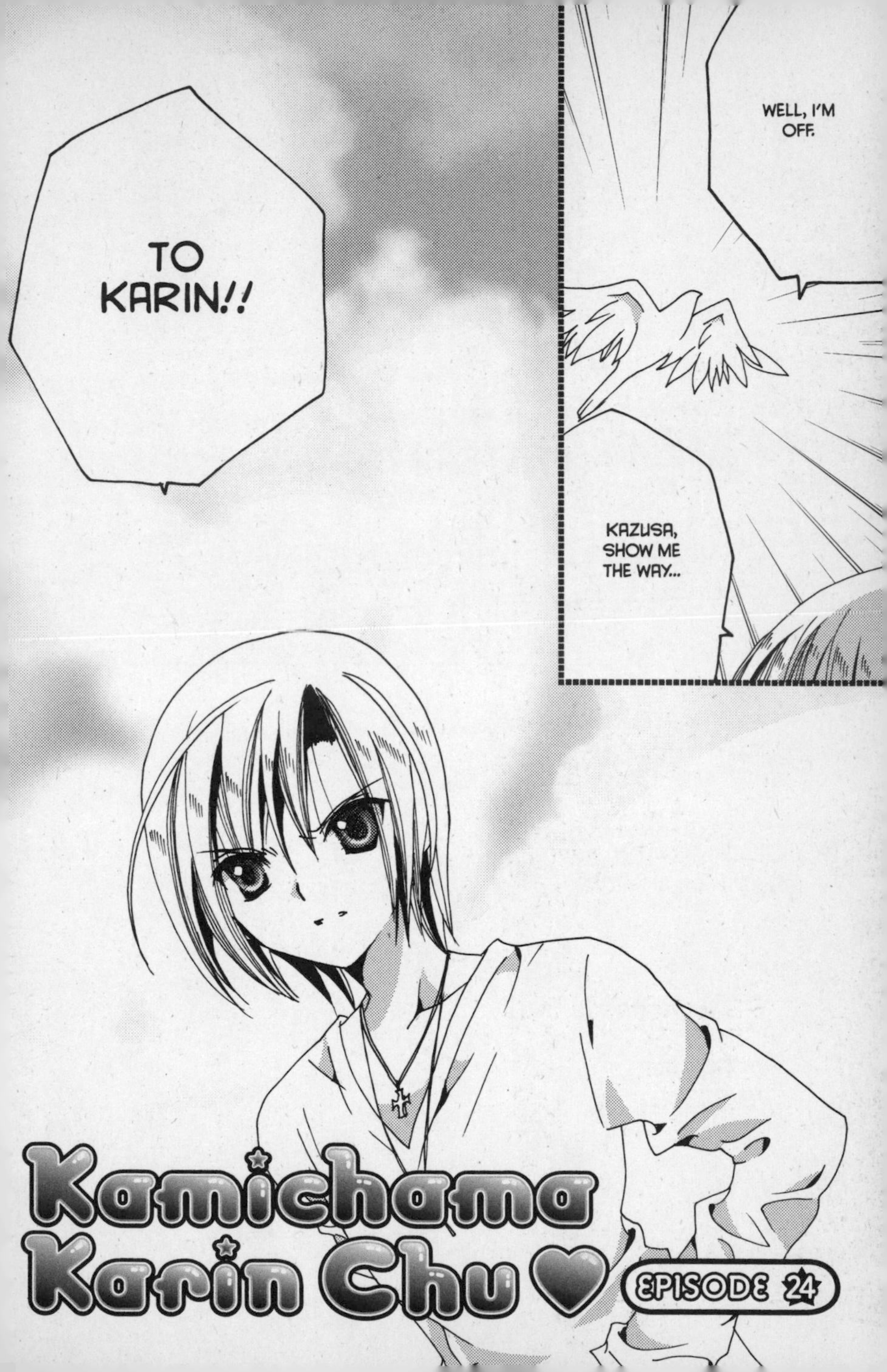
WELL, I'M OFF.
KAZUSA, SHOW ME THE WAY...
TO KARIN!!
Kamichama Karin Chu♥
EPISODE 24

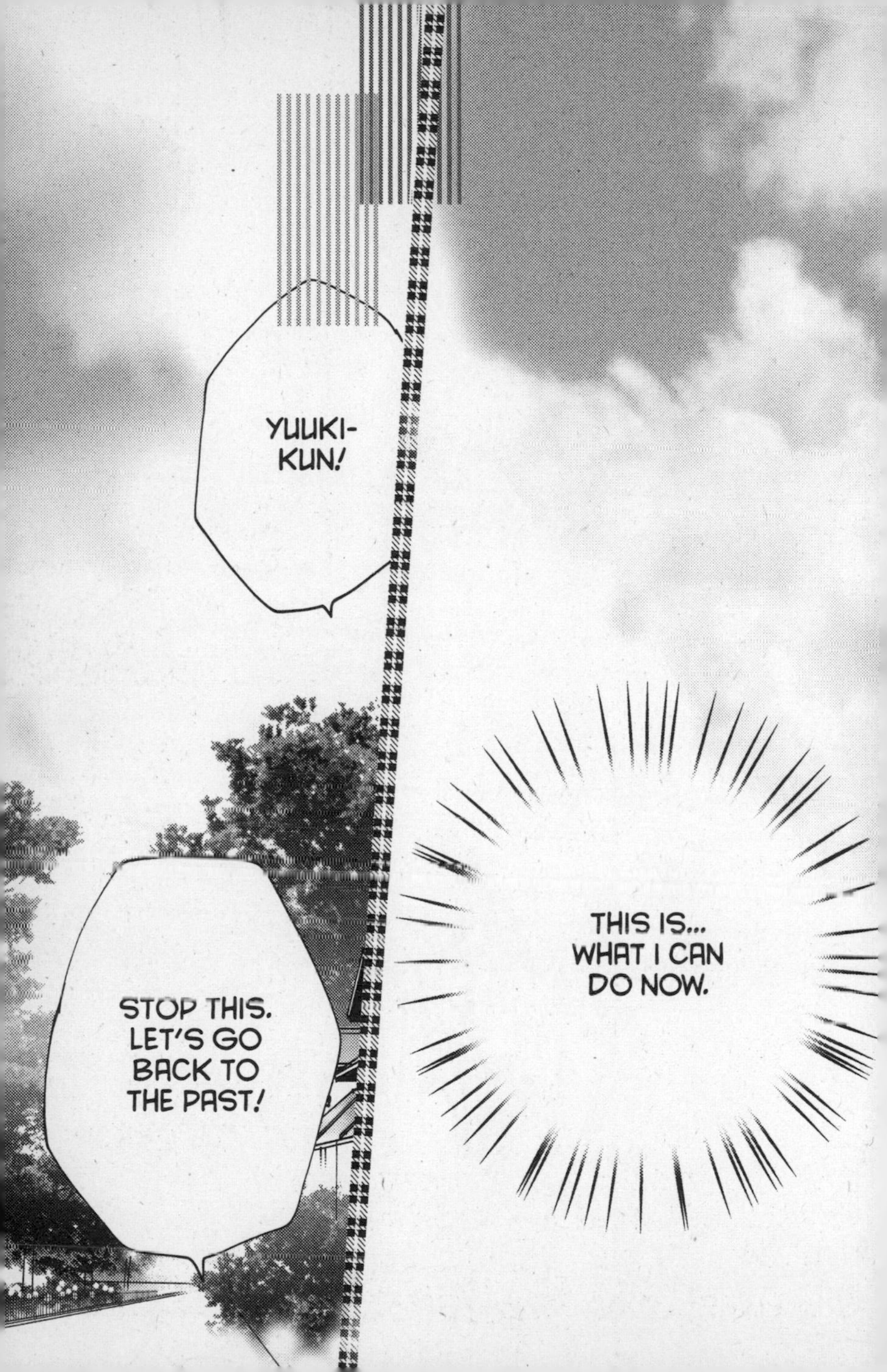
THIS IS...
WHAT I CAN
DO NOW.
YUUKI-
KUN!
STOP THIS.
LET'S GO
BACK TO
THE PAST!

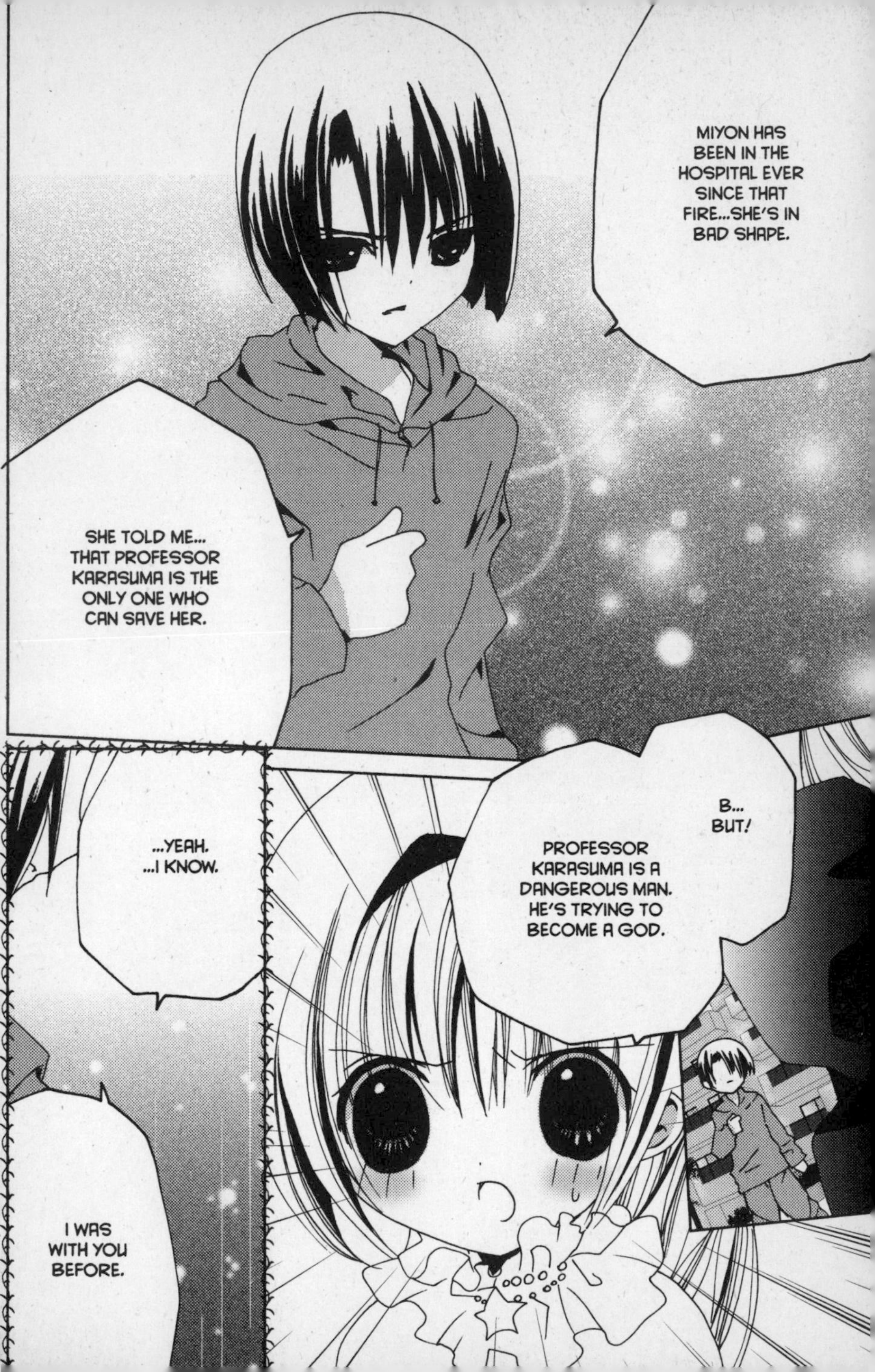
MIYON HAS BEEN IN THE HOSPITAL EVER SINCE THAT FIRE...SHE'S IN BAD SHAPE.
SHE TOLD ME... THAT PROFESSOR KARASUMA IS THE ONLY ONE WHO CAN SAVE HER.
B... BUT!
PROFESSOR KARASUMA IS A DANGEROUS MAN. HE'S TRYING TO BECOME A GOD.
...YEAH. ...I KNOW.
I WAS WITH YOU BEFORE.

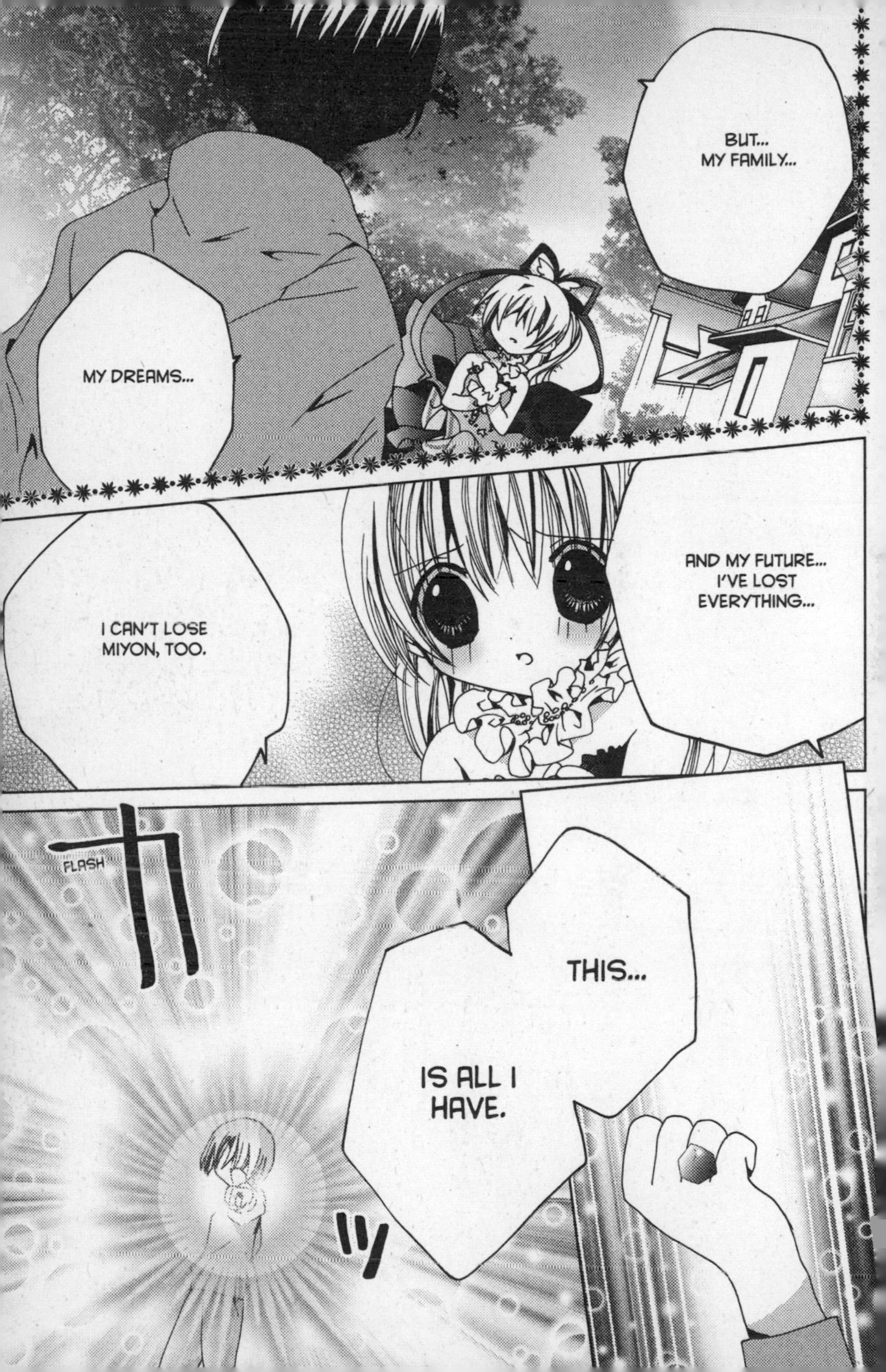
BUT...
MY FAMILY...
MY DREAMS...
AND MY FUTURE...
I'VE LOST
EVERYTHING...
I CAN'T LOSE
MIYON, TOO.
THIS...
IS ALL I
HAVE.
FLASH

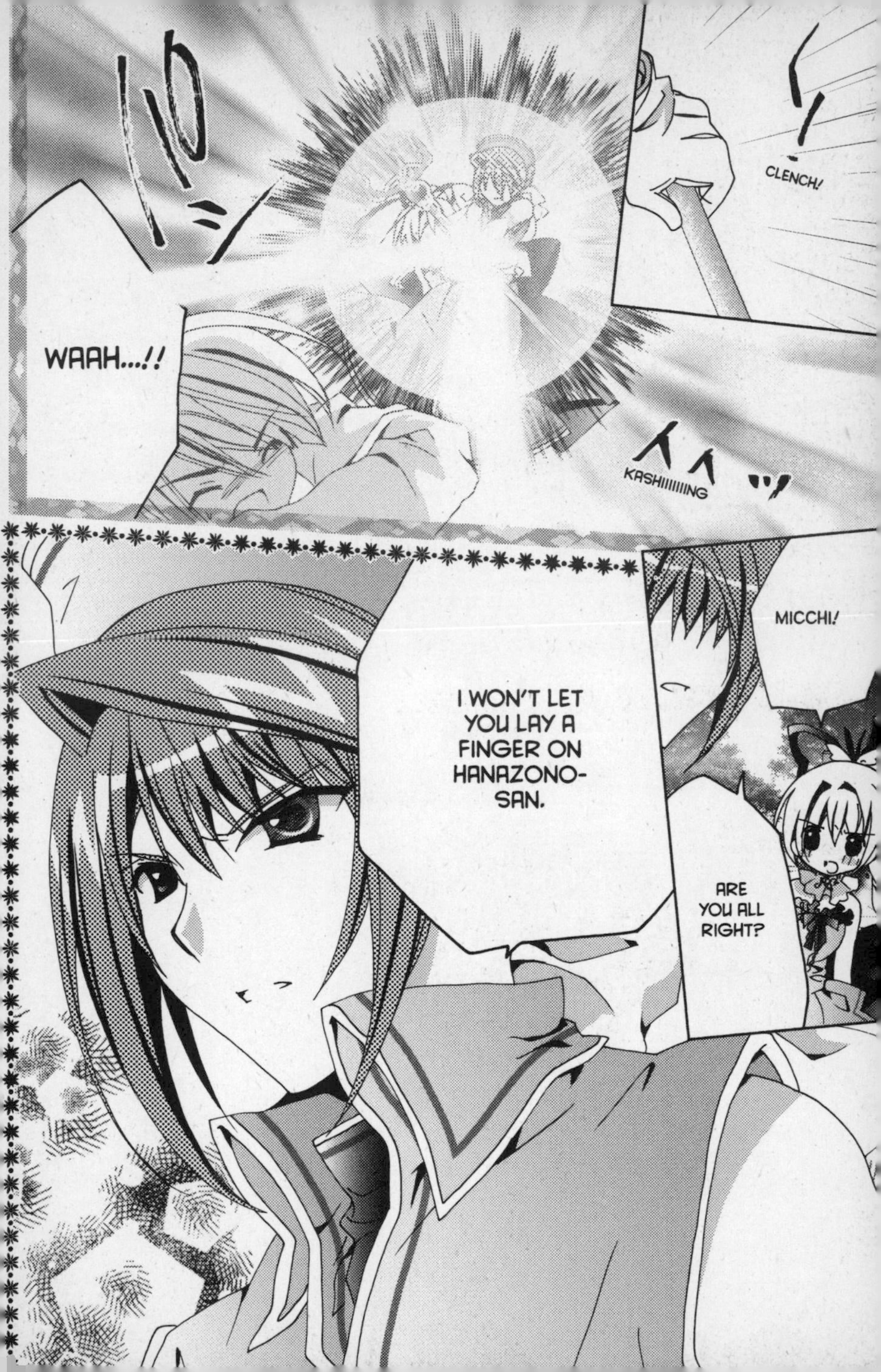
CLENCH!
WAAH...!!
KASHIIIIIIIIING
MICCHI!
ARE YOU ALL RIGHT?
I WON'T LET YOU LAY A FINGER ON HANAZONO-SAN.

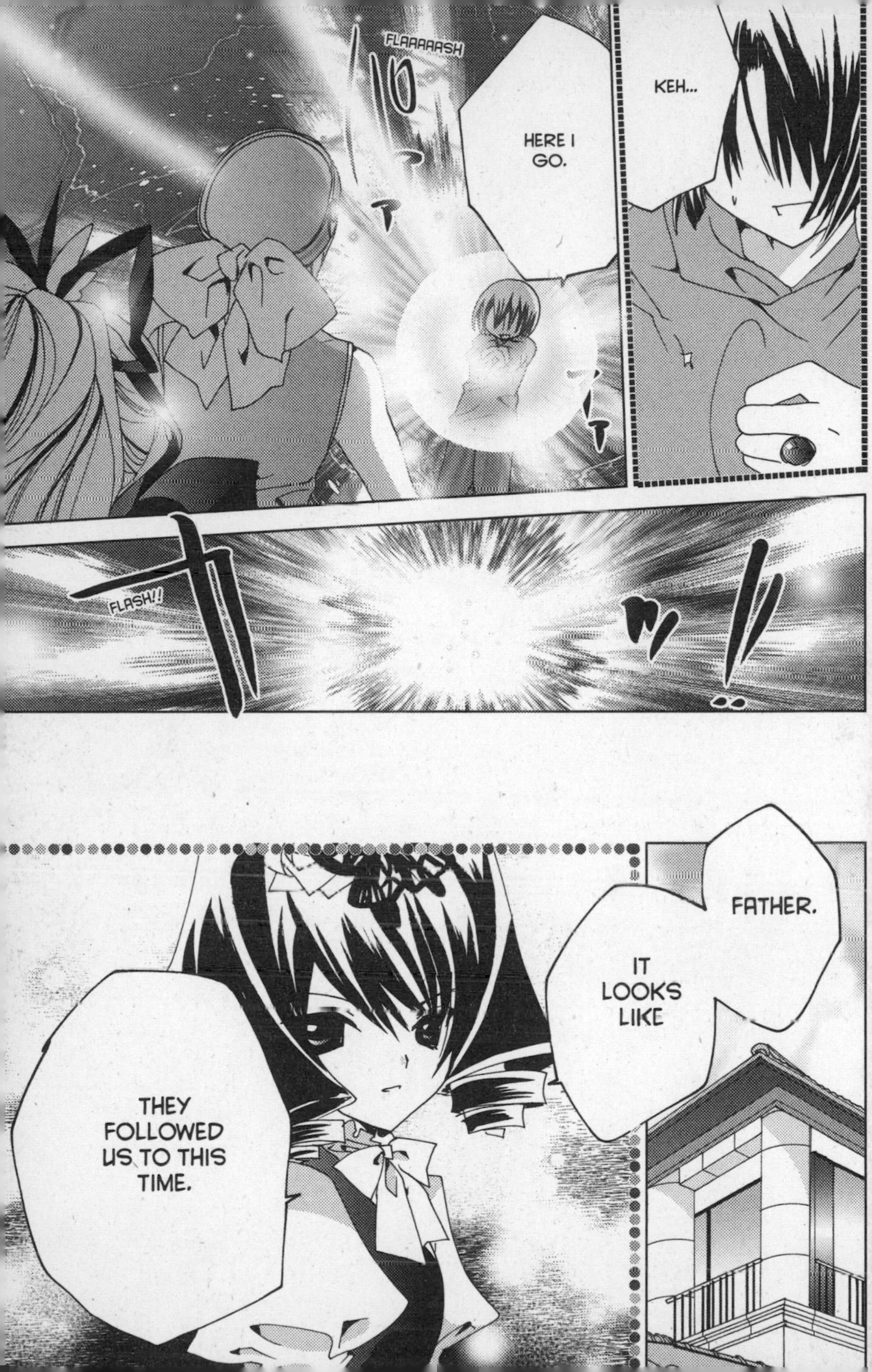
KEH...
HERE I GO.
FLAAAAASH
FLASH!!
FATHER.
IT LOOKS LIKE
THEY FOLLOWED US TO THIS TIME.

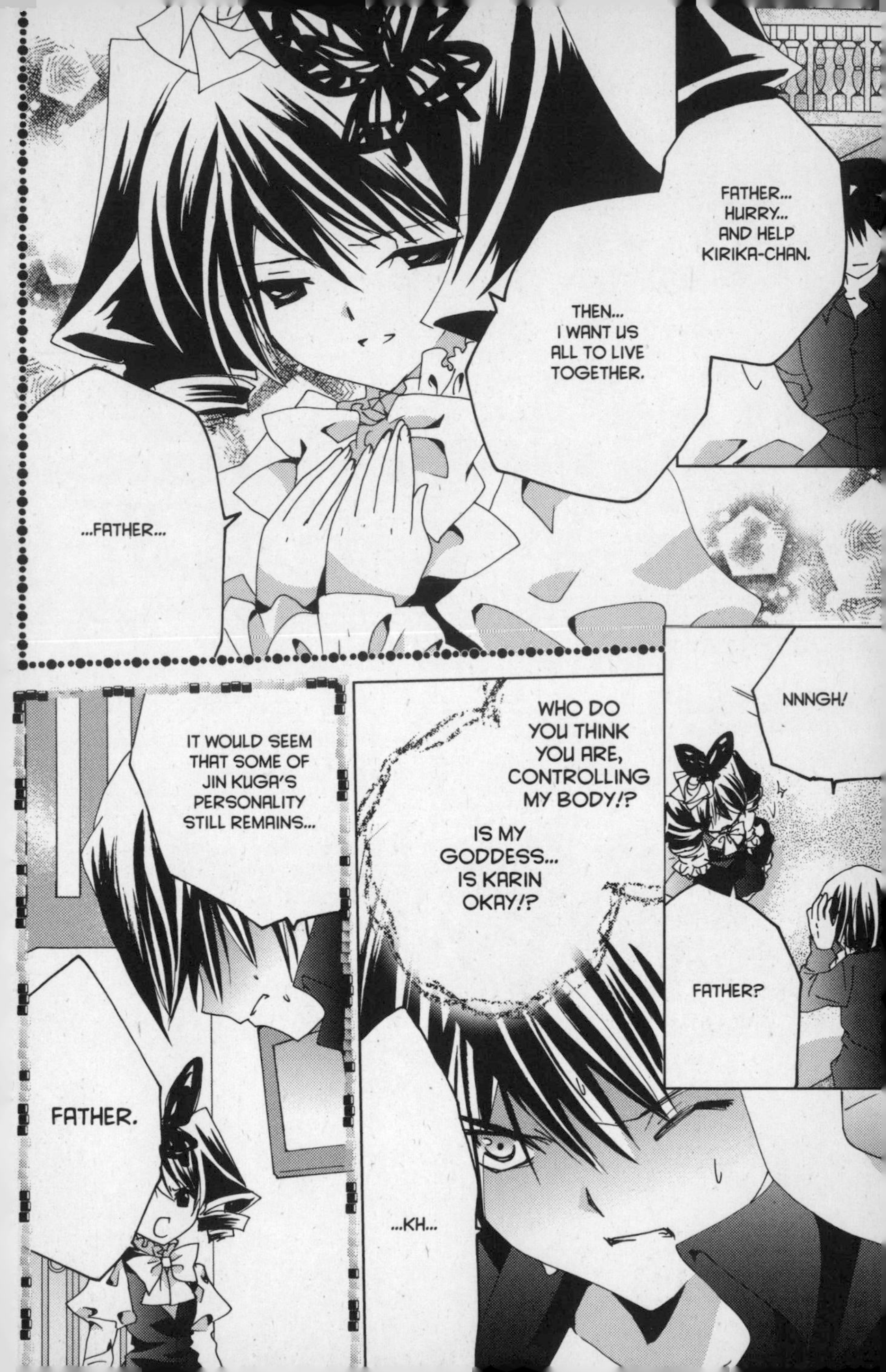
FATHER... HURRY... AND HELP KIRIKA-CHAN.
THEN... I WANT US ALL TO LIVE TOGETHER.
...FATHER...
NNNGH!
FATHER?
WHO DO YOU THINK YOU ARE, CONTROLLING MY BODY!?
IS MY GODDESS... IS KARIN OKAY!?
...KH...
IT WOULD SEEM THAT SOME OF JIN KUGA'S PERSONALITY STILL REMAINS...
FATHER.

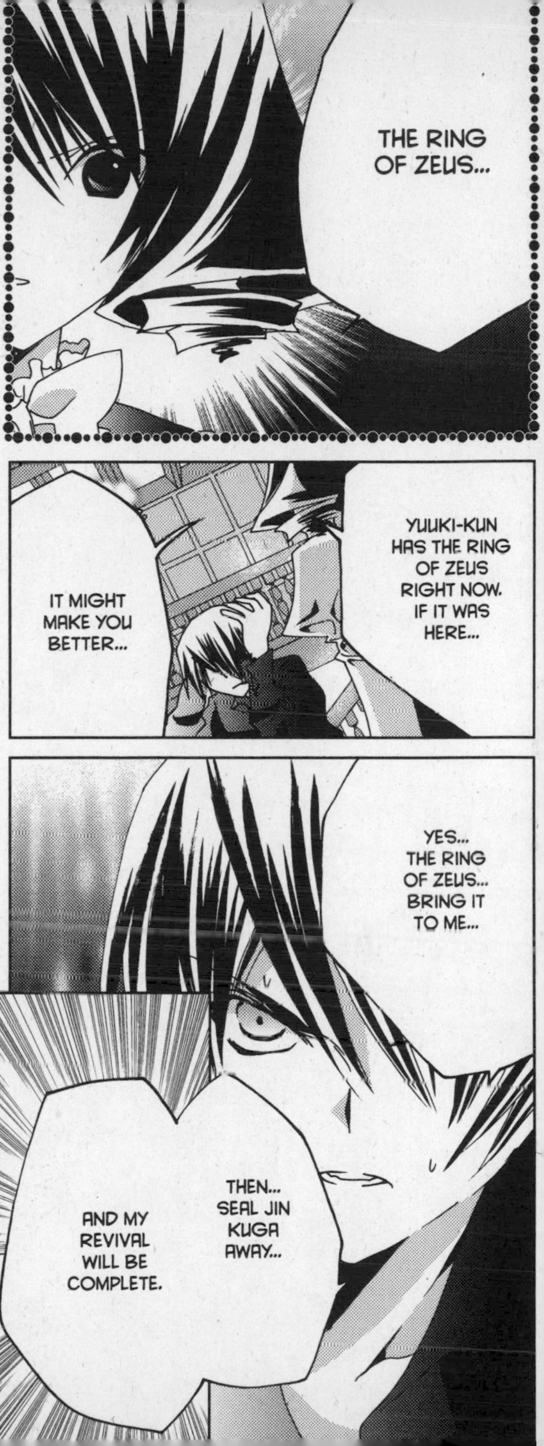
THE RING OF ZEUS...
YUUKI-KUN HAS THE RING OF ZEUS RIGHT NOW. IF IT WAS HERE...
IT MIGHT MAKE YOU BETTER...
YES... THE RING OF ZEUS... BRING IT TO ME...
THEN... SEAL JIN KUGA AWAY...
AND MY REVIVAL WILL BE COMPLETE.

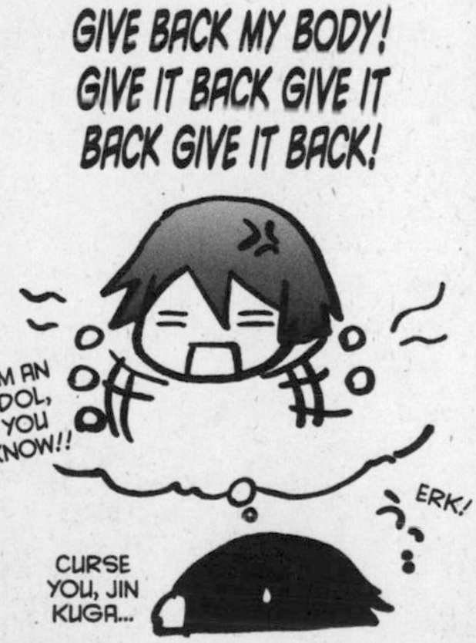
GIVE BACK MY BODY! GIVE IT BACK GIVE IT BACK GIVE IT BACK!
I'M AN IDOL, YOU KNOW!!
ERK!
CURSE YOU, JIN KUGA...

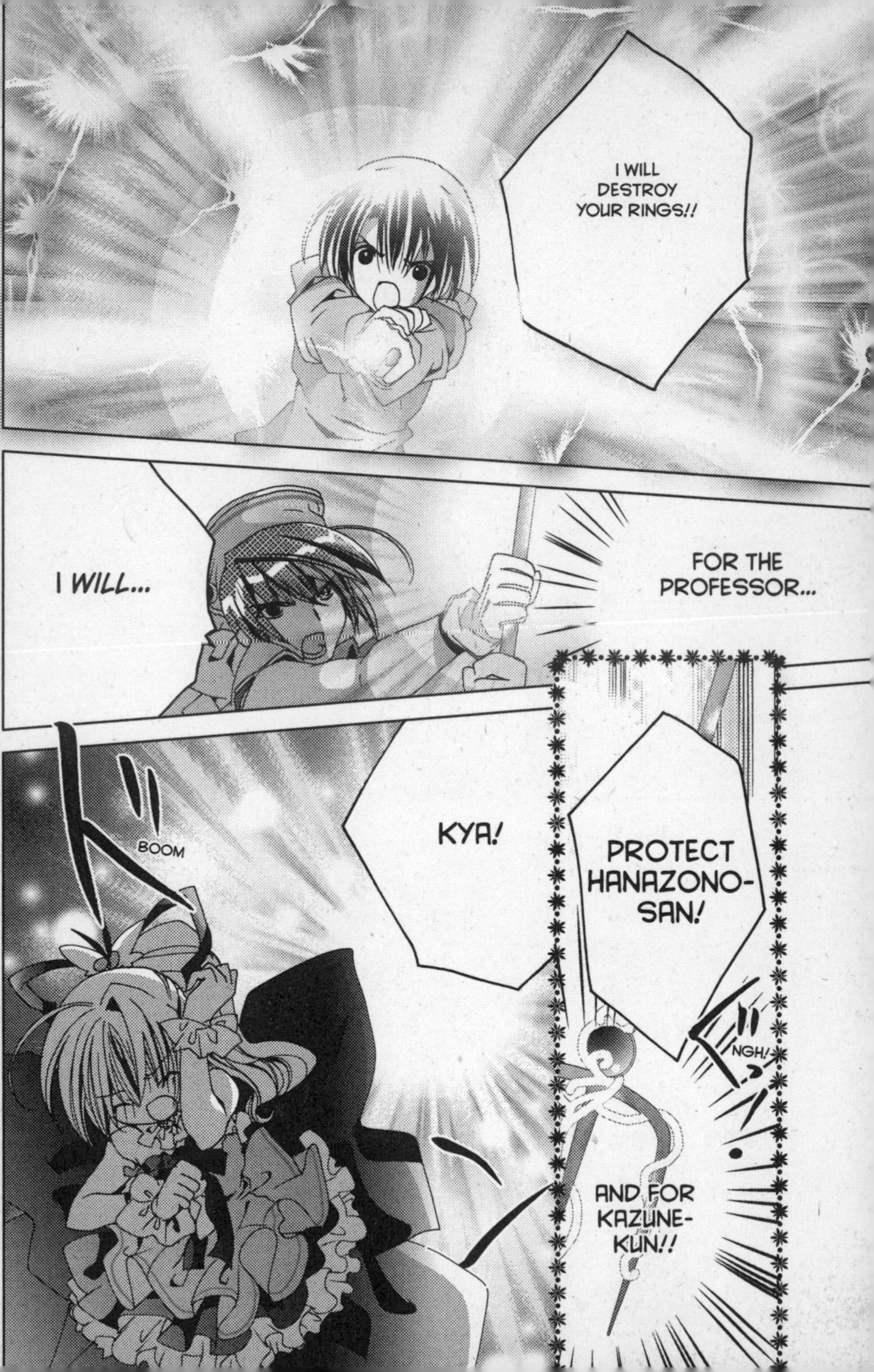
I WILL DESTROY YOUR RINGS!!
FOR THE PROFESSOR...
I WILL...
PROTECT HANAZONO-SAN!
NGH!
AND FOR KAZUNE-KUN!!
KYA!
BOOM

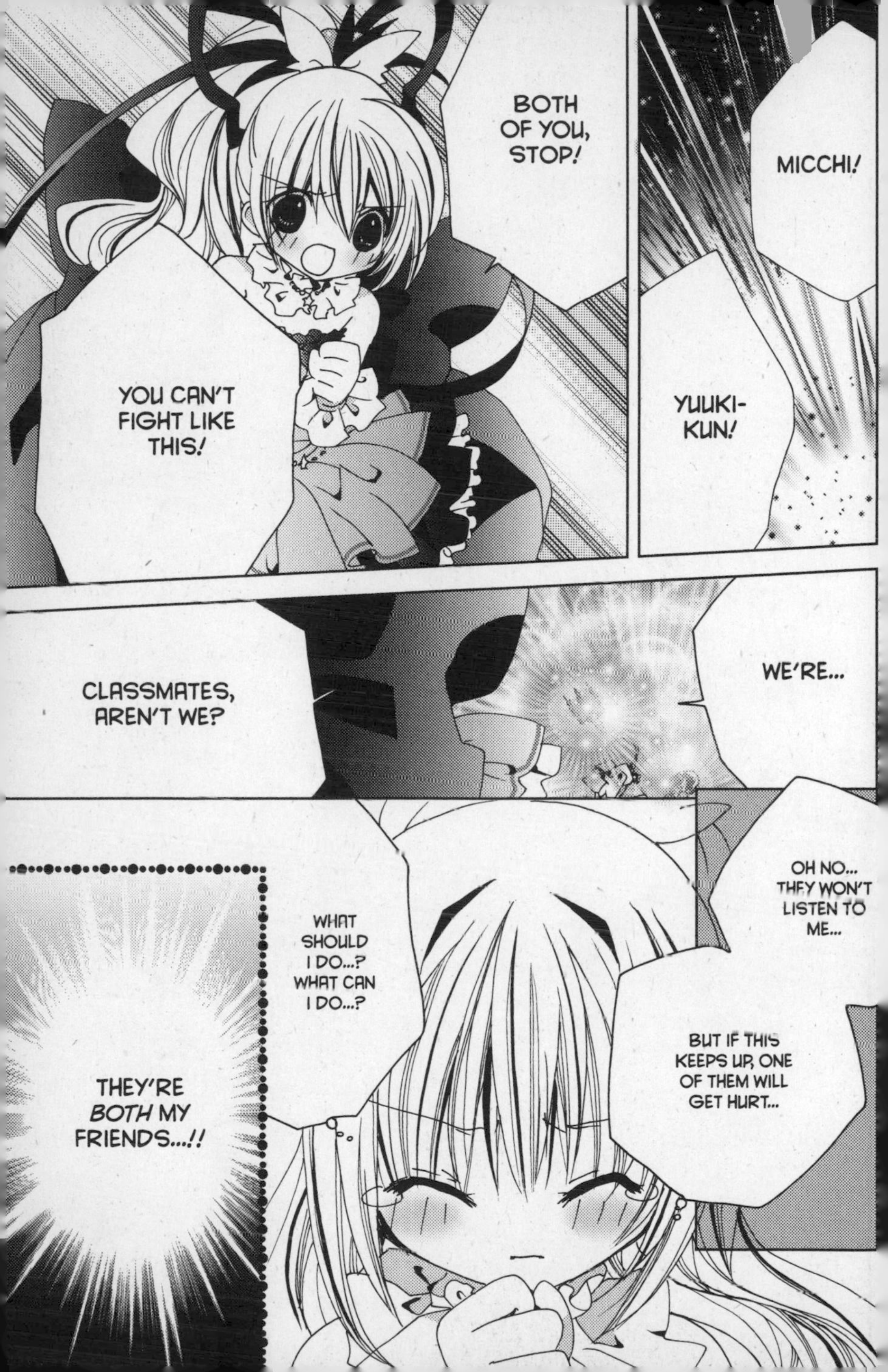
MICCHI!
YUUKI-KUN!
BOTH OF YOU, STOP!
YOU CAN'T FIGHT LIKE THIS!
WE'RE...
CLASSMATES, AREN'T WE?
OH NO... THEY WON'T LISTEN TO ME...
BUT IF THIS KEEPS UP, ONE OF THEM WILL GET HURT...
WHAT SHOULD I DO...? WHAT CAN I DO...?
THEY'RE *BOTH* MY FRIENDS...!!

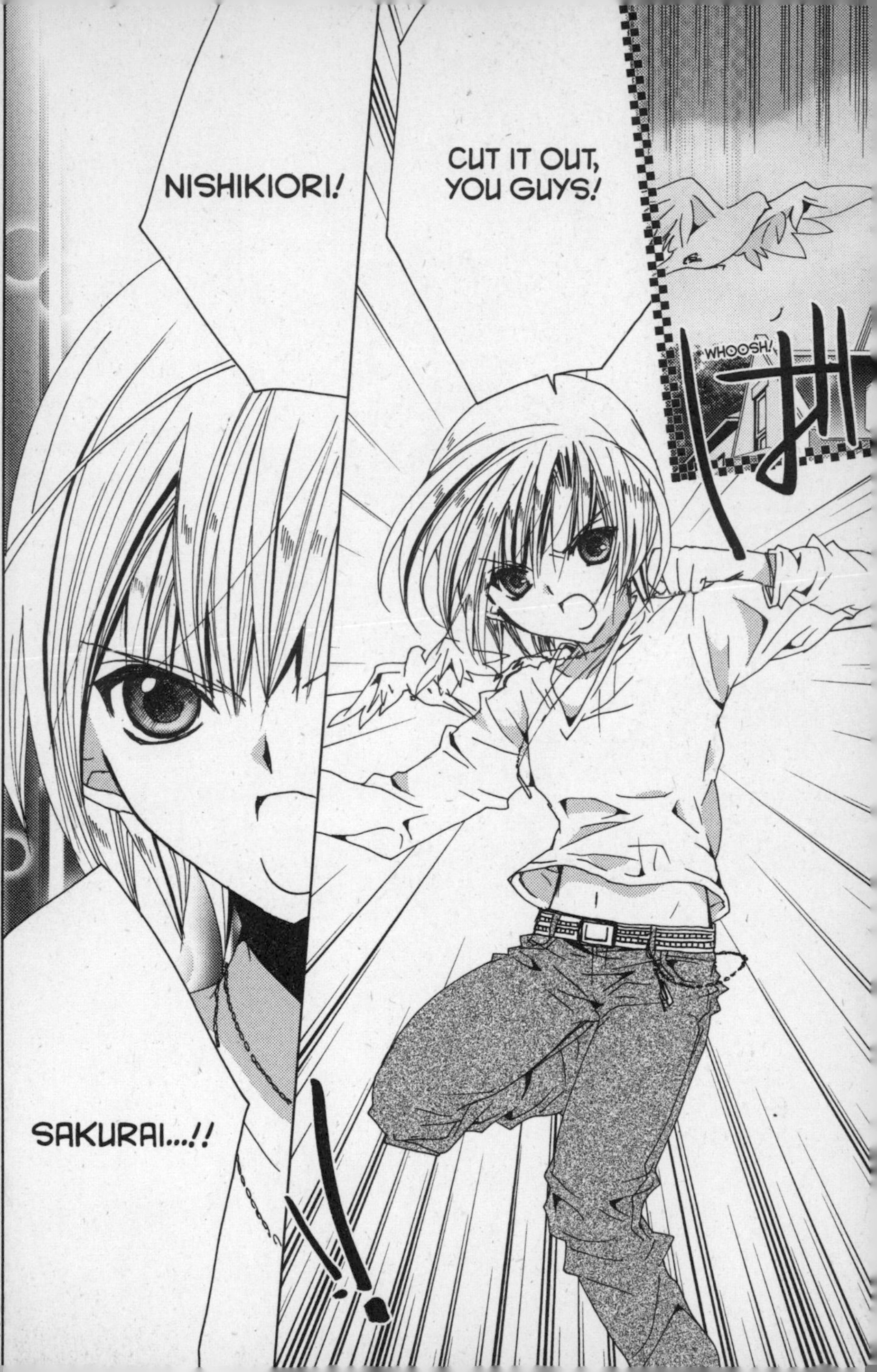
WHOOSH!
CUT IT OUT, YOU GUYS!
NISHIKIORI!
SAKURAI...!!

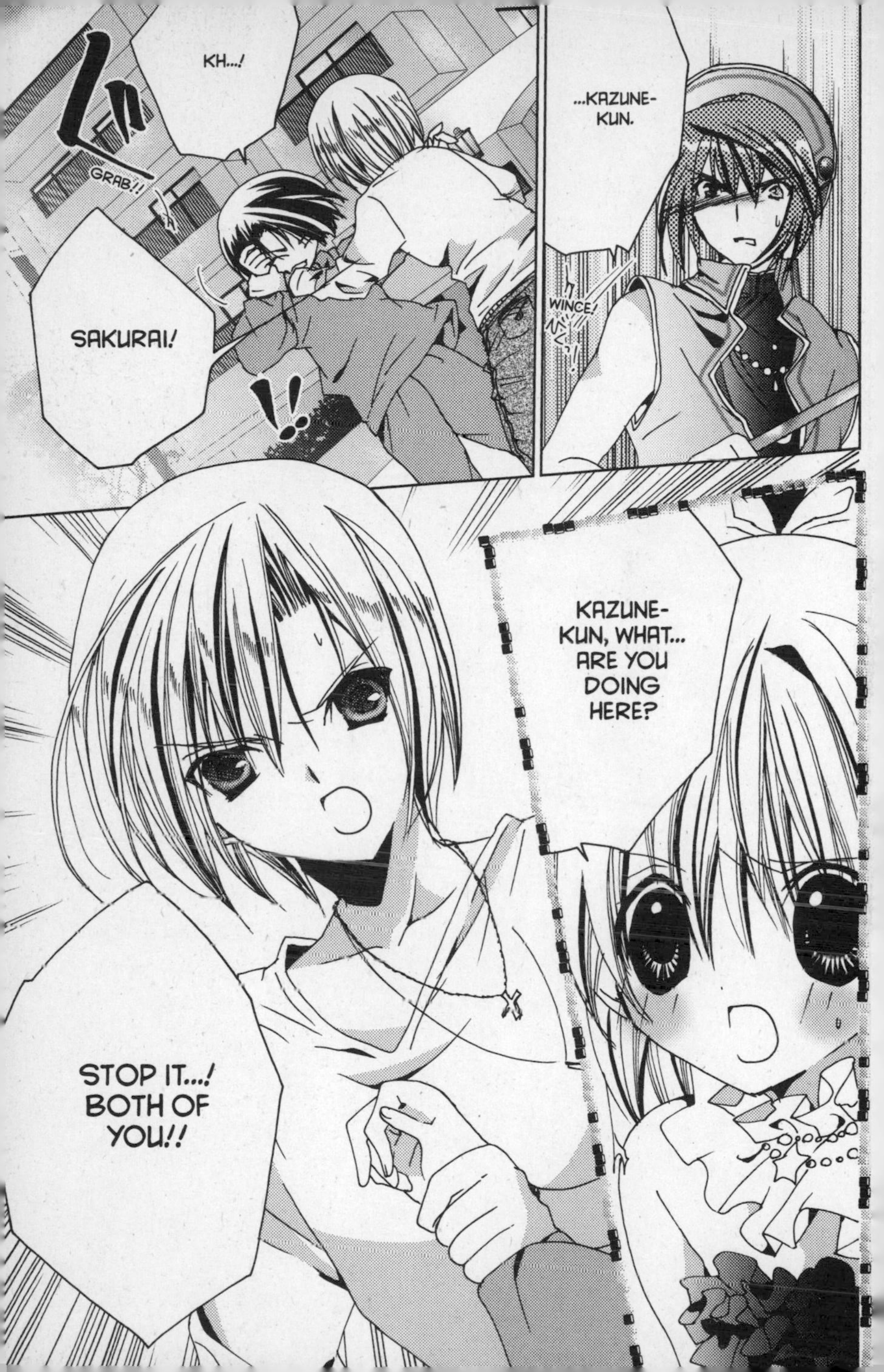
...KAZUNE-KUN.
WINCE!
KH...!
GRAB!!
SAKURAI!
!!
KAZUNE-KUN, WHAT... ARE YOU DOING HERE?
STOP IT...! BOTH OF YOU!!

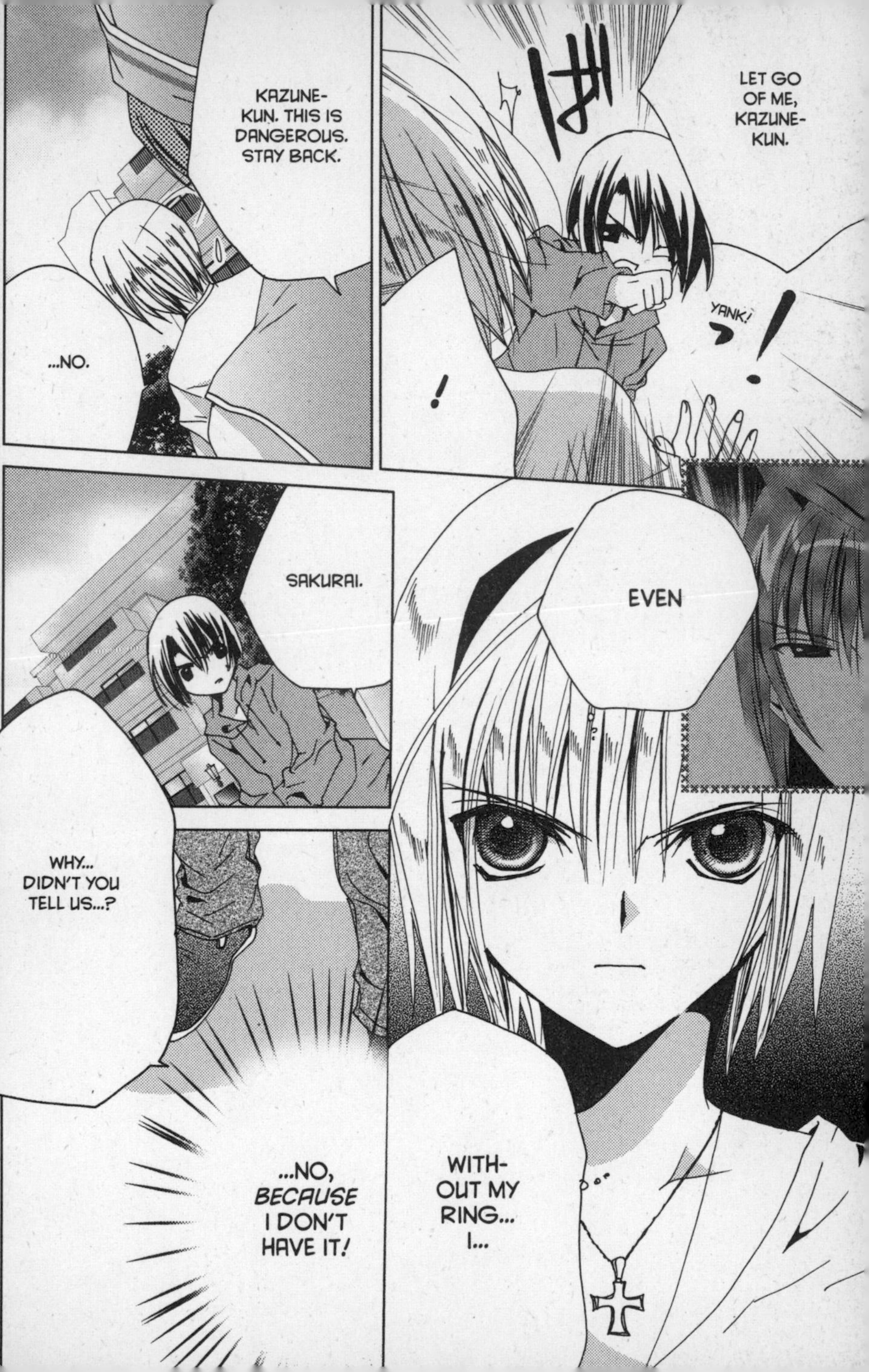
LET GO OF ME, KAZUNE-KUN.
YANK!
KAZUNE-KUN. THIS IS DANGEROUS. STAY BACK.
...NO.
EVEN
WITH-OUT MY RING... I...
SAKURAI.
WHY... DIDN'T YOU TELL US...?
...NO, *BECAUSE* I DON'T HAVE IT!

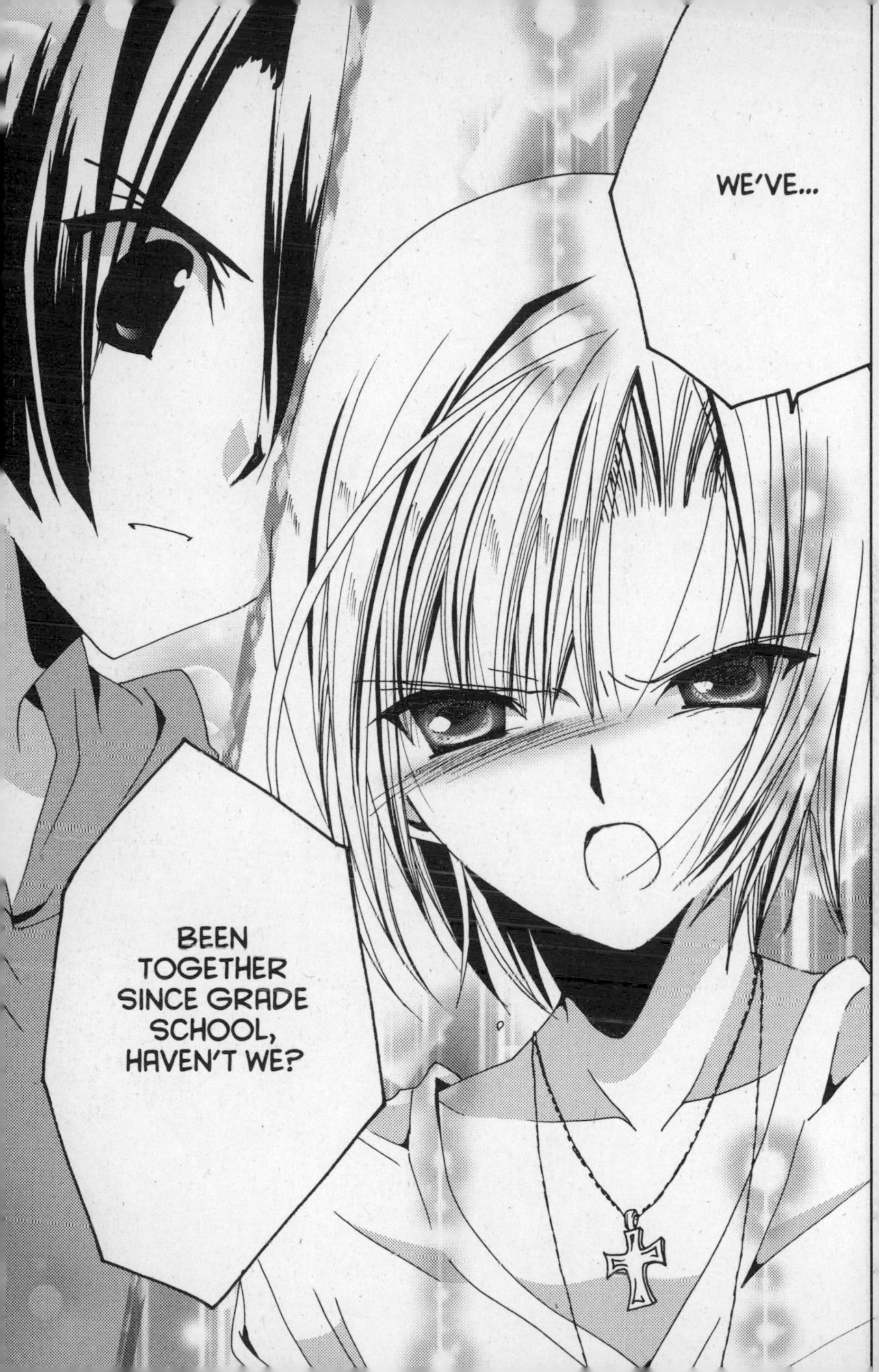
WE'VE...
BEEN TOGETHER SINCE GRADE SCHOOL, HAVEN'T WE?

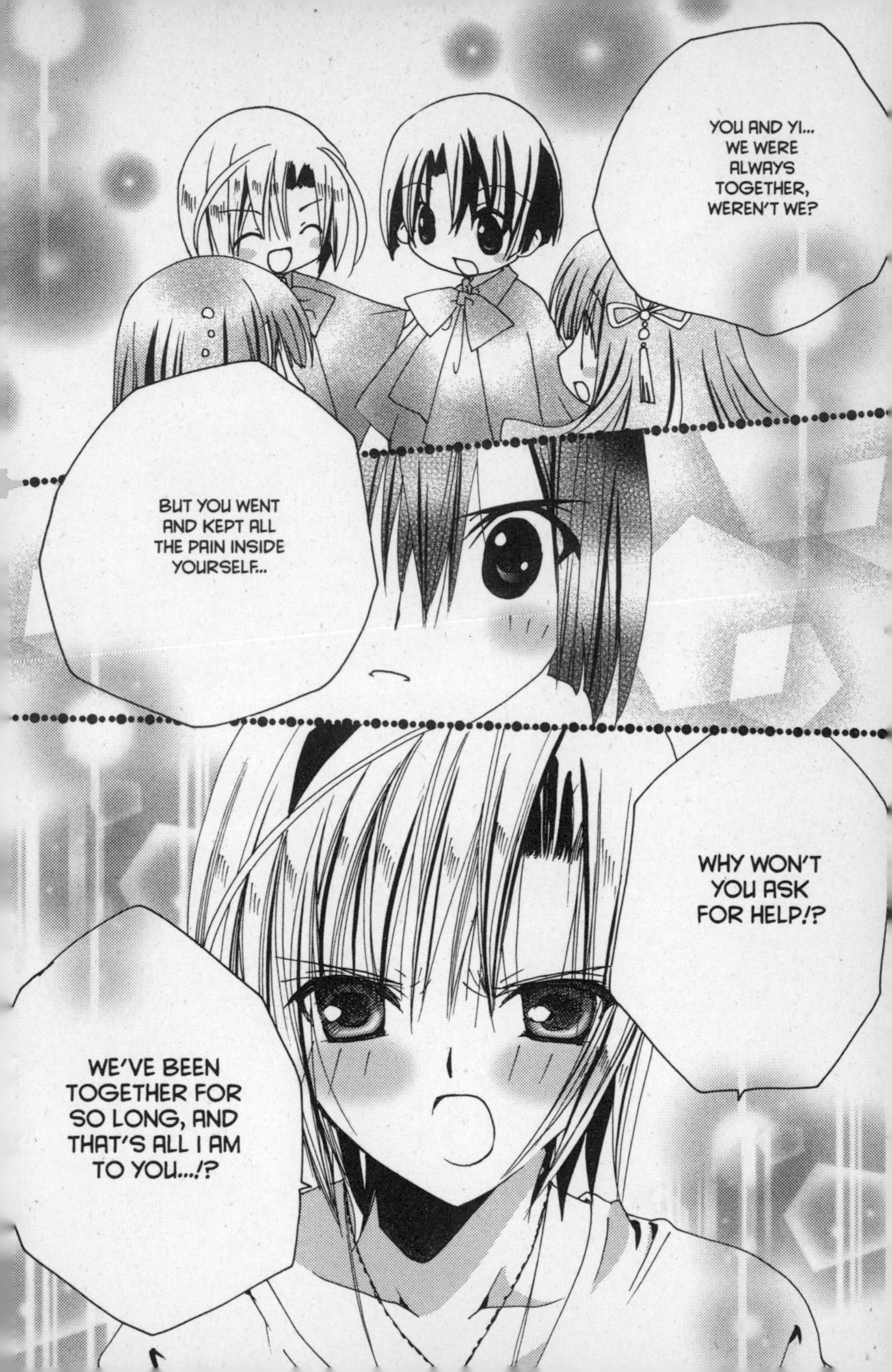
YOU AND YI... WE WERE ALWAYS TOGETHER, WEREN'T WE?
BUT YOU WENT AND KEPT ALL THE PAIN INSIDE YOURSELF...
WHY WON'T YOU ASK FOR HELP!?
WE'VE BEEN TOGETHER FOR SO LONG, AND THAT'S ALL I AM TO YOU...!?

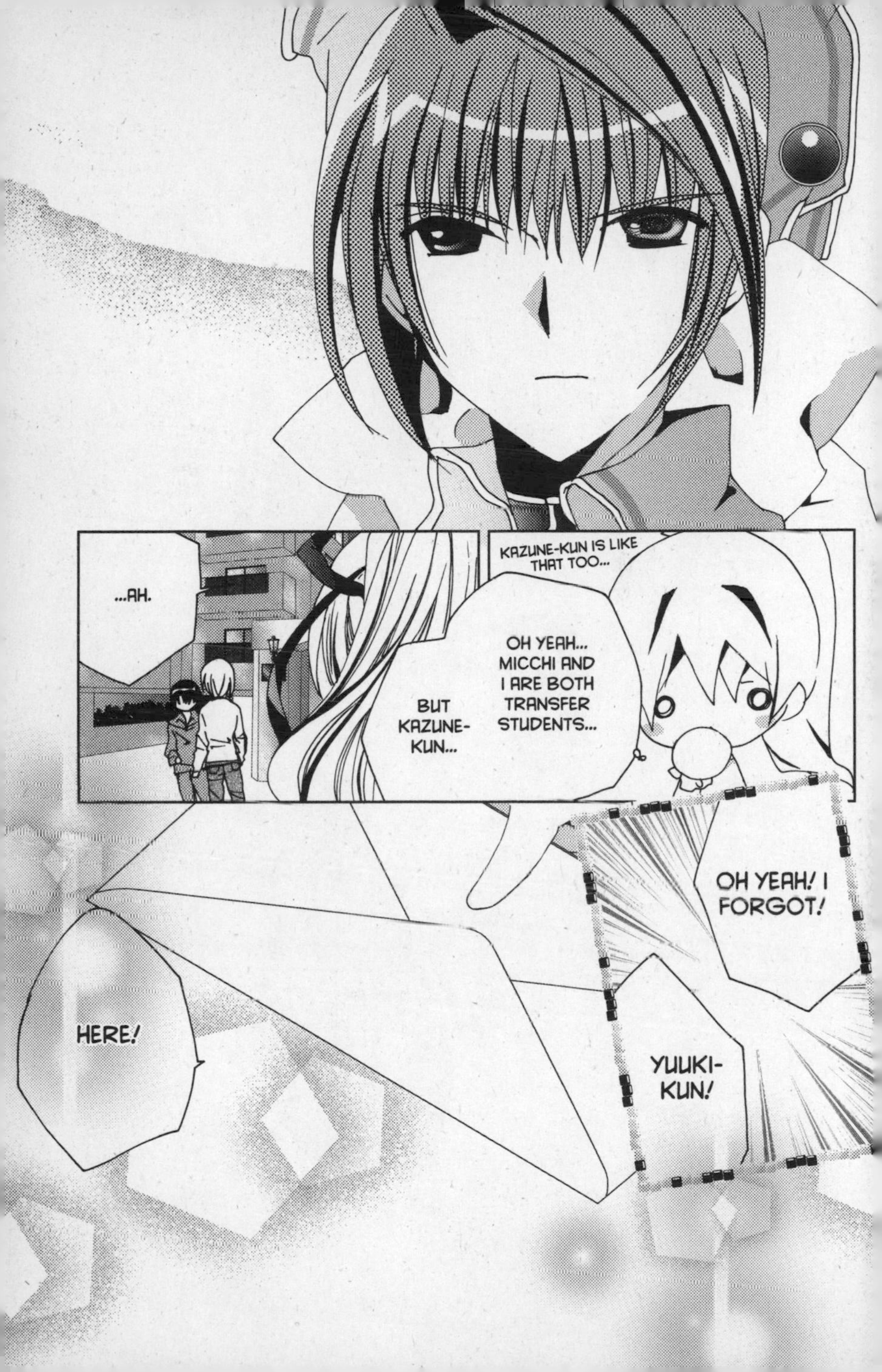
KAZUNE-KUN IS LIKE THAT TOO...
OH YEAH... MICCHI AND I ARE BOTH TRANSFER STUDENTS...
BUT KAZUNE-KUN...
...AH.
OH YEAH! I FORGOT!
YUUKI-KUN!
HERE!

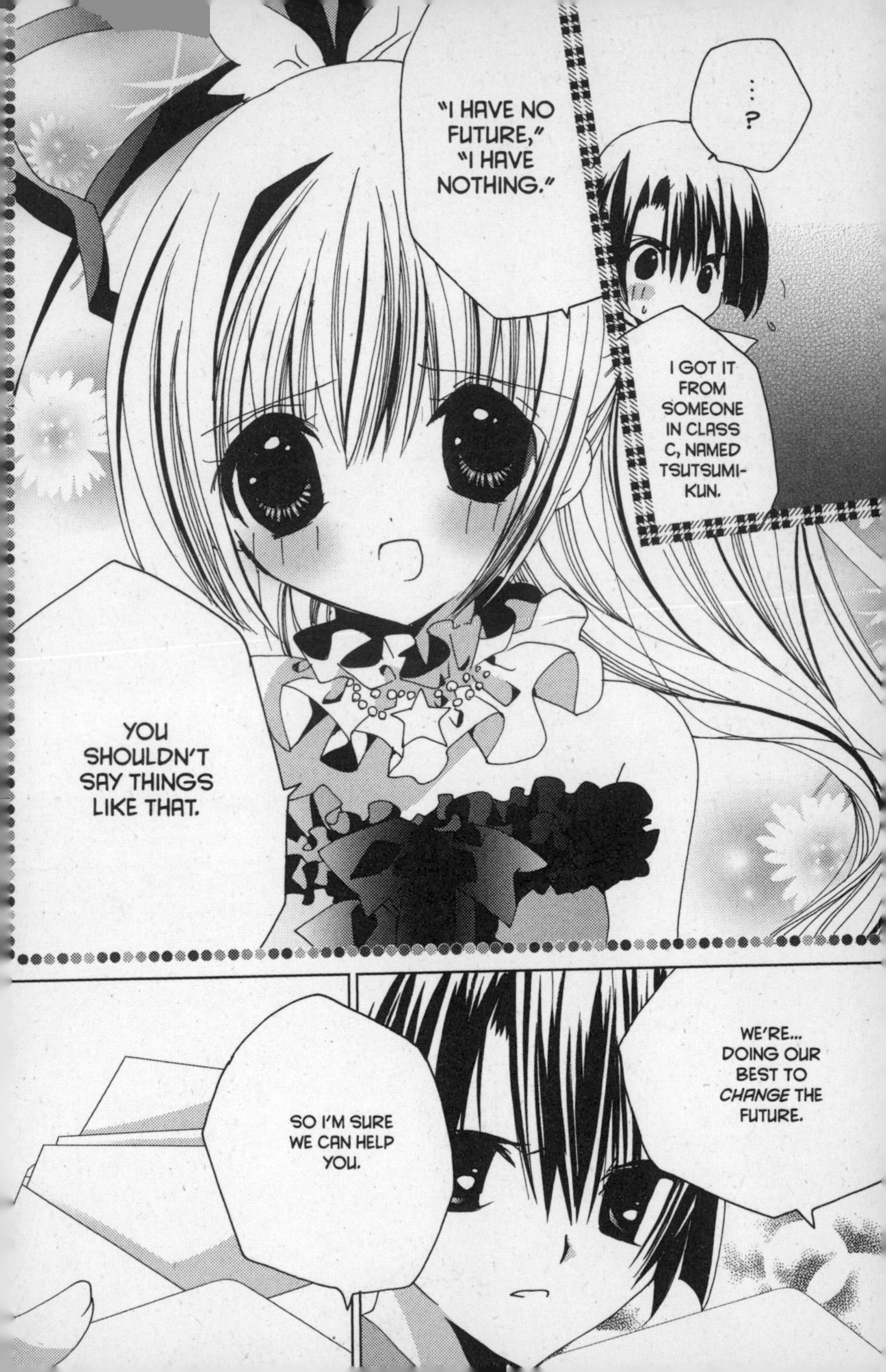
. . . ?
I GOT IT FROM SOMEONE IN CLASS C, NAMED TSUTSUMI-KUN.
"I HAVE NO FUTURE," "I HAVE NOTHING."
YOU SHOULDN'T SAY THINGS LIKE THAT.
WE'RE... DOING OUR BEST TO *CHANGE* THE FUTURE.
SO I'M SURE WE CAN HELP YOU.

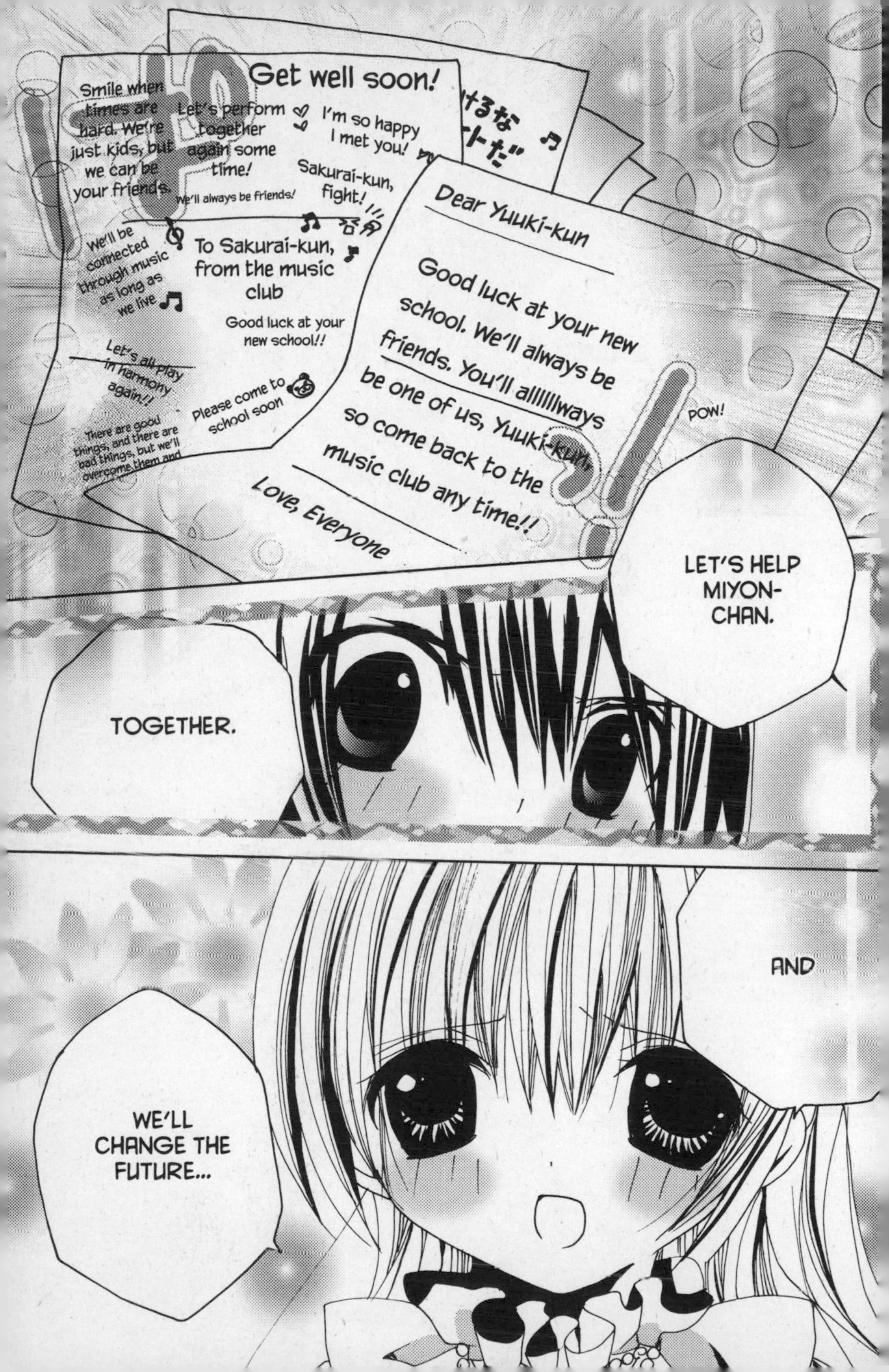
POW!
Dear Yuuki-kun
Good luck at your new school. We'll always be friends. You'll alllllways be one of us, Yuuki-kun, so come back to the music club any time!!
Love, Everyone
Get well soon!
I'm so happy I met you!
Let's perform together again some time!
Smile when times are hard. We're just kids, but we can be your friends.
Sakurai-kun, fight!
We'll always be friends!
To Sakurai-kun, from the music club
We'll be connected through music as long as we live
Good luck at your new school!!
Let's all play in harmony again!!
Please come to school soon
There are good things, and there are bad things, but we'll overcome them and
LET'S HELP MIYON-CHAN.
TOGETHER.
AND
WE'LL CHANGE THE FUTURE...

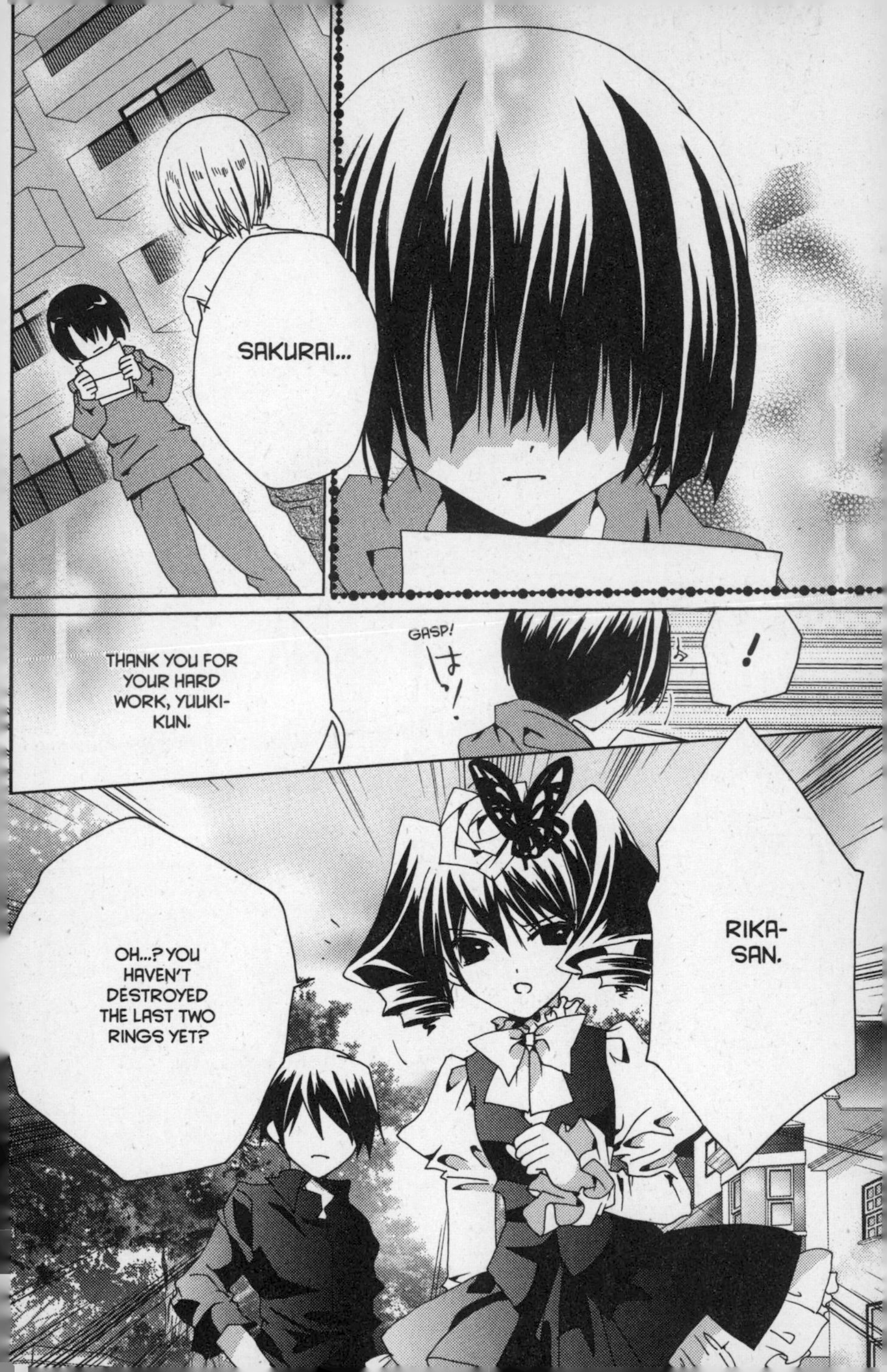
SAKURAI...
!
GASP!
はっ!
THANK YOU FOR YOUR HARD WORK, YUUKI-KUN.
RIKA-SAN.
OH...? YOU HAVEN'T DESTROYED THE LAST TWO RINGS YET?

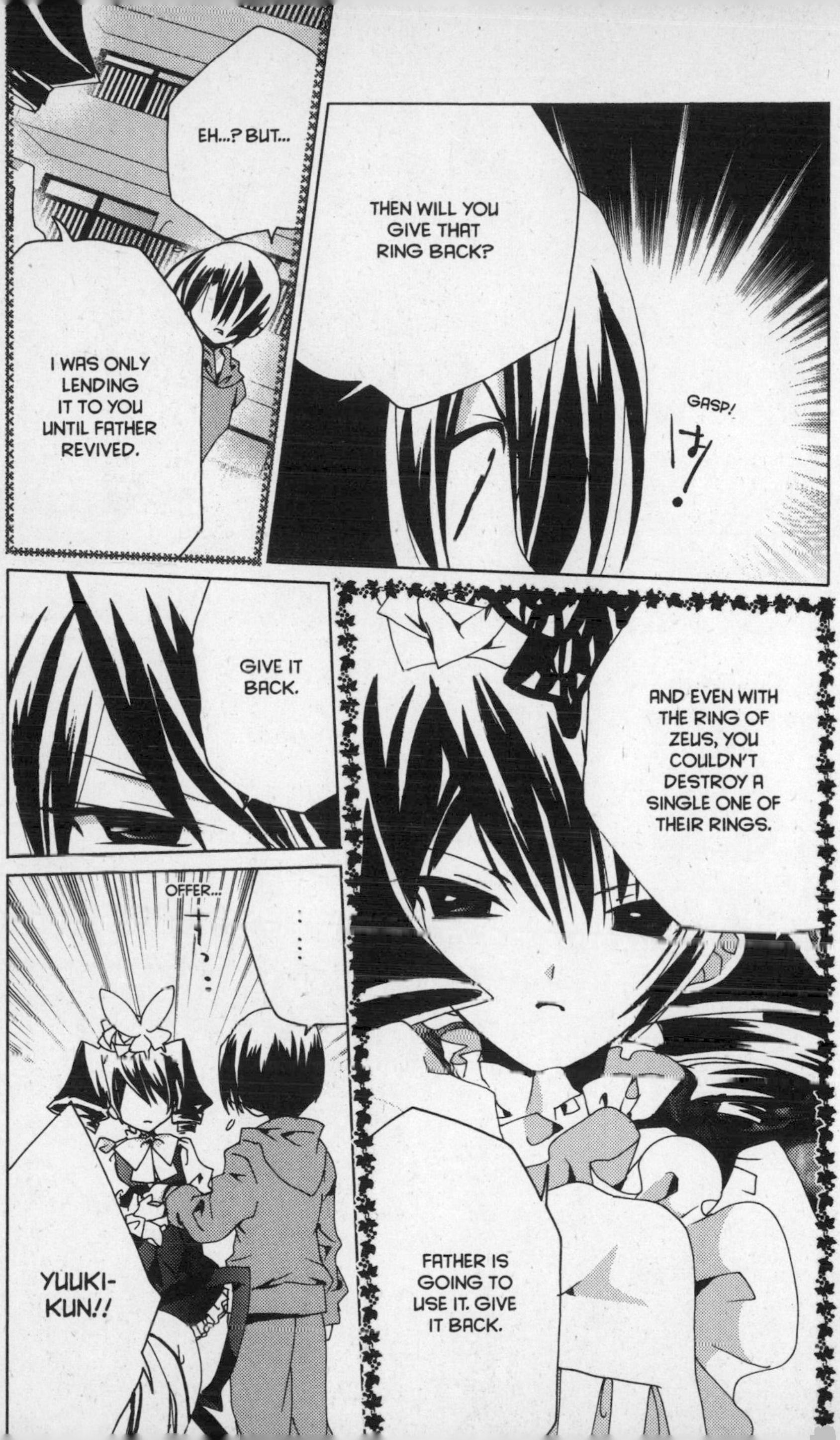
THEN WILL YOU GIVE THAT RING BACK?
GASP!
は!
EH...? BUT...
I WAS ONLY LENDING IT TO YOU UNTIL FATHER REVIVED.
AND EVEN WITH THE RING OF ZEUS, YOU COULDN'T DESTROY A SINGLE ONE OF THEIR RINGS.
FATHER IS GOING TO USE IT. GIVE IT BACK.
GIVE IT BACK.
OFFER...
......
YUUKI-KUN!!

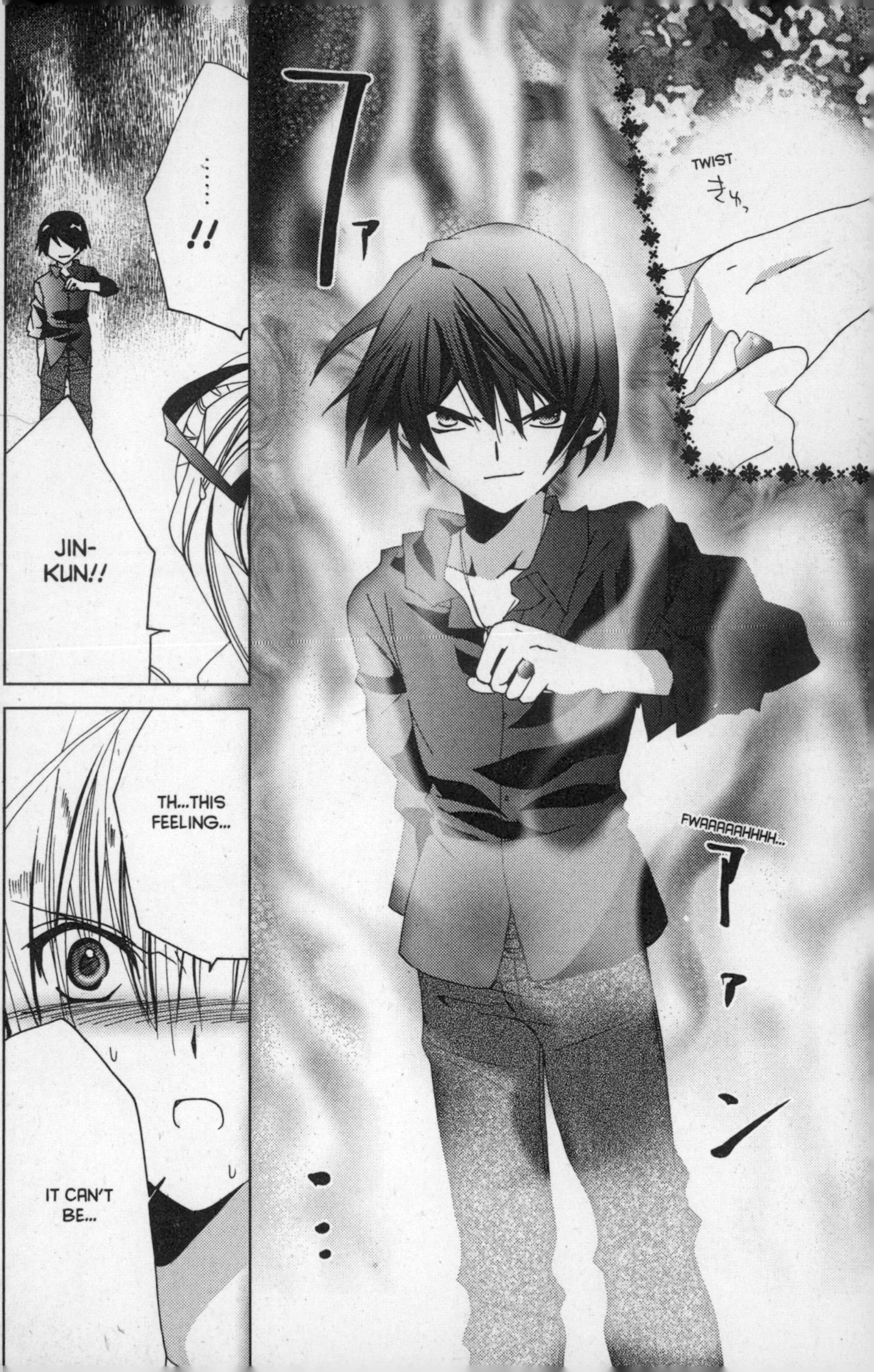

TWIST
きゅっ
ファ
FWAAAAAHHHH...
ァァン…
......!!
JIN-KUN!!
TH...THIS FEELING...
IT CAN'T BE...

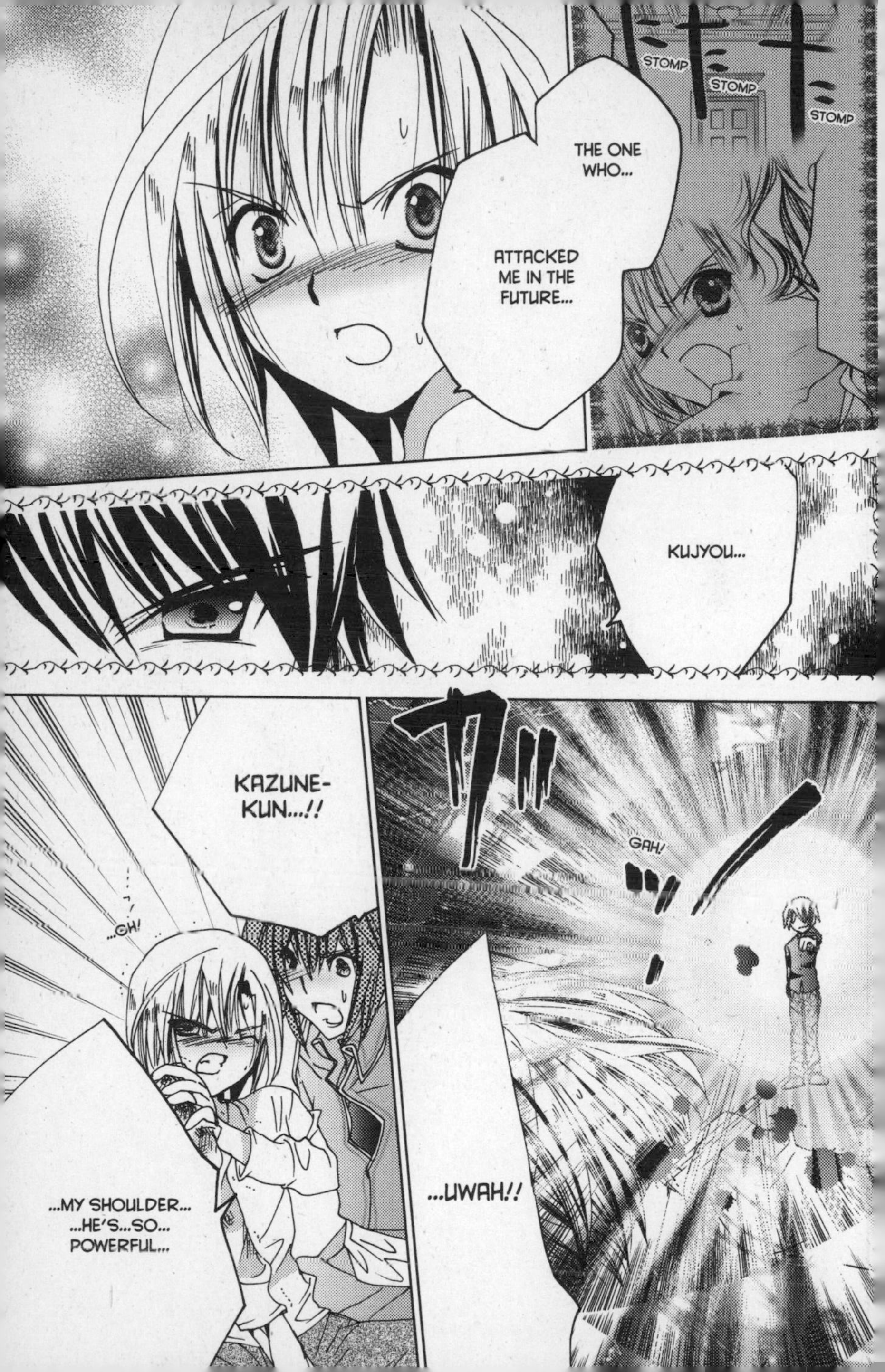
STOMP
STOMP
STOMP
THE ONE WHO...
ATTACKED ME IN THE FUTURE...
KUJYOU...
GAH!
...UWAH!!
KAZUNE-KUN...!!
...OH!
...MY SHOULDER... ...HE'S...SO... POWERFUL...

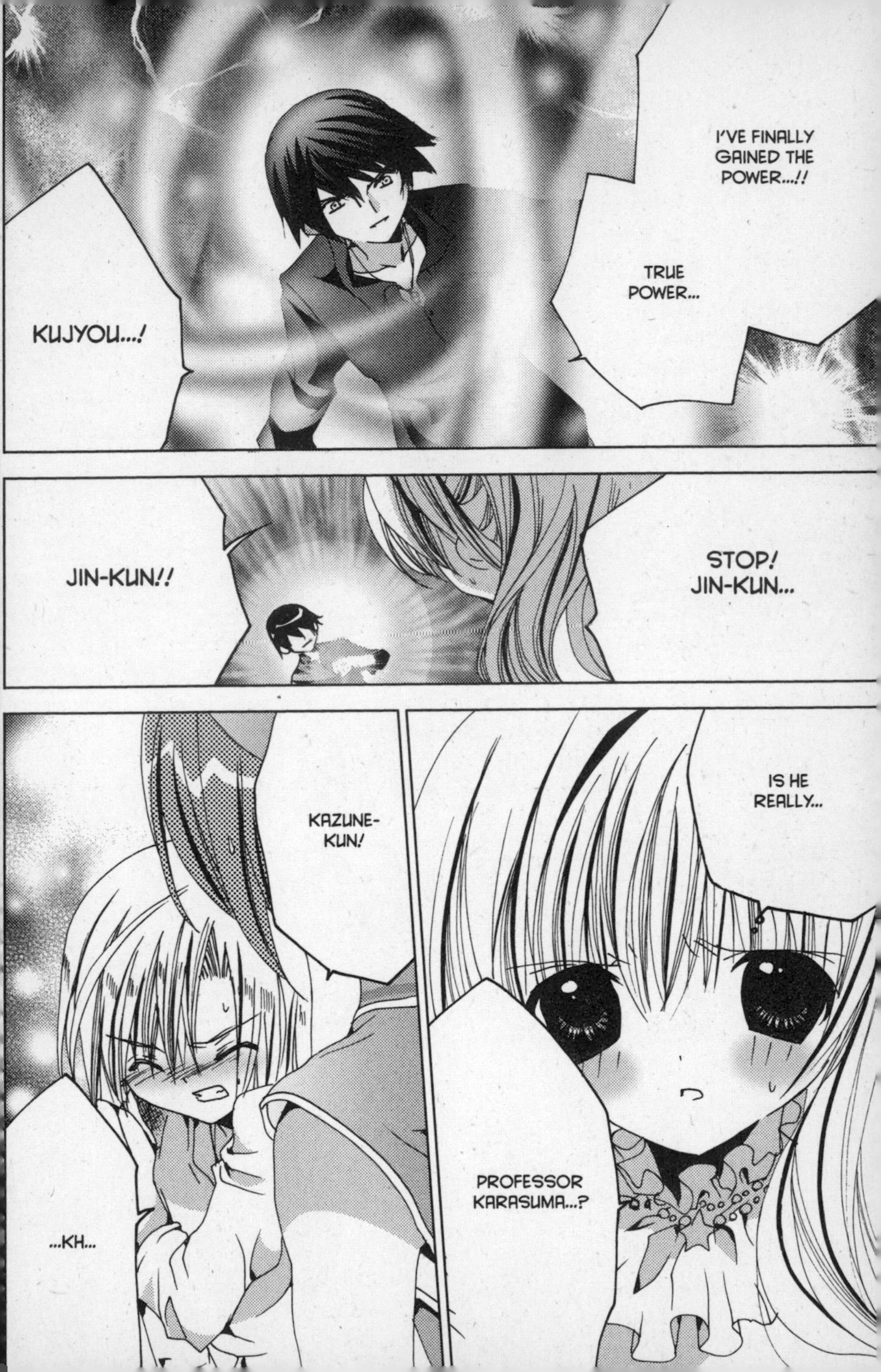
I'VE FINALLY GAINED THE POWER...!!
TRUE POWER...
KUJYOU...!
STOP! JIN-KUN...
JIN-KUN!!
IS HE REALLY...
PROFESSOR KARASUMA...?
KAZUNE-KUN!
...KH...

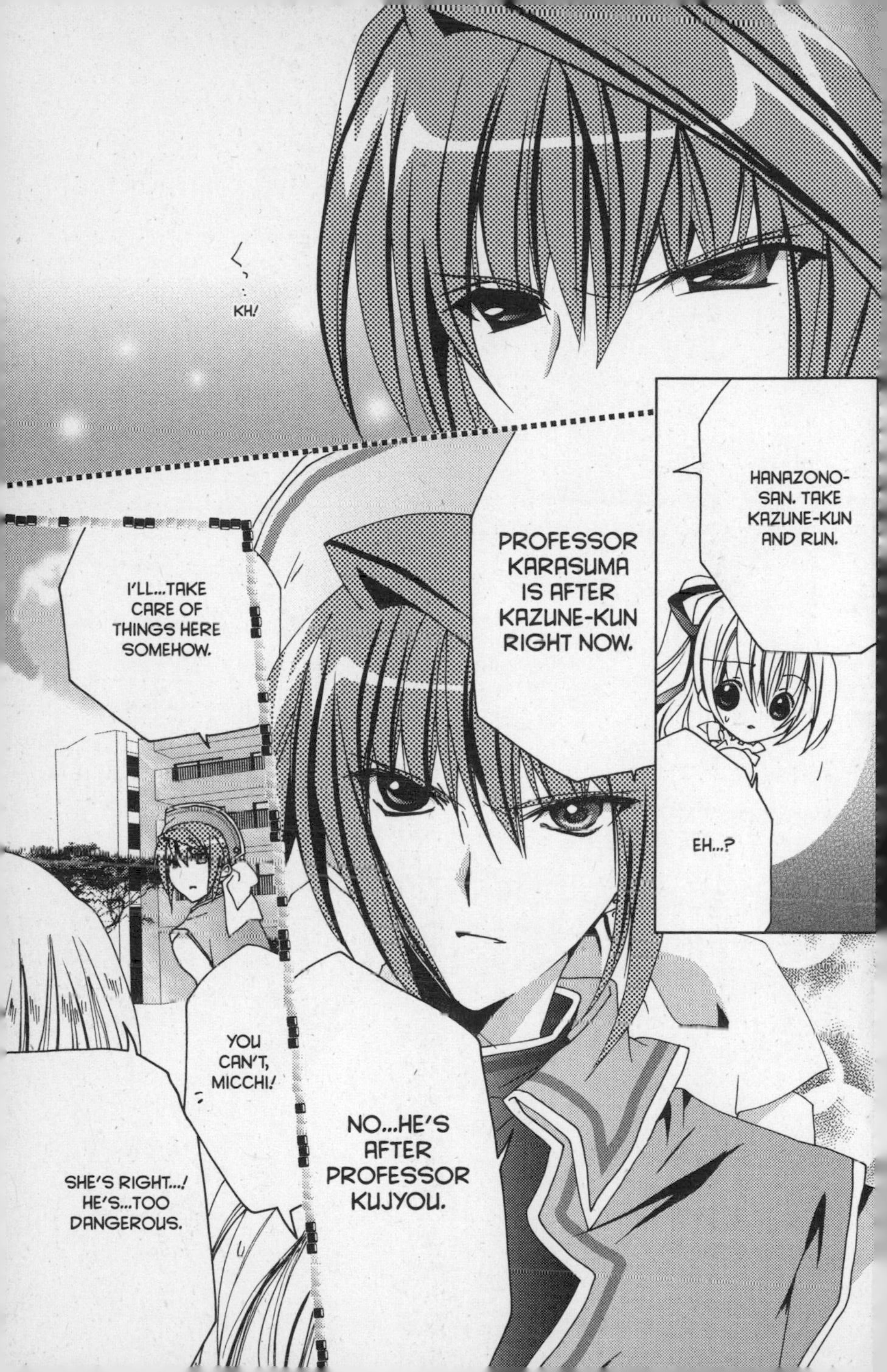

KH!
HANAZONO-SAN. TAKE KAZUNE-KUN AND RUN.
EH...?
PROFESSOR KARASUMA IS AFTER KAZUNE-KUN RIGHT NOW.
NO...HE'S AFTER PROFESSOR KUJYOU.
I'LL...TAKE CARE OF THINGS HERE SOMEHOW.
YOU CAN'T, MICCHI!
SHE'S RIGHT...! HE'S...TOO DANGEROUS.

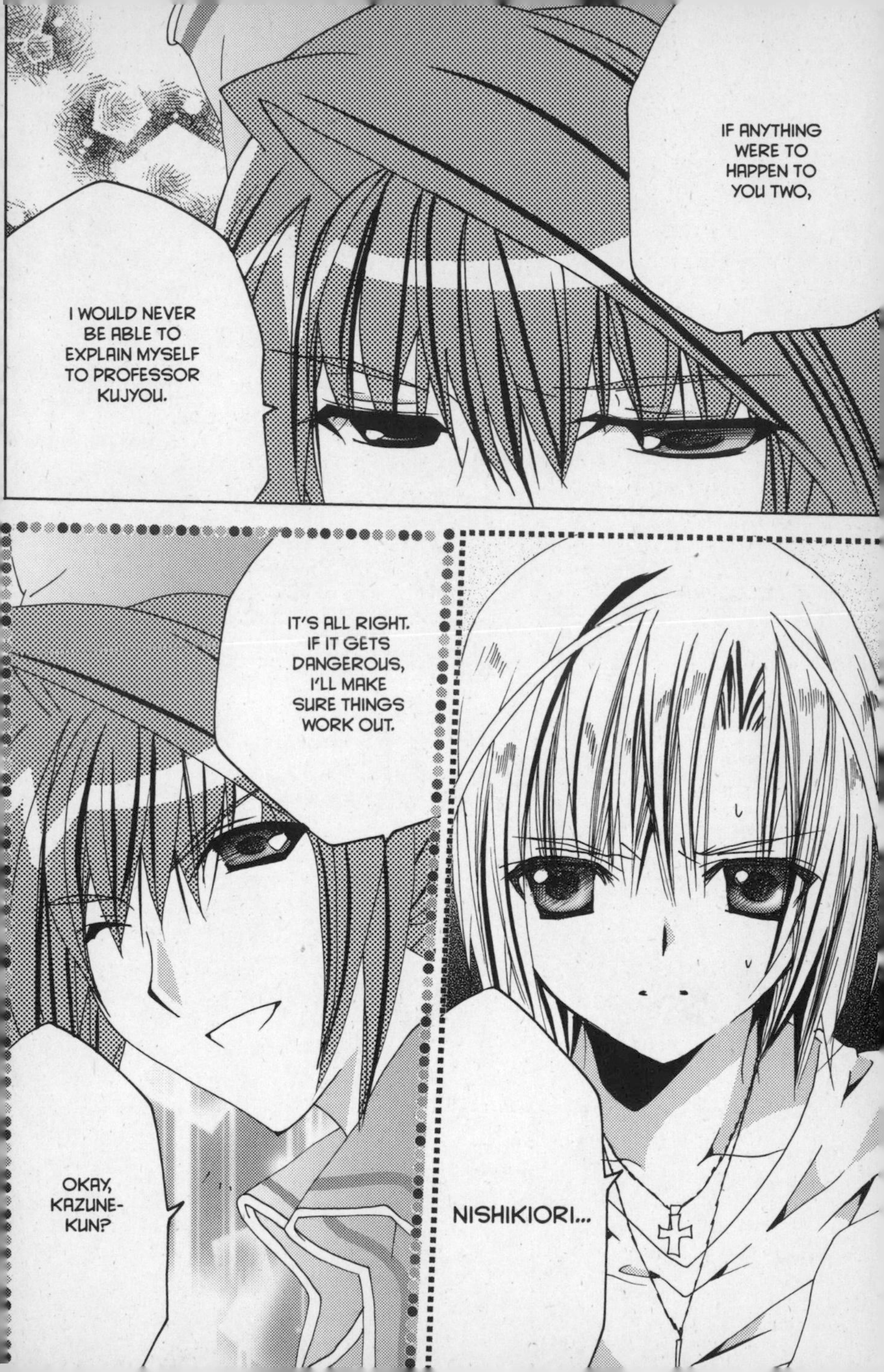
IF ANYTHING WERE TO HAPPEN TO YOU TWO,
I WOULD NEVER BE ABLE TO EXPLAIN MYSELF TO PROFESSOR KUJYOU.
NISHIKIORI...
IT'S ALL RIGHT. IF IT GETS DANGEROUS, I'LL MAKE SURE THINGS WORK OUT.
OKAY, KAZUNE-KUN?

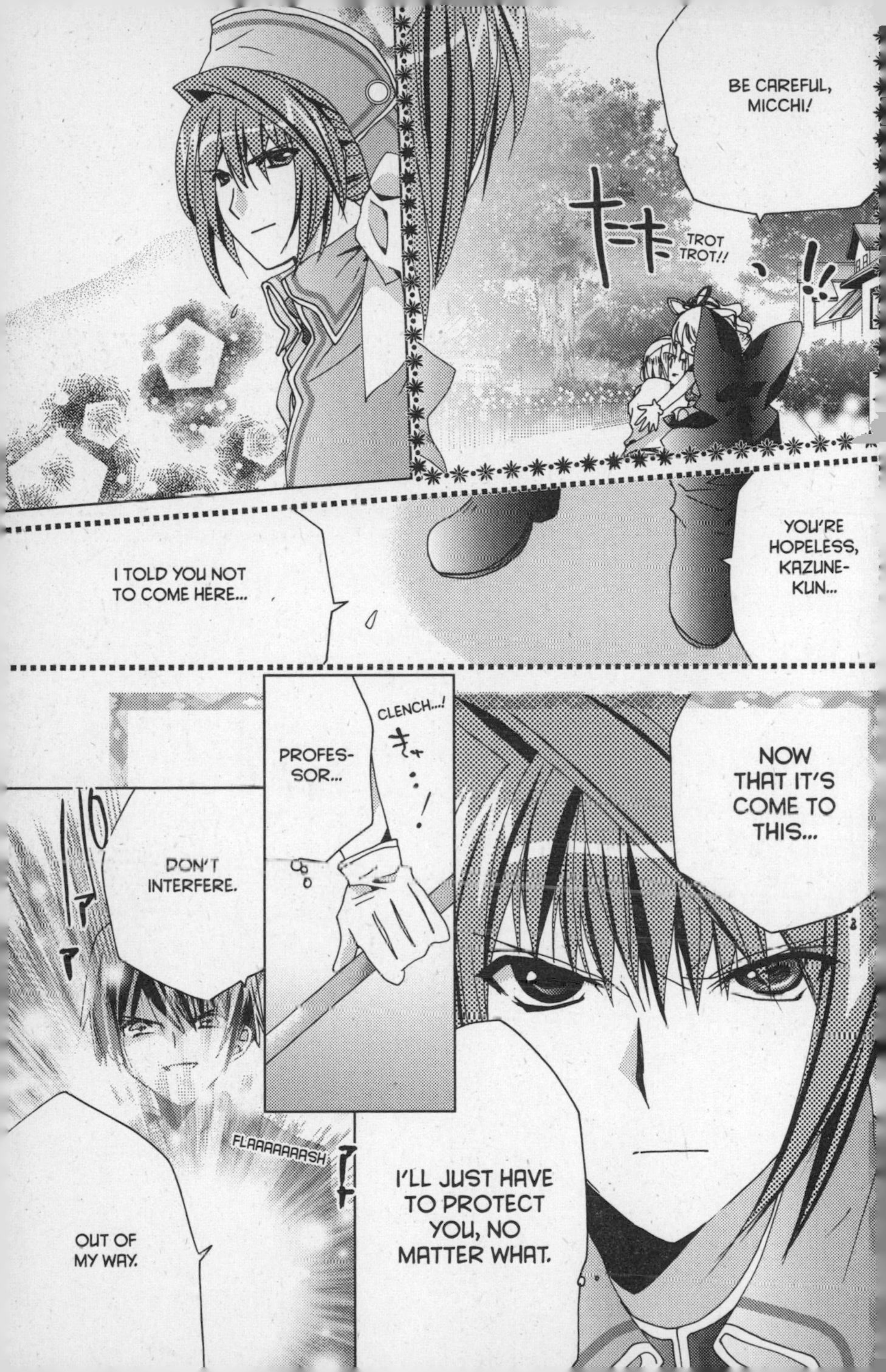
BE CAREFUL, MICCHI!
TROT TROT!!
YOU'RE HOPELESS, KAZUNE-KUN...
I TOLD YOU NOT TO COME HERE...
NOW THAT IT'S COME TO THIS...
I'LL JUST HAVE TO PROTECT YOU, NO MATTER WHAT.
CLENCH...!
PROFESSOR...
DON'T INTERFERE.
FLAAAAAAAASH
OUT OF MY WAY.

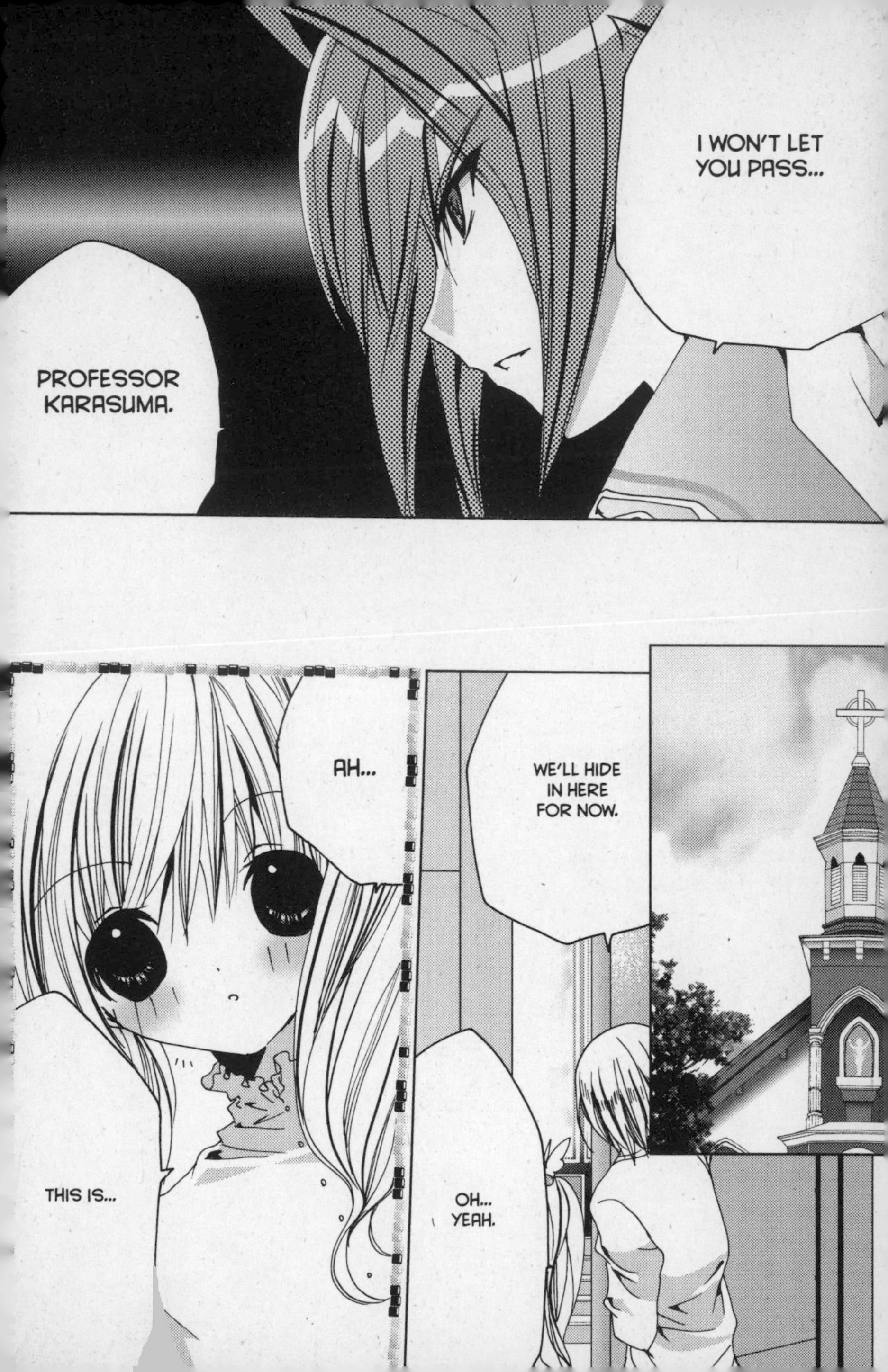
I WON'T LET YOU PASS...
PROFESSOR KARASUMA.
WE'LL HIDE IN HERE FOR NOW.
OH... YEAH.
AH...
THIS IS...

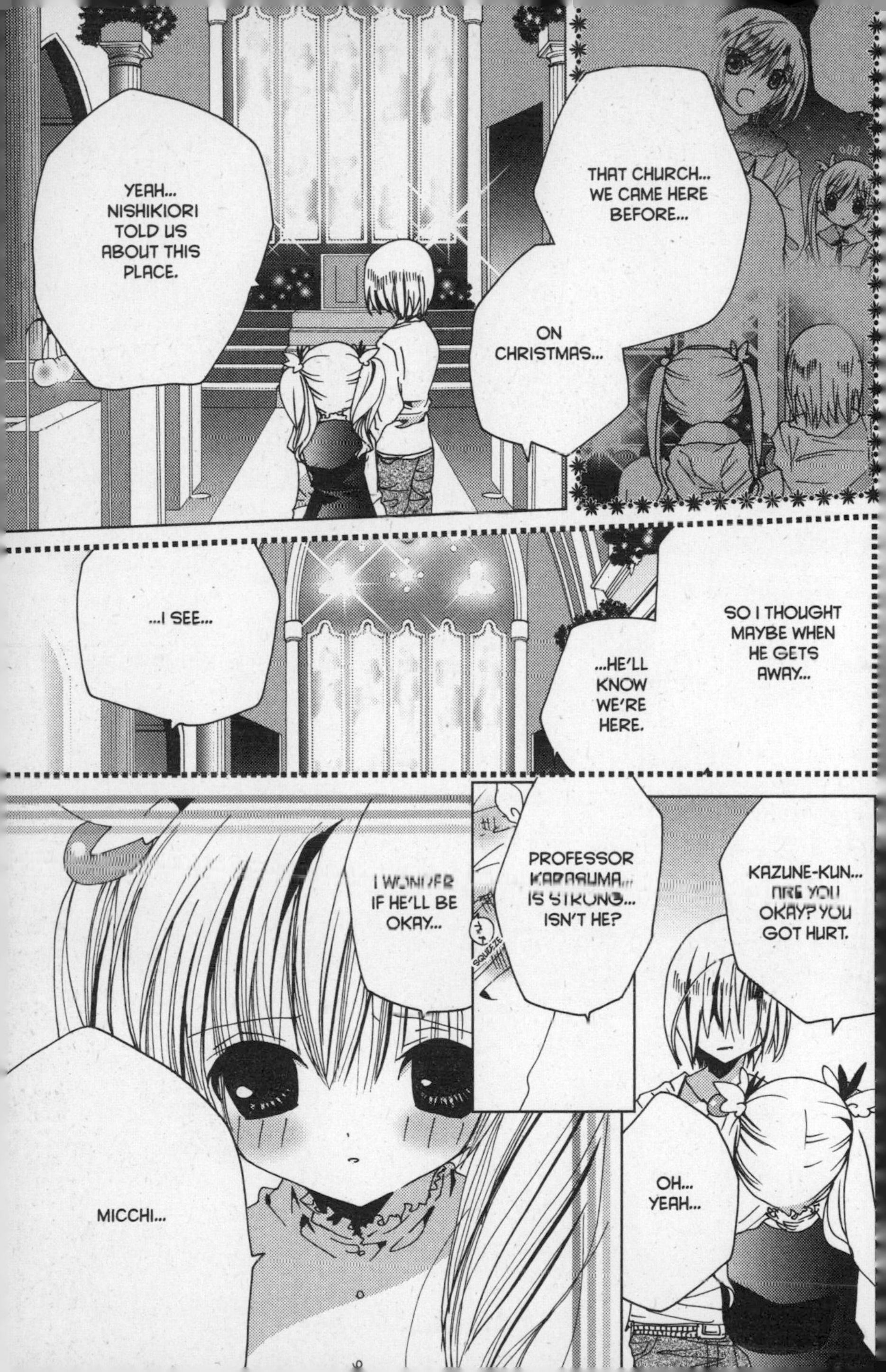
THAT CHURCH... WE CAME HERE BEFORE...
ON CHRISTMAS...
YEAH... NISHIKIORI TOLD US ABOUT THIS PLACE.
SO I THOUGHT MAYBE WHEN HE GETS AWAY...
...HE'LL KNOW WE'RE HERE.
...I SEE...
KAZUNE-KUN... ARE YOU OKAY? YOU GOT HURT.
OH... YEAH...
PROFESSOR KARASUMA... IS STRONG... ISN'T HE?
SQUEEZE
I WONDER IF HE'LL BE OKAY...
MICCHI...

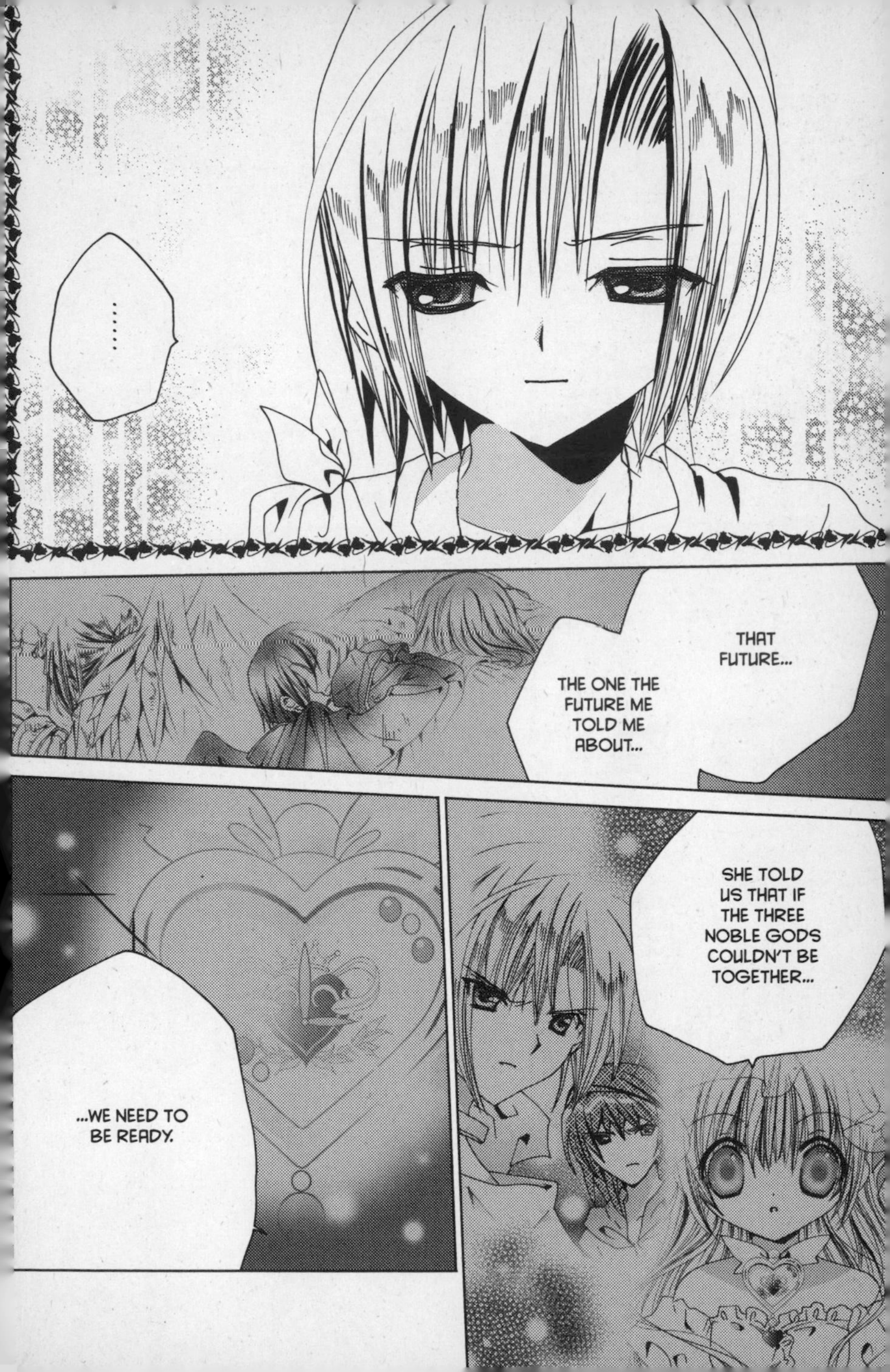
……
THAT FUTURE...
THE ONE THE FUTURE ME TOLD ME ABOUT...
SHE TOLD US THAT IF THE THREE NOBLE GODS COULDN'T BE TOGETHER...
...WE NEED TO BE READY.

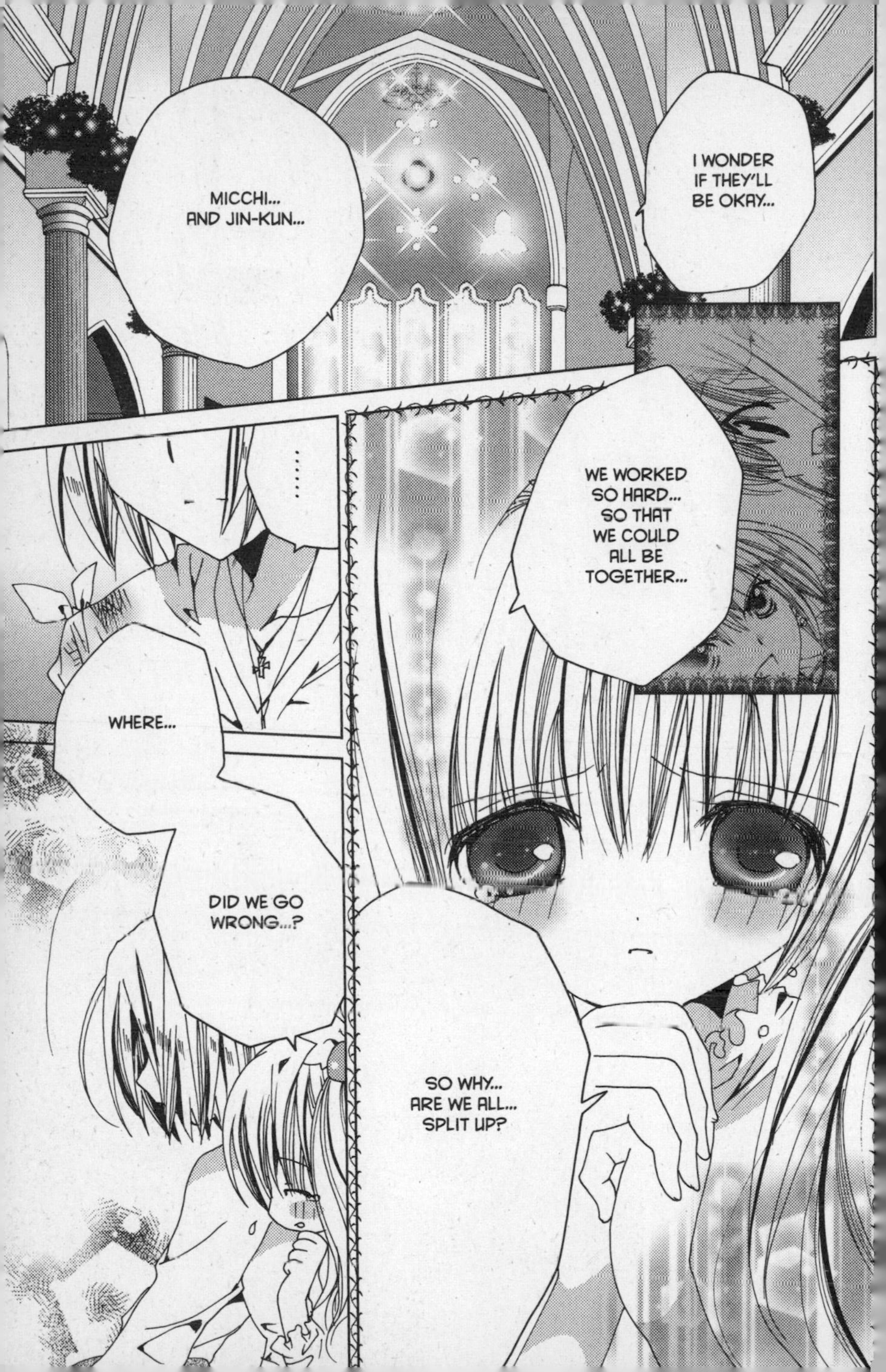
I WONDER IF THEY'LL BE OKAY...
MICCHI... AND JIN-KUN...
WE WORKED SO HARD... SO THAT WE COULD ALL BE TOGETHER...
SO WHY... ARE WE ALL... SPLIT UP?
......
WHERE...
DID WE GO WRONG...?

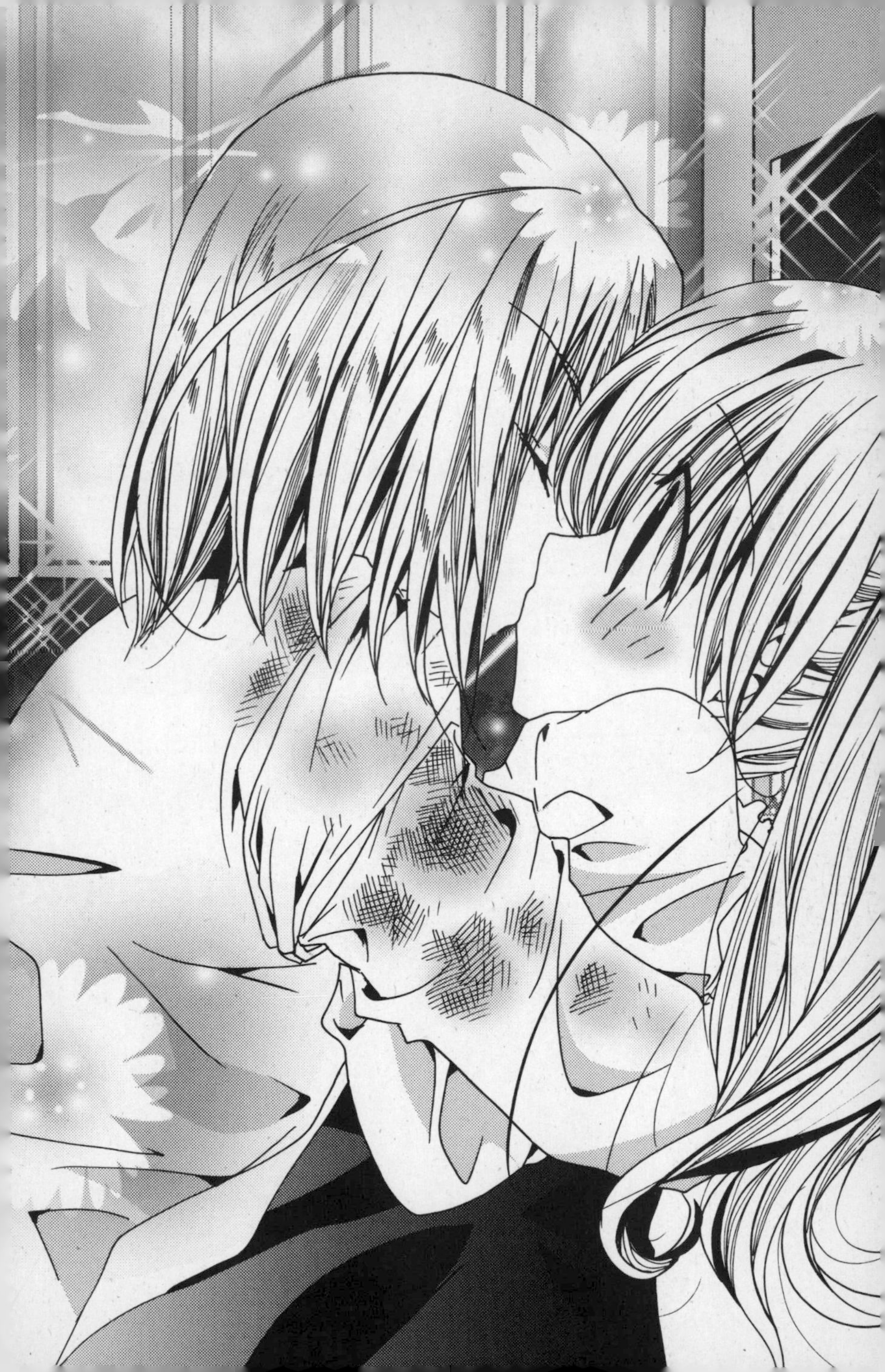

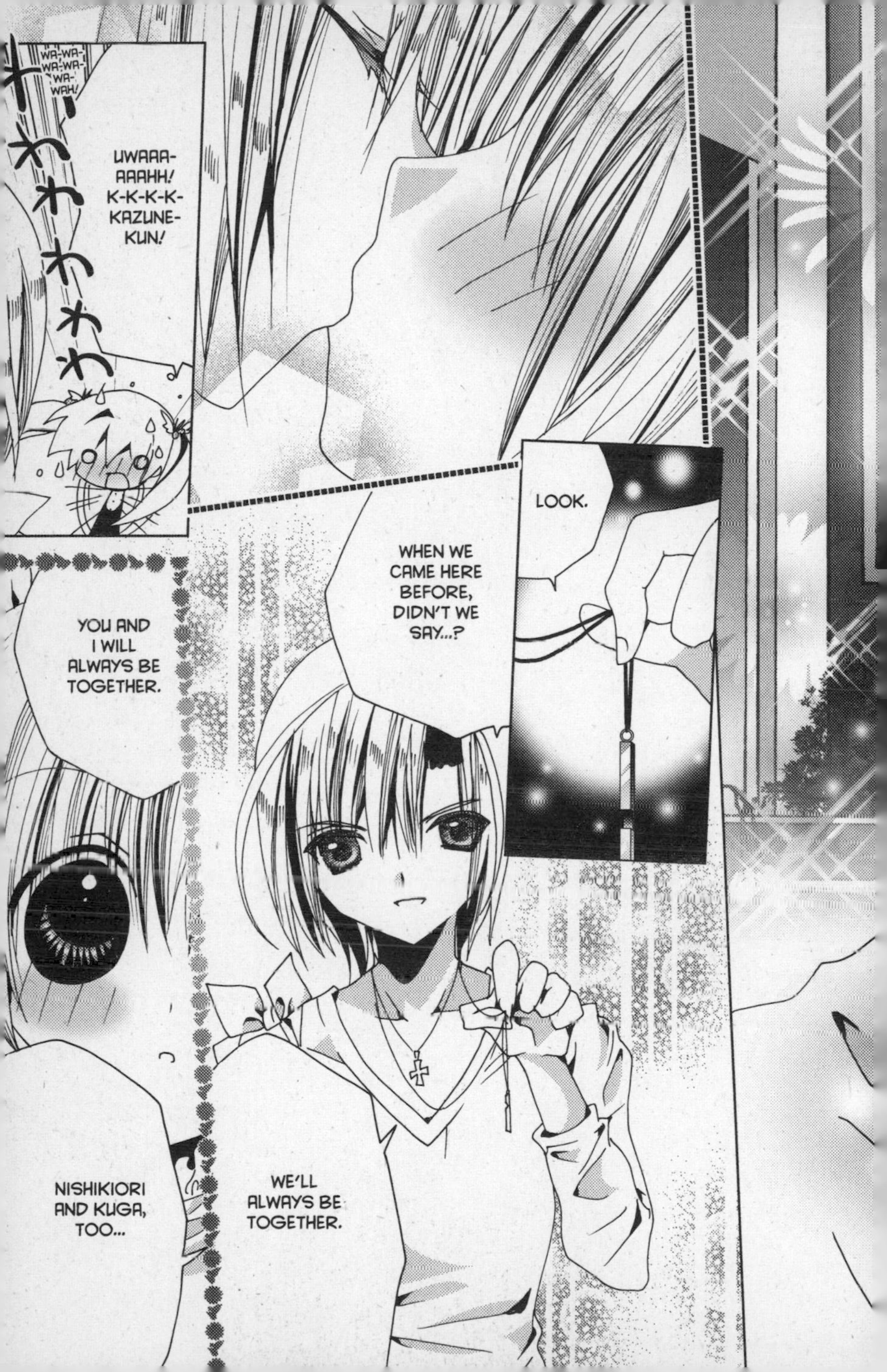
WA-WA-WA-WA-WA-WAH!
UWAAA-AAAHH! K-K-K-K-KAZUNE-KUN!
LOOK.
WHEN WE CAME HERE BEFORE, DIDN'T WE SAY...?
YOU AND I WILL ALWAYS BE TOGETHER.
WE'LL ALWAYS BE TOGETHER.
NISHIKIORI AND KUGA, TOO...

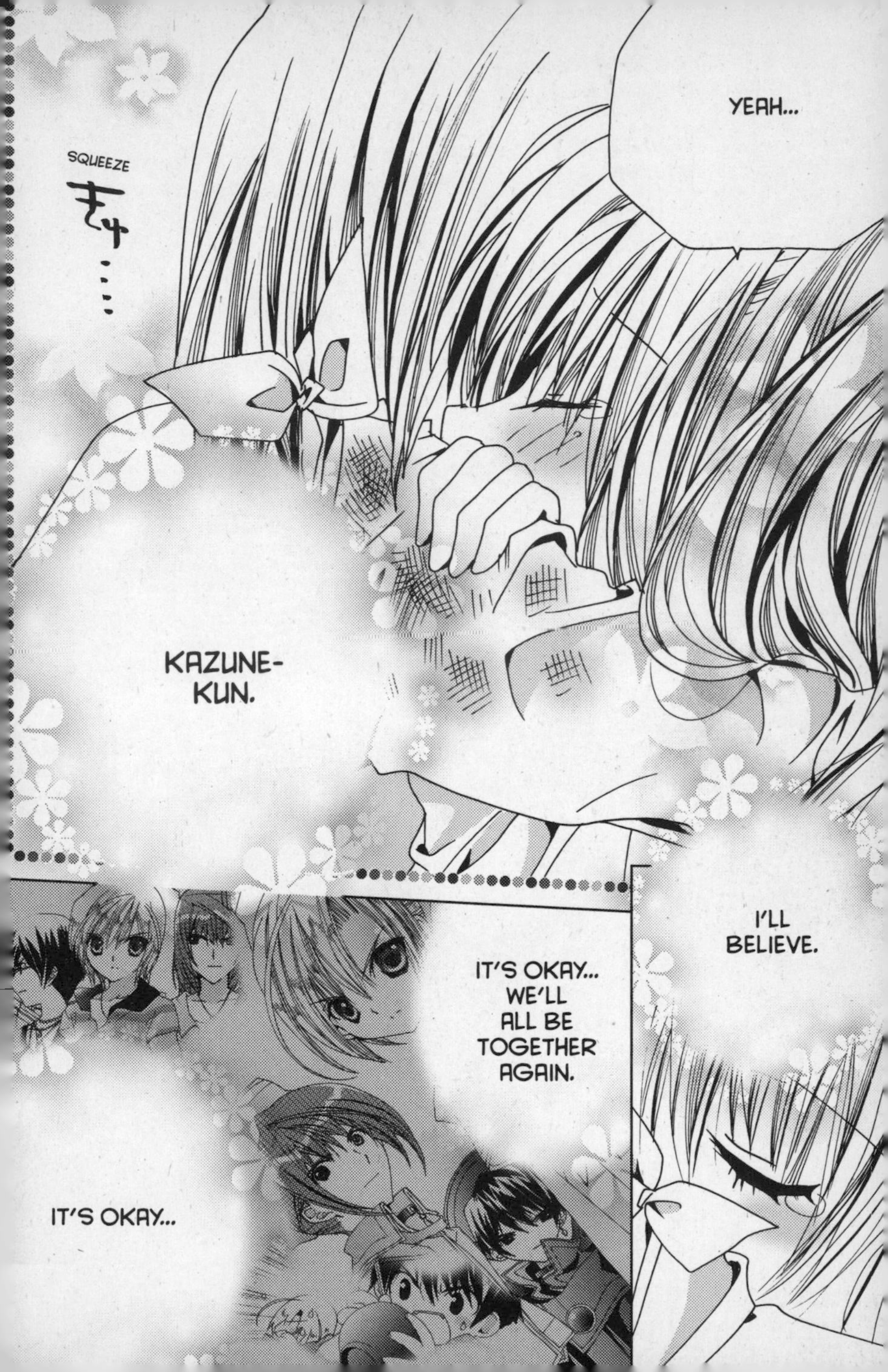
YEAH...
SQUEEZE
KAZUNE-KUN.
I'LL BELIEVE.
IT'S OKAY... WE'LL ALL BE TOGETHER AGAIN.
IT'S OKAY...

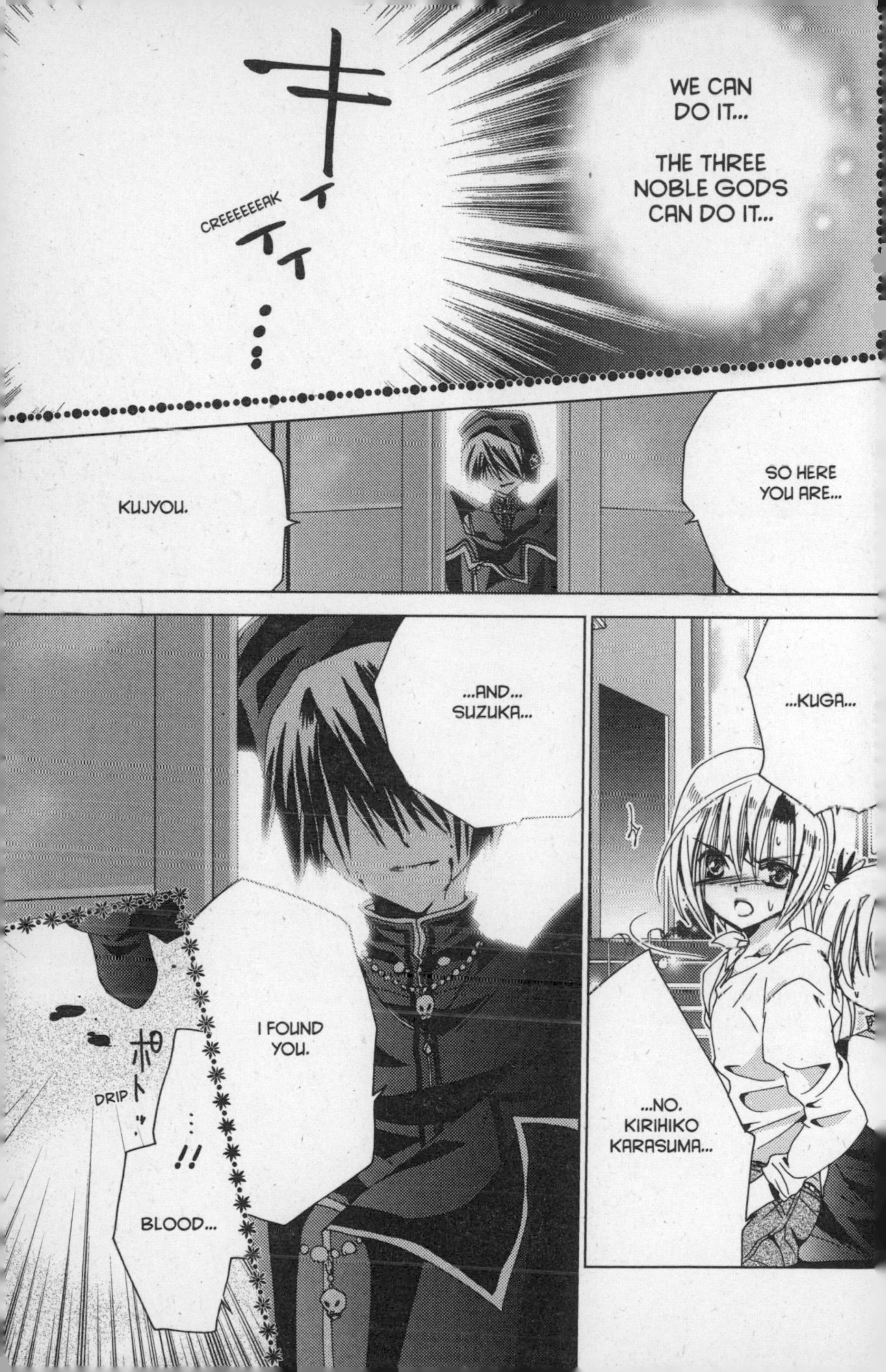
WE CAN DO IT...
THE THREE NOBLE GODS CAN DO IT...
キィィィ...
CREEEEEEAK
SO HERE YOU ARE...
KUJYOU.
...KUGA...
...NO. KIRIHIKO KARASUMA...
...AND... SUZUKA...
I FOUND YOU.
ポトッ
DRIP
...!!
BLOOD...

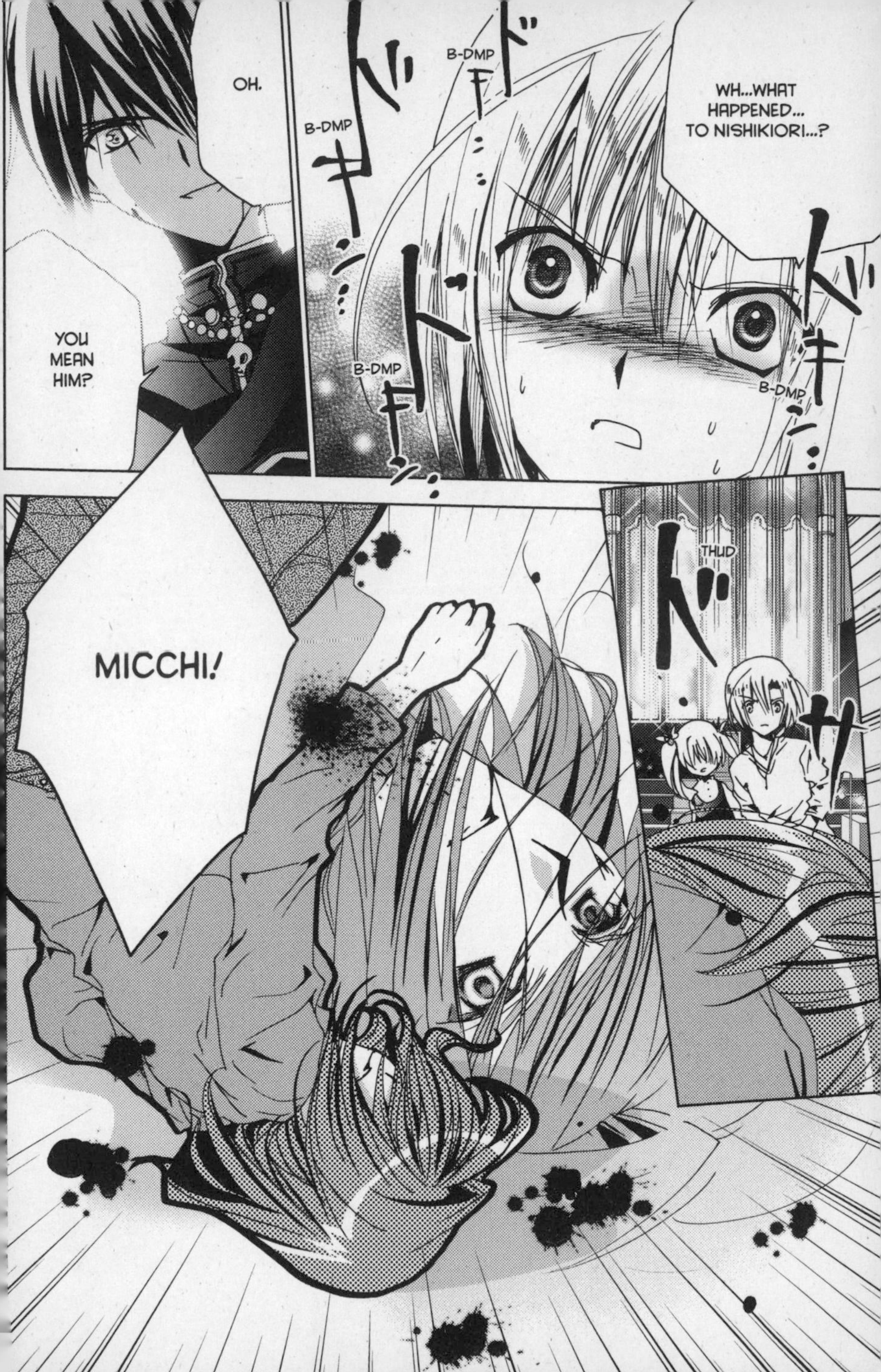
WH...WHAT HAPPENED... TO NISHIKIORI...?
B-DMP
B-DMP
B-DMP
B-DMP
OH.
YOU MEAN HIM?
THUD
MICCHI!

HERE HE IS.
I BROUGHT HIM.

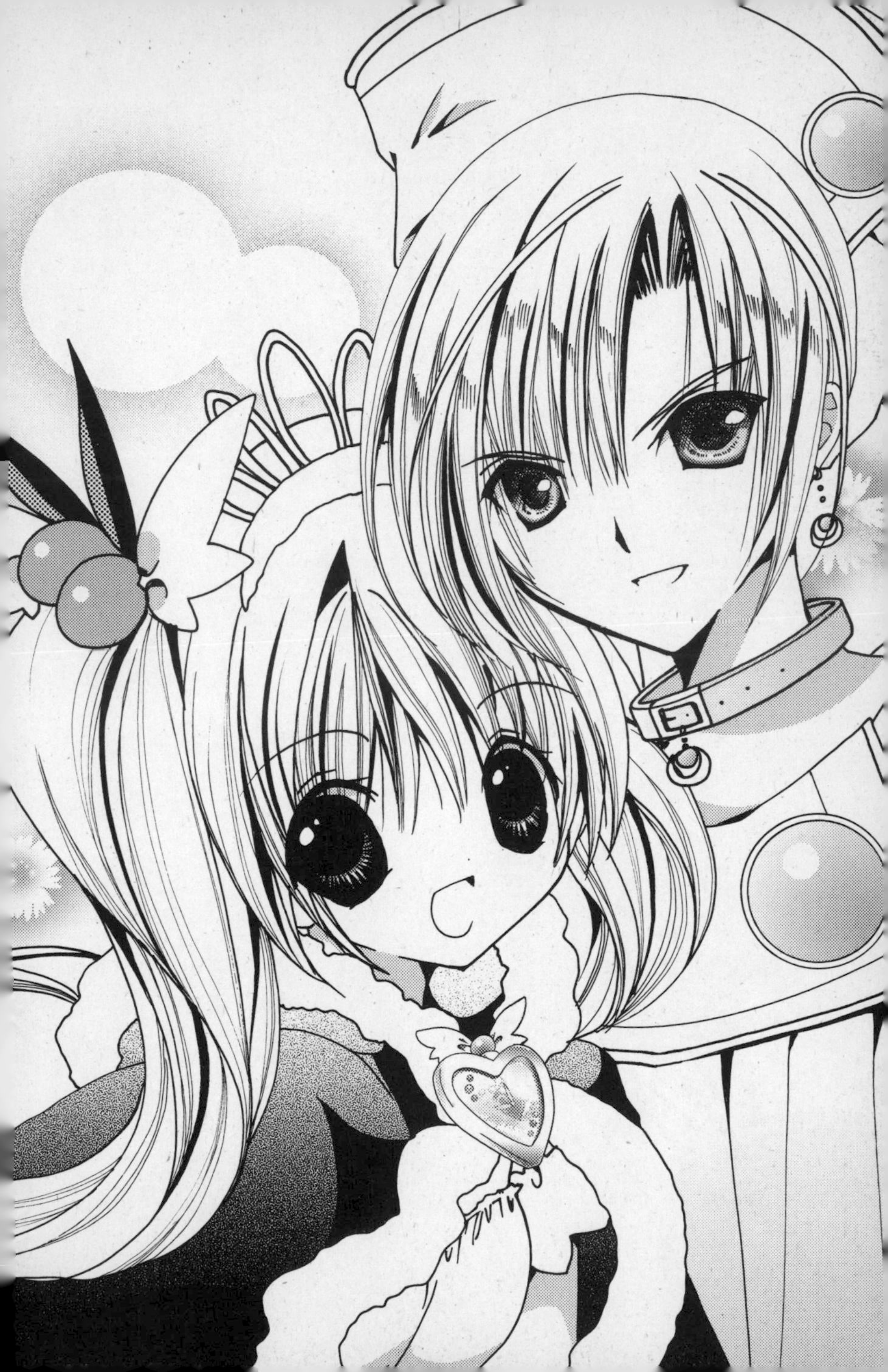

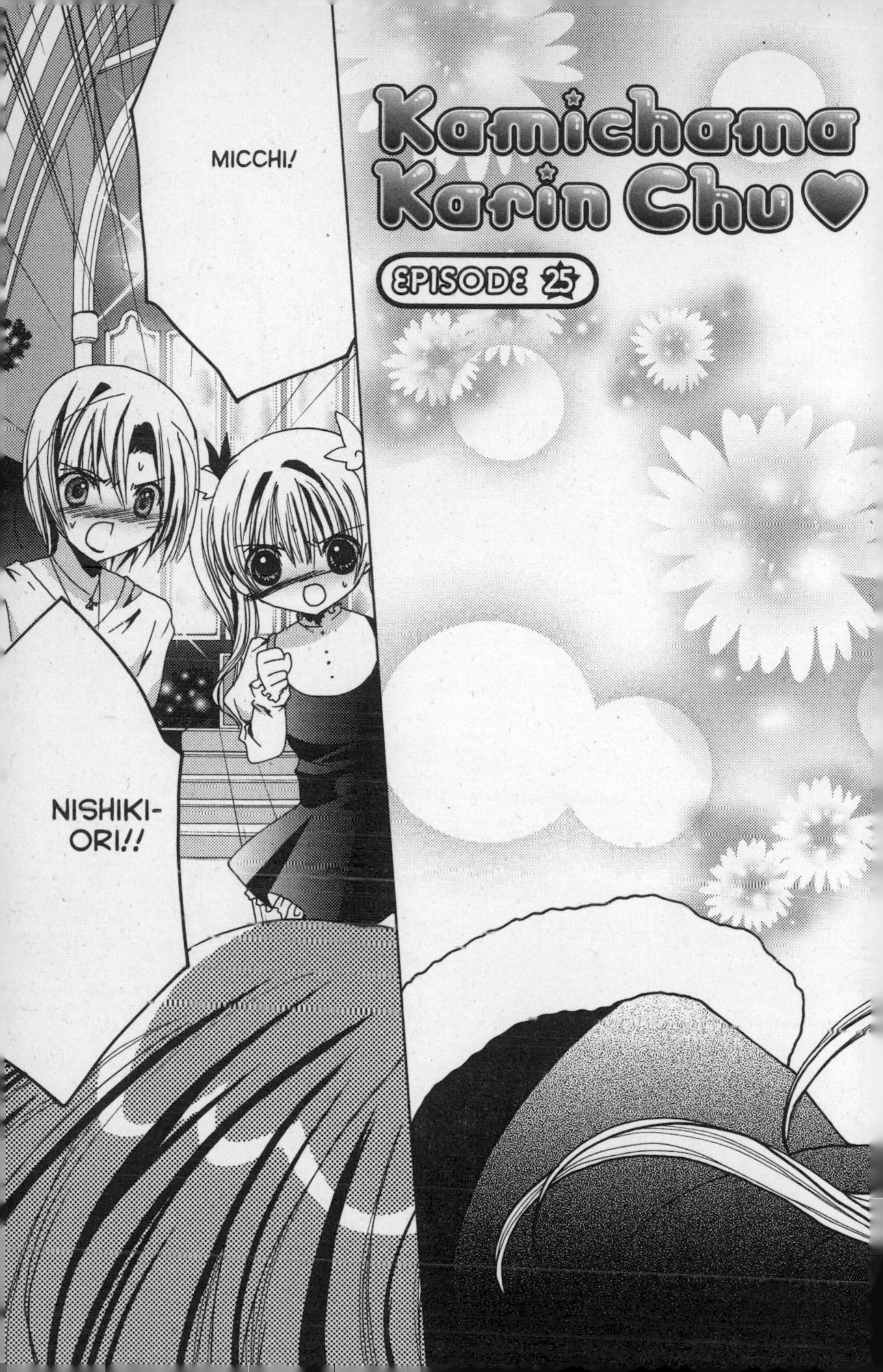
Kamichama Karin Chu♥
EPISODE 25
MICCHI!
NISHIKI-ORI!!

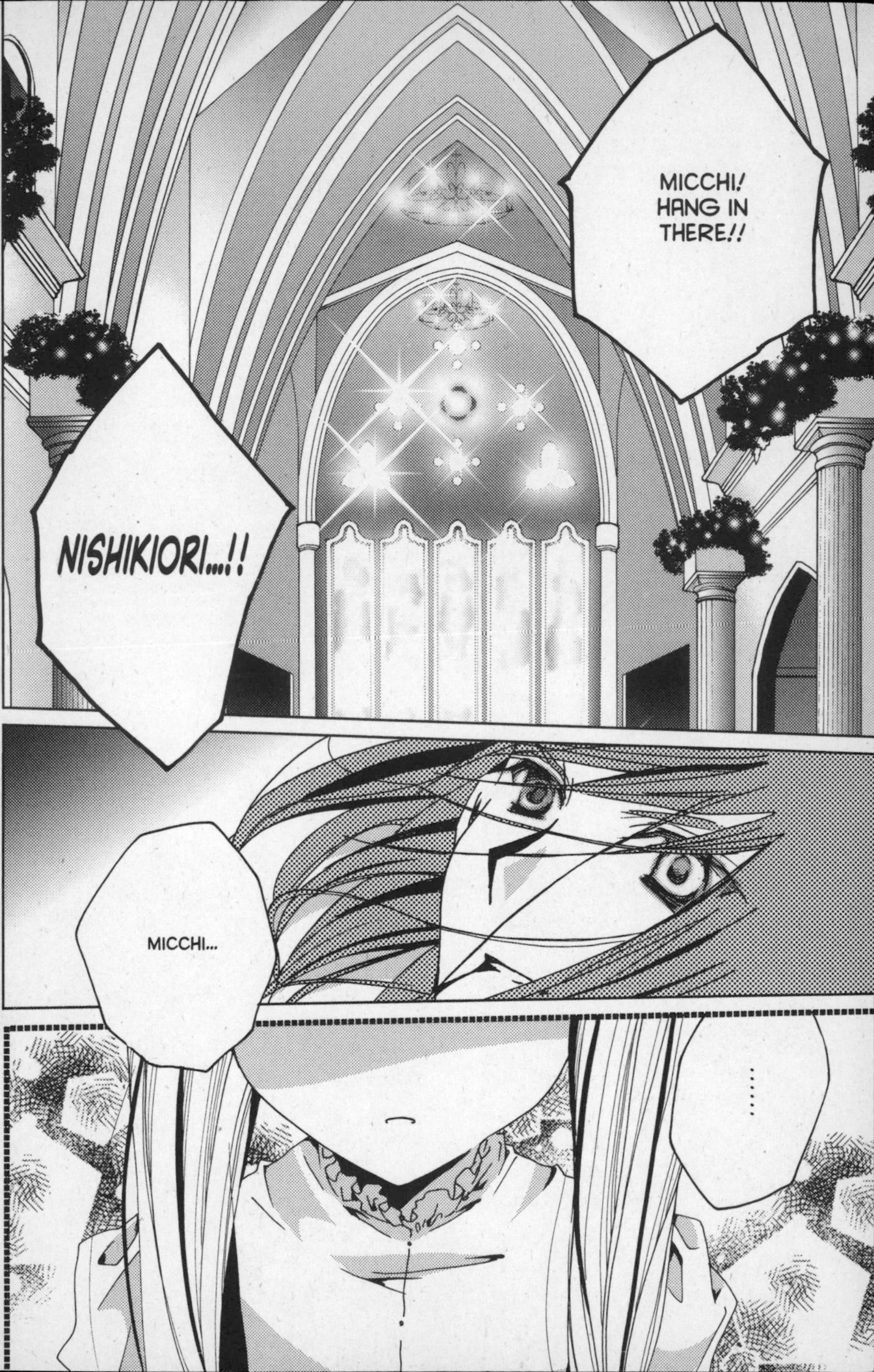
MICCHI! HANG IN THERE!!
NISHIKIORI...!!
MICCHI...
......

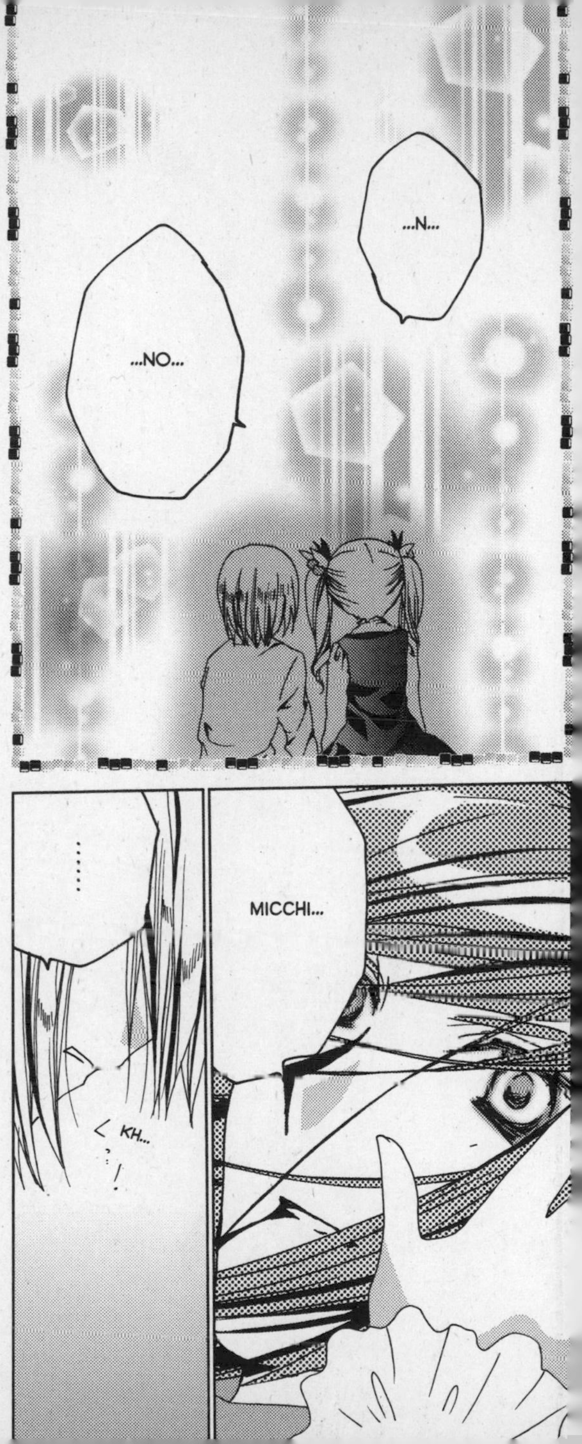
...N...
...NO...
MICCHI...
......
KH...
!
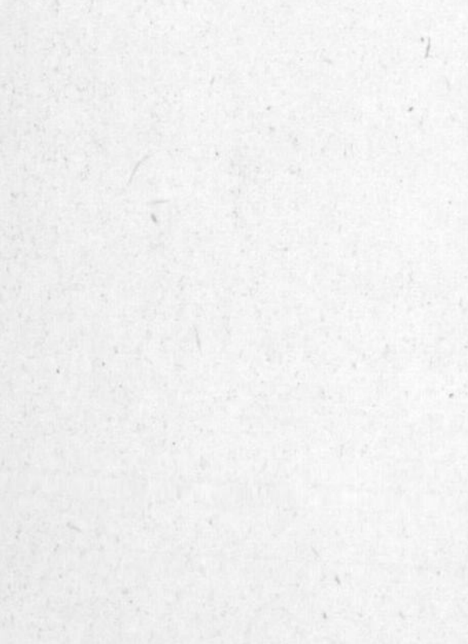
BUT ISN'T THIS A MANGA FOR YOUNGER READERS?!

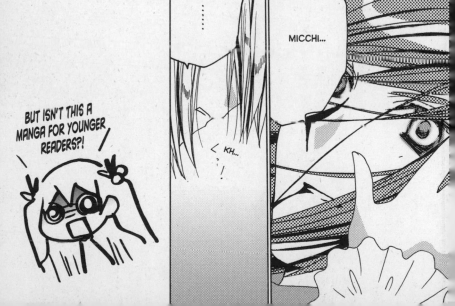

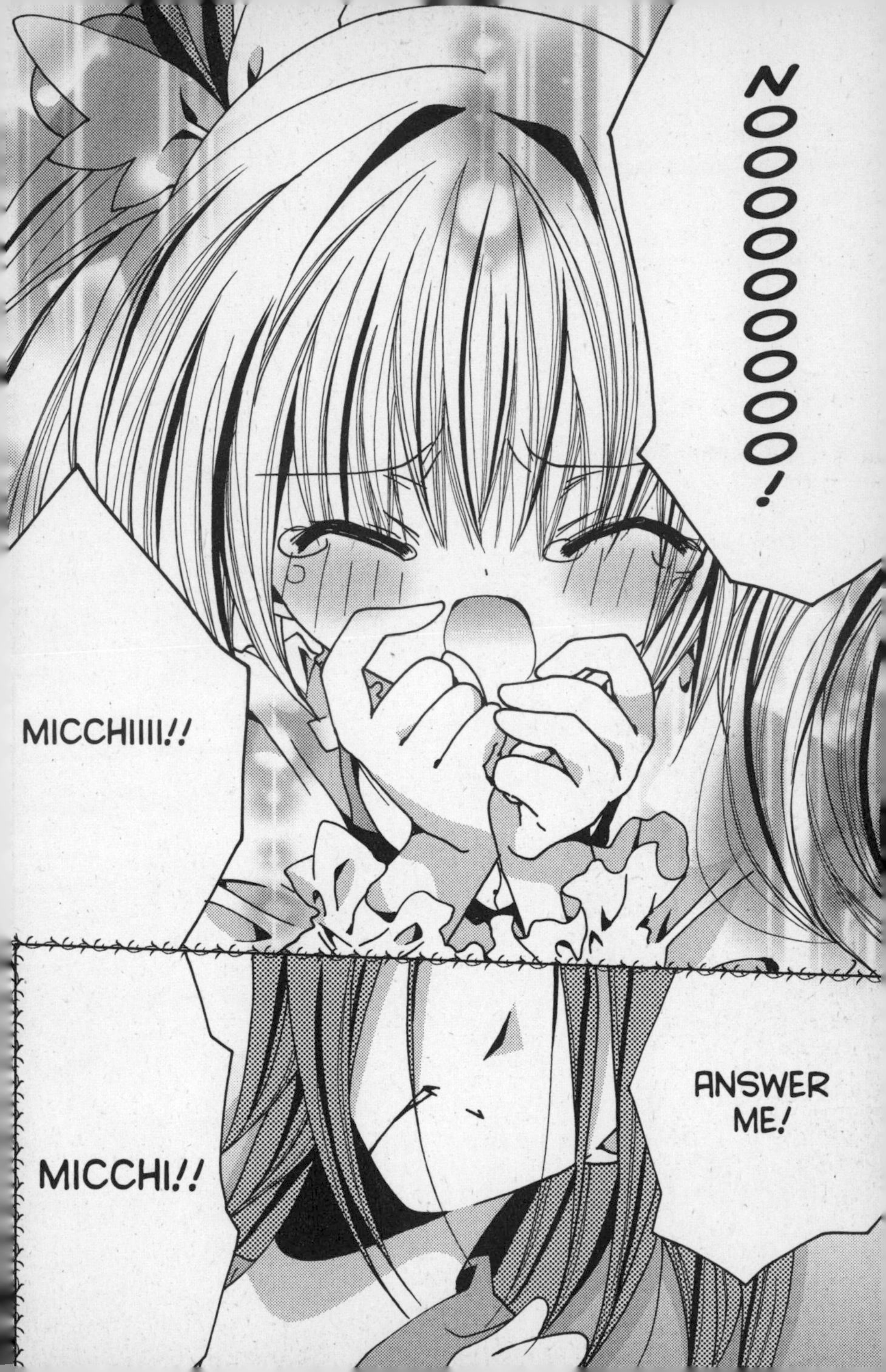
NOOOOOOOOO!
MICCHIIII!!
ANSWER ME!
MICCHI!!

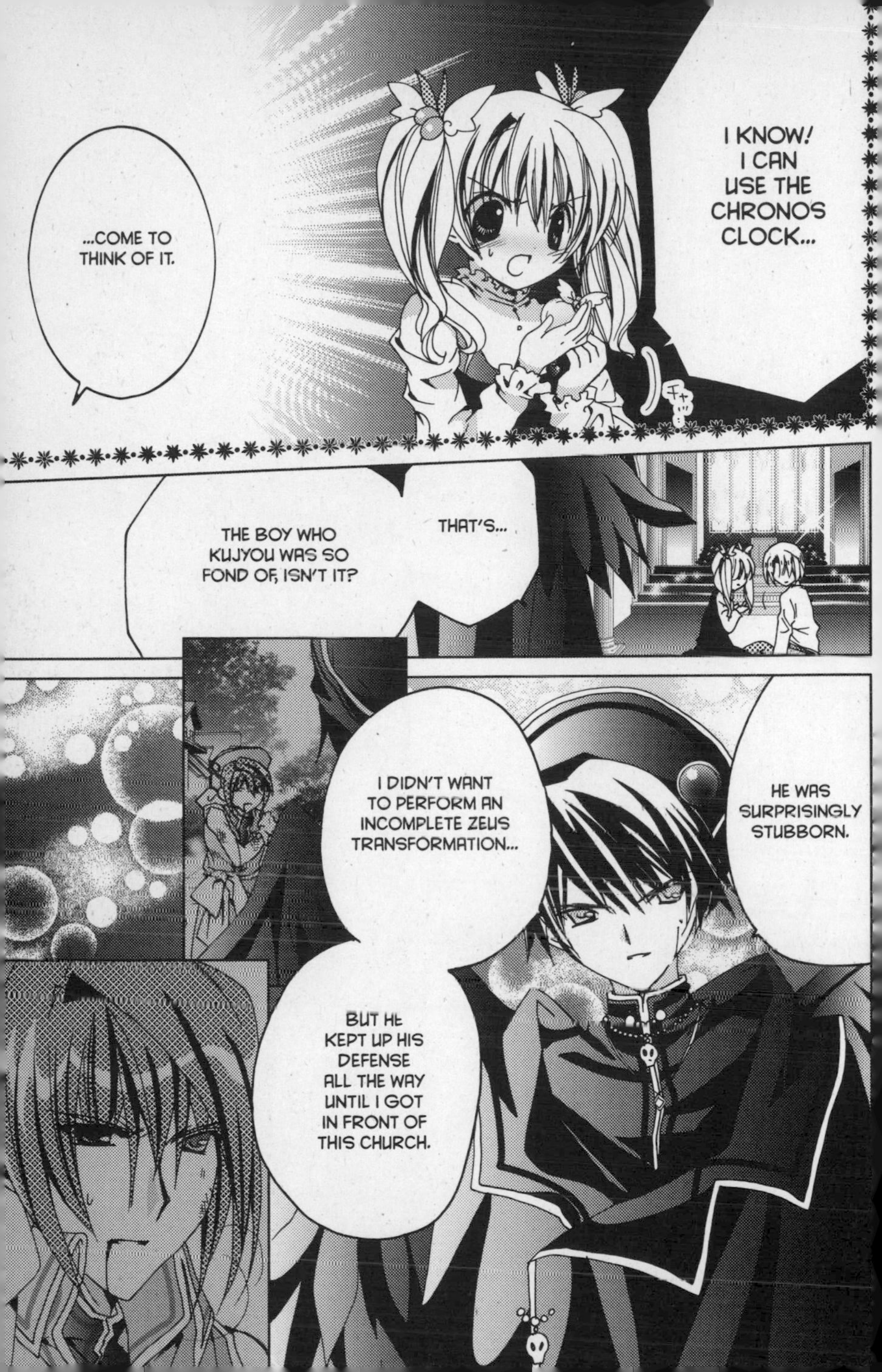
I KNOW! I CAN USE THE CHRONOS CLOCK...
...COME TO THINK OF IT.
THAT'S...
THE BOY WHO KUJYOU WAS SO FOND OF, ISN'T IT?
HE WAS SURPRISINGLY STUBBORN.
I DIDN'T WANT TO PERFORM AN INCOMPLETE ZEUS TRANSFORMATION...
BUT HE KEPT UP HIS DEFENSE ALL THE WAY UNTIL I GOT IN FRONT OF THIS CHURCH.

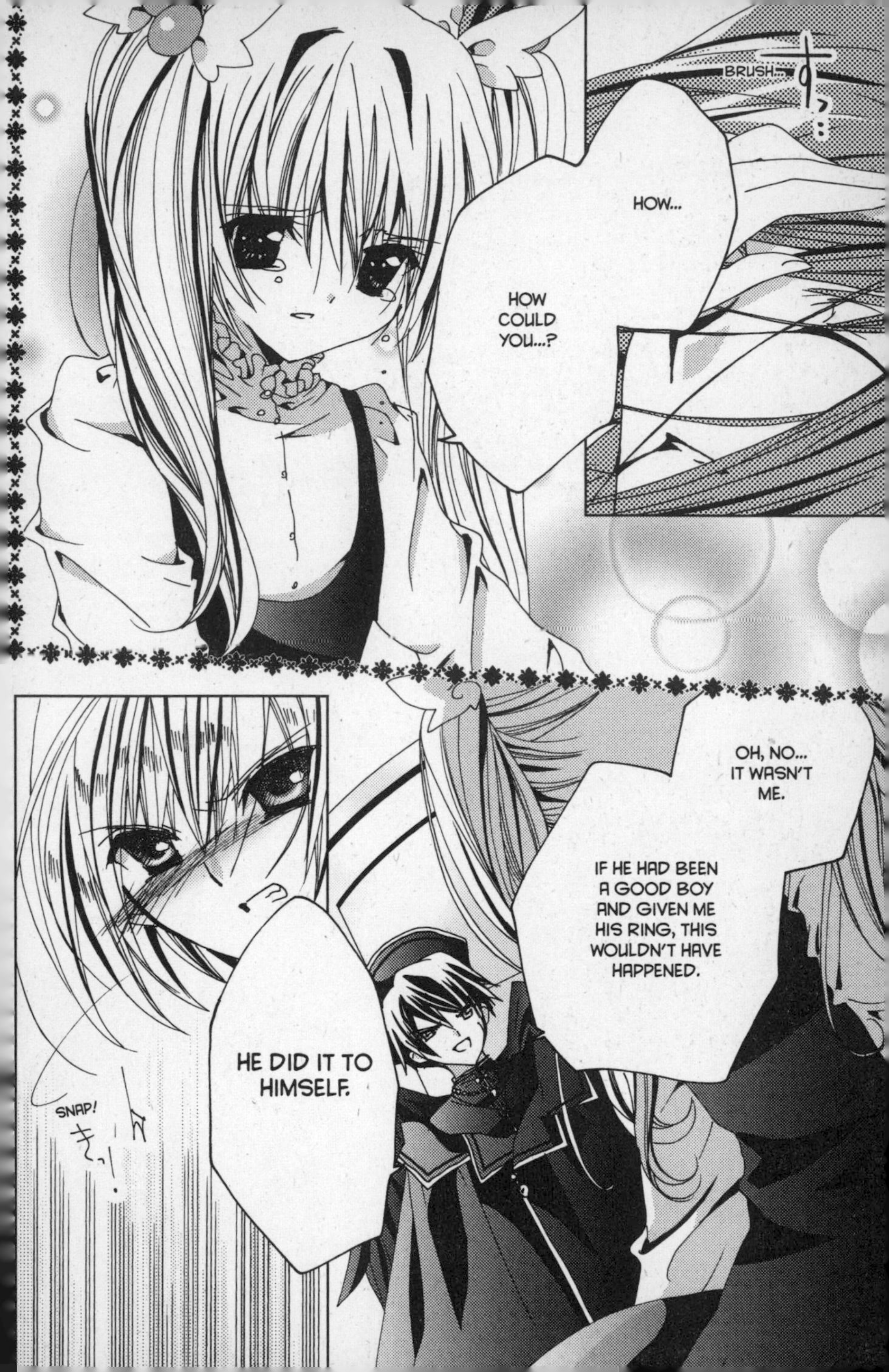
BRUSH...
HOW...
HOW COULD YOU...?
OH, NO... IT WASN'T ME.
IF HE HAD BEEN A GOOD BOY AND GIVEN ME HIS RING, THIS WOULDN'T HAVE HAPPENED.
HE DID IT TO HIMSELF.
SNAP!

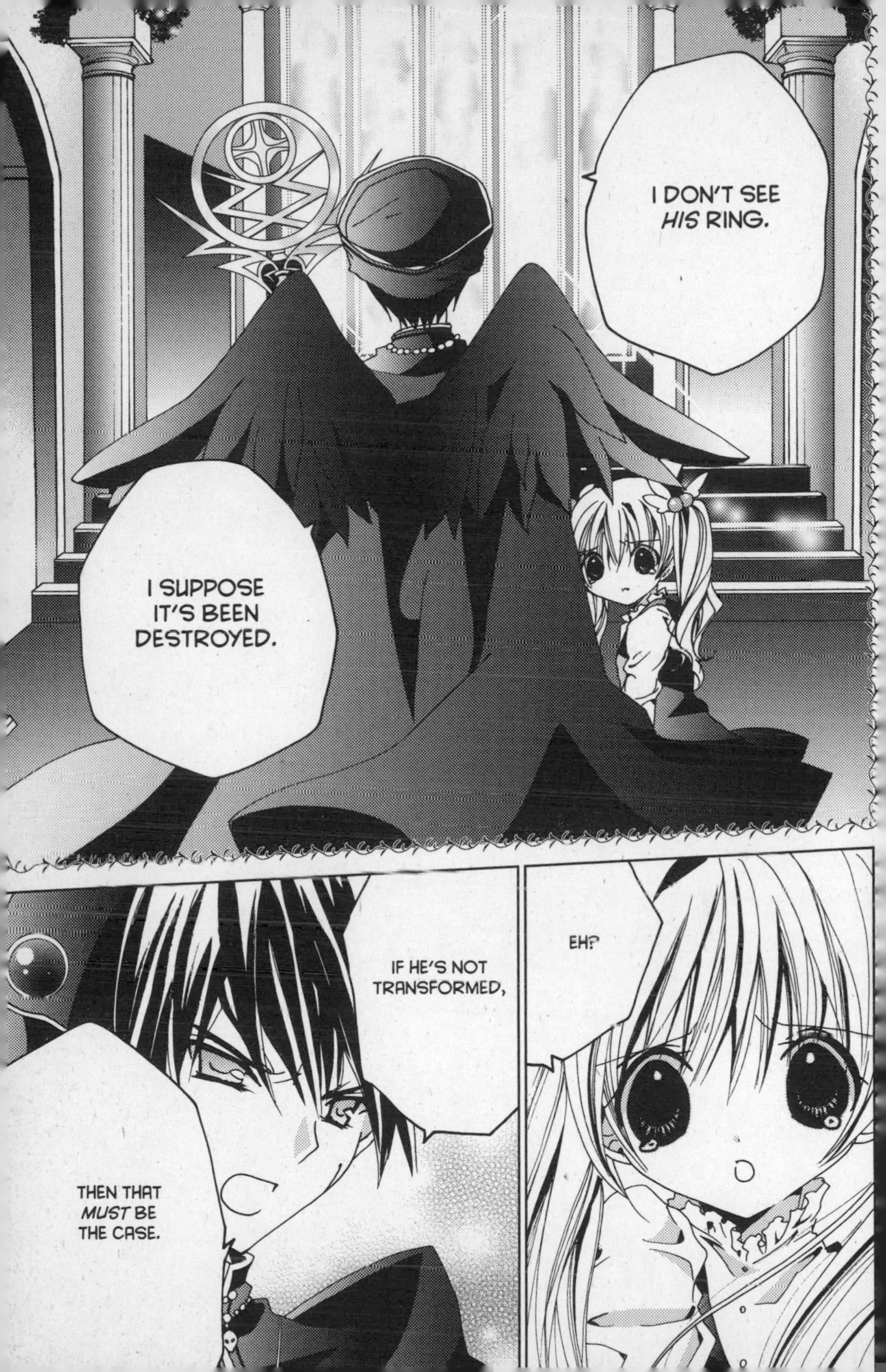
I DON'T SEE *HIS* RING.
I SUPPOSE IT'S BEEN DESTROYED.
EH?
IF HE'S NOT TRANSFORMED,
THEN THAT *MUST* BE THE CASE.

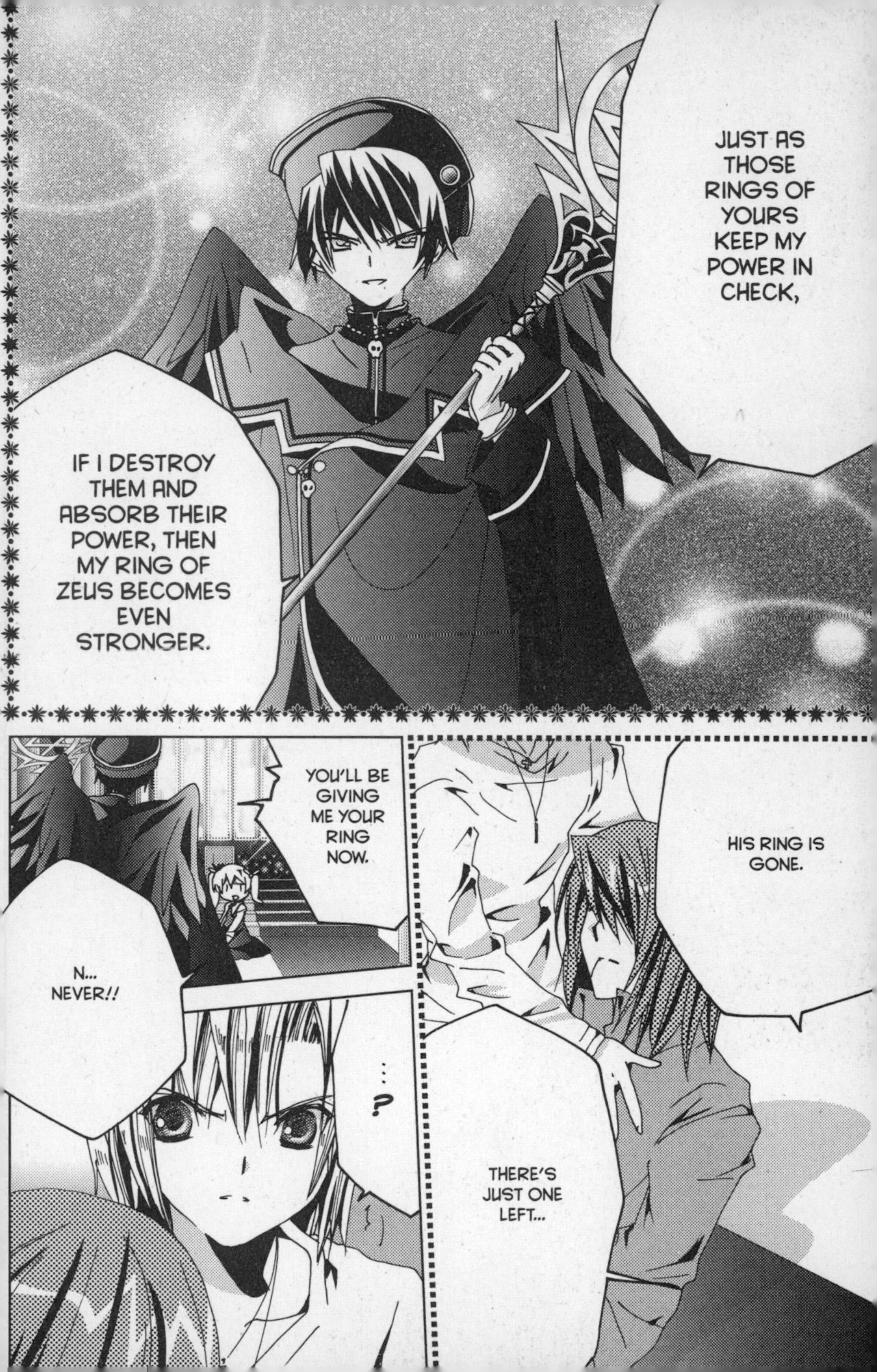
JUST AS THOSE RINGS OF YOURS KEEP MY POWER IN CHECK,
IF I DESTROY THEM AND ABSORB THEIR POWER, THEN MY RING OF ZEUS BECOMES EVEN STRONGER.
HIS RING IS GONE.
THERE'S JUST ONE LEFT...
YOU'LL BE GIVING ME YOUR RING NOW.
N... NEVER!!
...?

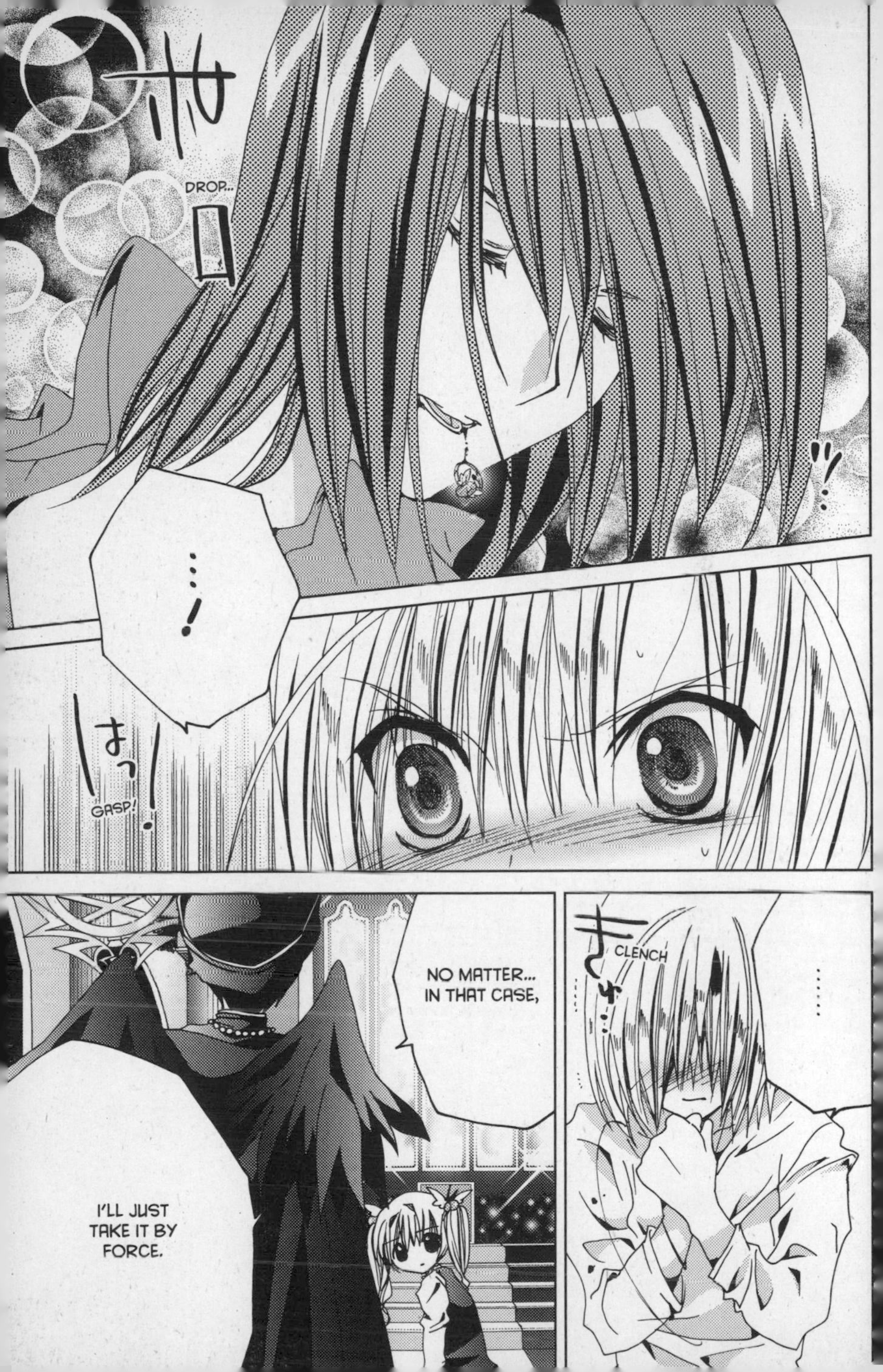
DROP...
!!
...!
はっ
GASP!
CLENCH
......
NO MATTER... IN THAT CASE,
I'LL JUST TAKE IT BY FORCE.

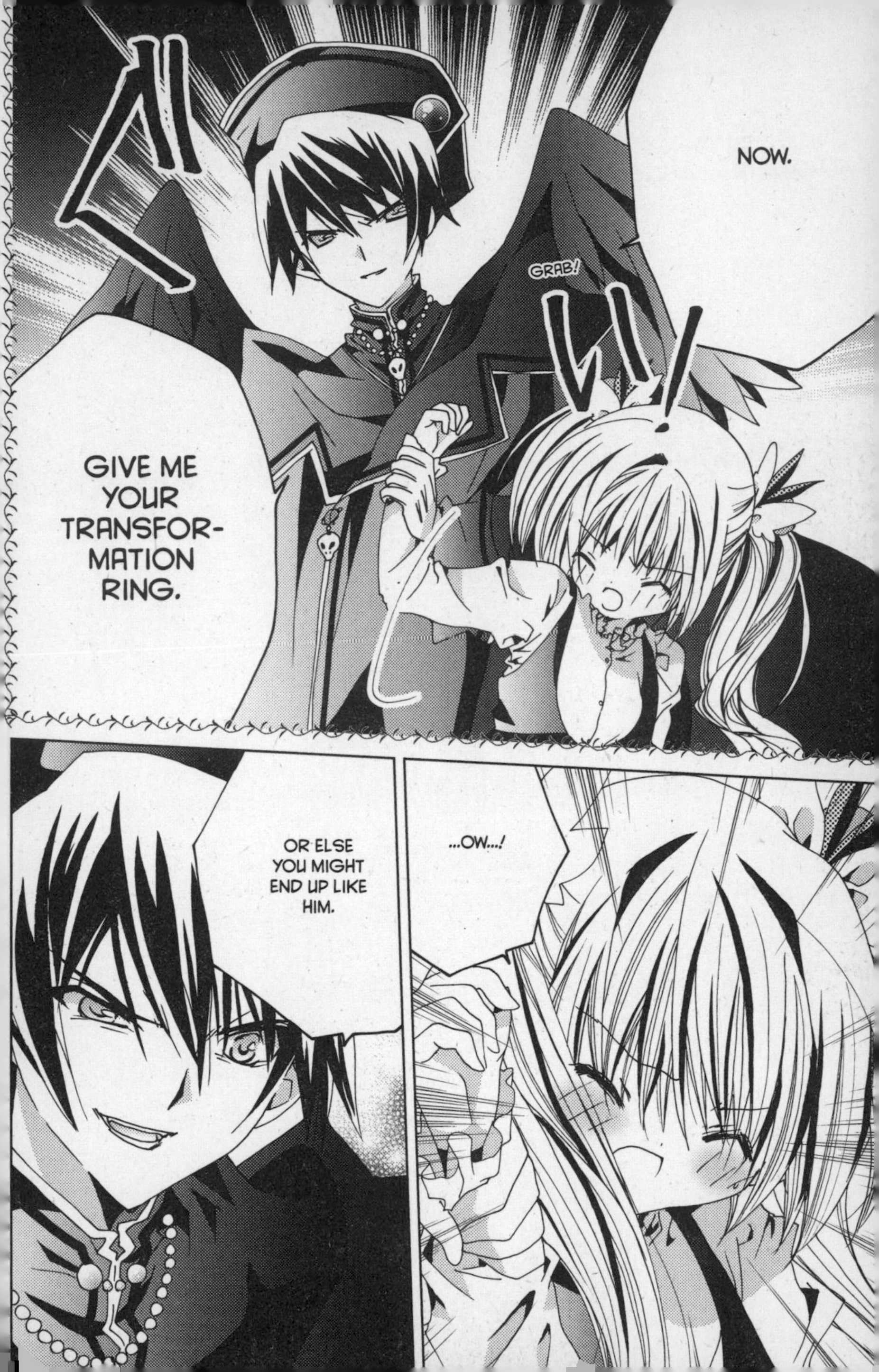
NOW.
GRAB!
GIVE ME YOUR TRANSFORMATION RING.
...OW...!
OR ELSE YOU MIGHT END UP LIKE HIM.

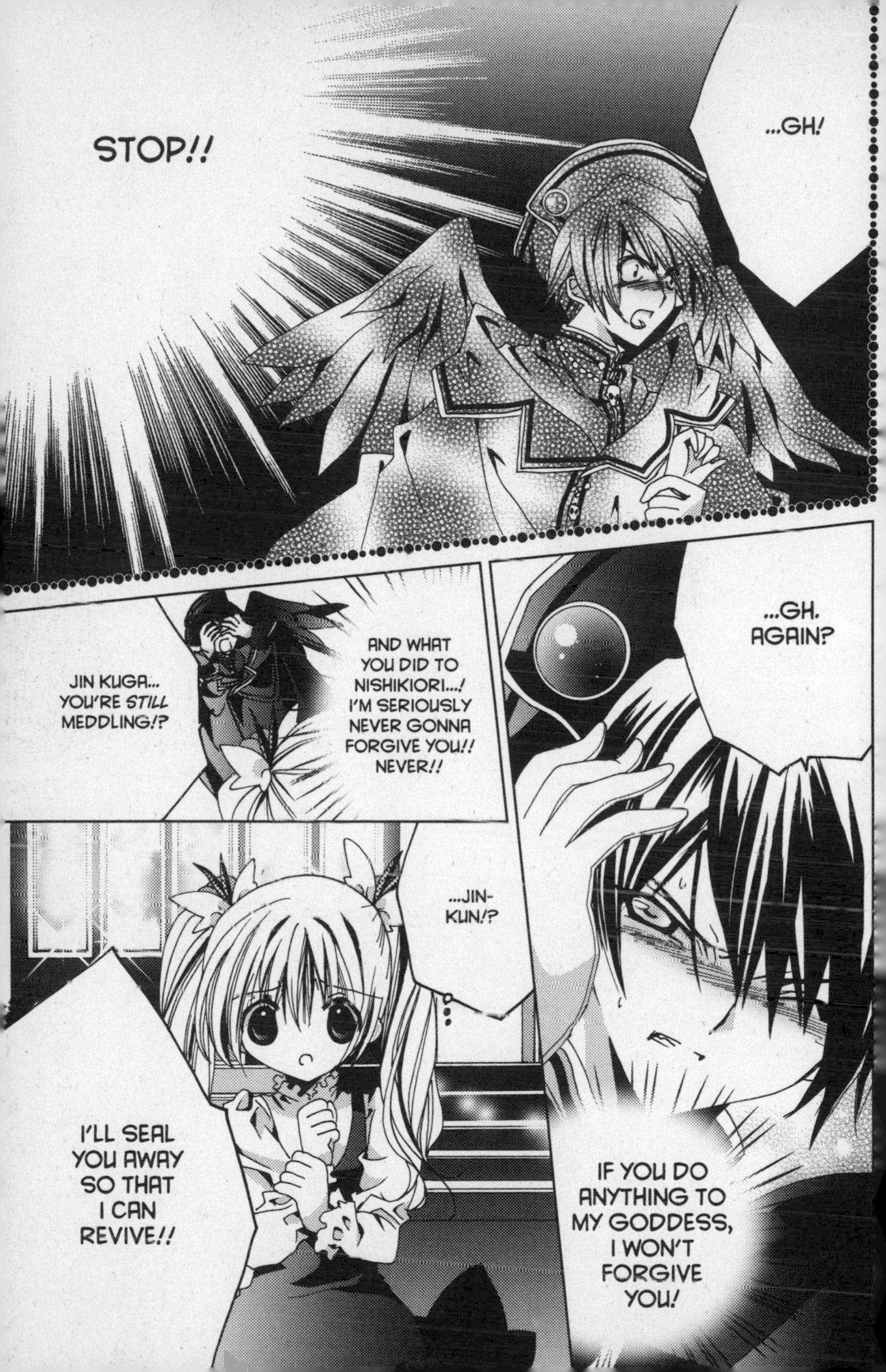
...GH!
STOP!!
...GH. AGAIN?
IF YOU DO ANYTHING TO MY GODDESS, I WON'T FORGIVE YOU!
AND WHAT YOU DID TO NISHIKIORI...! I'M SERIOUSLY NEVER GONNA FORGIVE YOU!! NEVER!!
JIN KUGA... YOU'RE *STILL* MEDDLING!?
...JIN-KUN!?
I'LL SEAL YOU AWAY SO THAT I CAN REVIVE!!

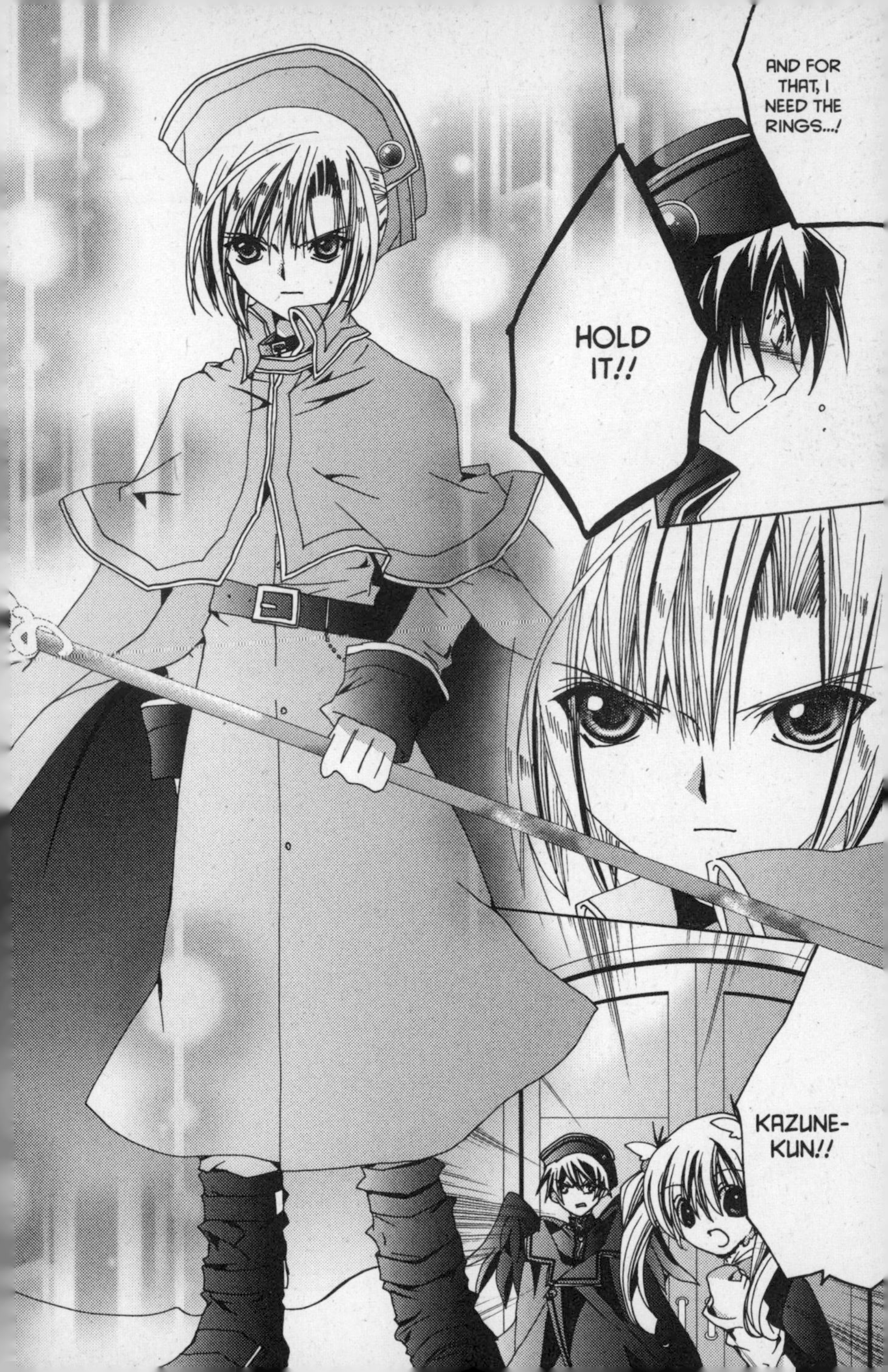
AND FOR THAT, I NEED THE RINGS...!
HOLD IT!!
KAZUNE-KUN!!

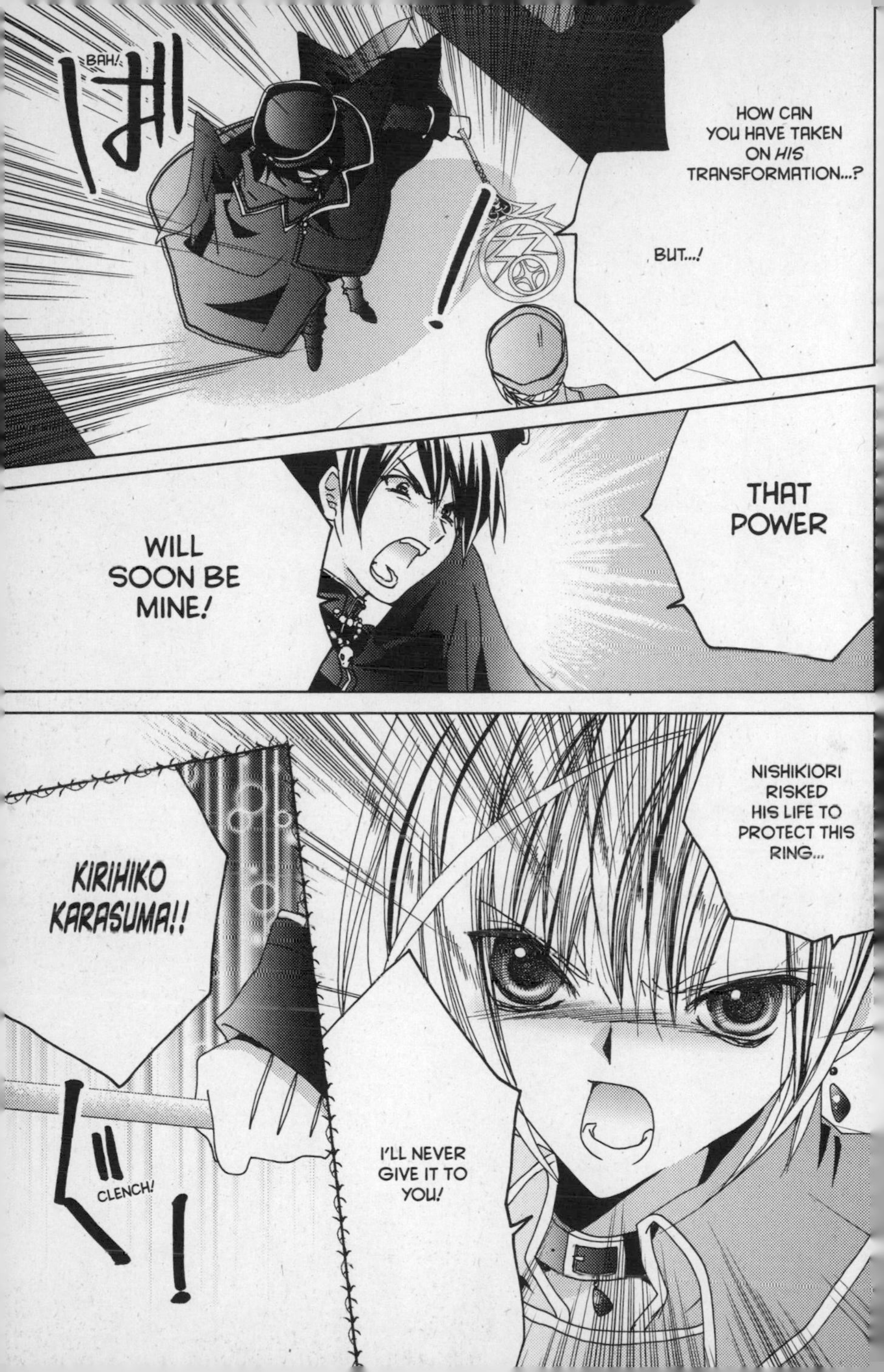
HOW CAN YOU HAVE TAKEN ON *HIS* TRANSFORMATION...?
BUT...!
BAH!
THAT POWER
WILL SOON BE MINE!
NISHIKIORI RISKED HIS LIFE TO PROTECT THIS RING...
I'LL NEVER GIVE IT TO YOU!
KIRIHIKO KARASUMA!!
CLENCH!

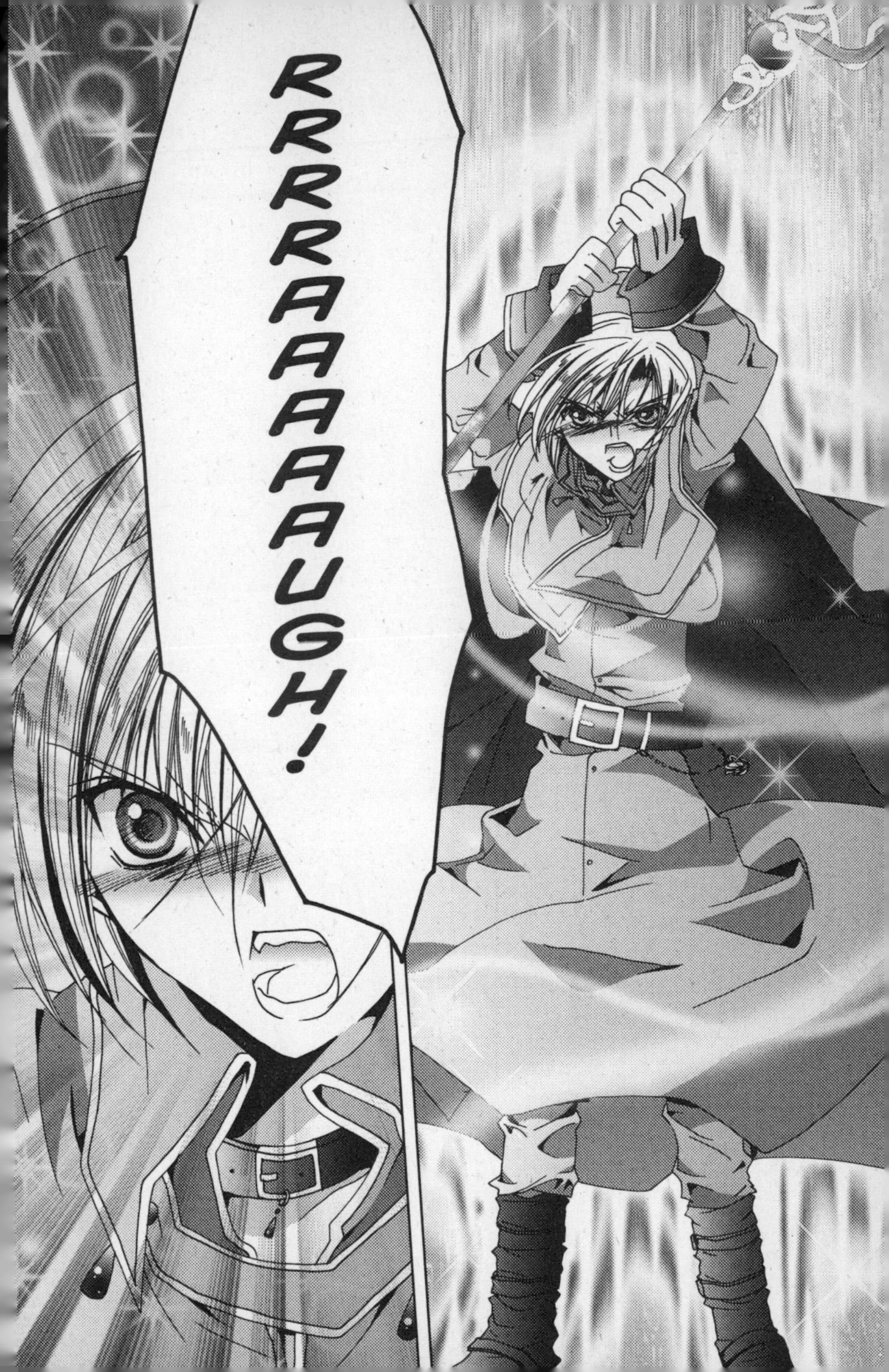
RRRRAAAAAUGH!

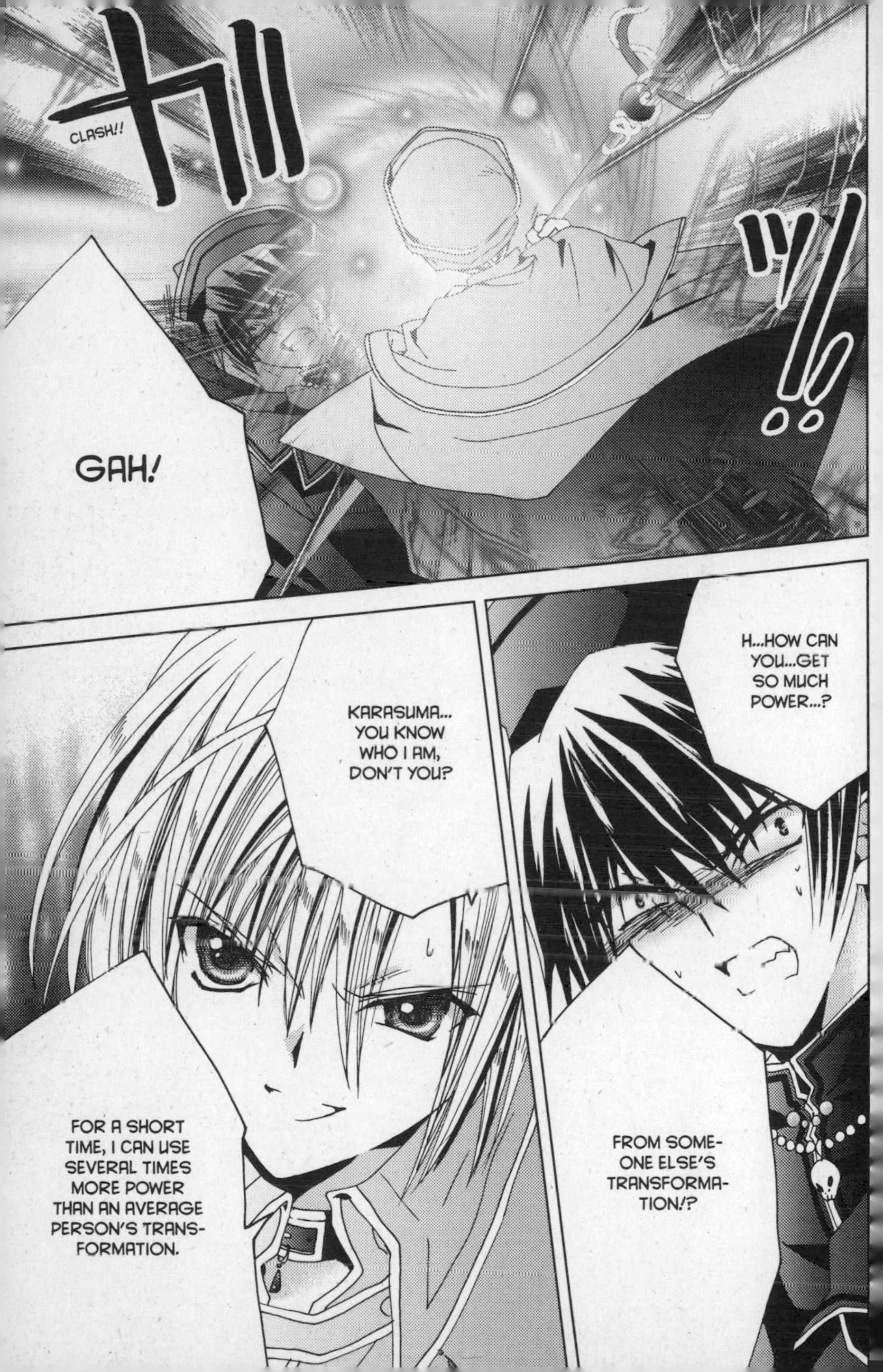
CLASH!!
GAH!
H...HOW CAN YOU...GET SO MUCH POWER...?
FROM SOME-ONE ELSE'S TRANSFORMA-TION!?
KARASUMA... YOU KNOW WHO I AM, DON'T YOU?
FOR A SHORT TIME, I CAN USE SEVERAL TIMES MORE POWER THAN AN AVERAGE PERSON'S TRANS-FORMATION.

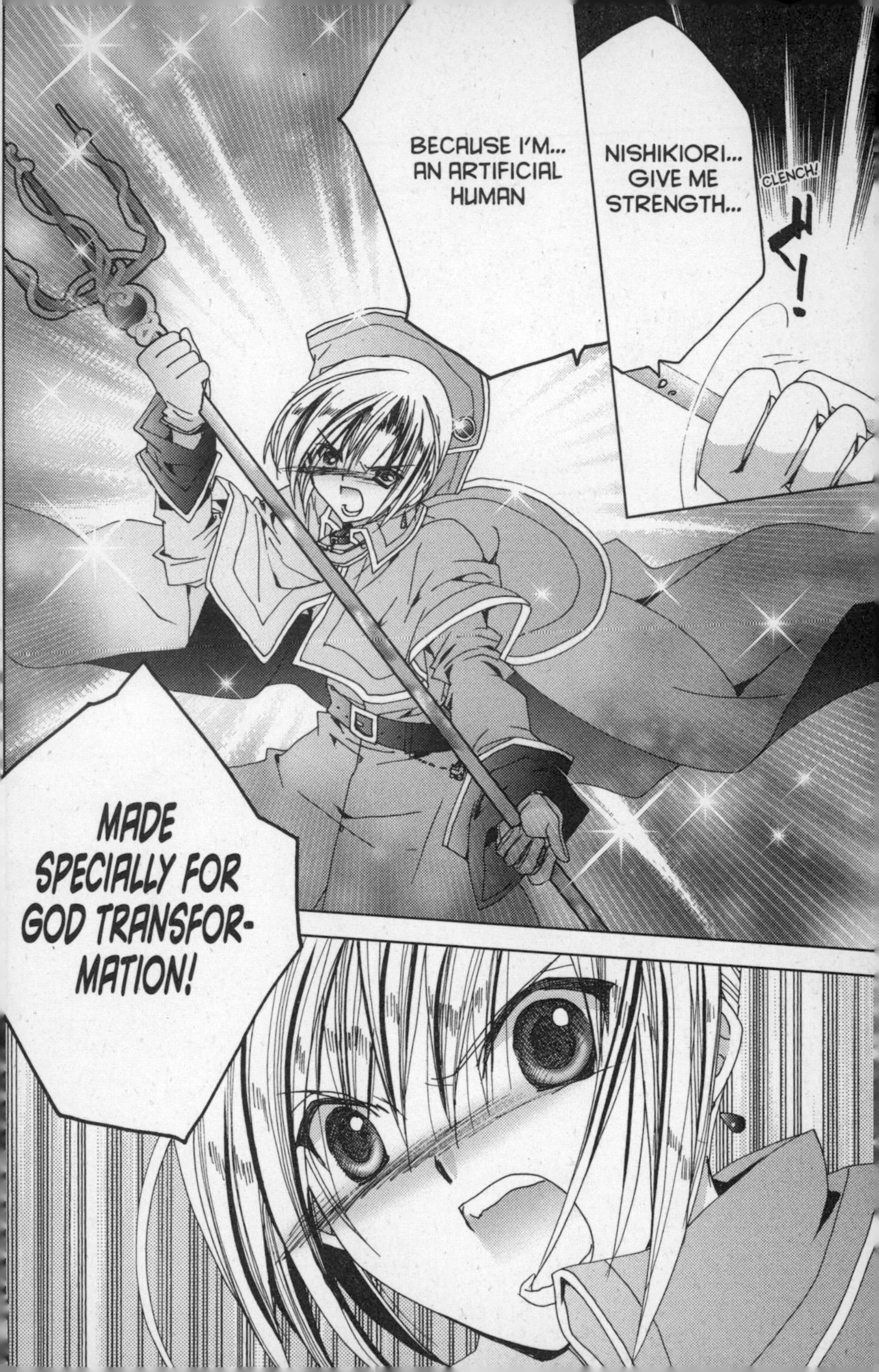
CLENCH!
NISHIKIORI... GIVE ME STRENGTH...
BECAUSE I'M... AN ARTIFICIAL HUMAN
MADE SPECIALLY FOR GOD TRANSFOR-MATION!

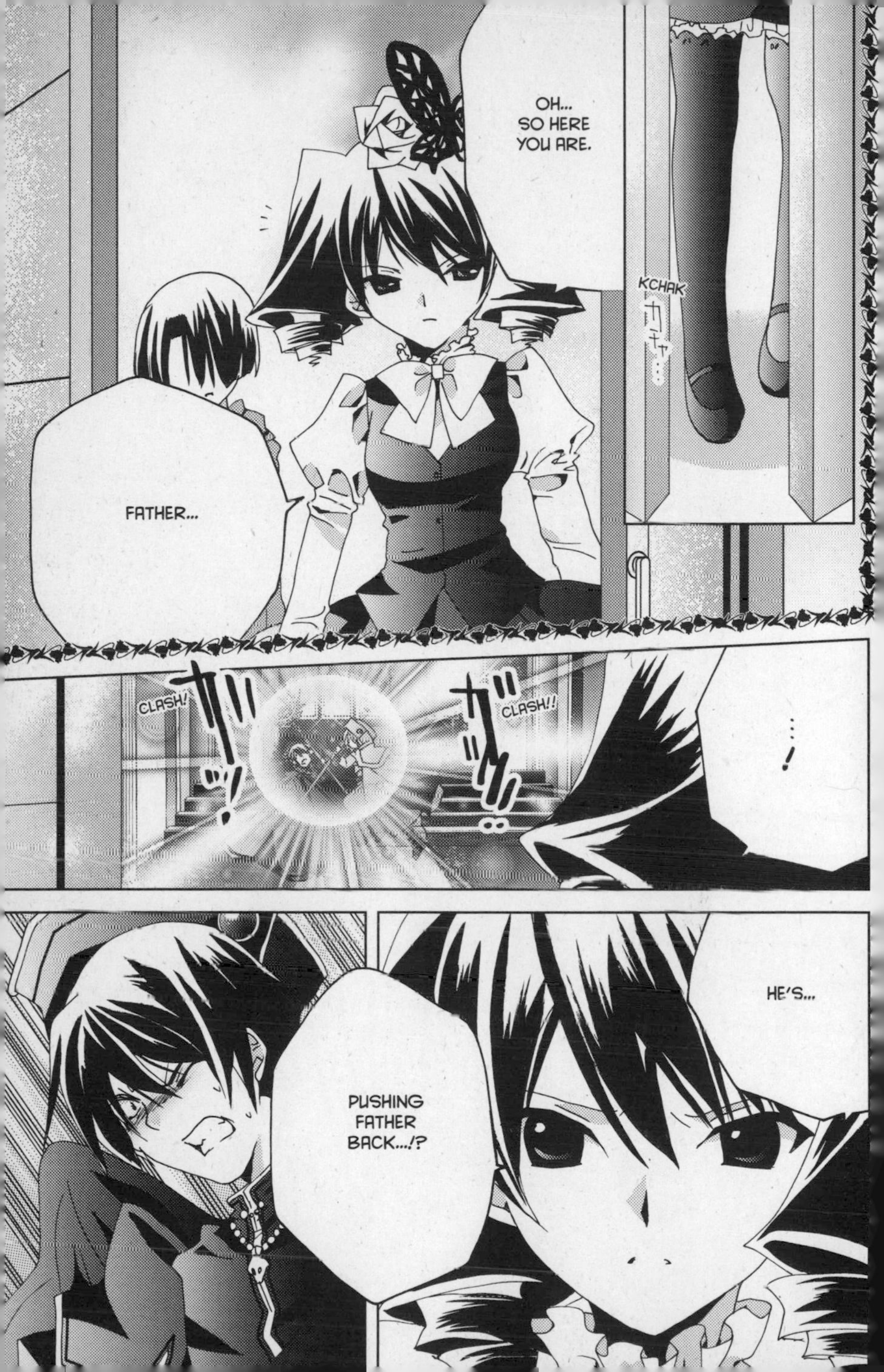
KCHAK
カチャ…
OH... SO HERE YOU ARE.
FATHER...
...!
CLASH!!
CLASH!
HE'S...
PUSHING FATHER BACK...!?

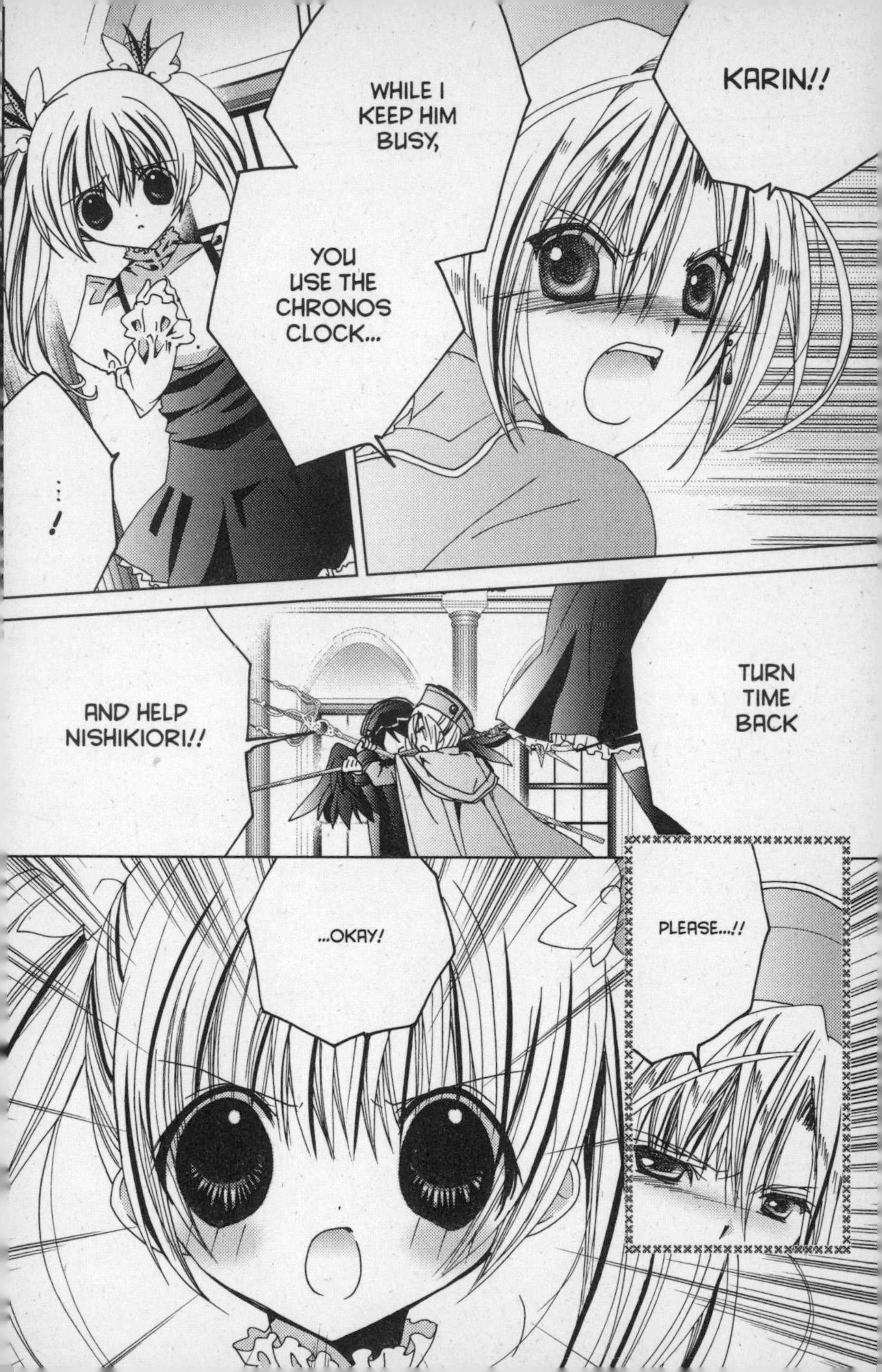
KARIN!!
WHILE I KEEP HIM BUSY,
YOU USE THE CHRONOS CLOCK...
...!
TURN TIME BACK
AND HELP NISHIKIORI!!
PLEASE...!!
...OKAY!

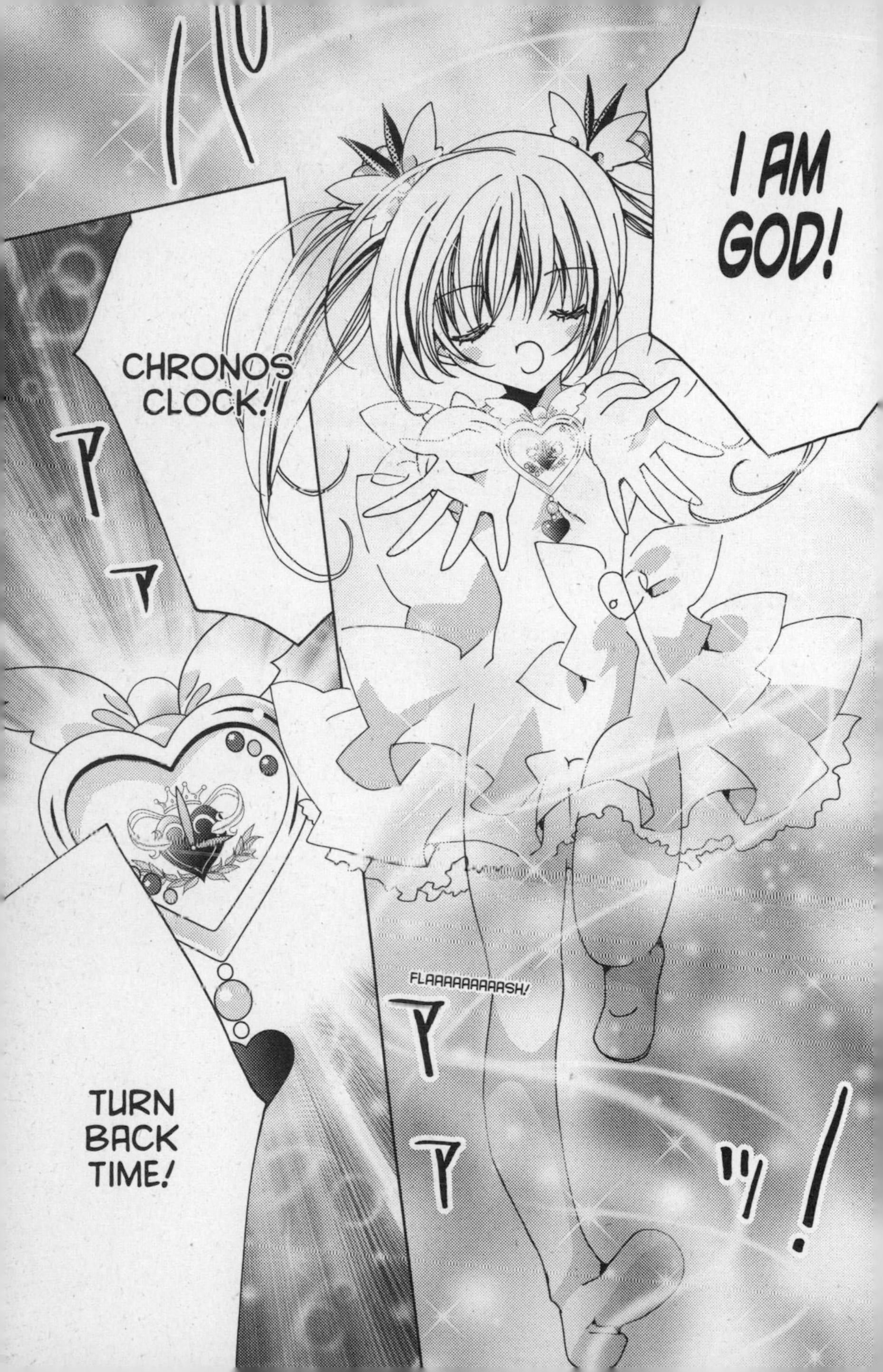
I AM GOD!
CHRONOS CLOCK!
TURN BACK TIME!
FLAAAAAAAAAASH!

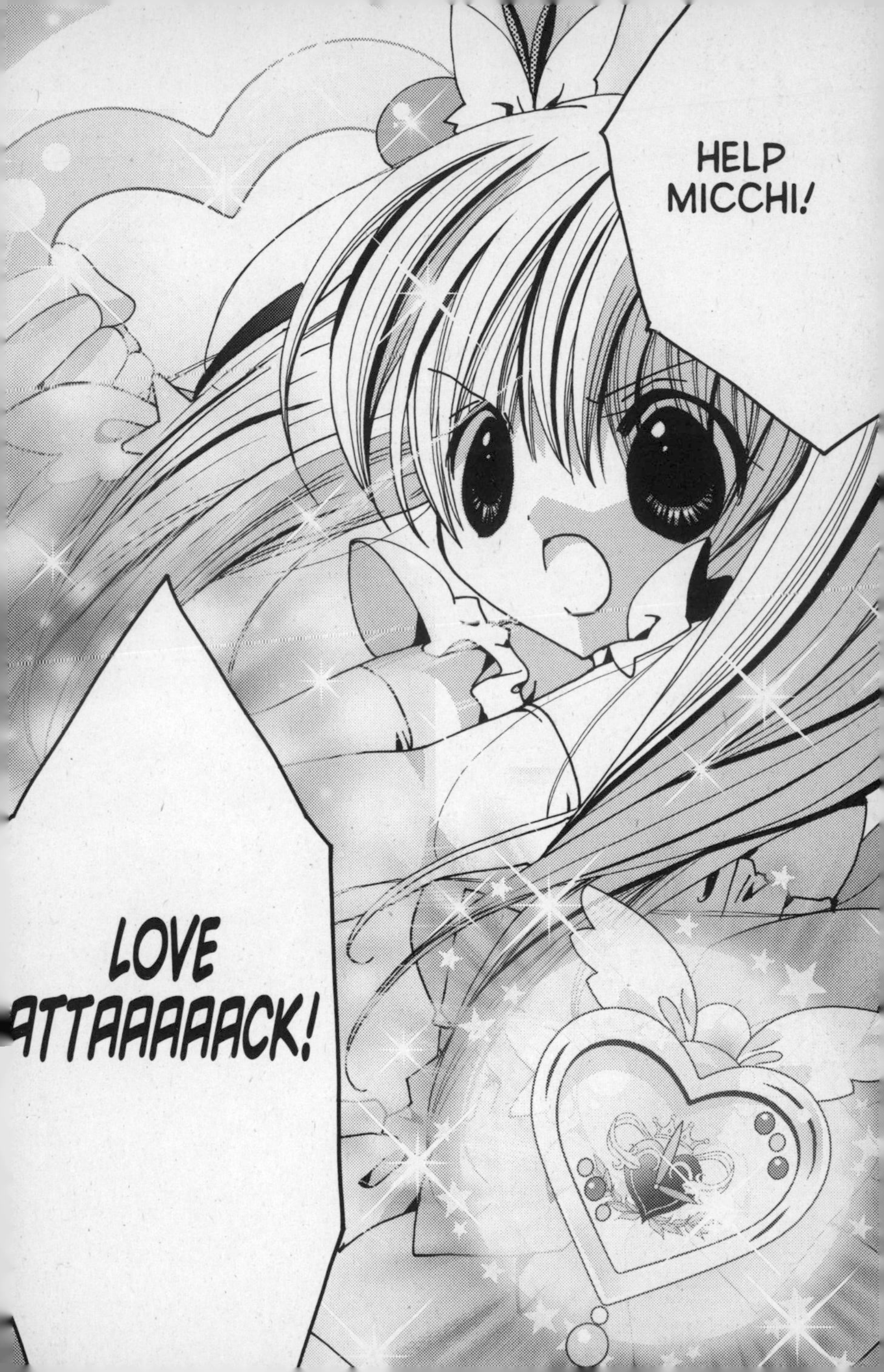
HELP MICCHI!
LOVE ATTAAAAACK!

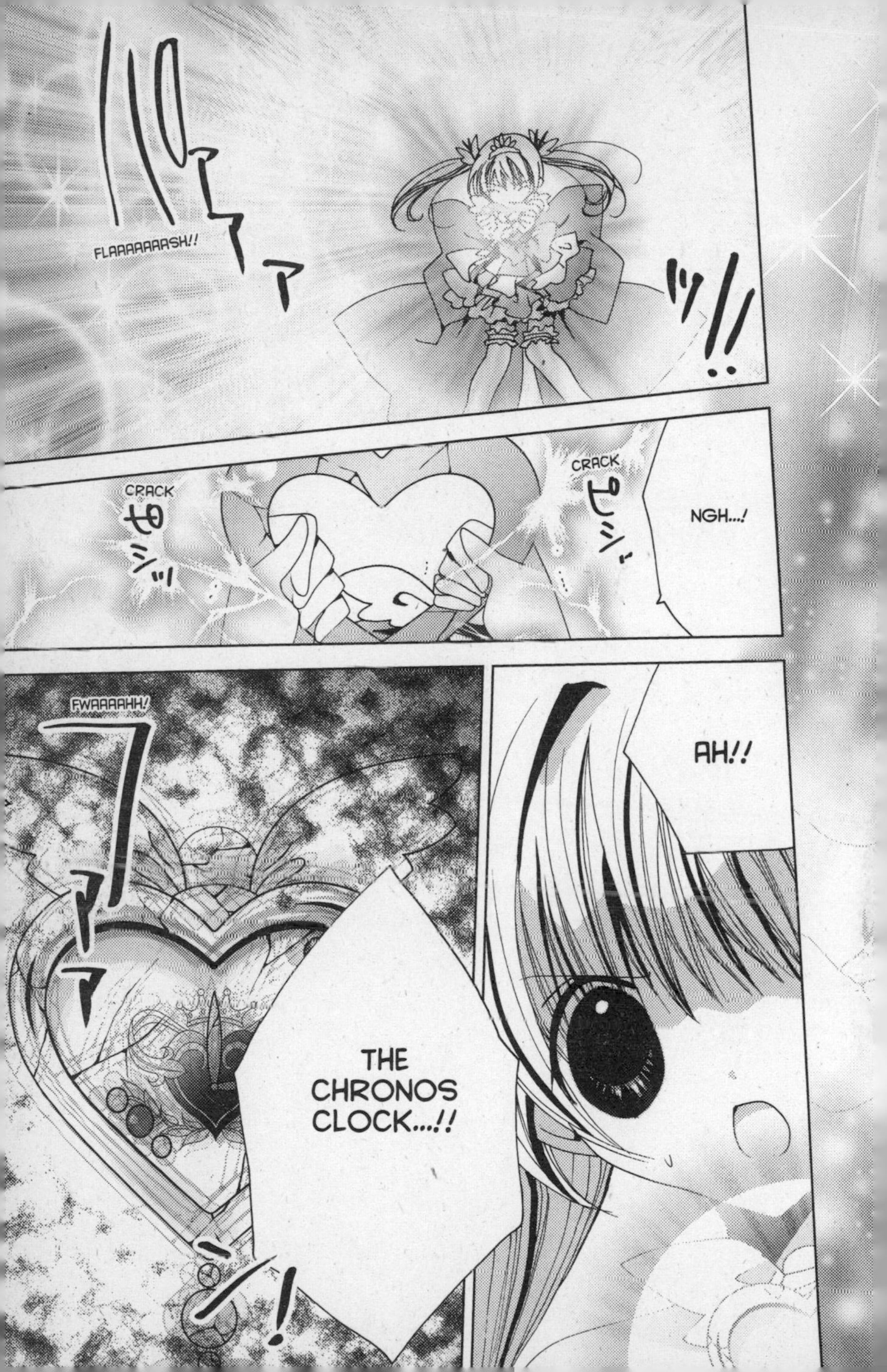
FLAAAAAAASH!!
NGH...!
CRACK
CRACK
AH!!
FWAAAAHH!
THE CHRONOS CLOCK...!!

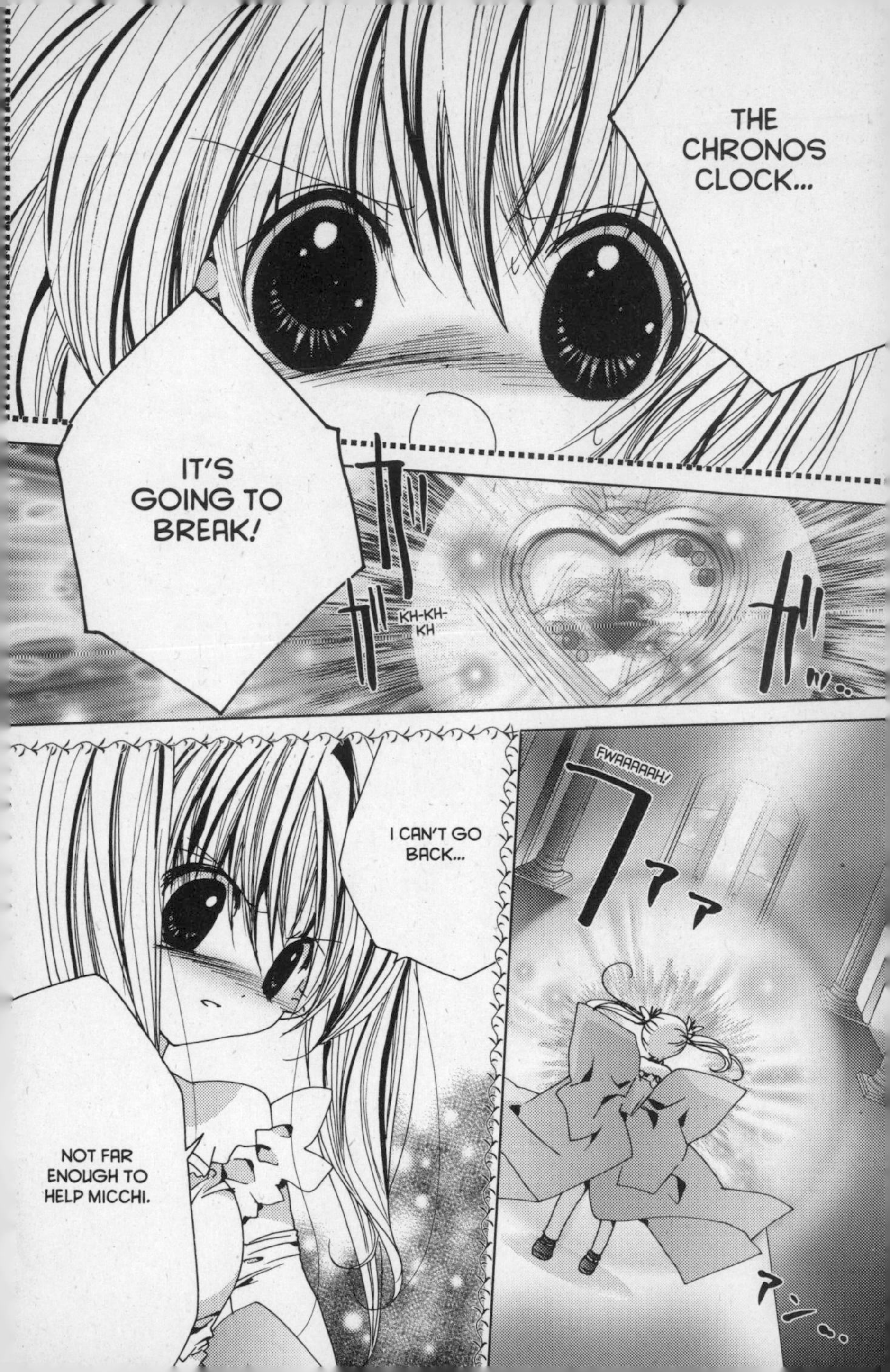
THE CHRONOS CLOCK...
IT'S GOING TO BREAK!
KH-KH-KH
FWAAAAAH!
I CAN'T GO BACK...
NOT FAR ENOUGH TO HELP MICCHI.

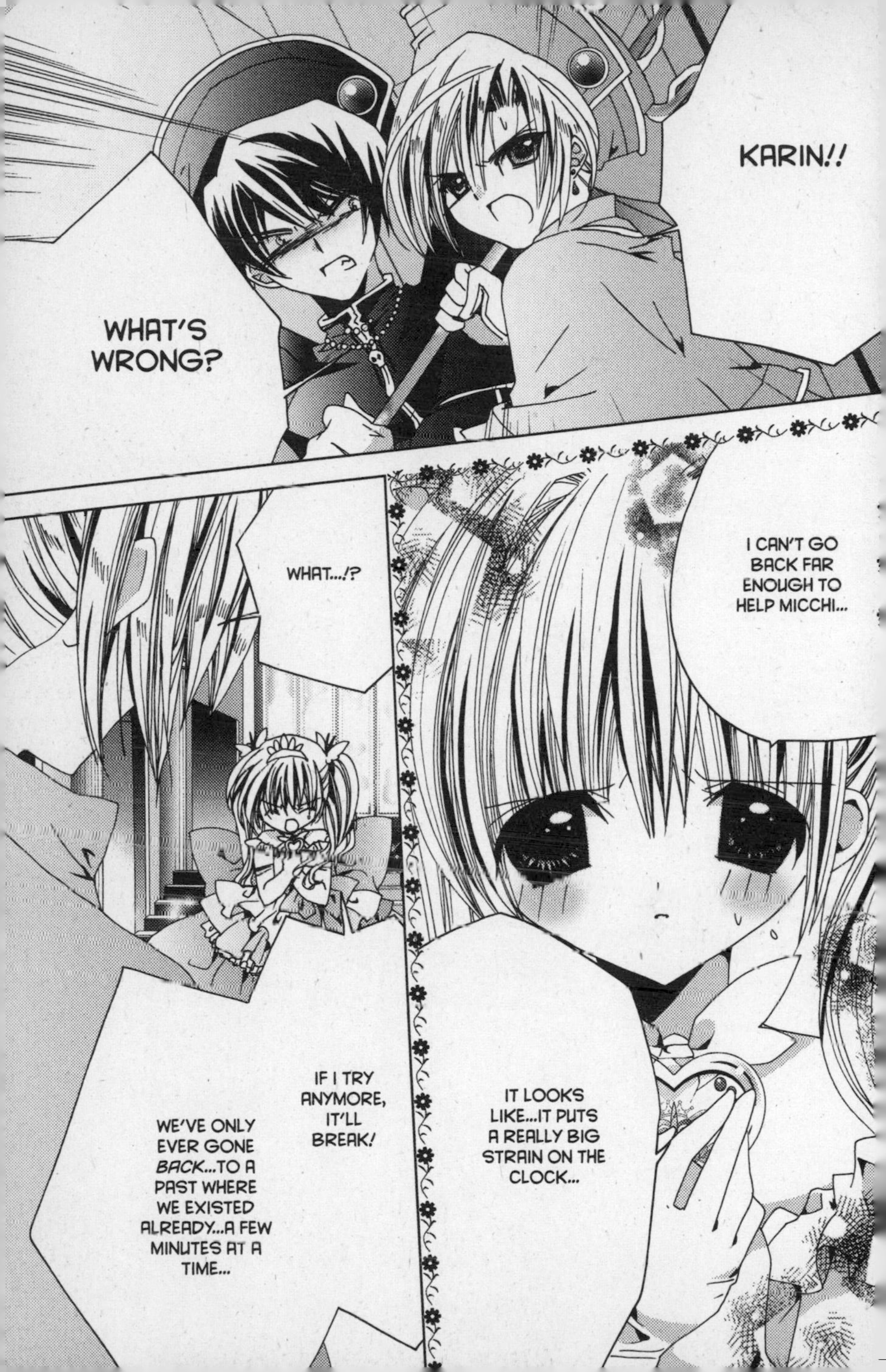
KARIN!!
WHAT'S WRONG?
I CAN'T GO BACK FAR ENOUGH TO HELP MICCHI...
IT LOOKS LIKE...IT PUTS A REALLY BIG STRAIN ON THE CLOCK...
WHAT...!?
IF I TRY ANYMORE, IT'LL BREAK!
WE'VE ONLY EVER GONE *BACK*...TO A PAST WHERE WE EXISTED ALREADY...A FEW MINUTES AT A TIME...

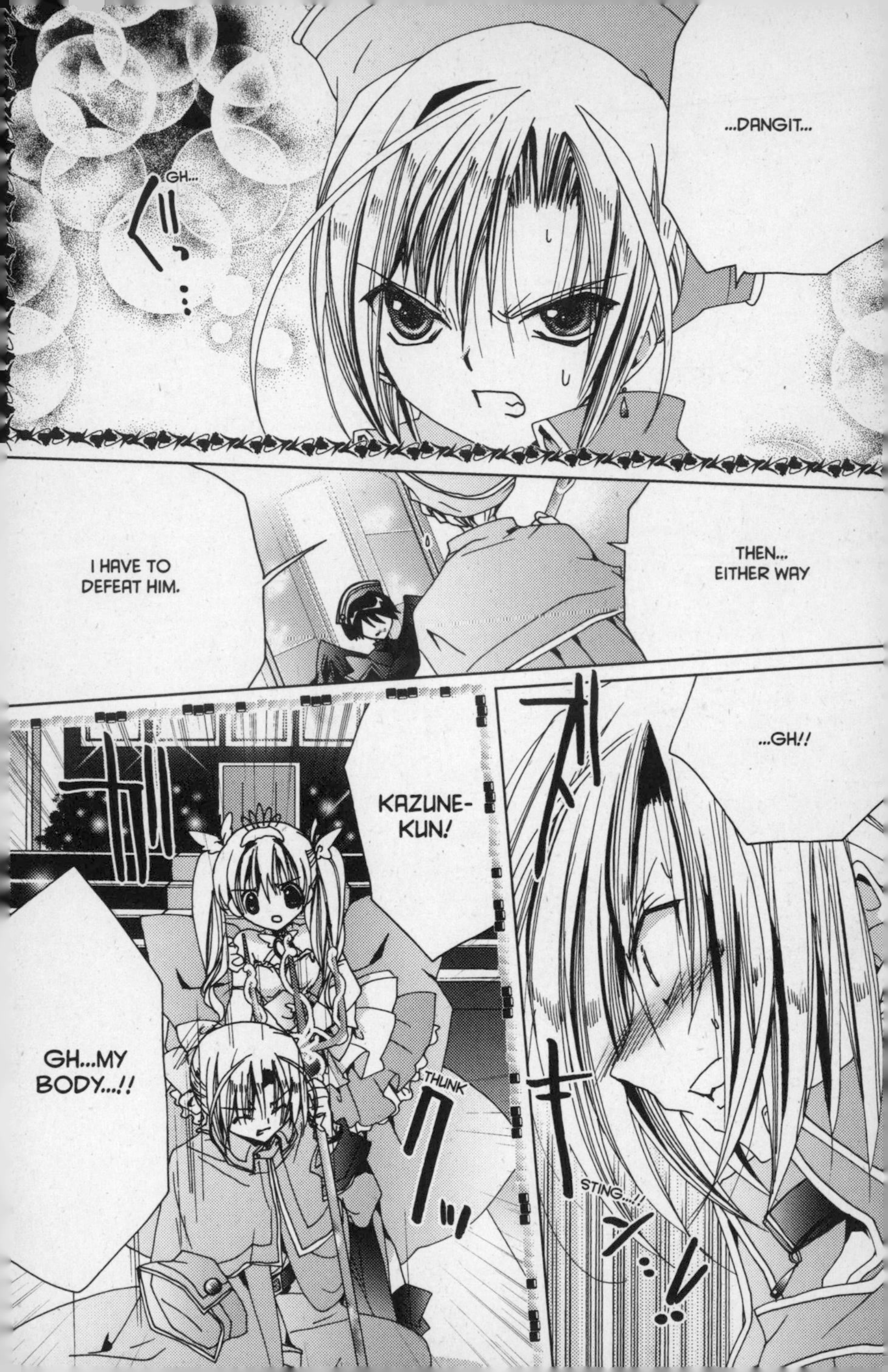
...DANGIT...
GH...
THEN... EITHER WAY
I HAVE TO DEFEAT HIM.
...GH!!
STING...!!
KAZUNE-KUN!
THUNK
GH...MY BODY...!!

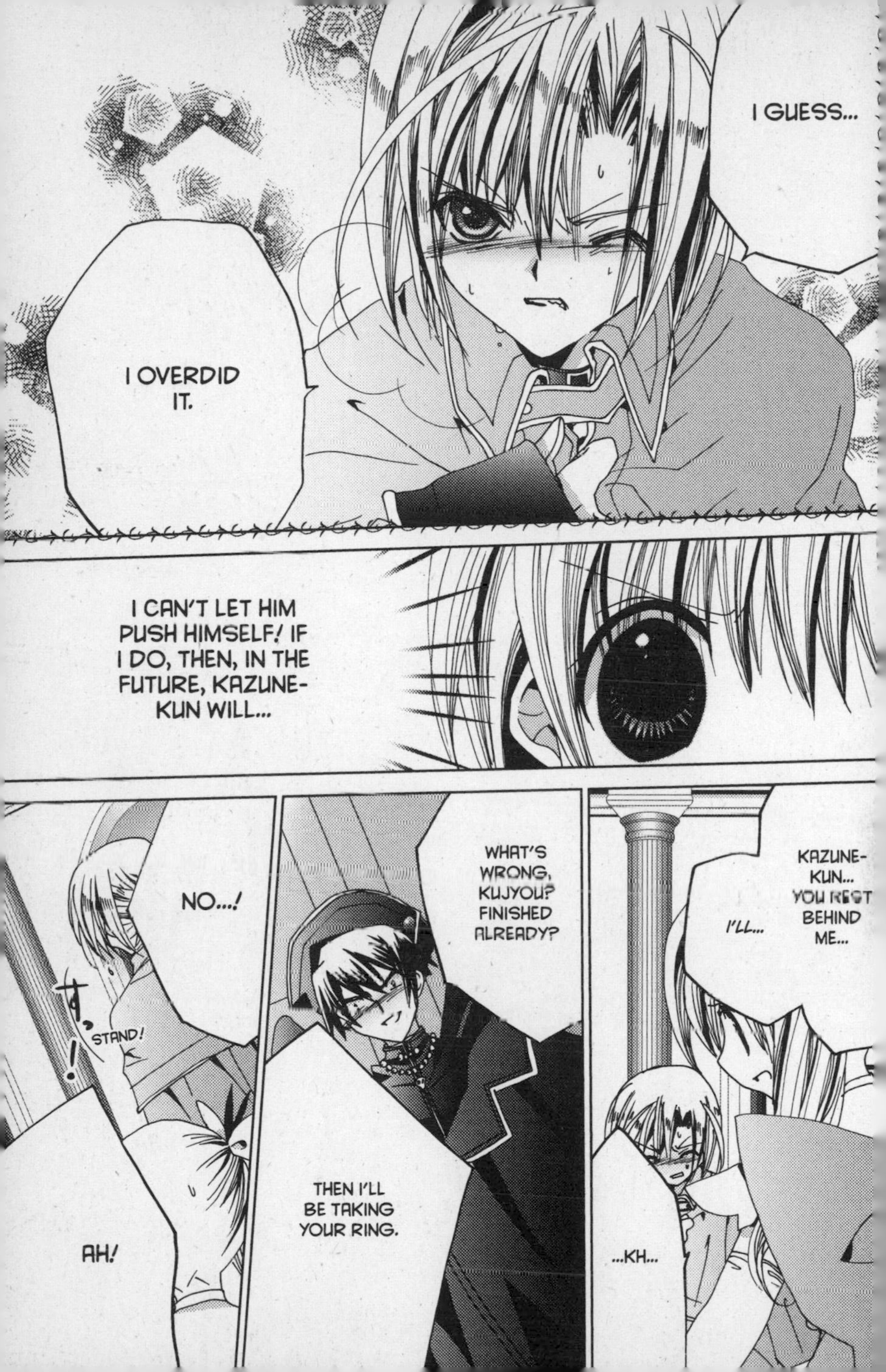
I GUESS...
I OVERDID IT.
I CAN'T LET HIM PUSH HIMSELF! IF I DO, THEN, IN THE FUTURE, KAZUNE-KUN WILL...
KAZUNE-KUN... YOU REST BEHIND ME...
I'LL...
...KH...
WHAT'S WRONG, KUJYOU? FINISHED ALREADY?
THEN I'LL BE TAKING YOUR RING.
NO...!
STAND!
AH!

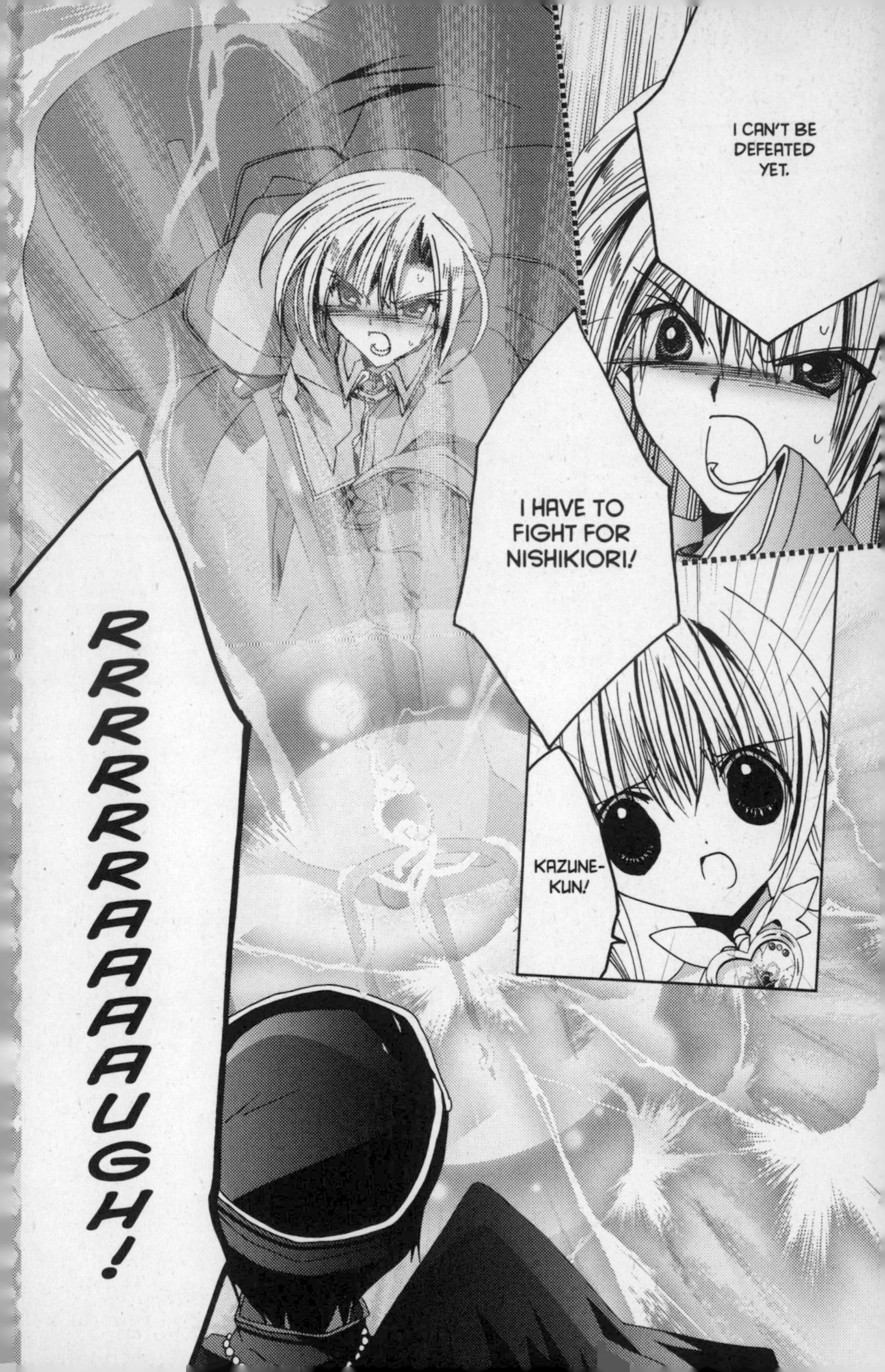
I CAN'T BE DEFEATED YET.
I HAVE TO FIGHT FOR NISHIKIORI!
KAZUNE-KUN!
RRRRRAAAAUGH!

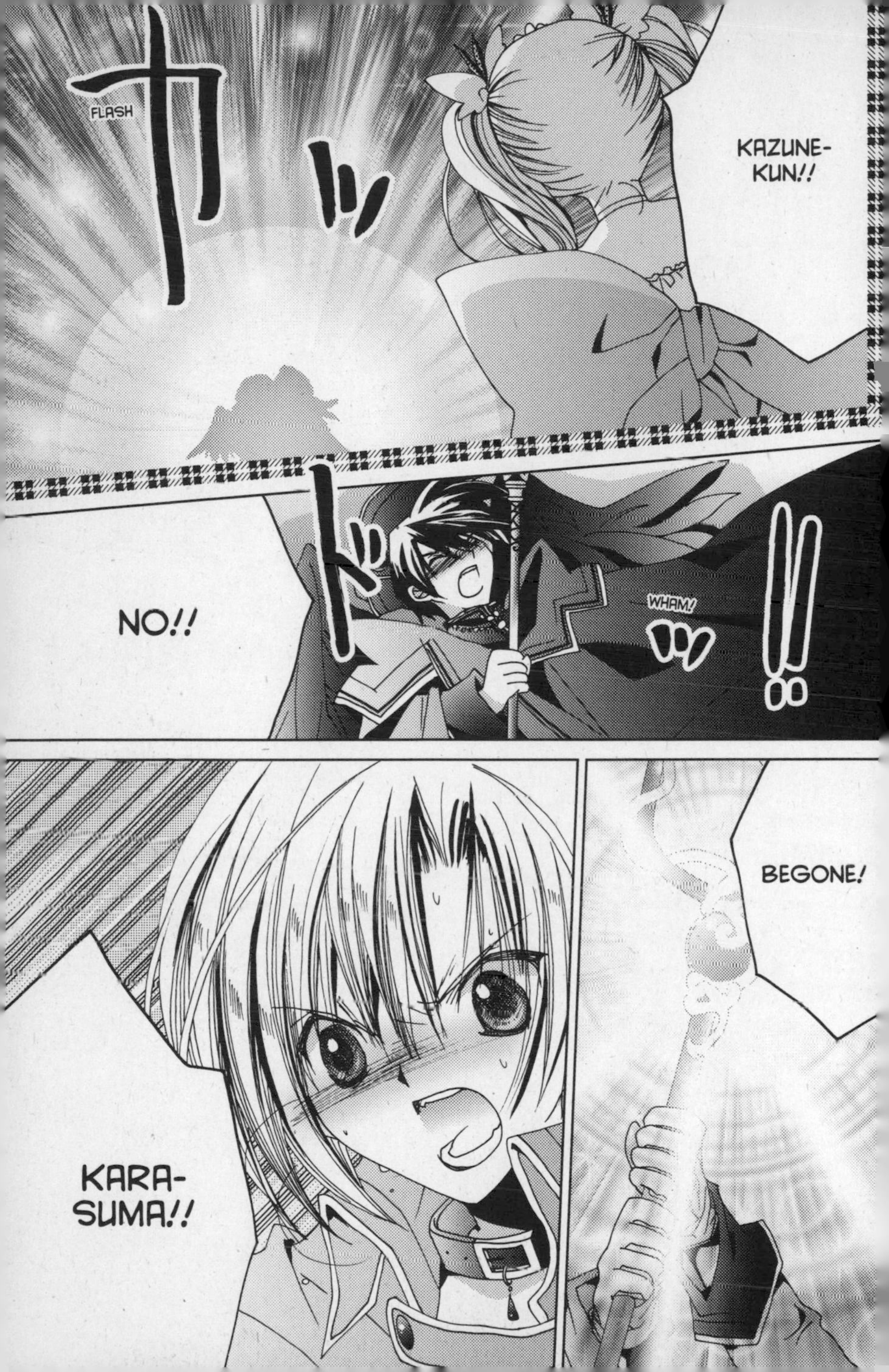
KAZUNE-KUN!!
FLASH
WHAM!
NO!!
BEGONE!
KARA-SUMA!!

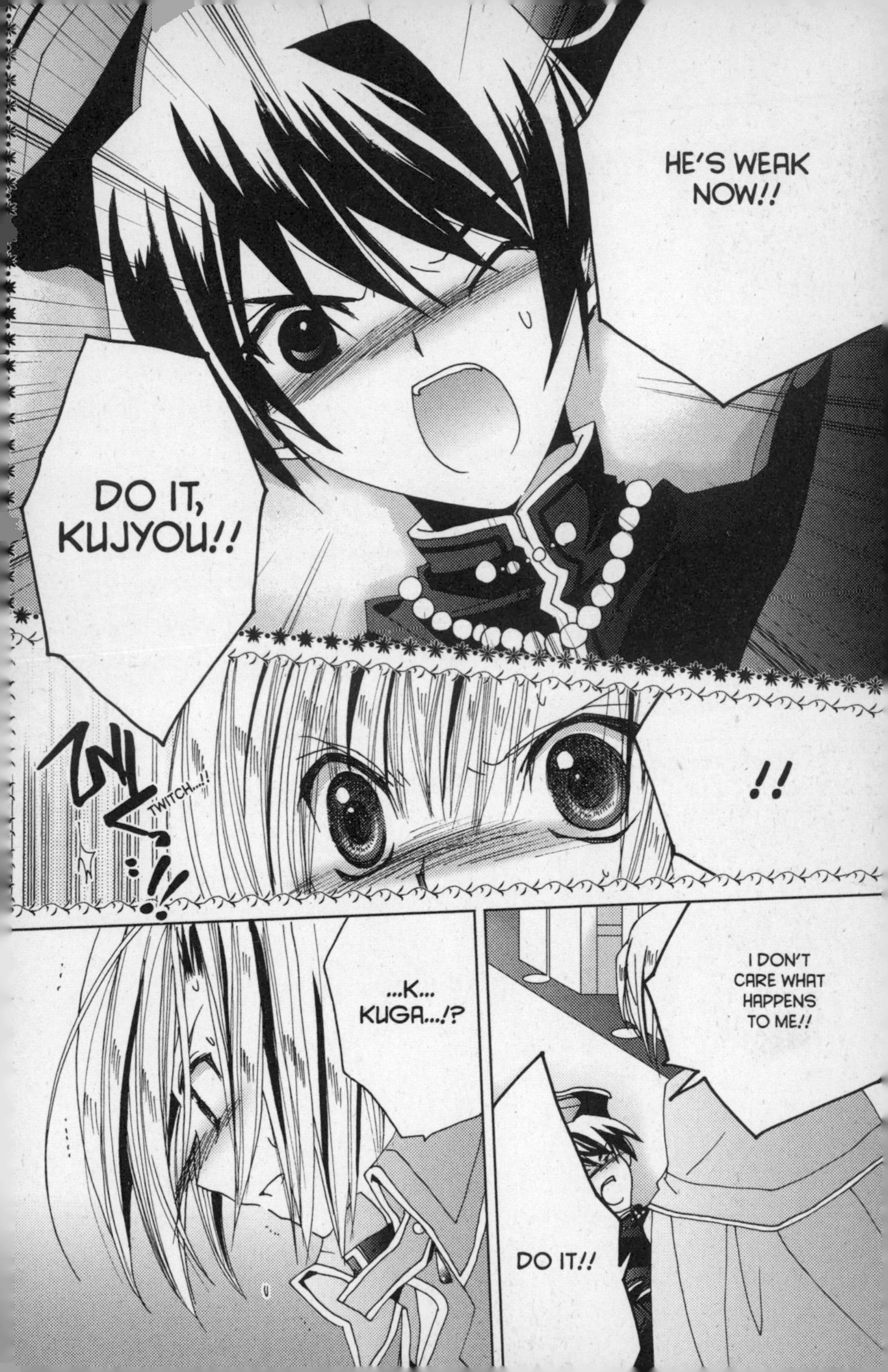
HE'S WEAK NOW!!
DO IT, KUJYOU!!
!!
TWITCH...!!
I DON'T CARE WHAT HAPPENS TO ME!!
DO IT!!
...K... KUGA...!?

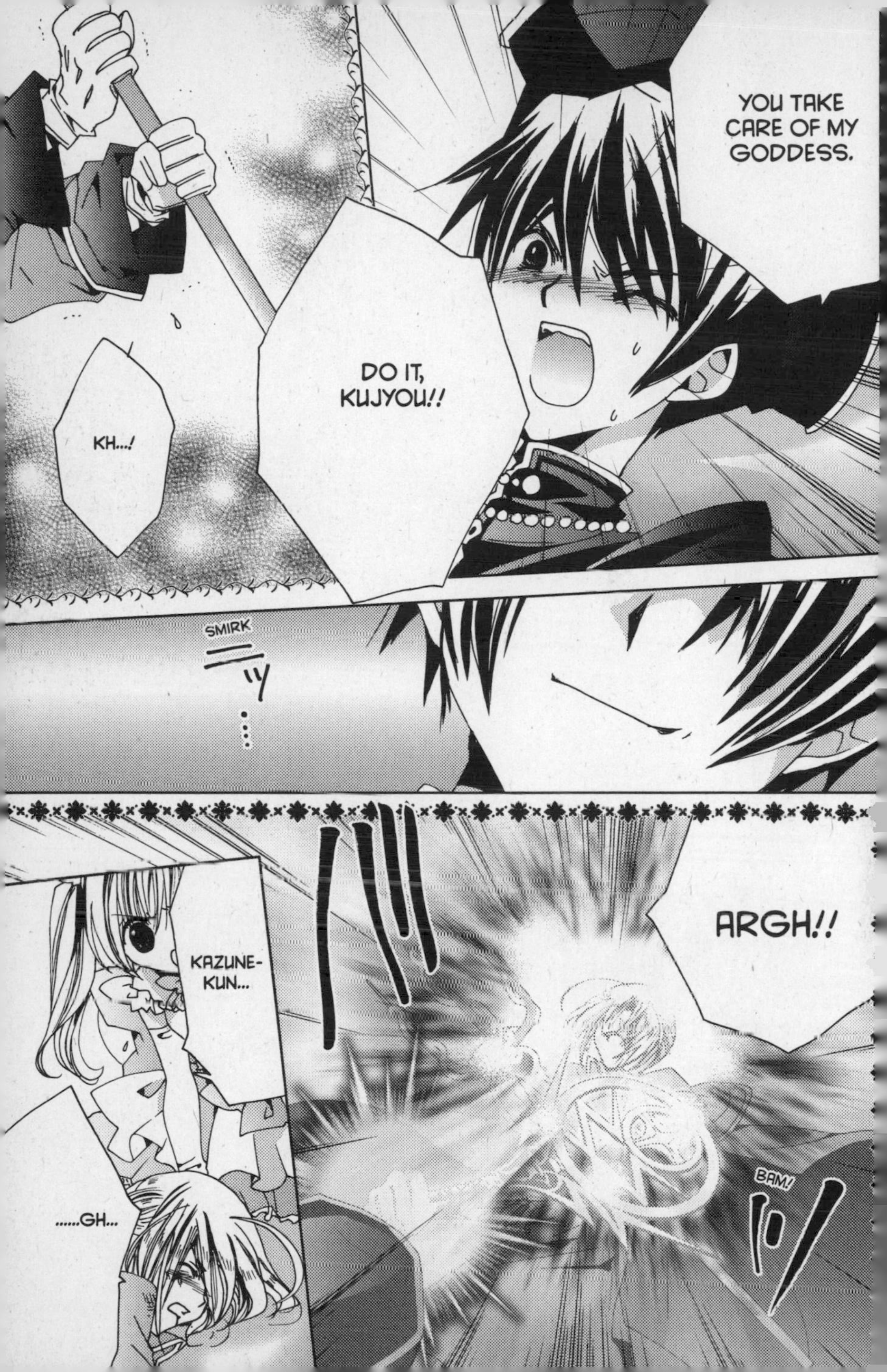
YOU TAKE CARE OF MY GODDESS.
DO IT, KUJYOU!!
KH...!
SMIRK
ARGH!!
BAM!
KAZUNE-KUN...
......GH...

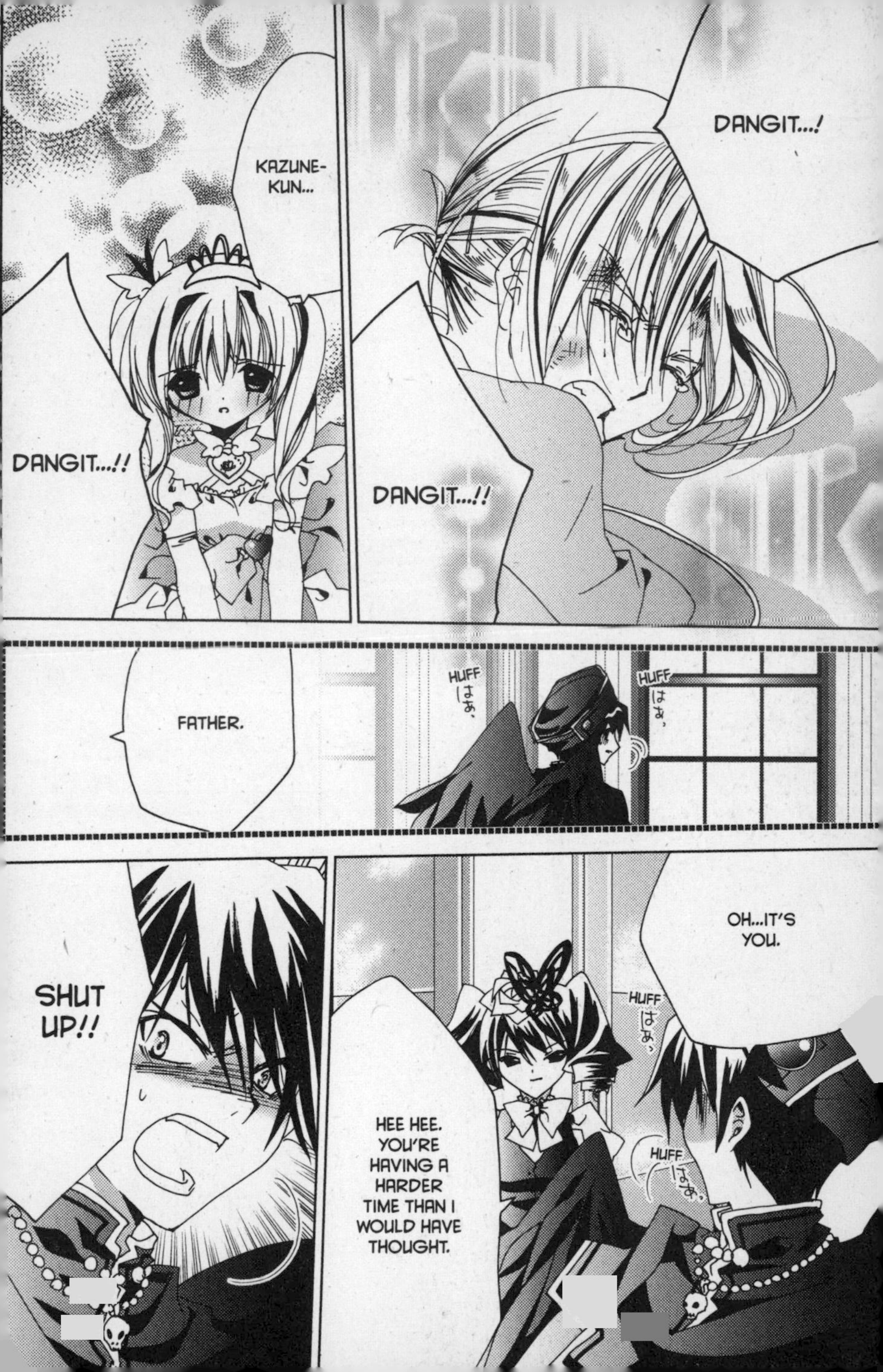
DANGIT...!
DANGIT...!!
KAZUNE-KUN...
DANGIT...!!
HUFF はぁ、
HUFF はぁ、
FATHER.
OH...IT'S YOU.
HUFF はぁ、
HEE HEE. YOU'RE HAVING A HARDER TIME THAN I WOULD HAVE THOUGHT.
HUFF はぁ、
SHUT UP!!

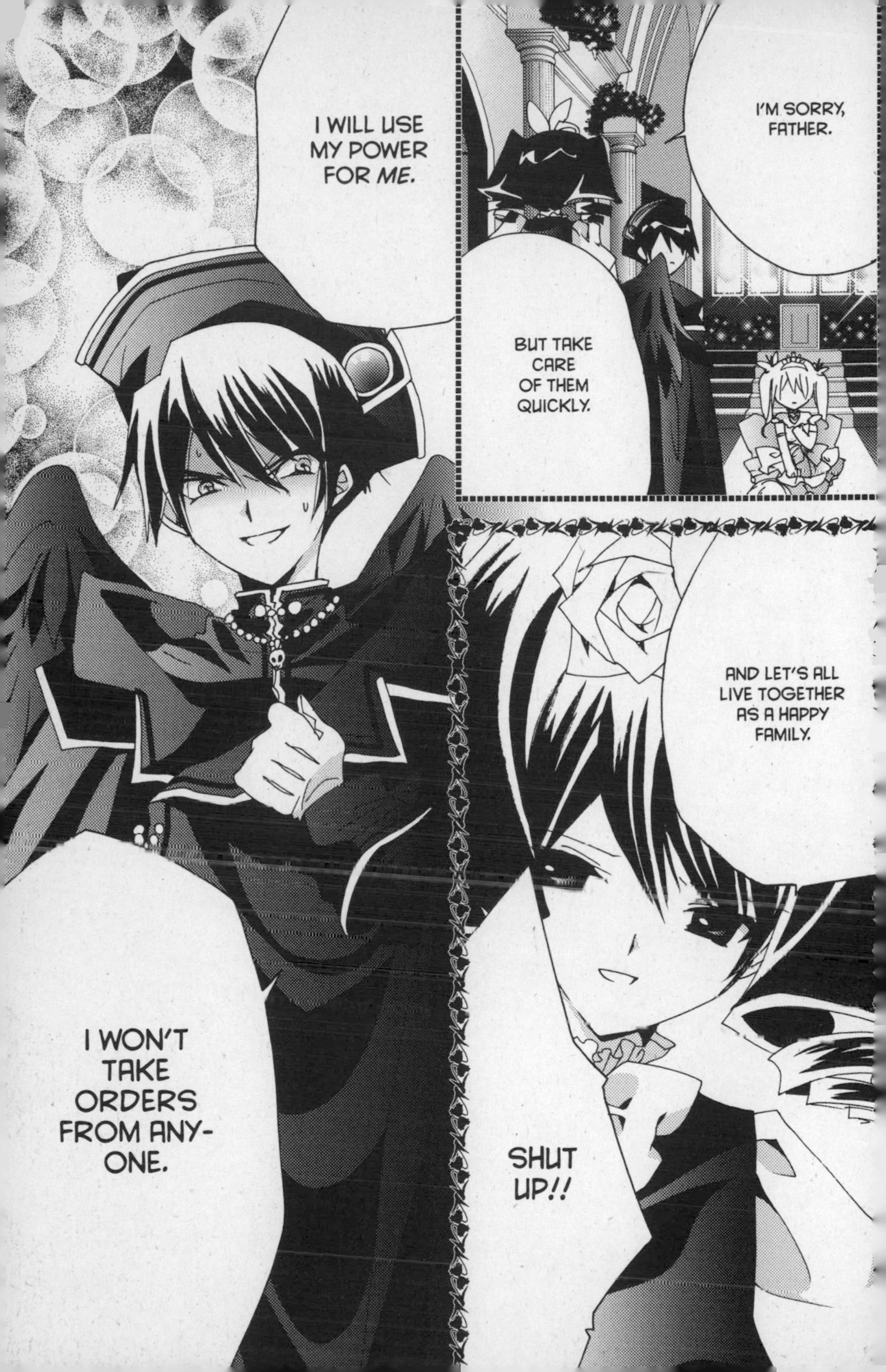
I'M SORRY, FATHER.
BUT TAKE CARE OF THEM QUICKLY.
AND LET'S ALL LIVE TOGETHER AS A HAPPY FAMILY.
SHUT UP!!
I WILL USE MY POWER FOR *ME*.
I WON'T TAKE ORDERS FROM ANY-ONE.

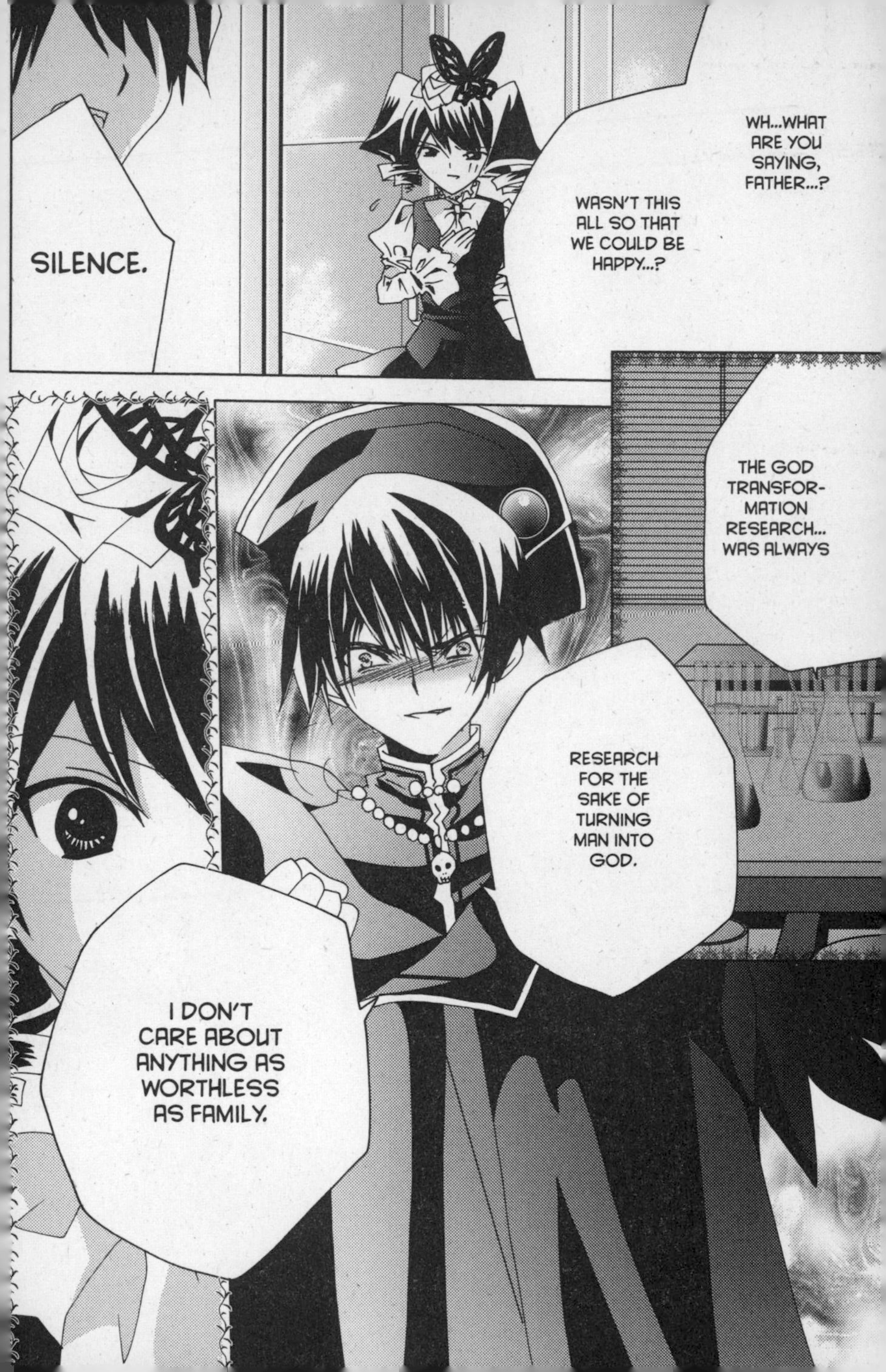
WH...WHAT ARE YOU SAYING, FATHER...?
WASN'T THIS ALL SO THAT WE COULD BE HAPPY...?
SILENCE.
THE GOD TRANSFOR-MATION RESEARCH... WAS ALWAYS
RESEARCH FOR THE SAKE OF TURNING MAN INTO GOD.
I DON'T CARE ABOUT ANYTHING AS WORTHLESS AS FAMILY.

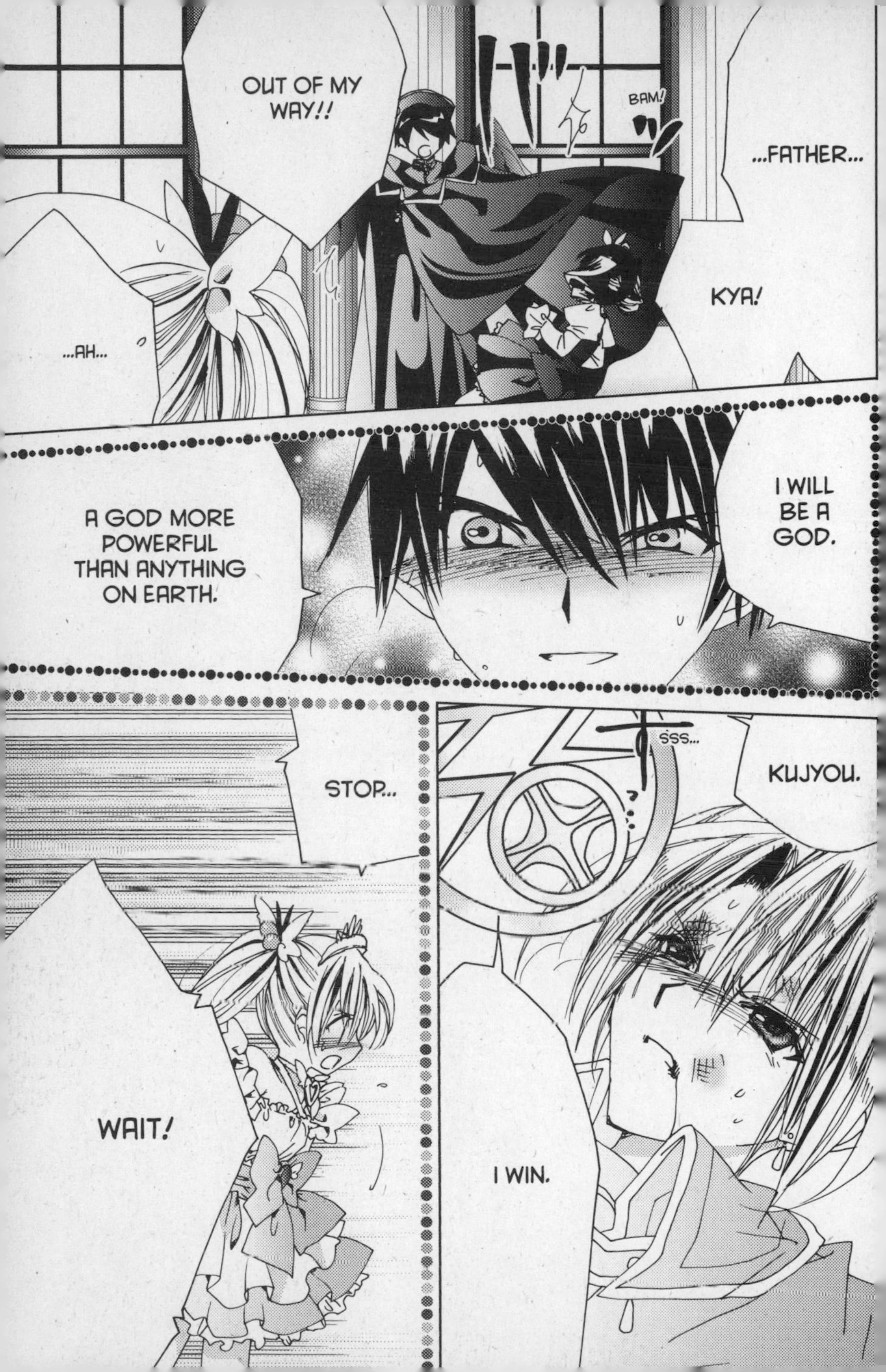
...FATHER...
BAM!
OUT OF MY WAY!!
KYA!
...AH...
I WILL BE A GOD.
A GOD MORE POWERFUL THAN ANYTHING ON EARTH.
SSS...
KUJYOU.
I WIN.
STOP...
WAIT!

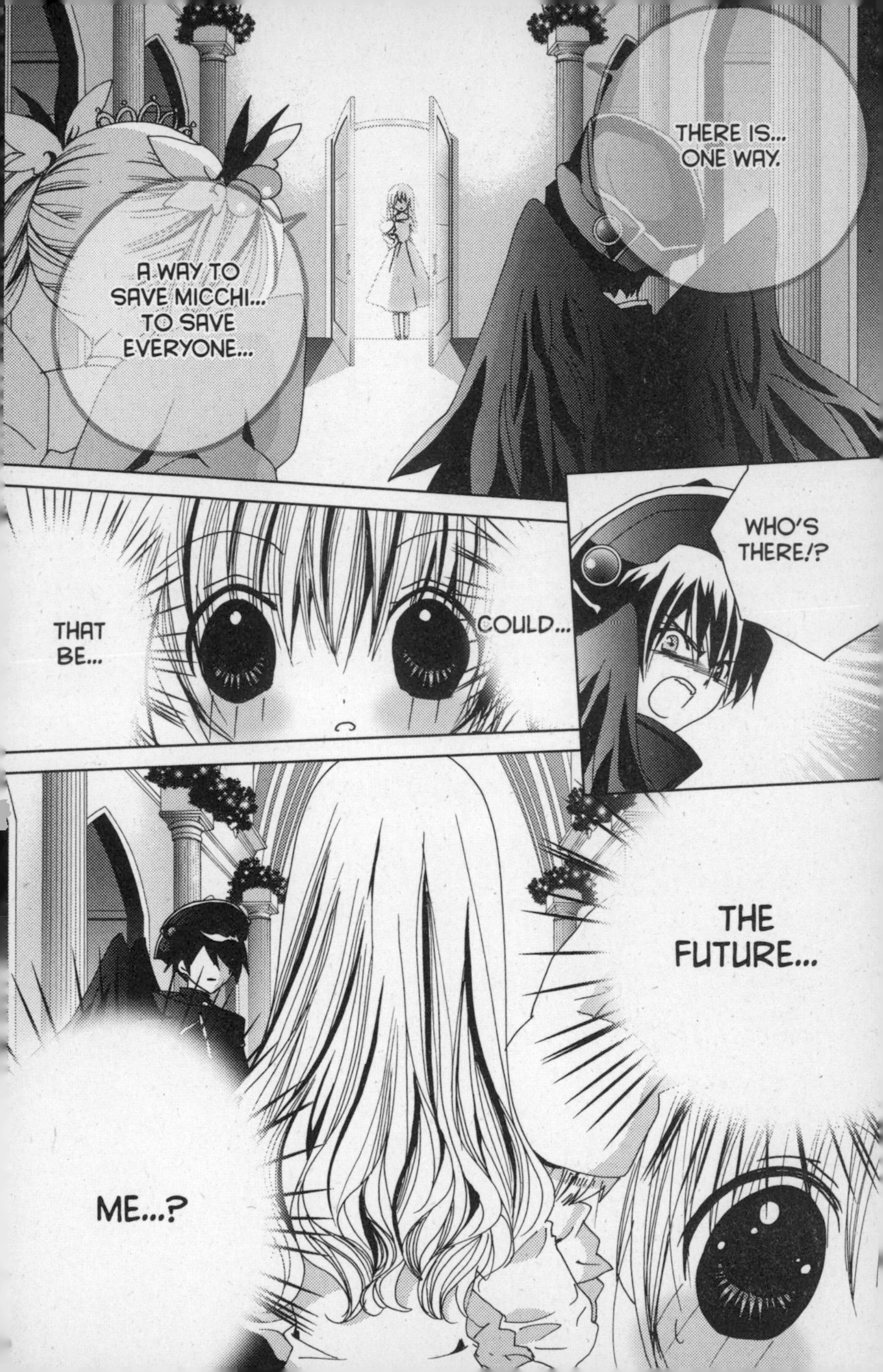
THERE IS... ONE WAY.
A WAY TO SAVE MICCHI... TO SAVE EVERYONE...
WHO'S THERE!?
COULD...
THAT BE...
THE FUTURE...
ME...?

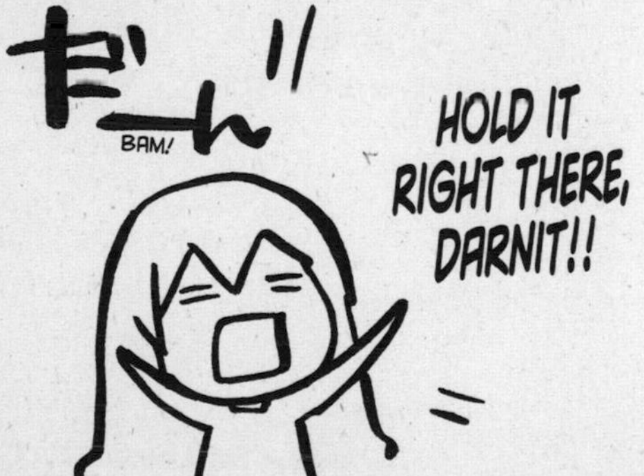
だーん!!
BAM!
HOLD IT RIGHT THERE, DARNIT!!

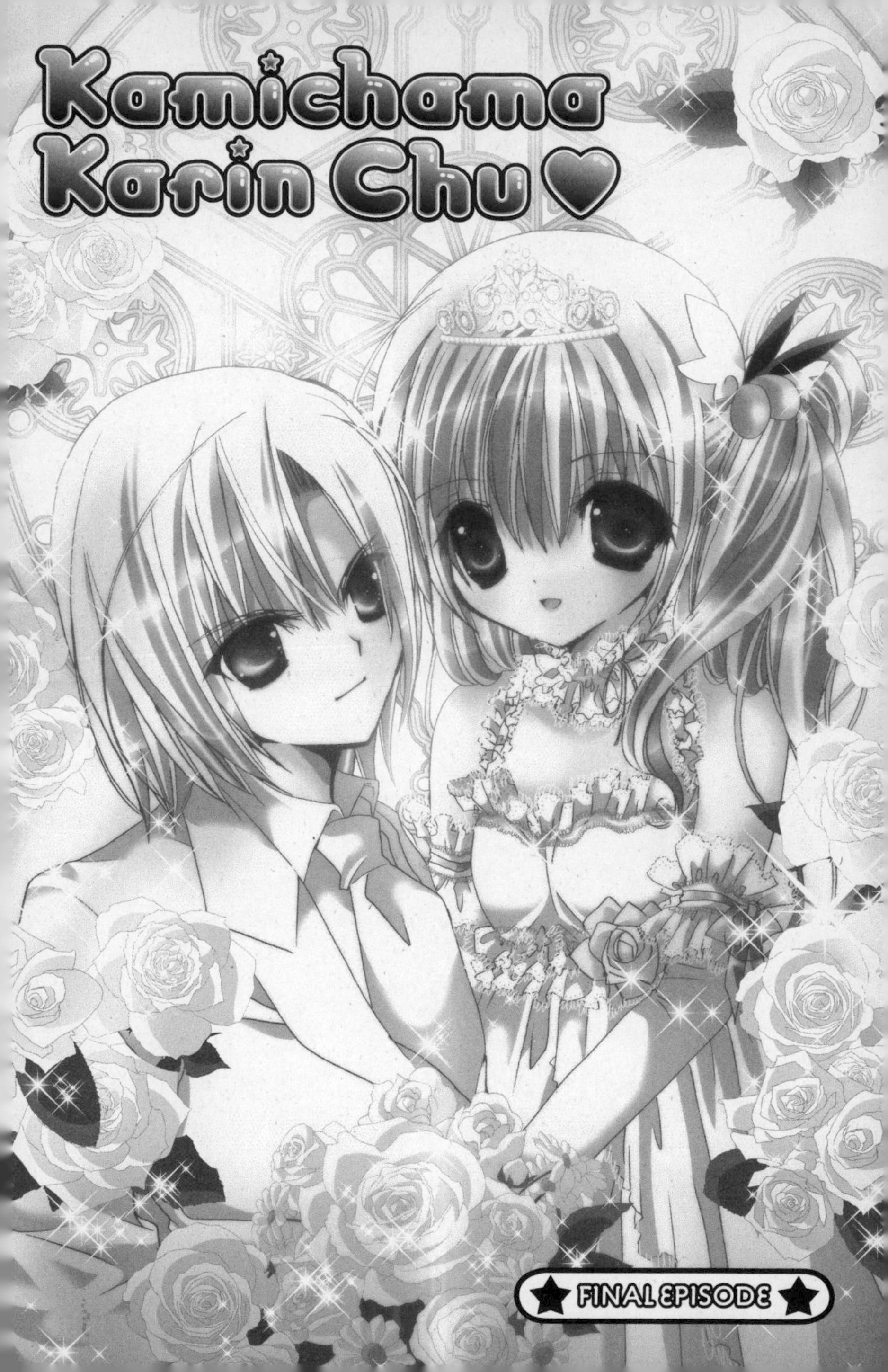
Kamichama Karin Chu♥
FINAL EPISODE

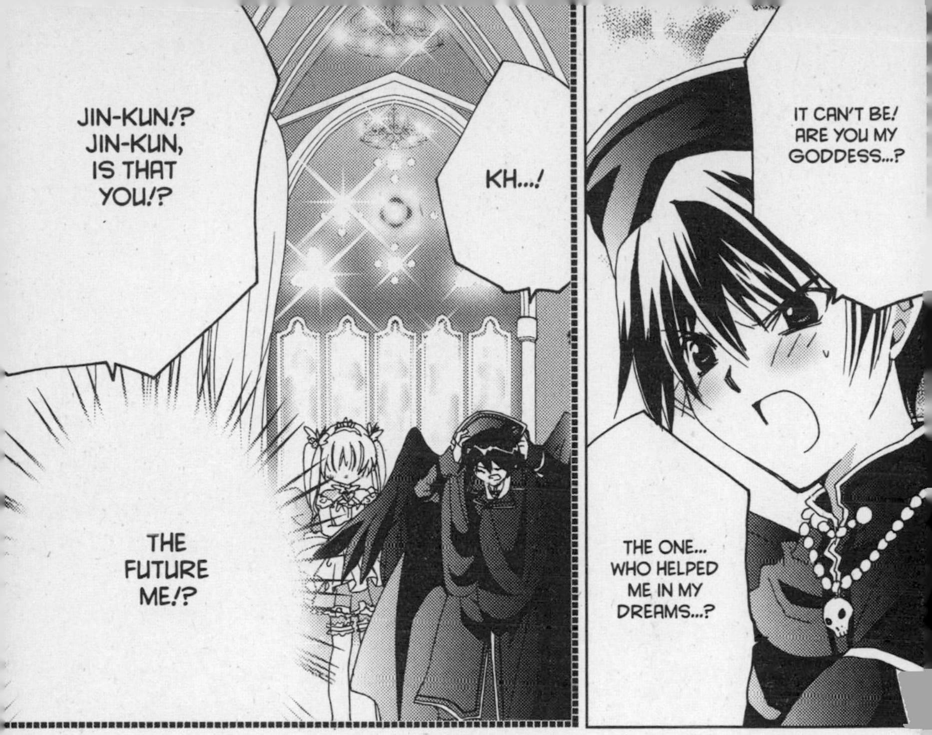
IT CAN'T BE! ARE YOU MY GODDESS...?
THE ONE... WHO HELPED ME IN MY DREAMS...?
KH...!
JIN-KUN!? JIN-KUN, IS THAT YOU!?
THE FUTURE ME!?

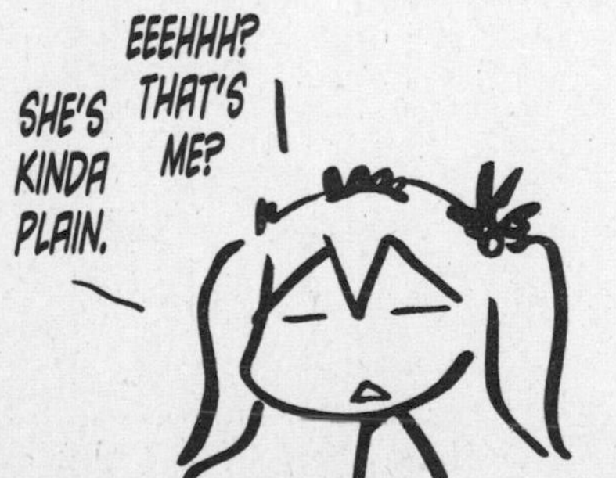
EEEHHH? THAT'S ME?
SHE'S KINDA PLAIN.

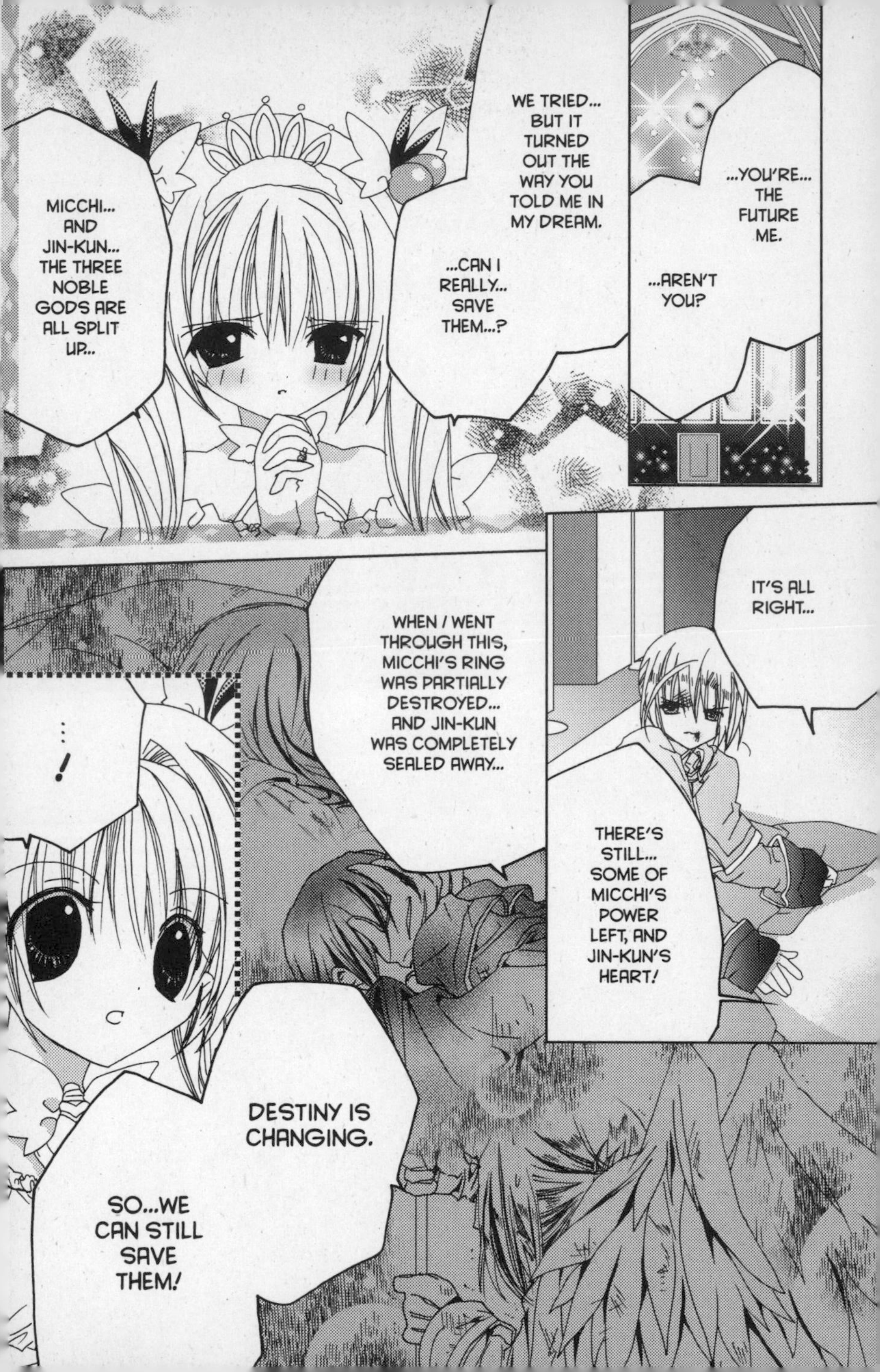
...YOU'RE... THE FUTURE ME.
...AREN'T YOU?
WE TRIED... BUT IT TURNED OUT THE WAY YOU TOLD ME IN MY DREAM.
...CAN I REALLY... SAVE THEM...?
MICCHI... AND JIN-KUN... THE THREE NOBLE GODS ARE ALL SPLIT UP...
IT'S ALL RIGHT...
THERE'S STILL... SOME OF MICCHI'S POWER LEFT, AND JIN-KUN'S HEART!
WHEN I WENT THROUGH THIS, MICCHI'S RING WAS PARTIALLY DESTROYED... AND JIN-KUN WAS COMPLETELY SEALED AWAY...
...!
DESTINY IS CHANGING.
SO...WE CAN STILL SAVE THEM!

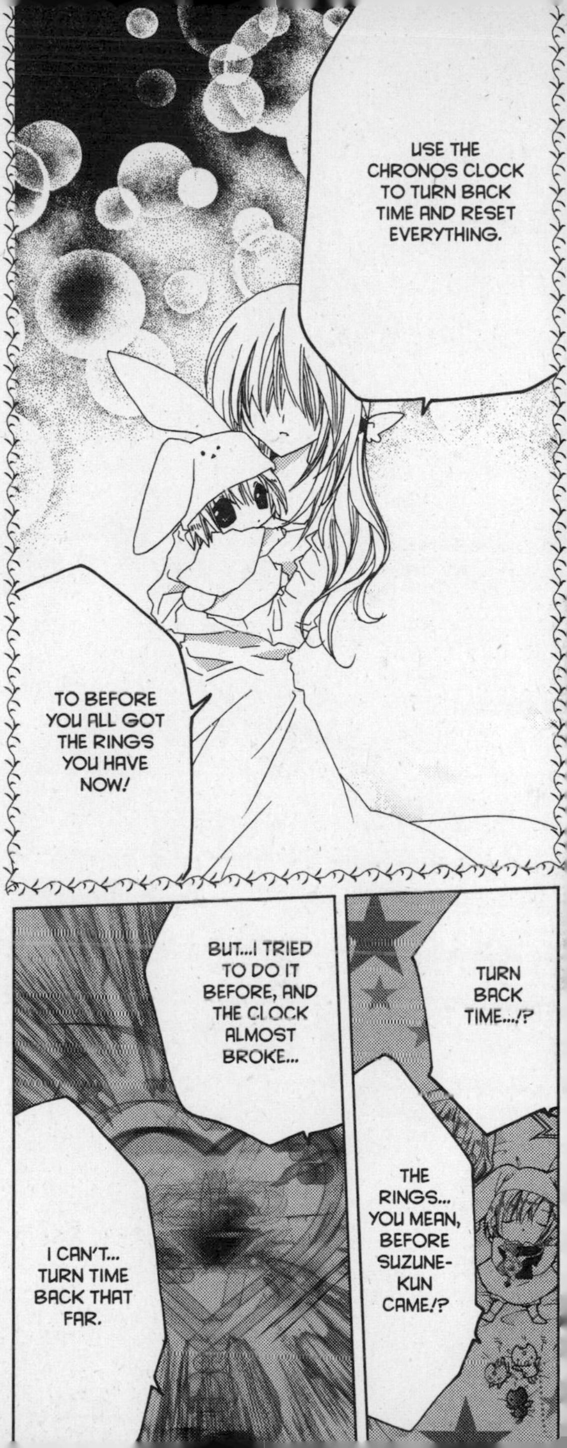
USE THE CHRONOS CLOCK TO TURN BACK TIME AND RESET EVERYTHING.
TO BEFORE YOU ALL GOT THE RINGS YOU HAVE NOW!
TURN BACK TIME...!?
THE RINGS... YOU MEAN, BEFORE SUZUNE-KUN CAME!?
BUT...I TRIED TO DO IT BEFORE, AND THE CLOCK ALMOST BROKE...
I CAN'T... TURN TIME BACK THAT FAR.

CAN I RELY ON SOMETHING THAT *I* THOUGHT OF?

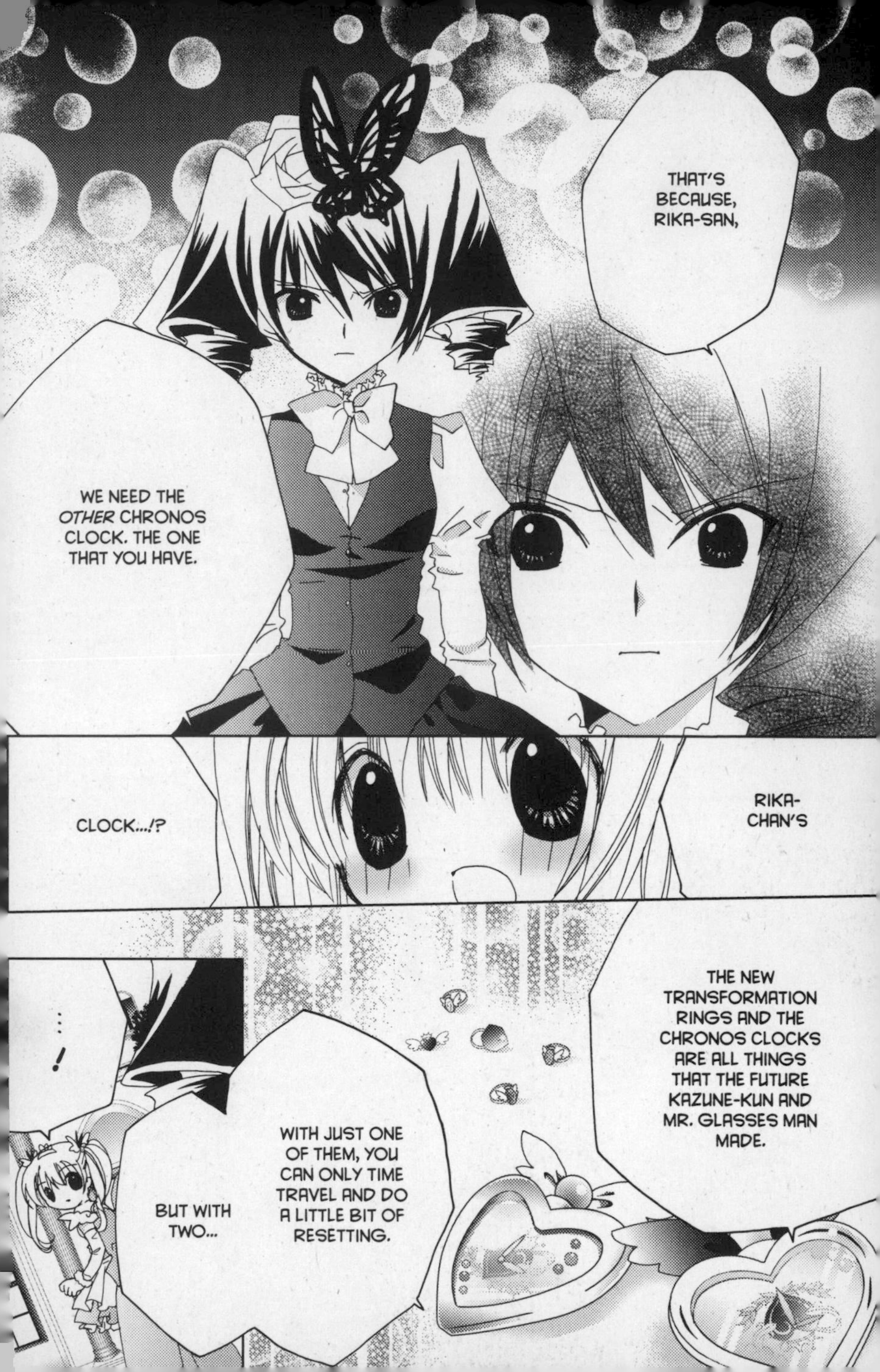
THAT'S BECAUSE, RIKA-SAN,
WE NEED THE *OTHER* CHRONOS CLOCK. THE ONE THAT YOU HAVE.
RIKA-CHAN'S
CLOCK...!?
THE NEW TRANSFORMATION RINGS AND THE CHRONOS CLOCKS ARE ALL THINGS THAT THE FUTURE KAZUNE-KUN AND MR. GLASSES MAN MADE.
WITH JUST ONE OF THEM, YOU CAN ONLY TIME TRAVEL AND DO A LITTLE BIT OF RESETTING.
BUT WITH TWO...
...!

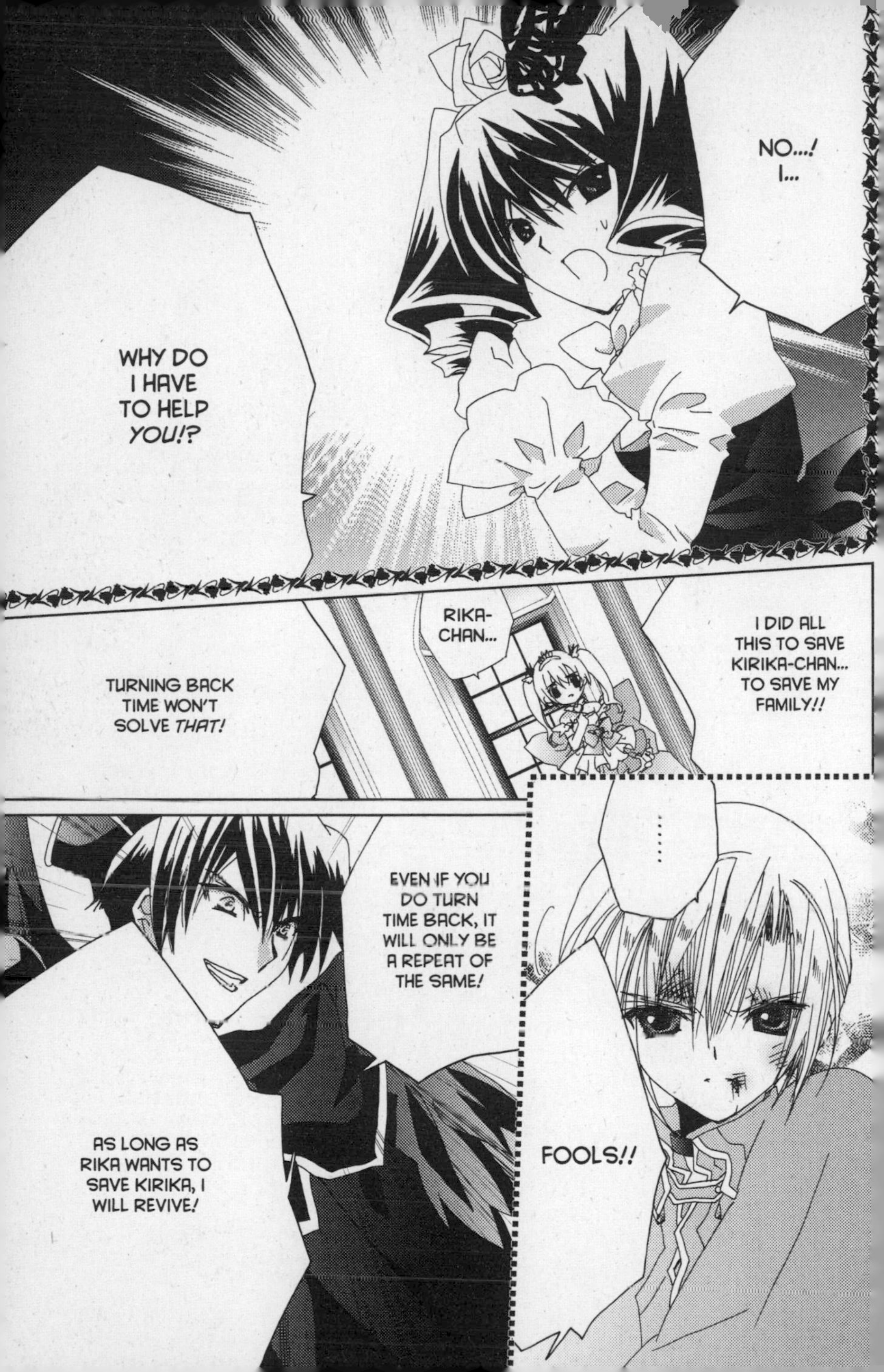
NO...! I...
WHY DO I HAVE TO HELP *YOU*!?
I DID ALL THIS TO SAVE KIRIKA-CHAN... TO SAVE MY FAMILY!!
RIKA-CHAN...
TURNING BACK TIME WON'T SOLVE *THAT*!
......
FOOLS!!
EVEN IF YOU DO TURN TIME BACK, IT WILL ONLY BE A REPEAT OF THE SAME!
AS LONG AS RIKA WANTS TO SAVE KIRIKA, I WILL REVIVE!

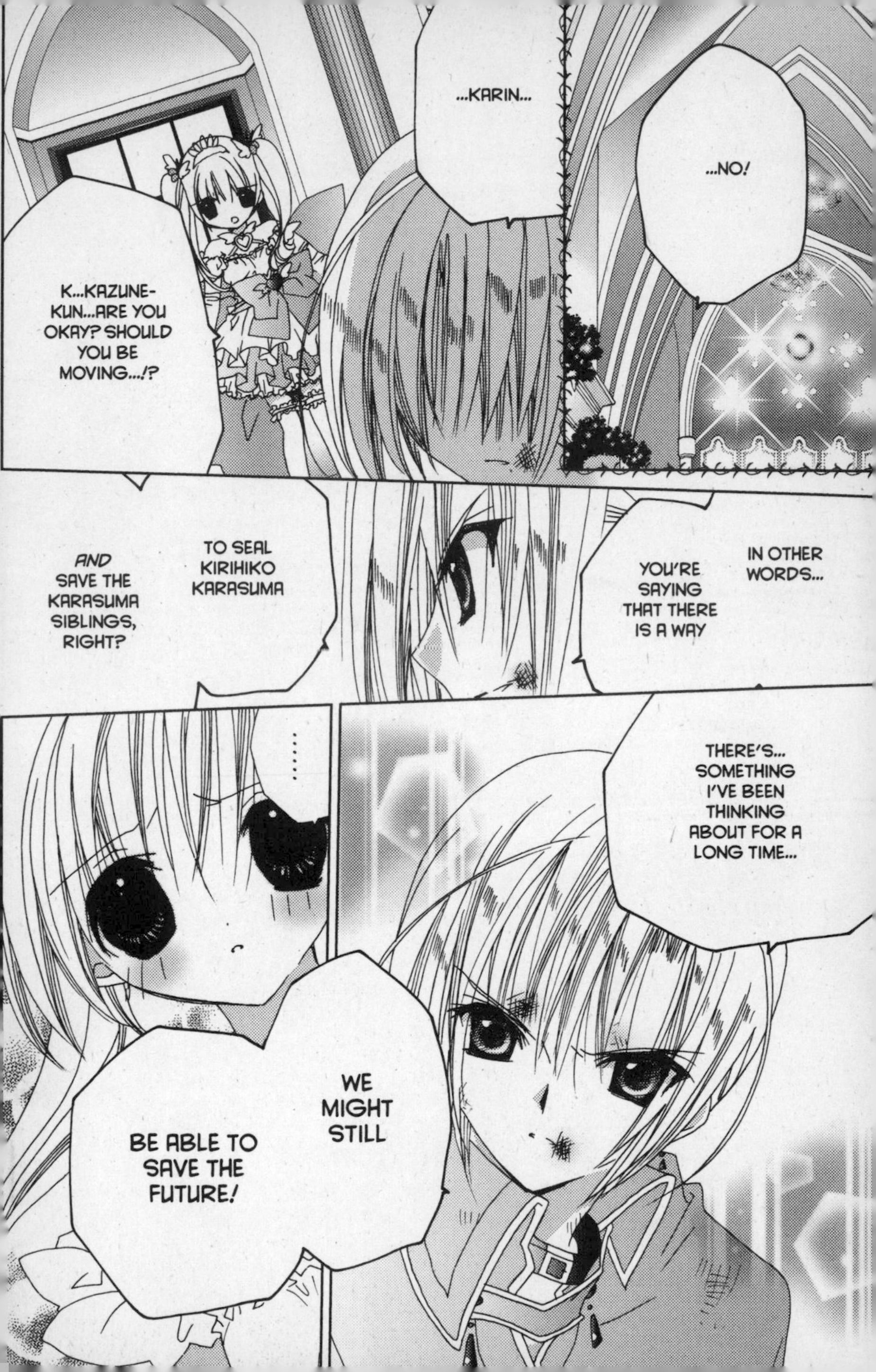
...NO!
...KARIN...
K...KAZUNE-KUN...ARE YOU OKAY? SHOULD YOU BE MOVING...!?
IN OTHER WORDS...
YOU'RE SAYING THAT THERE IS A WAY
TO SEAL KIRIHIKO KARASUMA
AND SAVE THE KARASUMA SIBLINGS, RIGHT?
THERE'S... SOMETHING I'VE BEEN THINKING ABOUT FOR A LONG TIME...
WE MIGHT STILL
BE ABLE TO SAVE THE FUTURE!
......

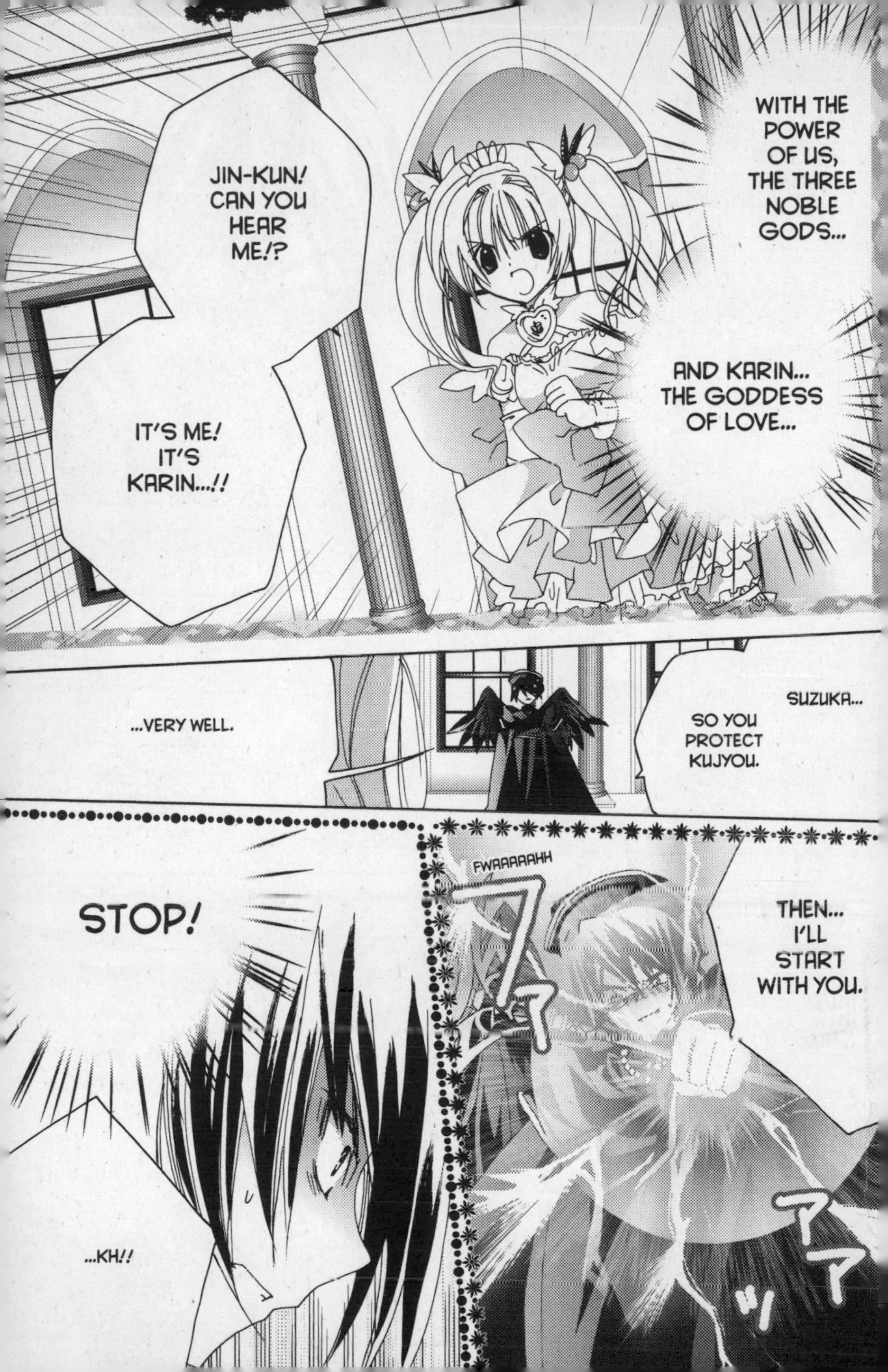
WITH THE POWER OF US, THE THREE NOBLE GODS...
AND KARIN... THE GODDESS OF LOVE...
JIN-KUN! CAN YOU HEAR ME!?
IT'S ME! IT'S KARIN...!!
SUZUKA...
SO YOU PROTECT KUJYOU.
...VERY WELL.
FWAAAAAAHH
THEN... I'LL START WITH YOU.
STOP!
...KH!!

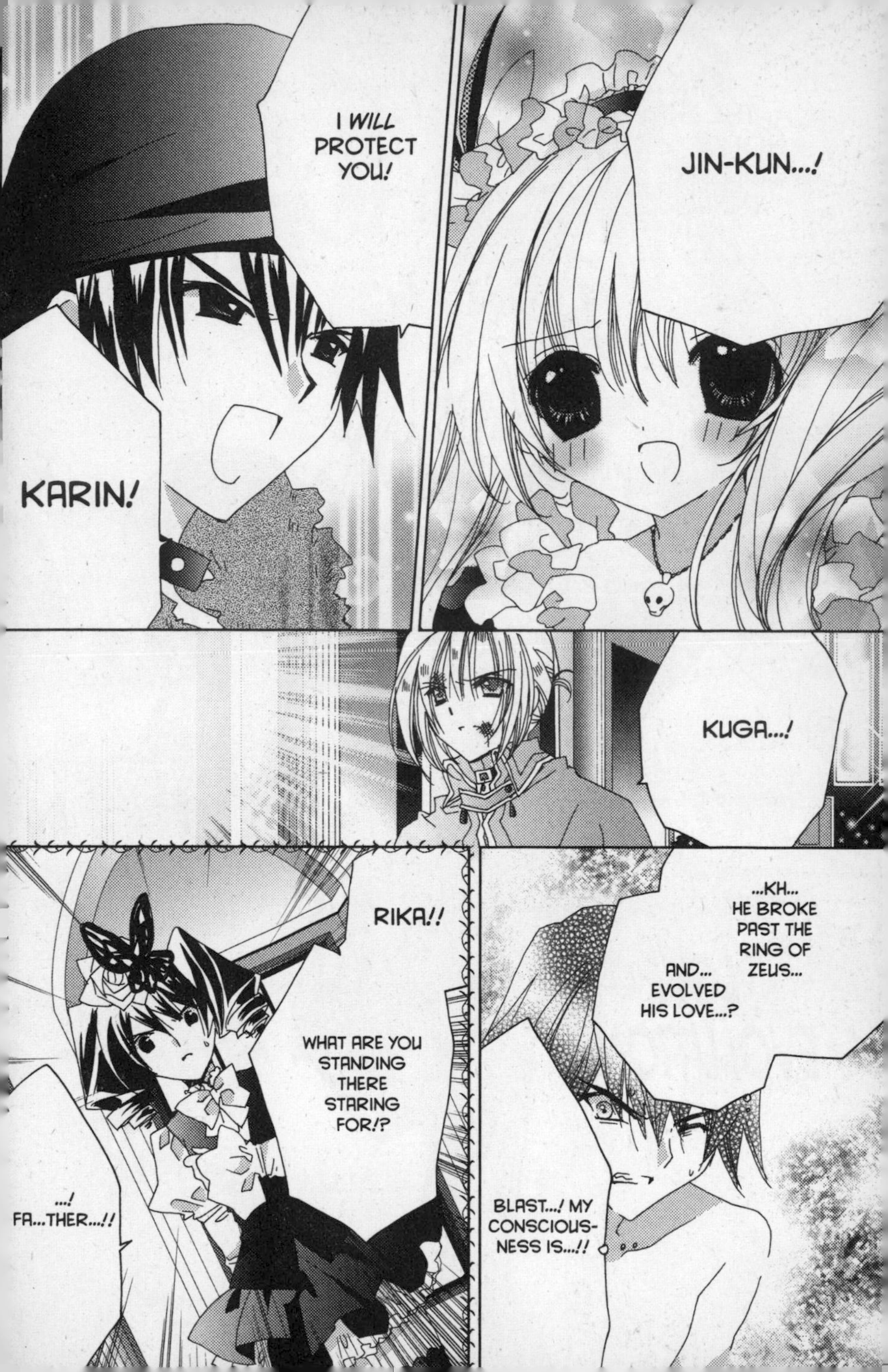
JIN-KUN...!
I WILL PROTECT YOU!
KARIN!
KUGA...!
...KH... HE BROKE PAST THE RING OF ZEUS...
AND... EVOLVED HIS LOVE...?
BLAST...! MY CONSCIOUS-NESS IS...!!
RIKA!!
WHAT ARE YOU STANDING THERE STARING FOR!?
...! FA...THER...!!

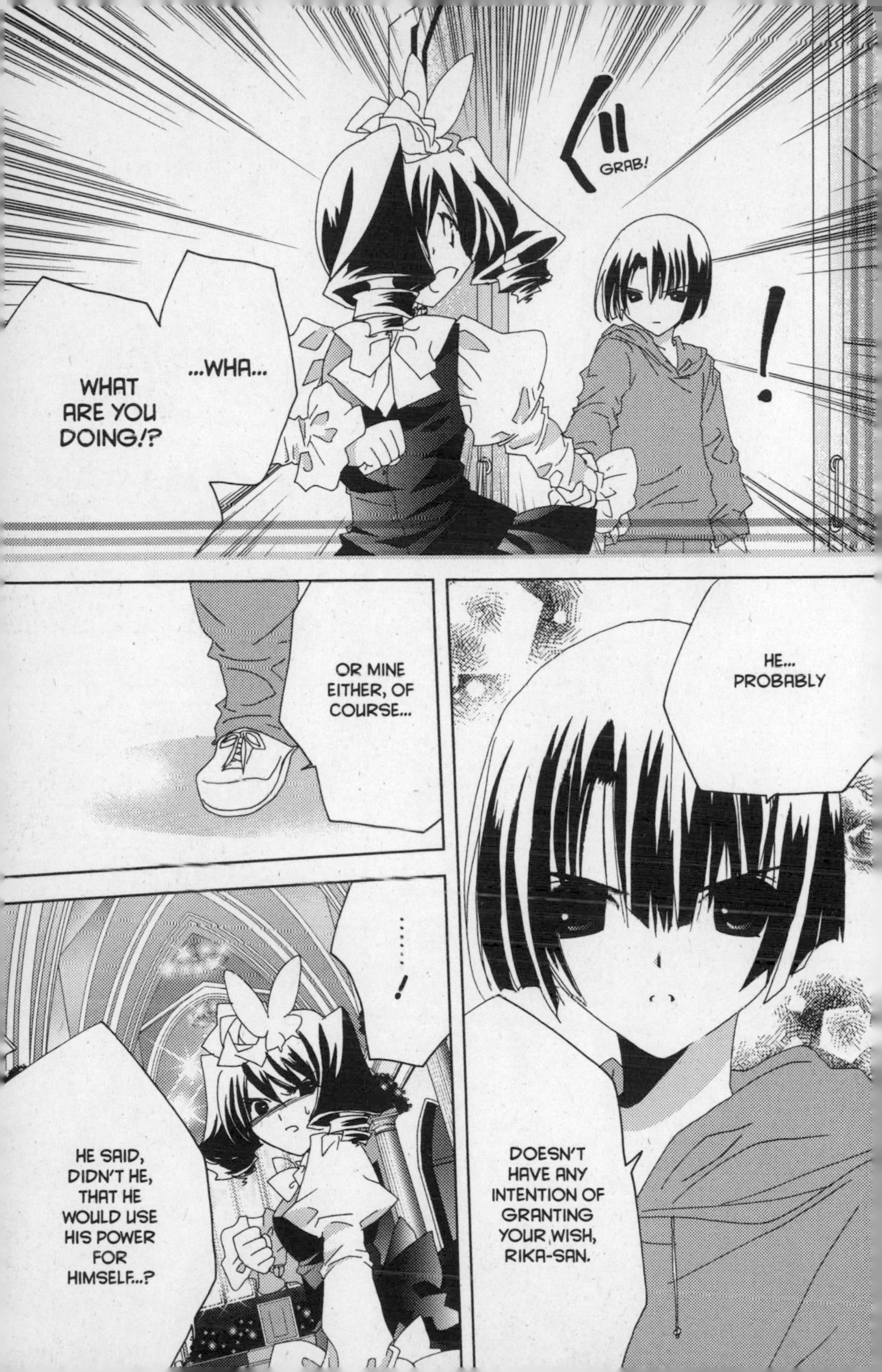
GRAB!
!
...WHA...
WHAT ARE YOU DOING!?
HE... PROBABLY
DOESN'T HAVE ANY INTENTION OF GRANTING YOUR WISH, RIKA-SAN.
OR MINE EITHER, OF COURSE...
......!
HE SAID, DIDN'T HE, THAT HE WOULD USE HIS POWER FOR HIMSELF...?

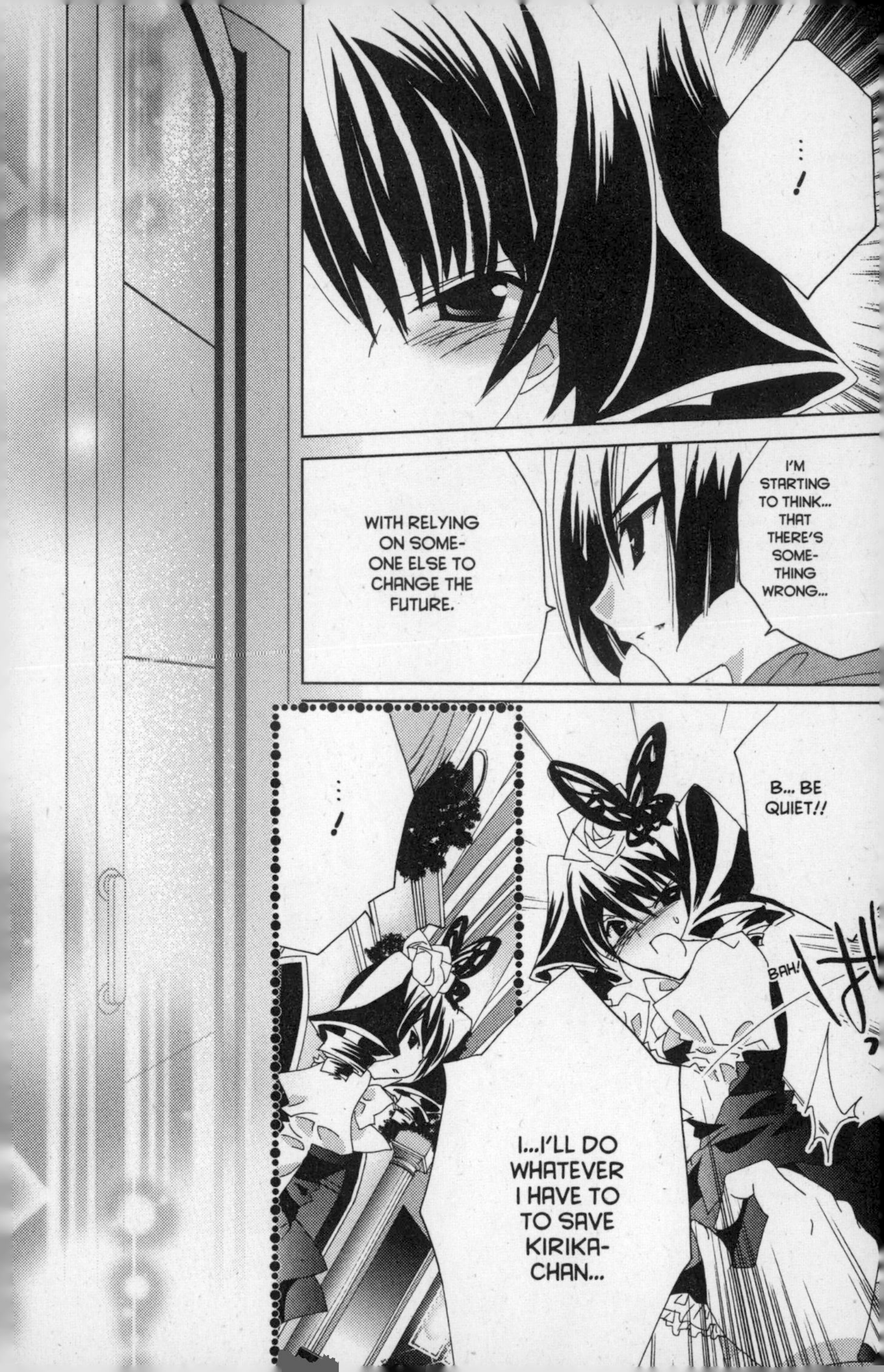
...!
I'M STARTING TO THINK... THAT THERE'S SOME-THING WRONG...
WITH RELYING ON SOME-ONE ELSE TO CHANGE THE FUTURE.
B... BE QUIET!!
BAH!
I...I'LL DO WHATEVER I HAVE TO TO SAVE KIRIKA-CHAN...
...!

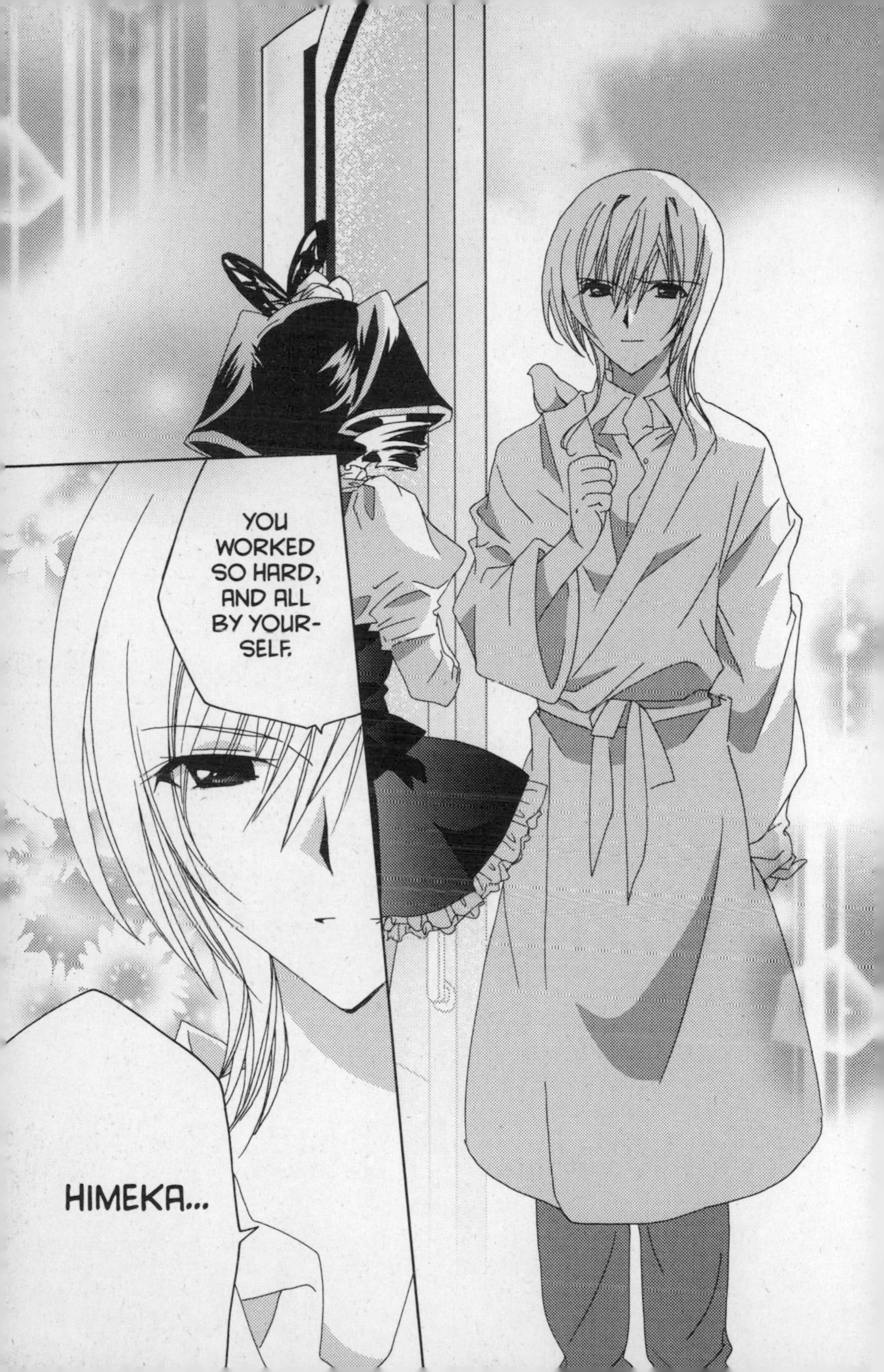
YOU WORKED SO HARD, AND ALL BY YOUR-SELF.
HIMEKA...

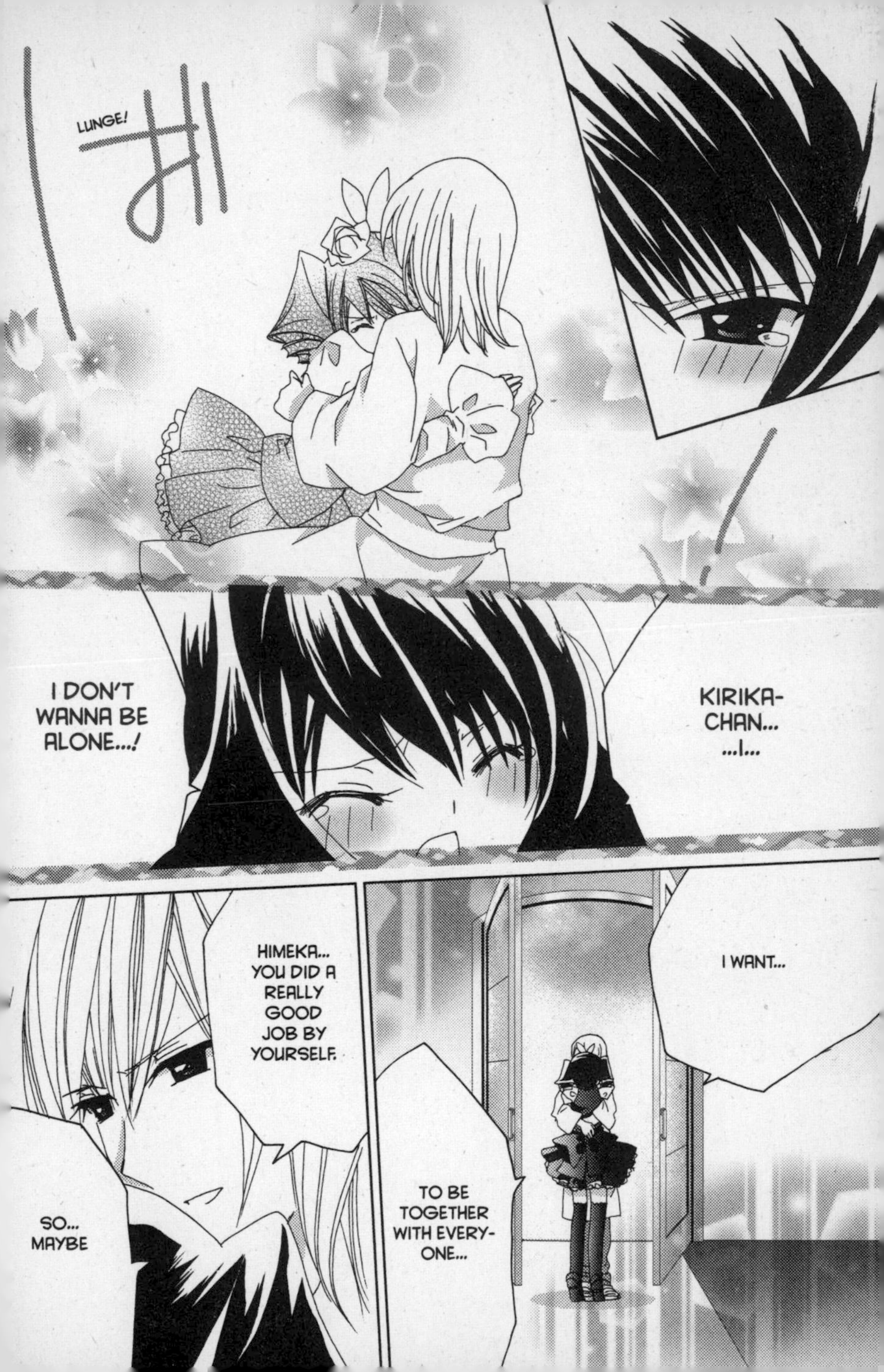

LUNGE!
KIRIKA-CHAN... ...I...
I DON'T WANNA BE ALONE...!
I WANT...
TO BE TOGETHER WITH EVERY-ONE...
HIMEKA... YOU DID A REALLY GOOD JOB BY YOURSELF.
SO... MAYBE

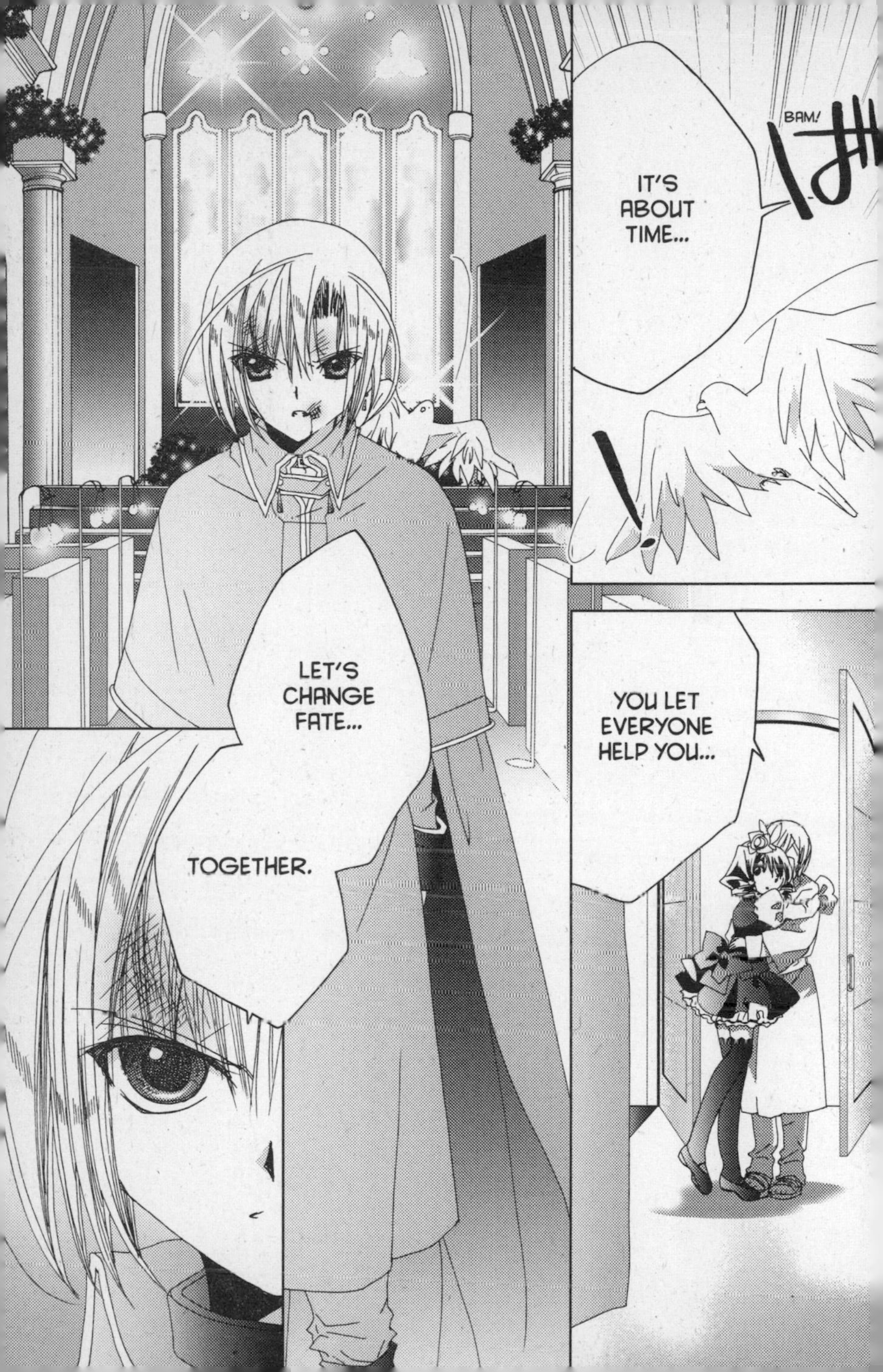
IT'S ABOUT TIME...
BAM!
YOU LET EVERYONE HELP YOU...
LET'S CHANGE FATE...
TOGETHER.

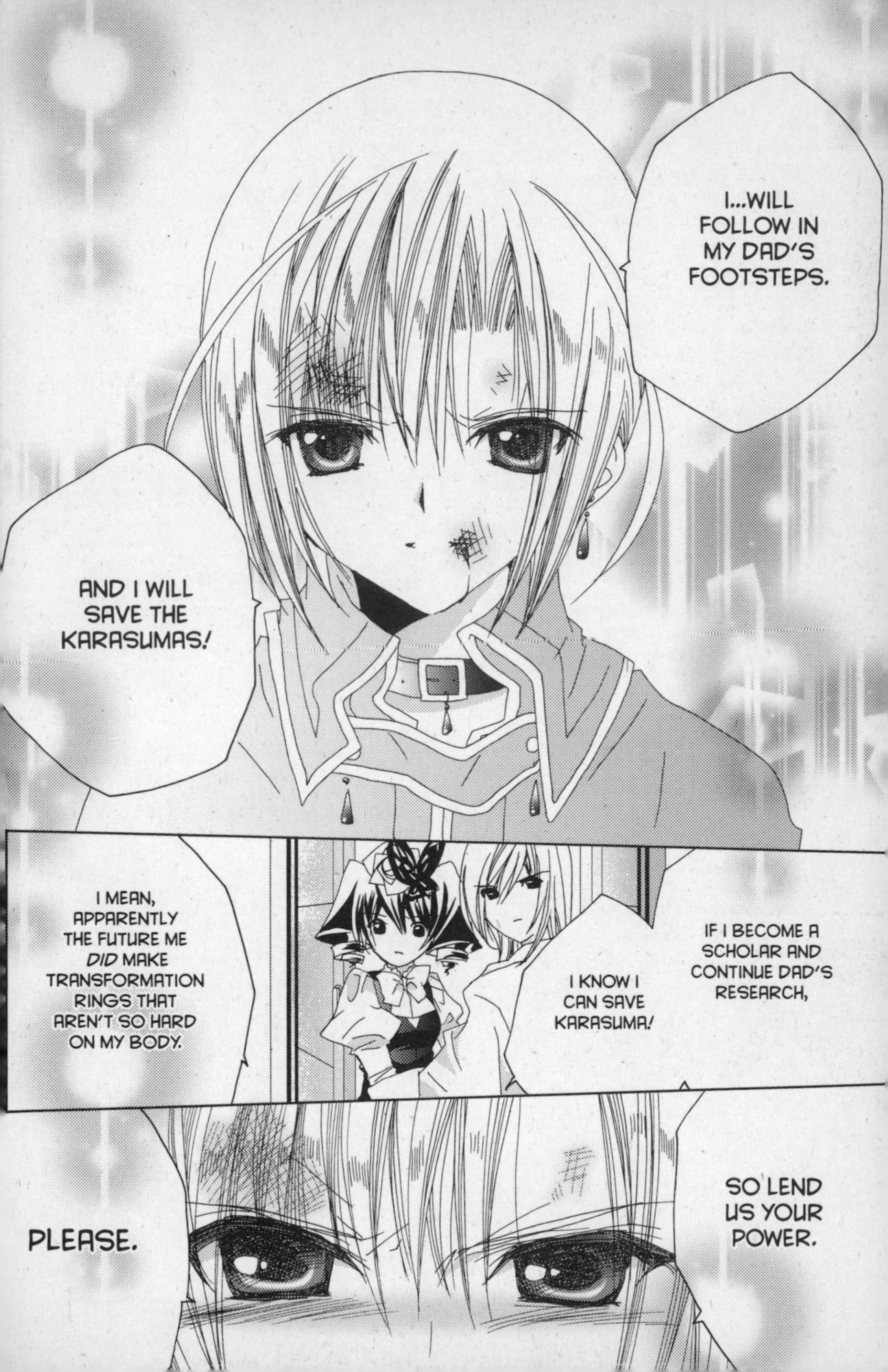
I...WILL FOLLOW IN MY DAD'S FOOTSTEPS.
AND I WILL SAVE THE KARASUMAS!
IF I BECOME A SCHOLAR AND CONTINUE DAD'S RESEARCH,
I KNOW I CAN SAVE KARASUMA!
I MEAN, APPARENTLY THE FUTURE ME *DID* MAKE TRANSFORMATION RINGS THAT AREN'T SO HARD ON MY BODY.
SO LEND US YOUR POWER.
PLEASE.

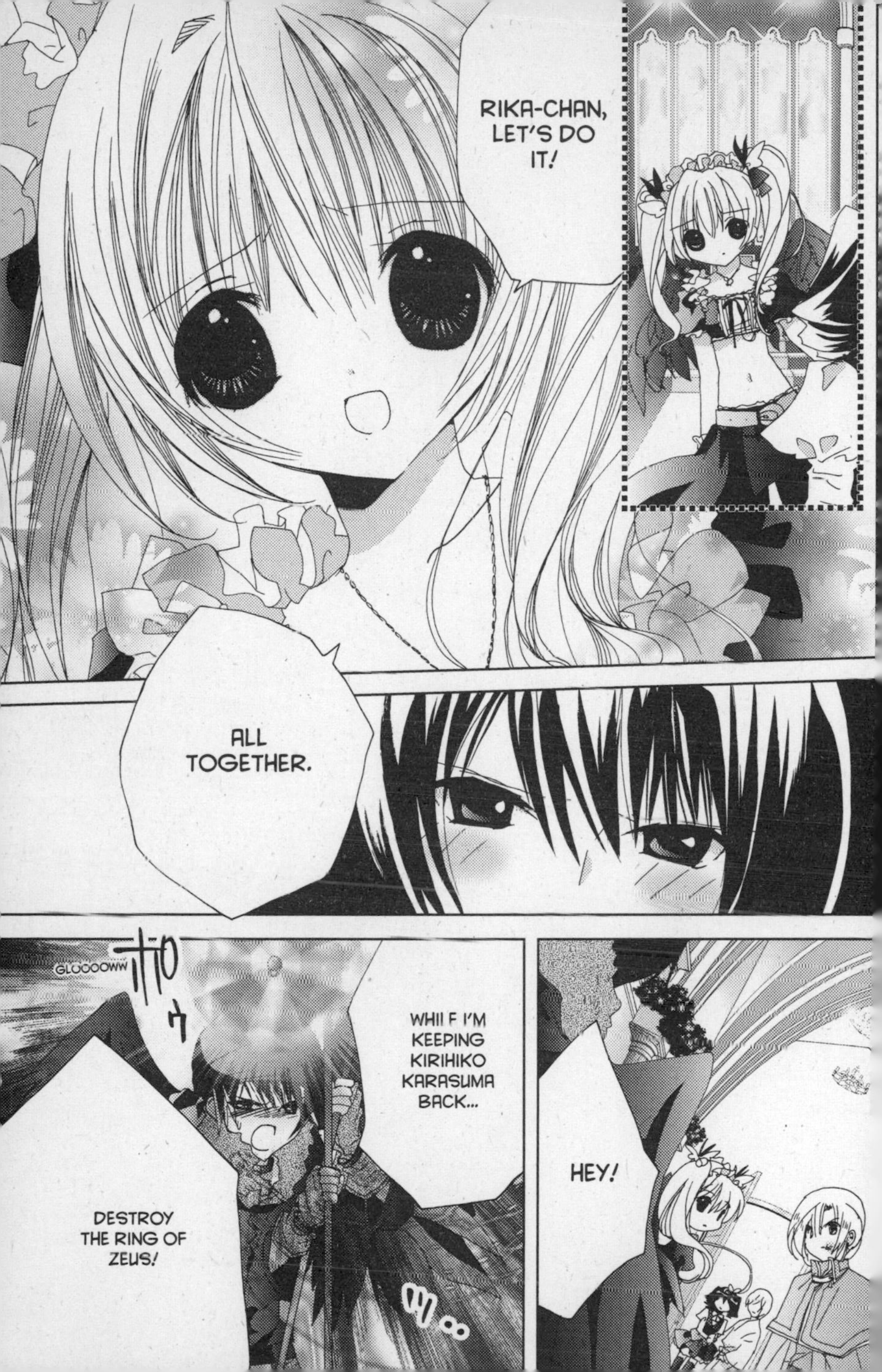
RIKA-CHAN, LET'S DO IT!
ALL TOGETHER.
HEY!
GLOOOOWW
WHILE I'M KEEPING KIRIHIKO KARASUMA BACK...
DESTROY THE RING OF ZEUS!

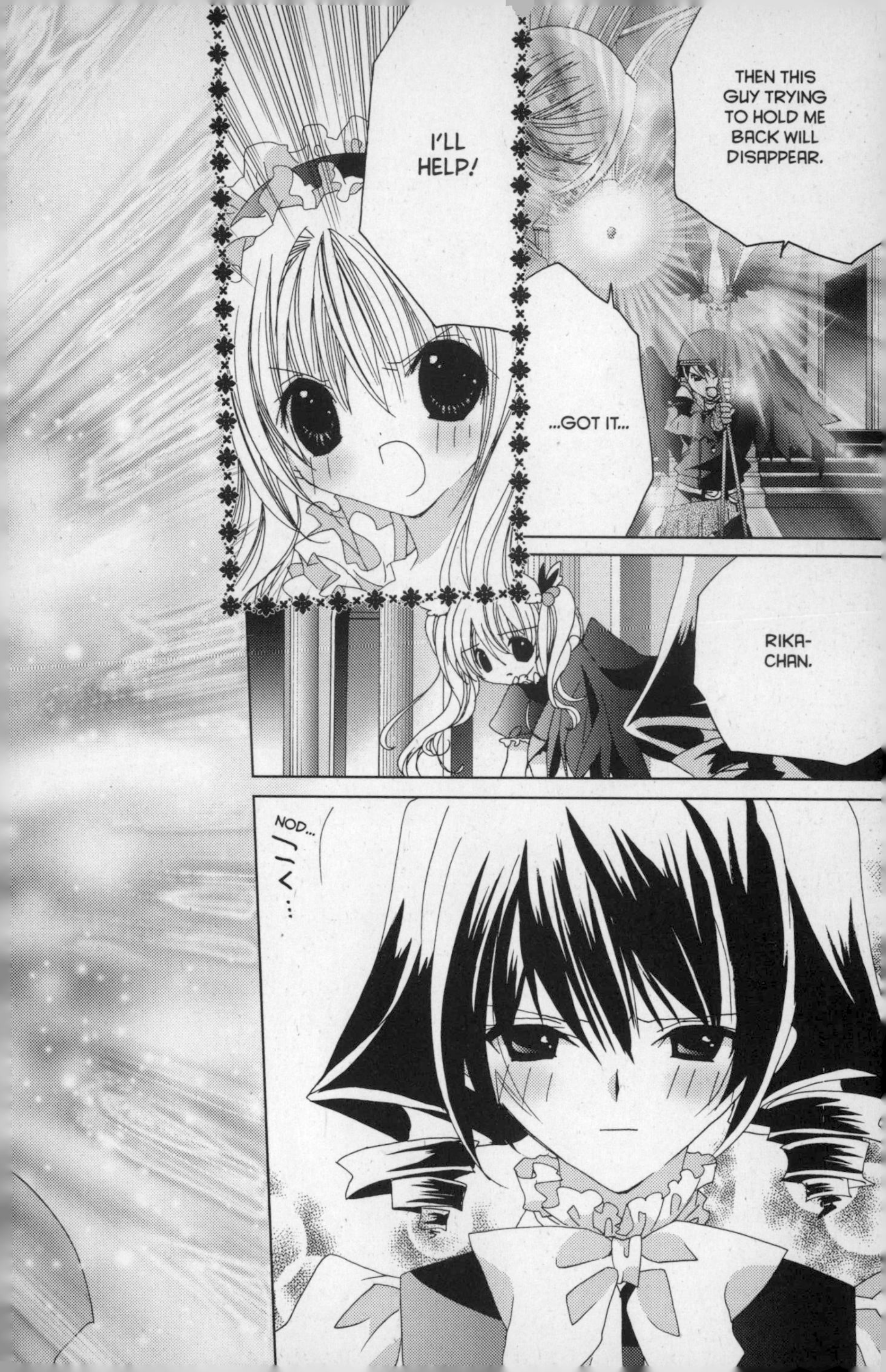
THEN THIS GUY TRYING TO HOLD ME BACK WILL DISAPPEAR.
...GOT IT...
RIKA-CHAN.
I'LL HELP!
NOD...

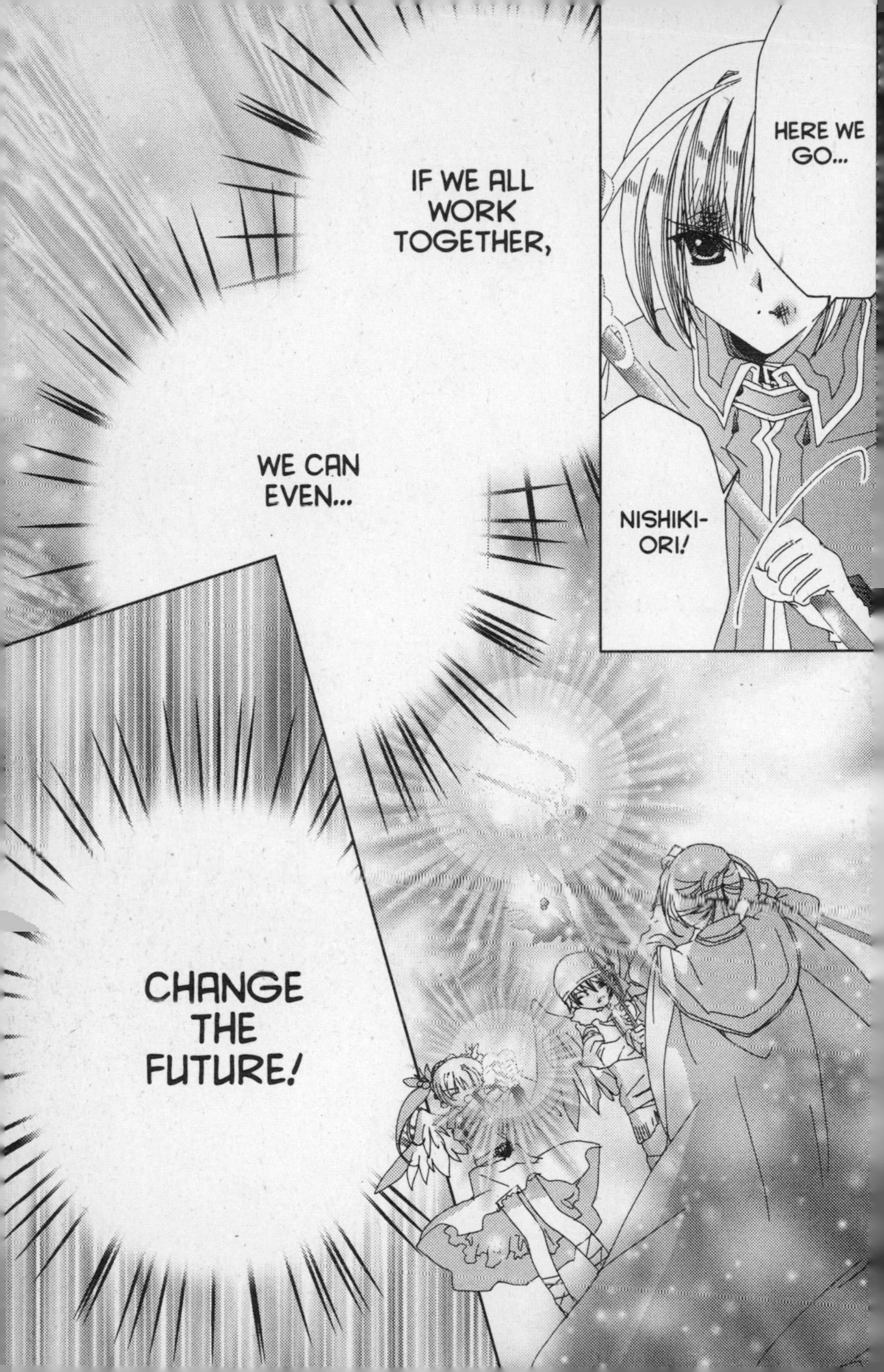
HERE WE GO...
NISHIKI-ORI!
IF WE ALL WORK TOGETHER,
WE CAN EVEN...
CHANGE THE FUTURE!

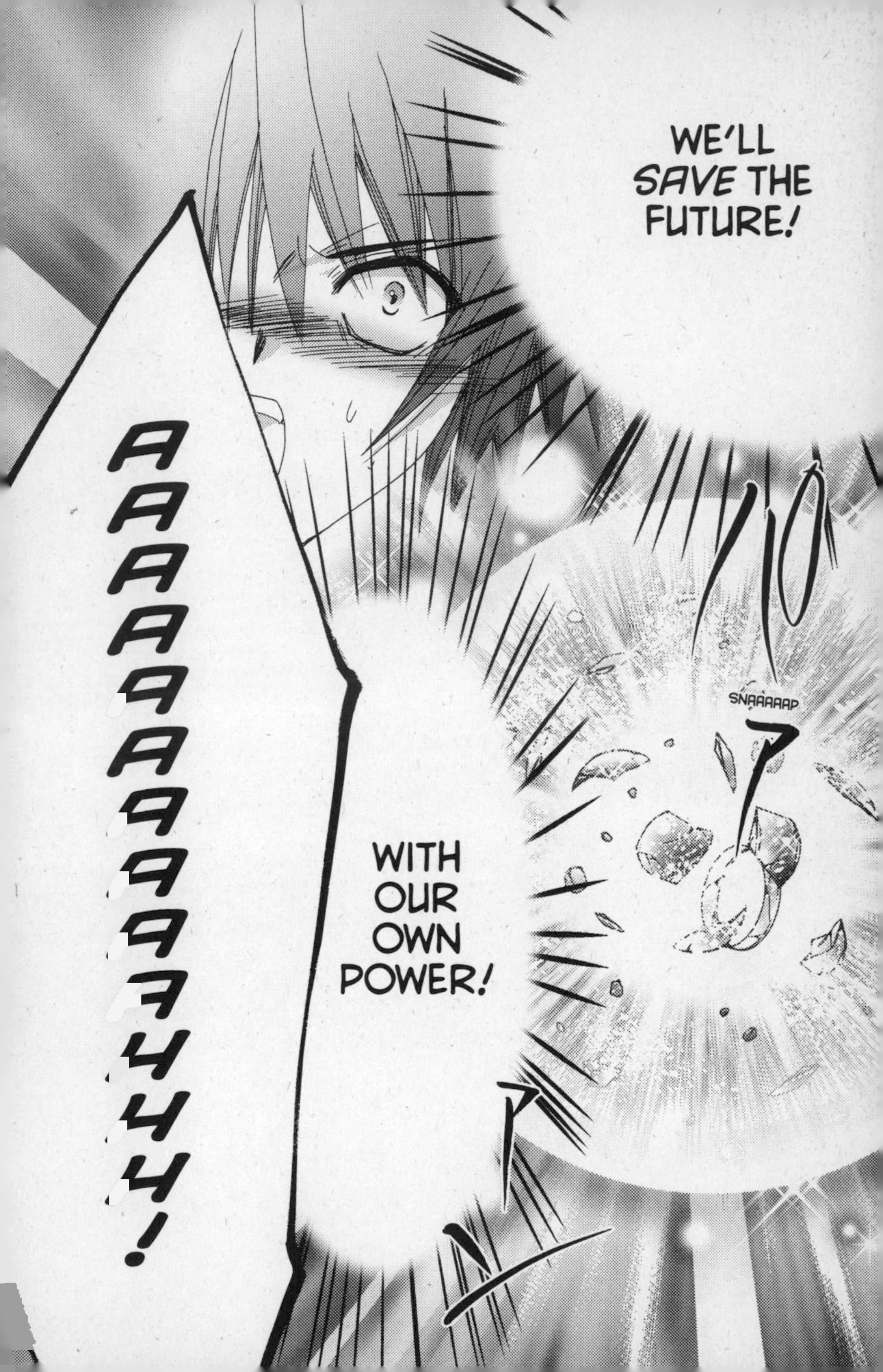
WE'LL SAVE THE FUTURE!
WITH OUR OWN POWER!
SNAAAAAP
AAAAAAAAAAAAHHH!

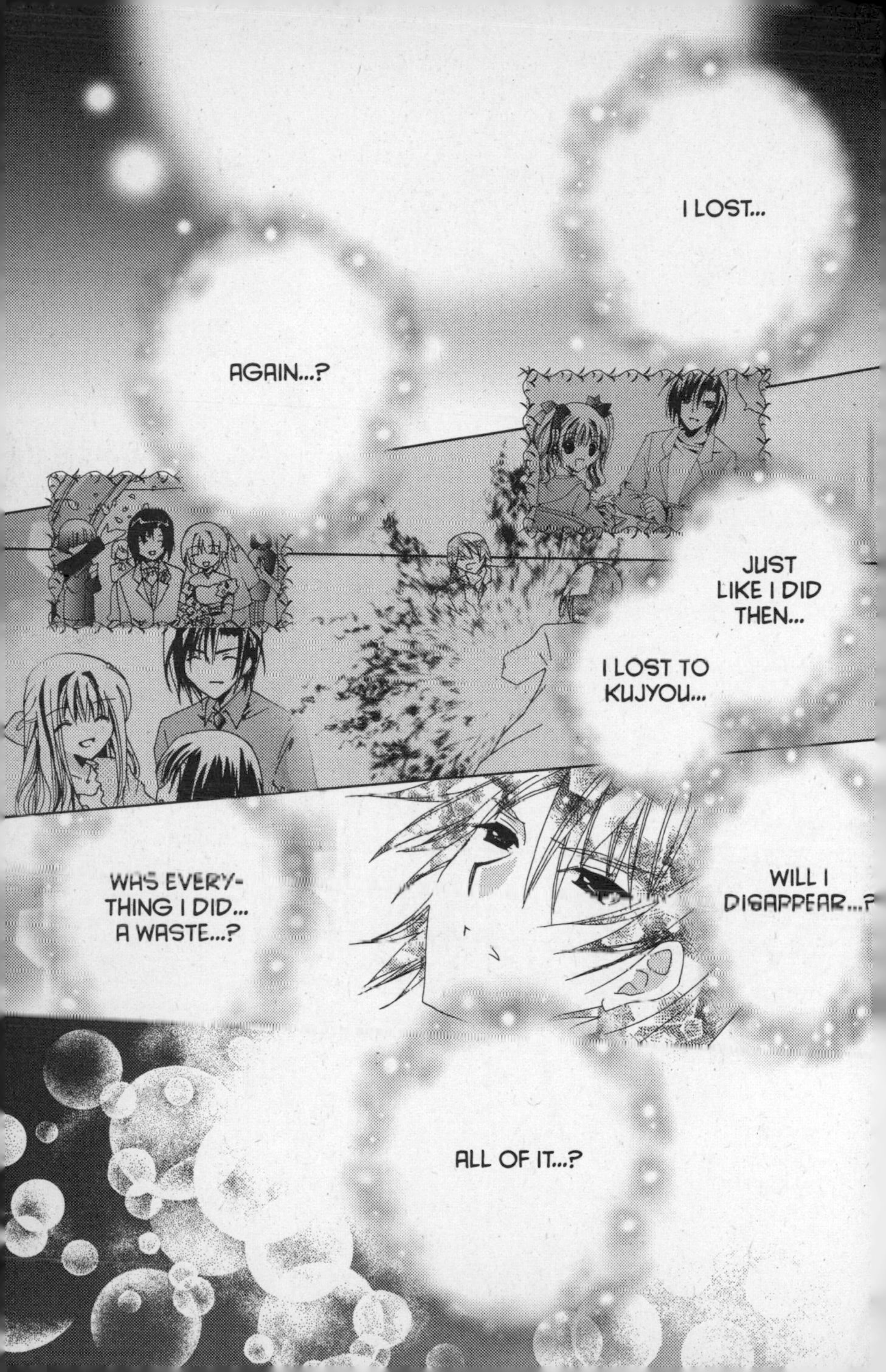
I LOST...
AGAIN...?
JUST LIKE I DID THEN...
I LOST TO KUJYOU...
WILL I DISAPPEAR...?
WAS EVERY-THING I DID... A WASTE...?
ALL OF IT...?

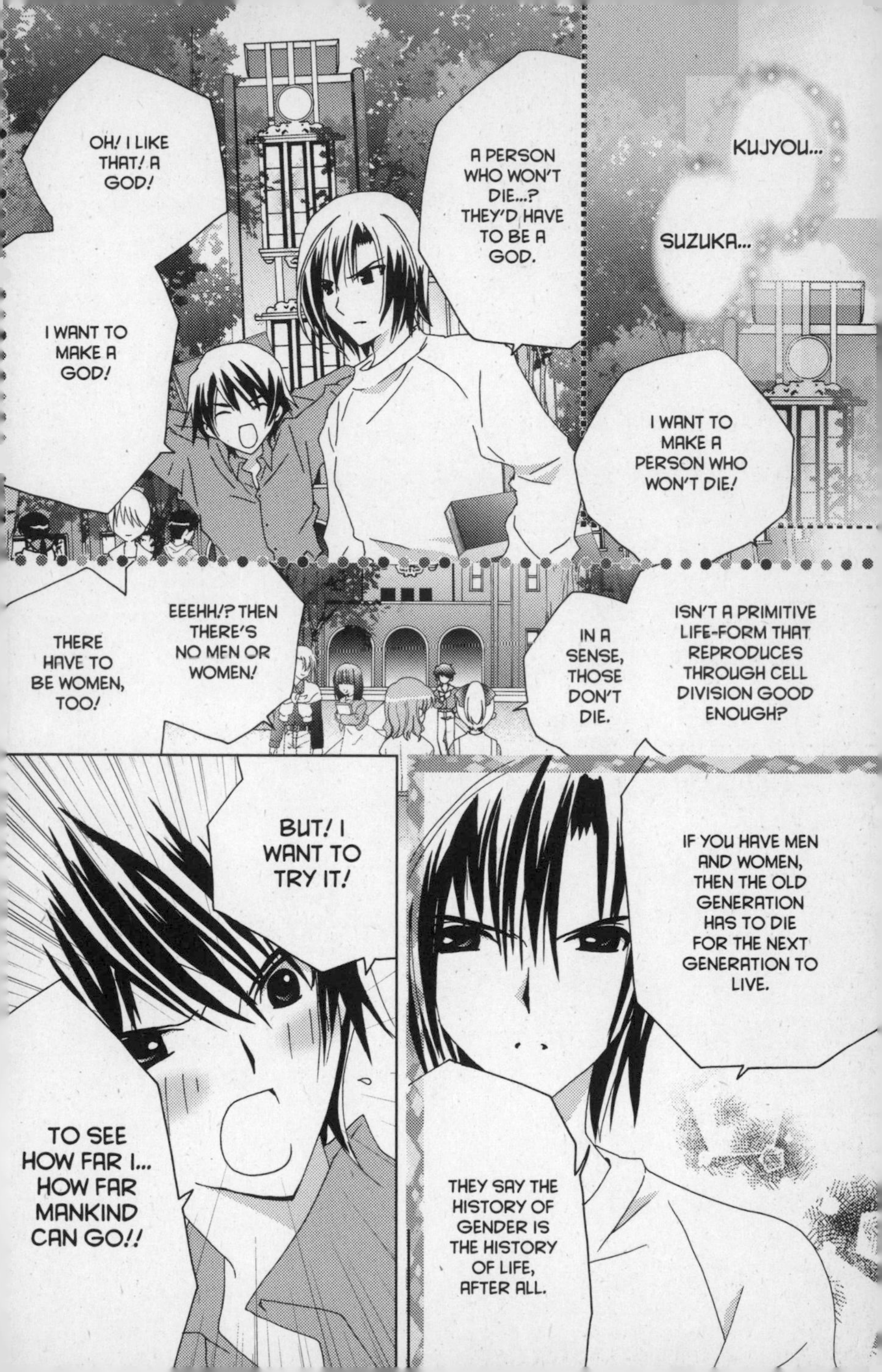
KUJYOU...
SUZUKA...
I WANT TO MAKE A PERSON WHO WON'T DIE!
A PERSON WHO WON'T DIE...? THEY'D HAVE TO BE A GOD.
OH! I LIKE THAT! A GOD!
I WANT TO MAKE A GOD!
ISN'T A PRIMITIVE LIFE-FORM THAT REPRODUCES THROUGH CELL DIVISION GOOD ENOUGH?
IN A SENSE, THOSE DON'T DIE.
EEEHH!? THEN THERE'S NO MEN OR WOMEN!
THERE HAVE TO BE WOMEN, TOO!
IF YOU HAVE MEN AND WOMEN, THEN THE OLD GENERATION HAS TO DIE FOR THE NEXT GENERATION TO LIVE.
THEY SAY THE HISTORY OF GENDER IS THE HISTORY OF LIFE, AFTER ALL.
BUT! I WANT TO TRY IT!
TO SEE HOW FAR I... HOW FAR MANKIND CAN GO!!

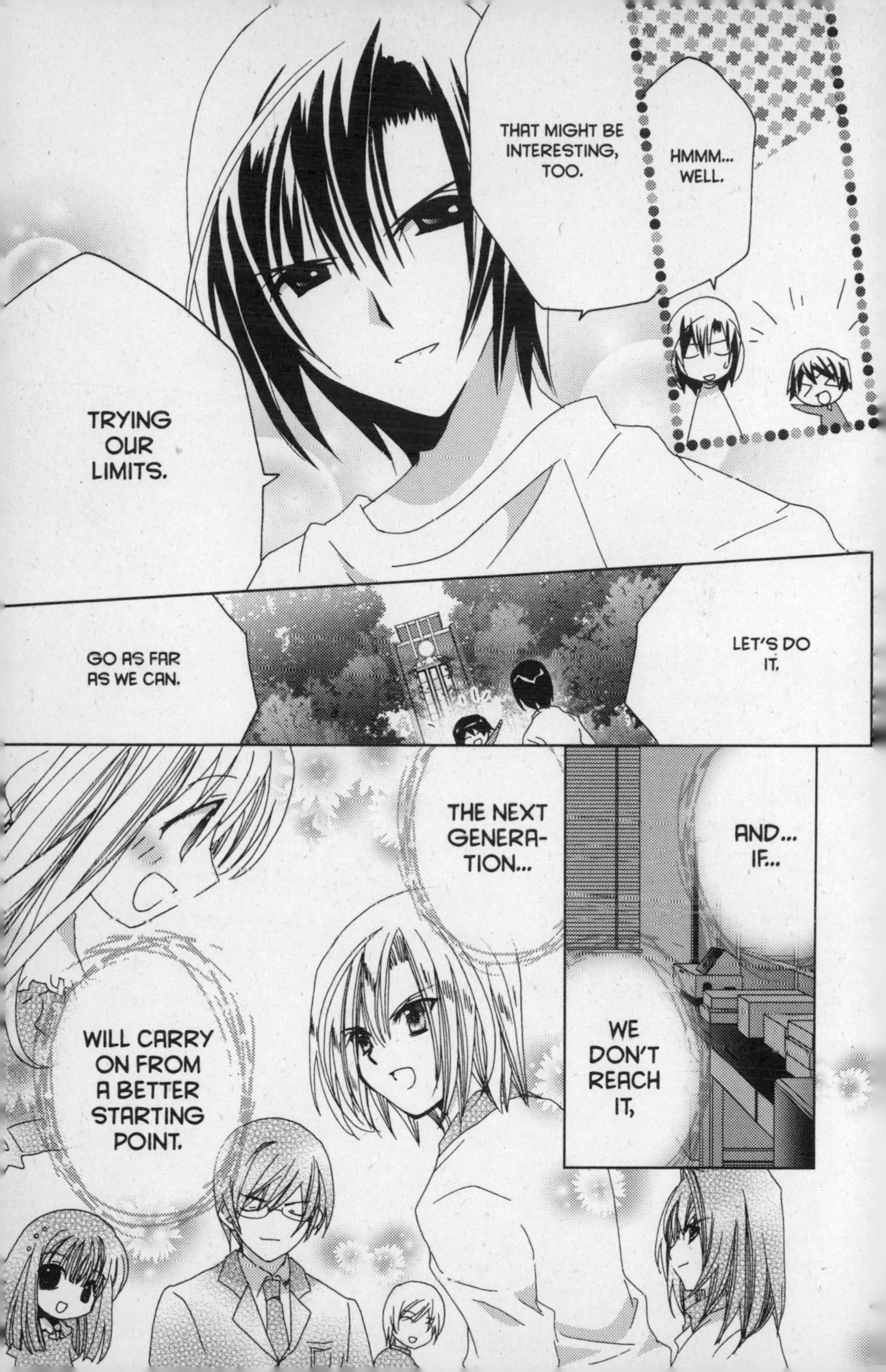
HMMM... WELL.
THAT MIGHT BE INTERESTING, TOO.
TRYING OUR LIMITS.
LET'S DO IT.
GO AS FAR AS WE CAN.
AND... IF...
WE DON'T REACH IT,
THE NEXT GENERA-TION...
WILL CARRY ON FROM A BETTER STARTING POINT.

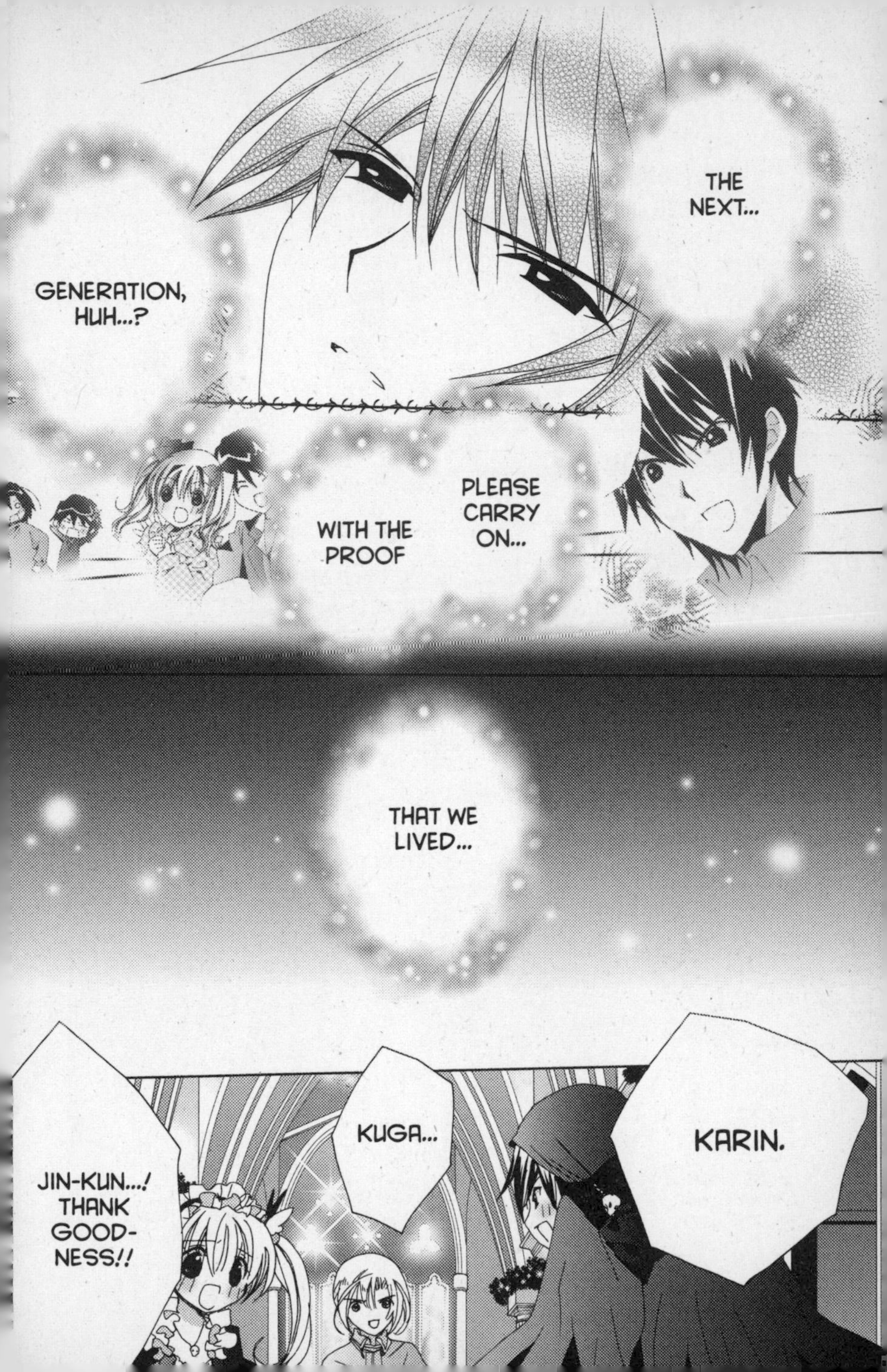
THE NEXT...
GENERATION, HUH...?
PLEASE CARRY ON...
WITH THE PROOF
THAT WE LIVED...
KARIN.
KUGA...
JIN-KUN...! THANK GOOD-NESS!!

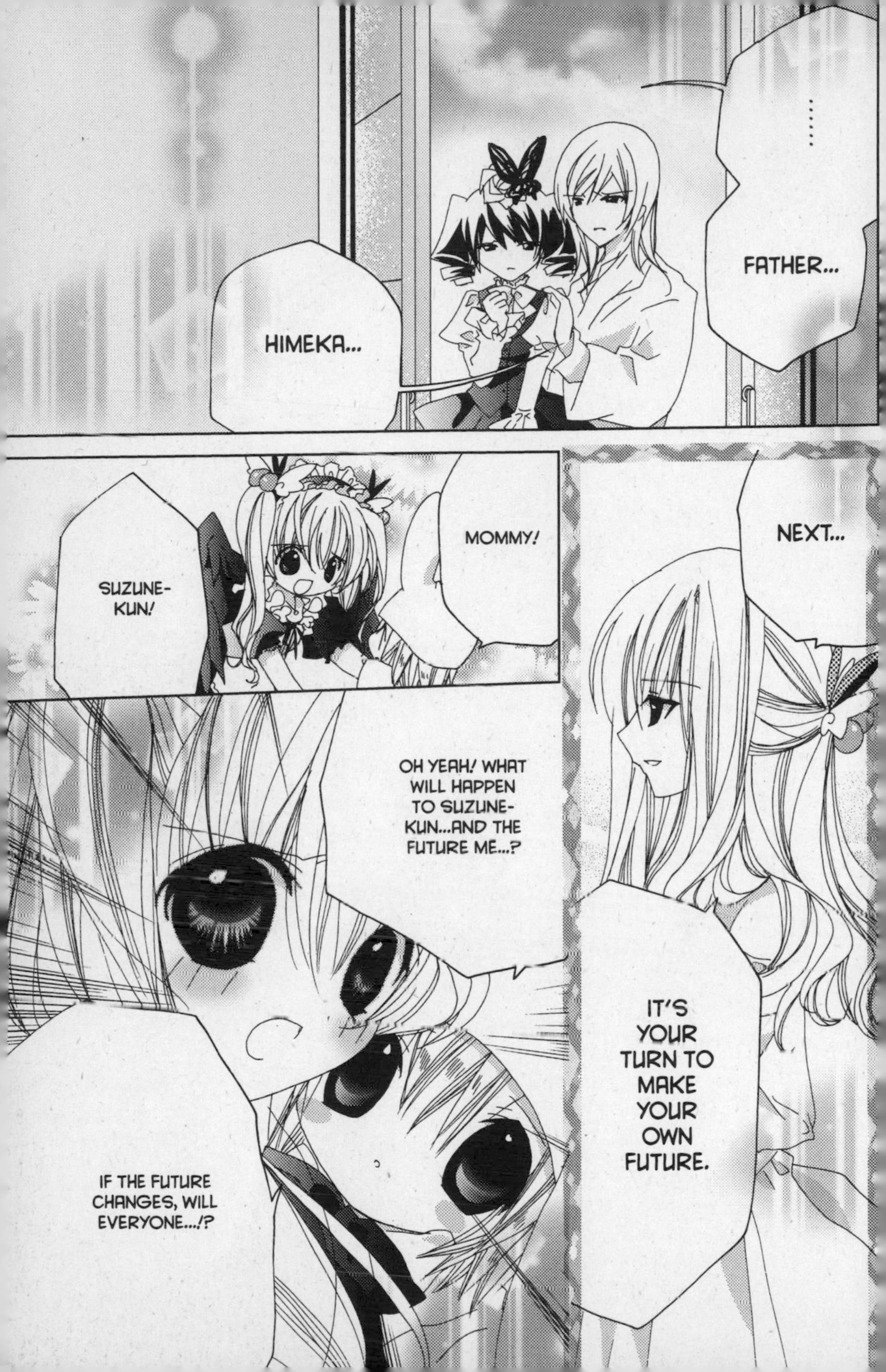
......
FATHER...
HIMEKA...
NEXT...
IT'S YOUR TURN TO MAKE YOUR OWN FUTURE.
MOMMY!
SUZUNE-KUN!
OH YEAH! WHAT WILL HAPPEN TO SUZUNE-KUN...AND THE FUTURE ME...?
IF THE FUTURE CHANGES, WILL EVERYONE...!?

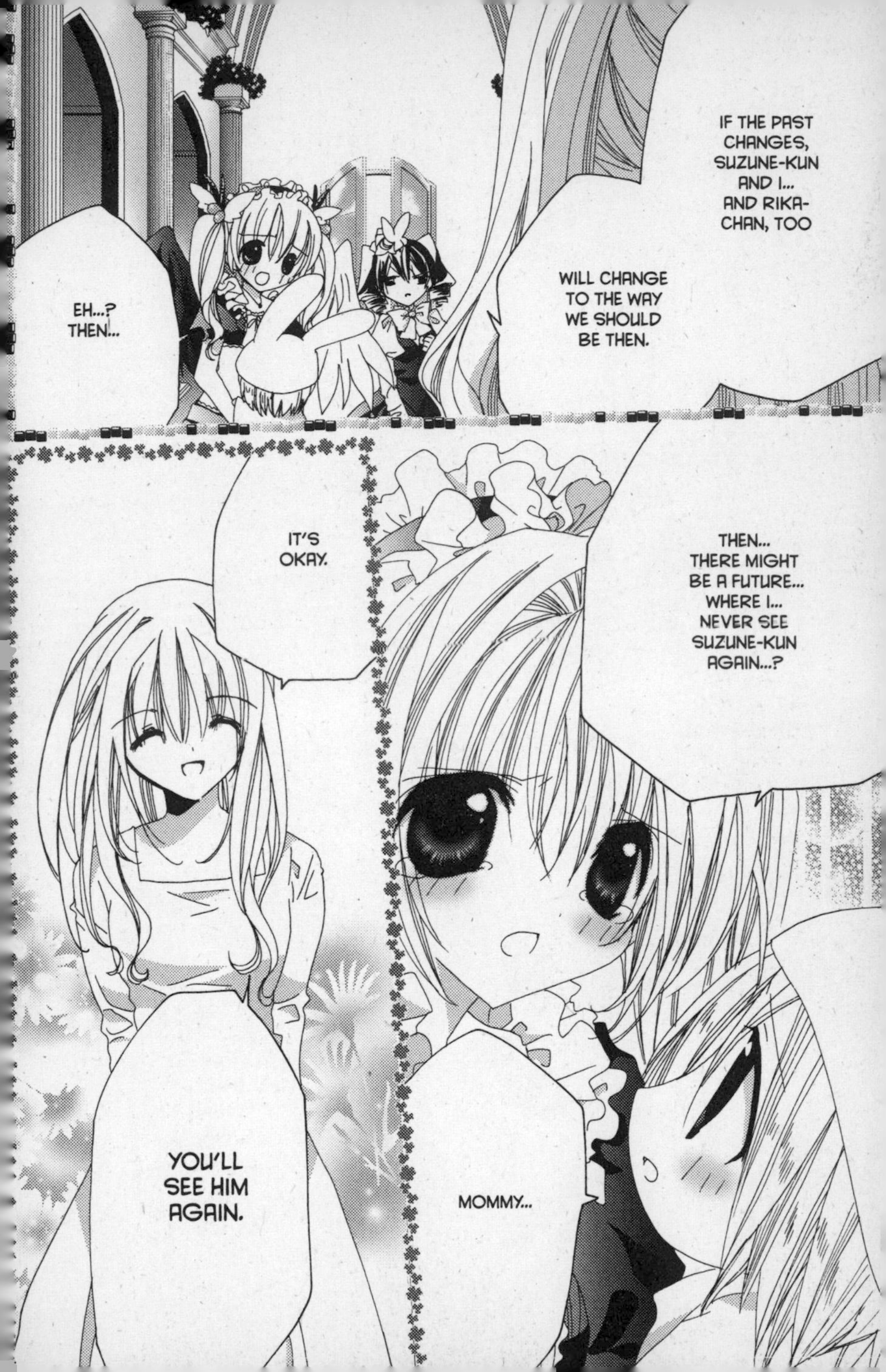
IF THE PAST CHANGES, SUZUNE-KUN AND I... AND RIKA-CHAN, TOO
WILL CHANGE TO THE WAY WE SHOULD BE THEN.
EH...? THEN...
THEN... THERE MIGHT BE A FUTURE... WHERE I... NEVER SEE SUZUNE-KUN AGAIN...?
MOMMY...
IT'S OKAY.
YOU'LL SEE HIM AGAIN.

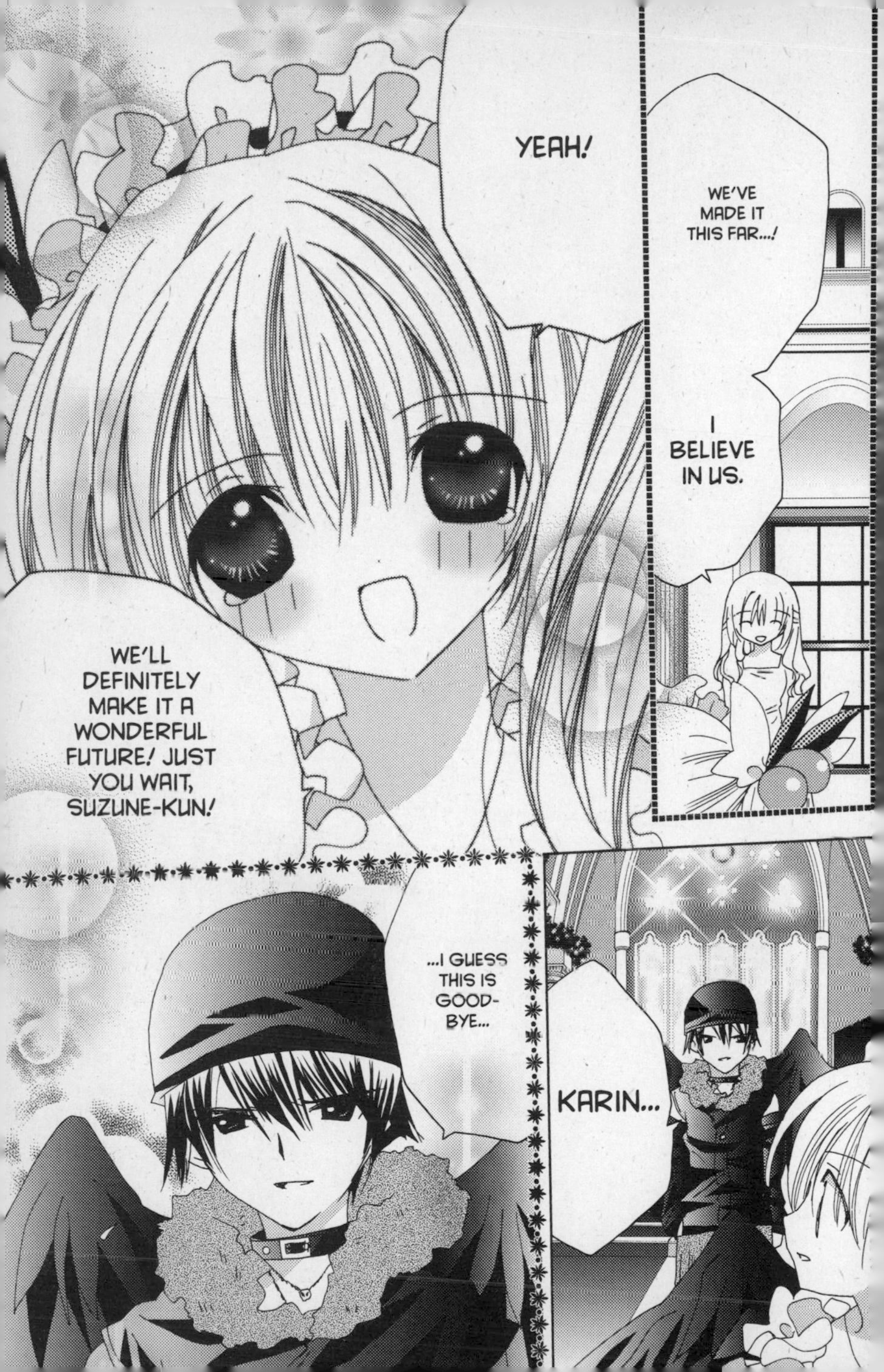
WE'VE MADE IT THIS FAR...!
I BELIEVE IN US.
YEAH!
WE'LL DEFINITELY MAKE IT A WONDERFUL FUTURE! JUST YOU WAIT, SUZUNE-KUN!
KARIN...
...I GUESS THIS IS GOOD-BYE...

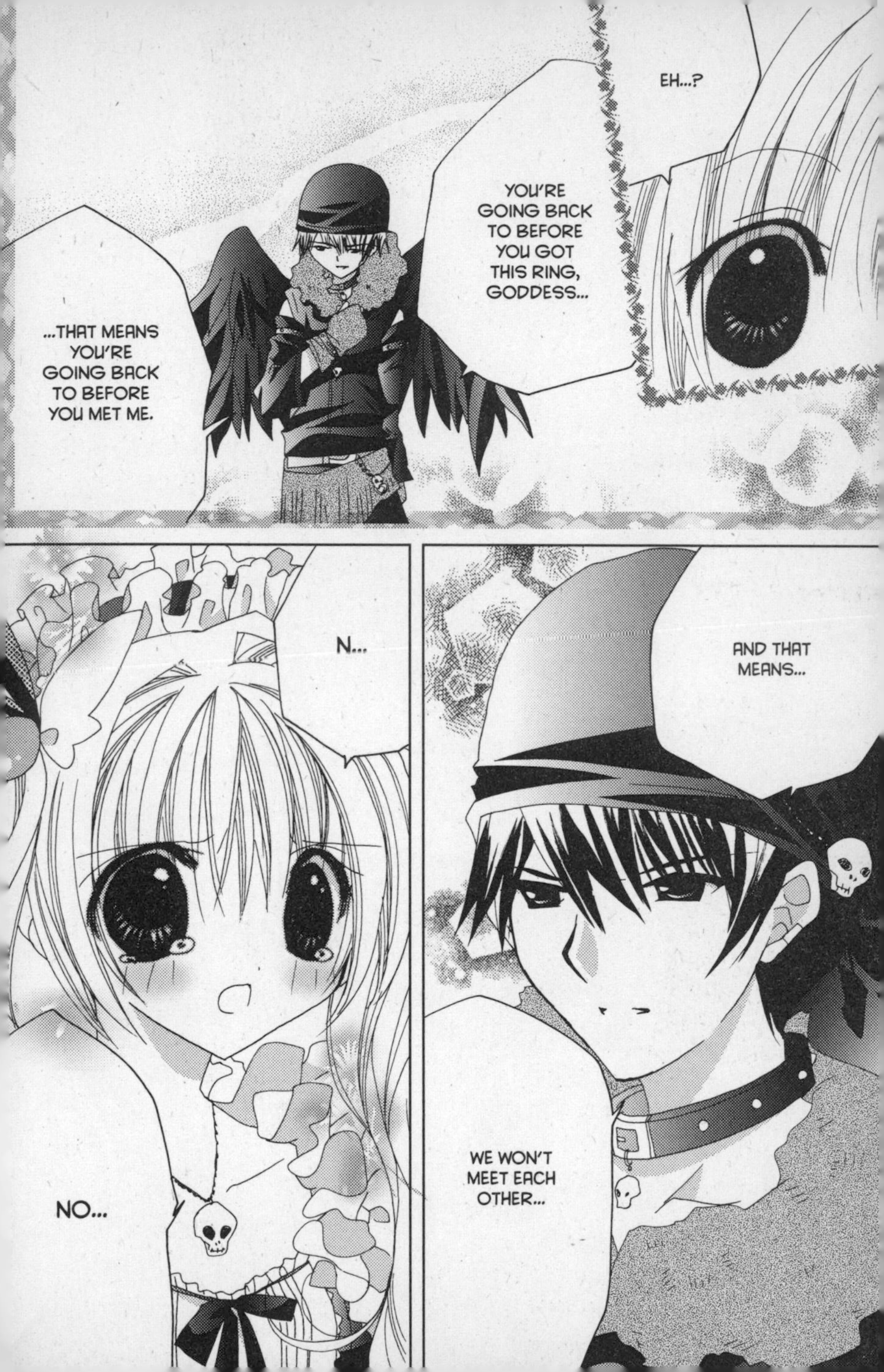
EH...?
YOU'RE GOING BACK TO BEFORE YOU GOT THIS RING, GODDESS...
...THAT MEANS YOU'RE GOING BACK TO BEFORE YOU MET ME.
AND THAT MEANS...
WE WON'T MEET EACH OTHER...
N...
NO...

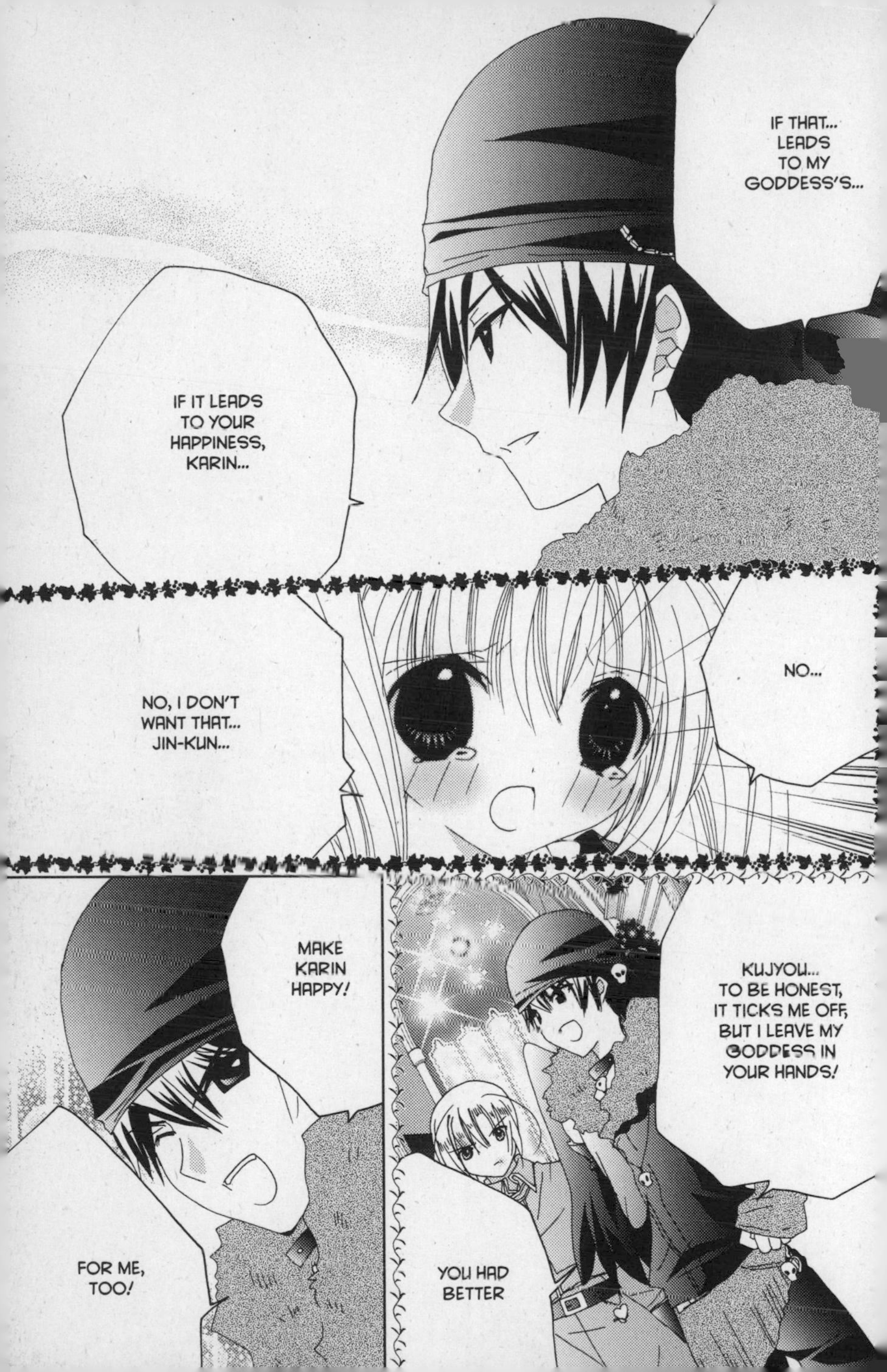
IF THAT... LEADS TO MY GODDESS'S...
IF IT LEADS TO YOUR HAPPINESS, KARIN...
NO...
NO, I DON'T WANT THAT... JIN-KUN...
KUJYOU... TO BE HONEST, IT TICKS ME OFF, BUT I LEAVE MY GODDESS IN YOUR HANDS!
YOU HAD BETTER
MAKE KARIN HAPPY!
FOR ME, TOO!

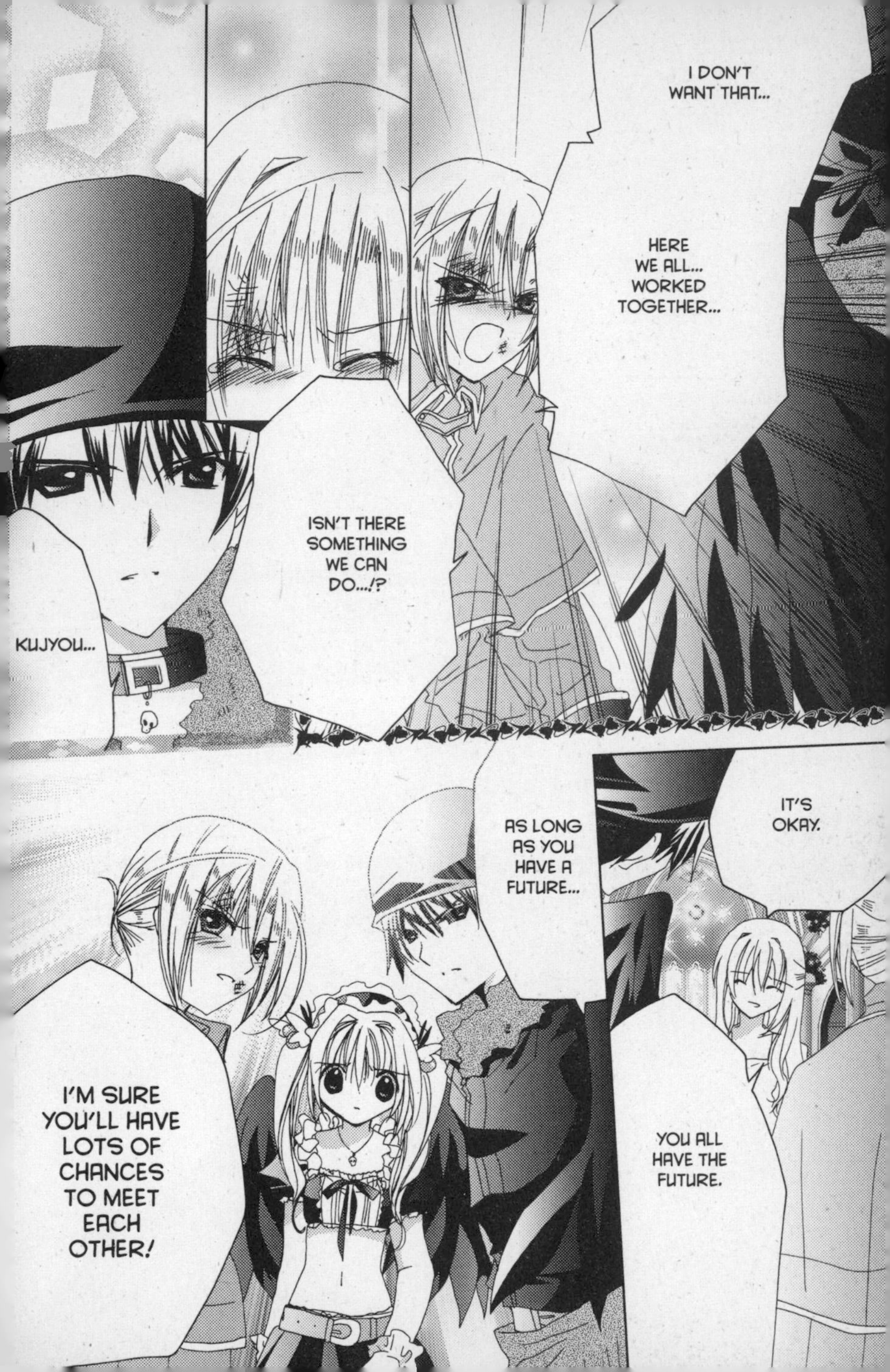
I DON'T WANT THAT...
HERE WE ALL... WORKED TOGETHER...
ISN'T THERE SOMETHING WE CAN DO...!?
KUJYOU...
IT'S OKAY.
YOU ALL HAVE THE FUTURE.
AS LONG AS YOU HAVE A FUTURE...
I'M SURE YOU'LL HAVE LOTS OF CHANCES TO MEET EACH OTHER!

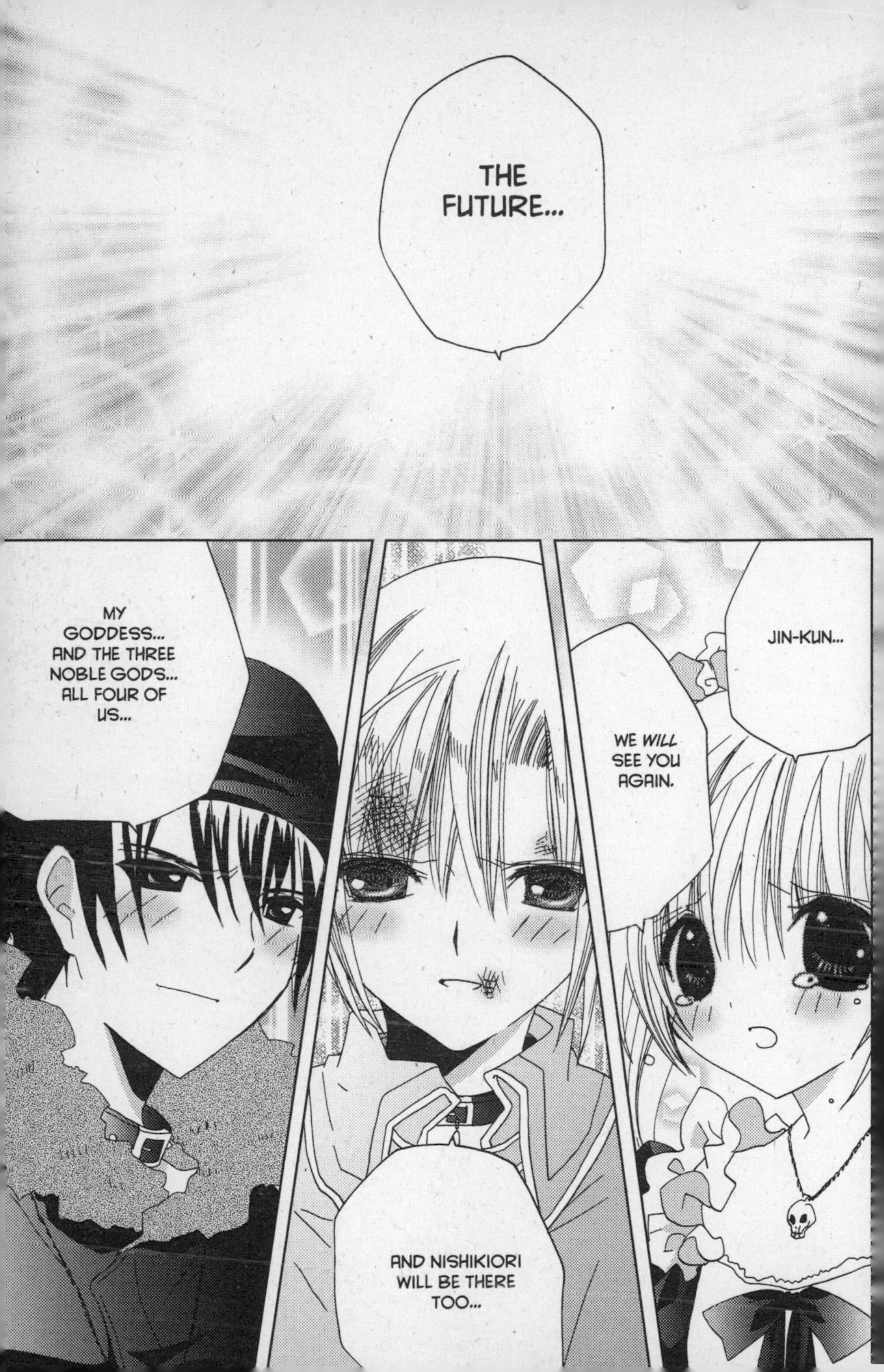
THE FUTURE...
JIN-KUN...
WE *WILL* SEE YOU AGAIN.
AND NISHIKIORI WILL BE THERE TOO...
MY GODDESS... AND THE THREE NOBLE GODS... ALL FOUR OF US...

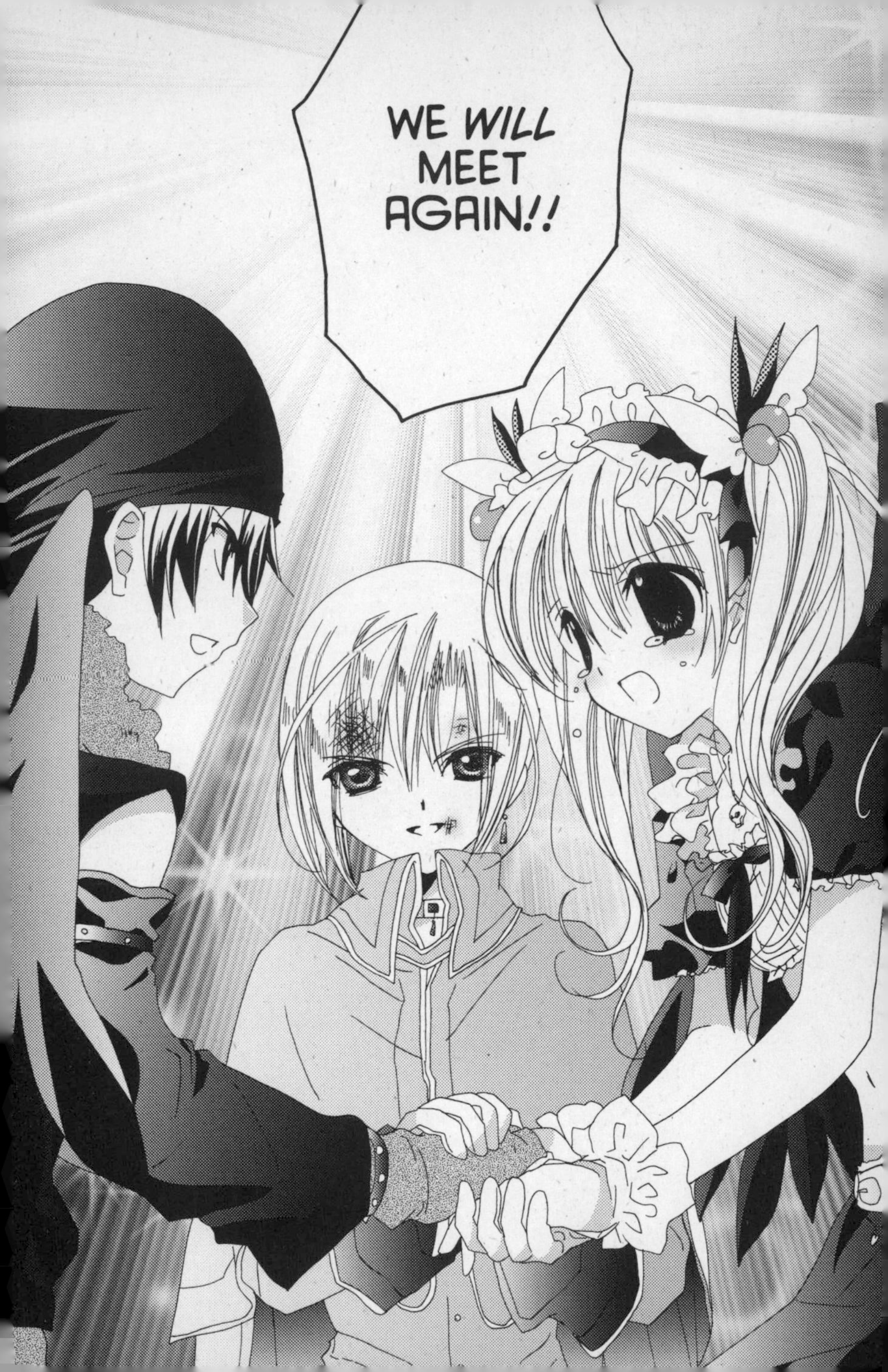
WE WILL MEET AGAIN!!

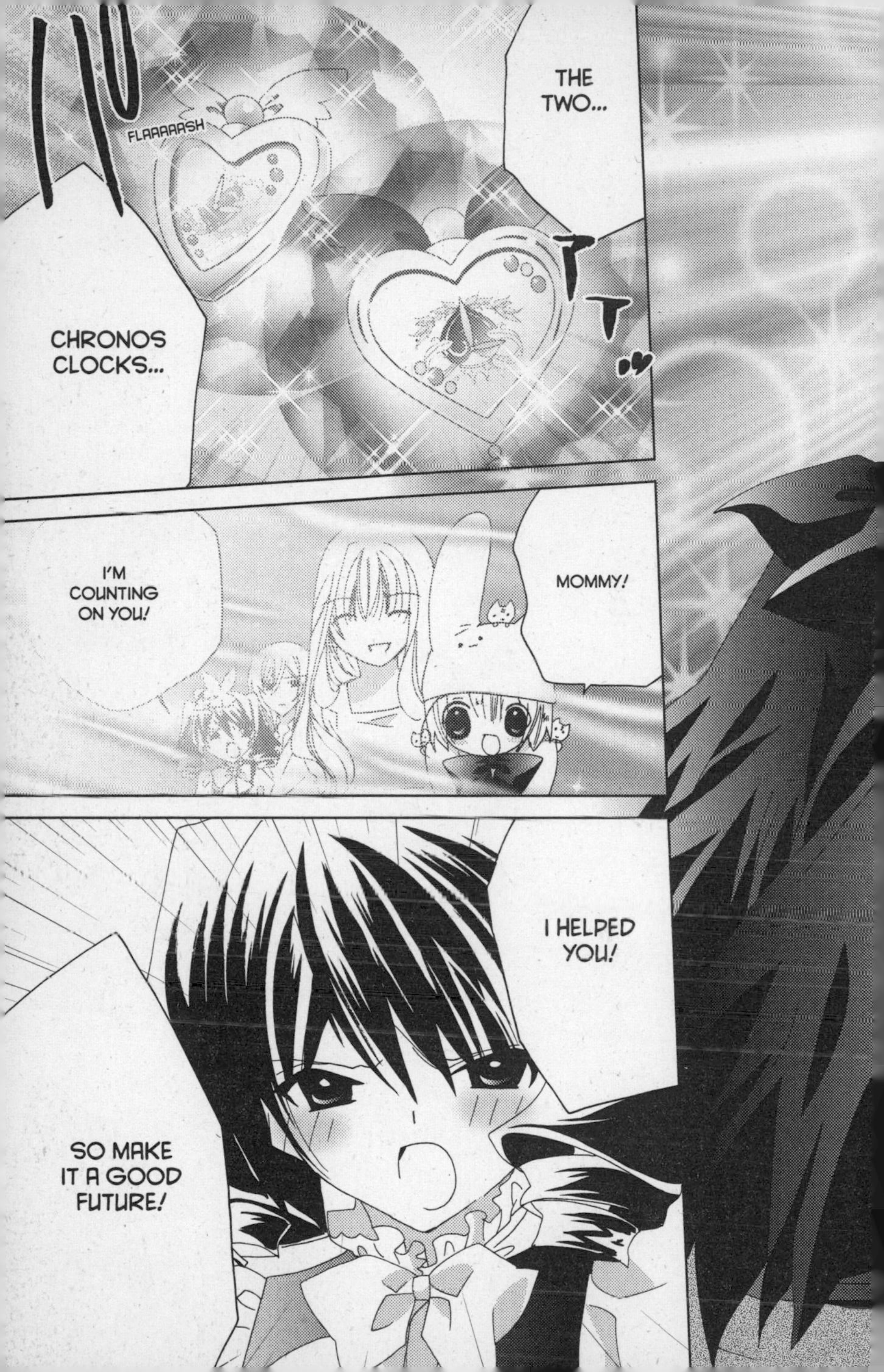
THE TWO...
FLAAAAASH
CHRONOS CLOCKS...
MOMMY!
I'M COUNTING ON YOU!
I HELPED YOU!
SO MAKE IT A GOOD FUTURE!

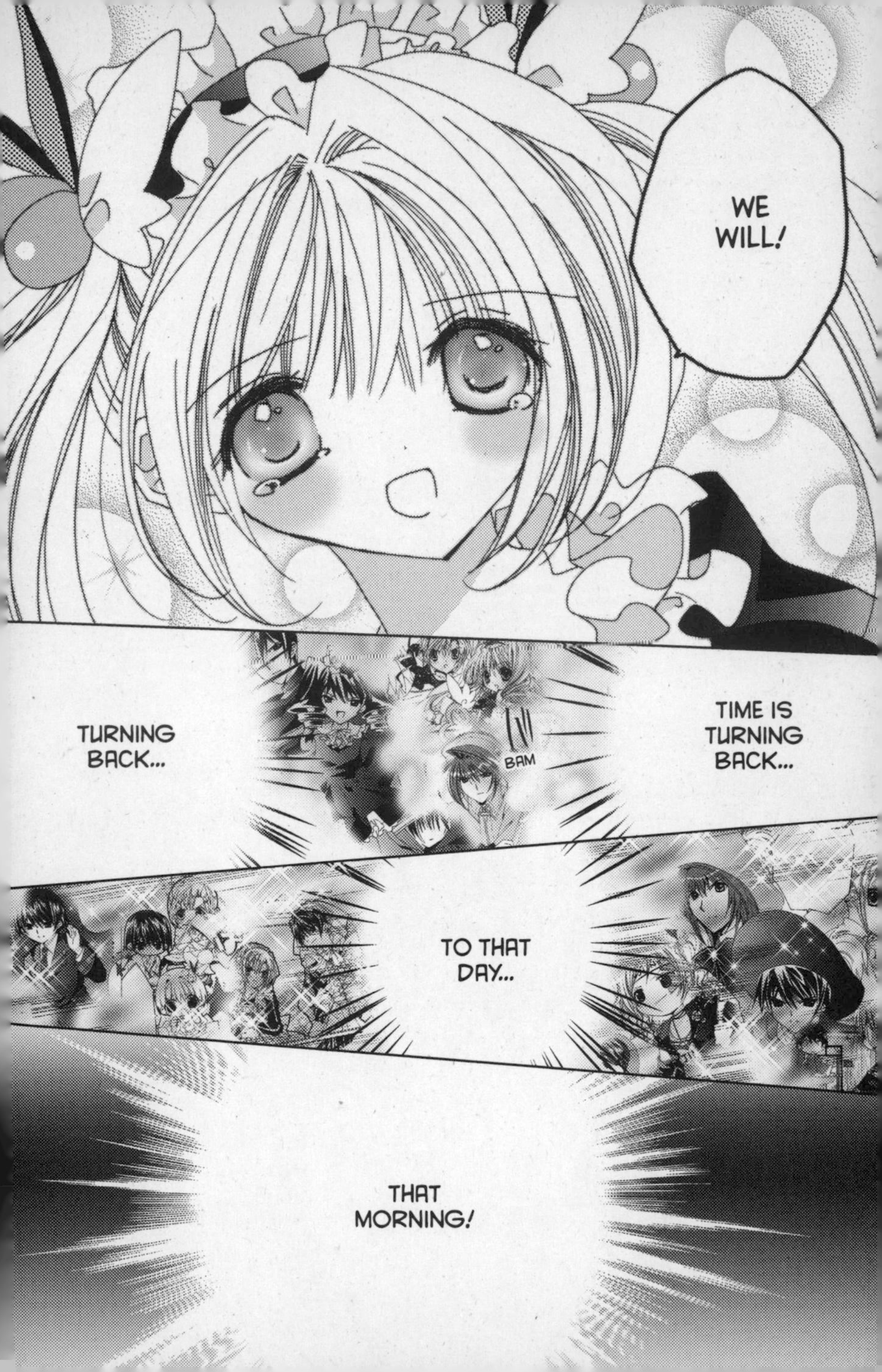
WE WILL!
TIME IS TURNING BACK...
BAM
TURNING BACK...
TO THAT DAY...
THAT MORNING!

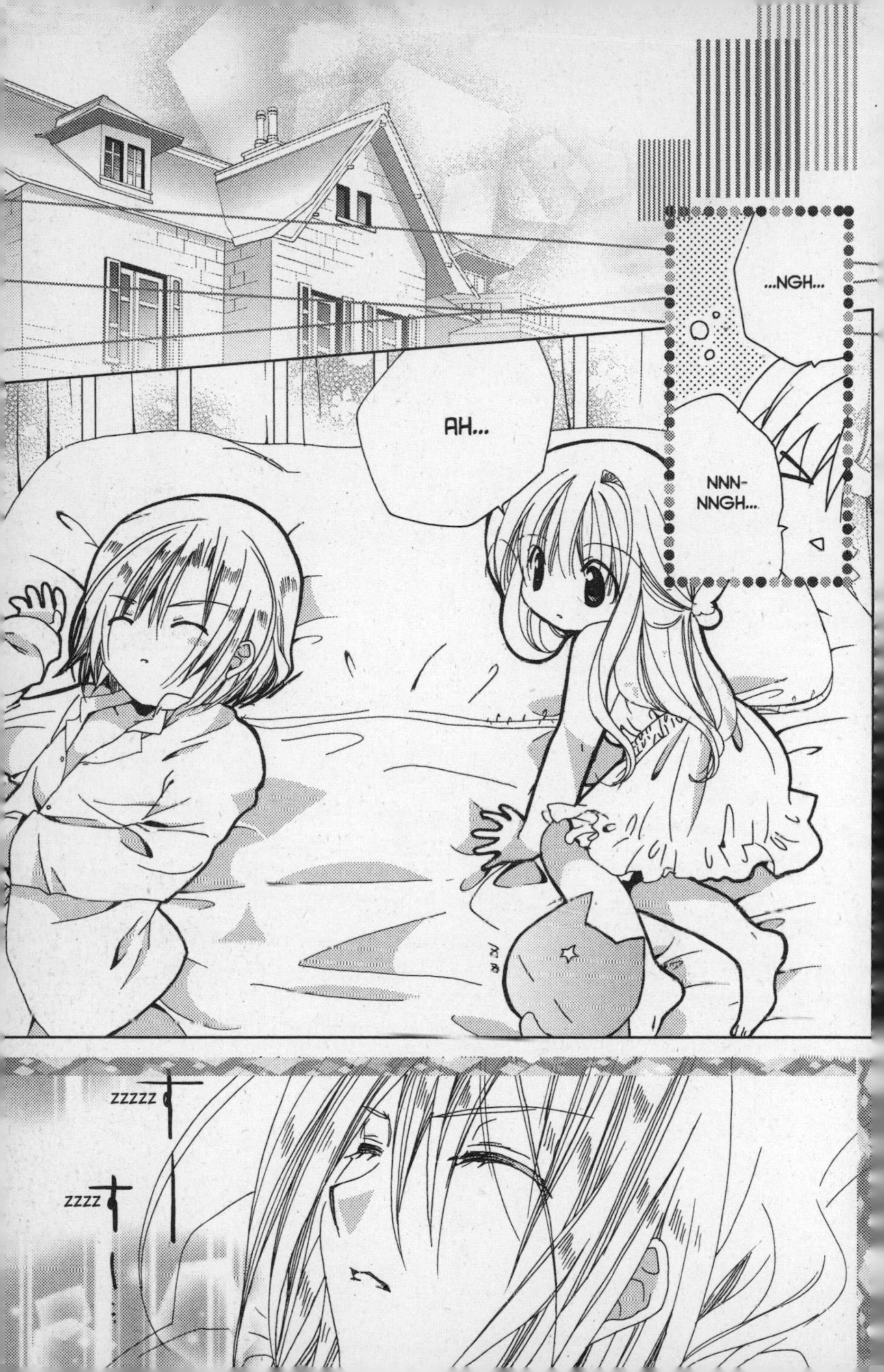
...NGH...
NNN-NNGH...
AH...
ZZZZZ
ZZZZ

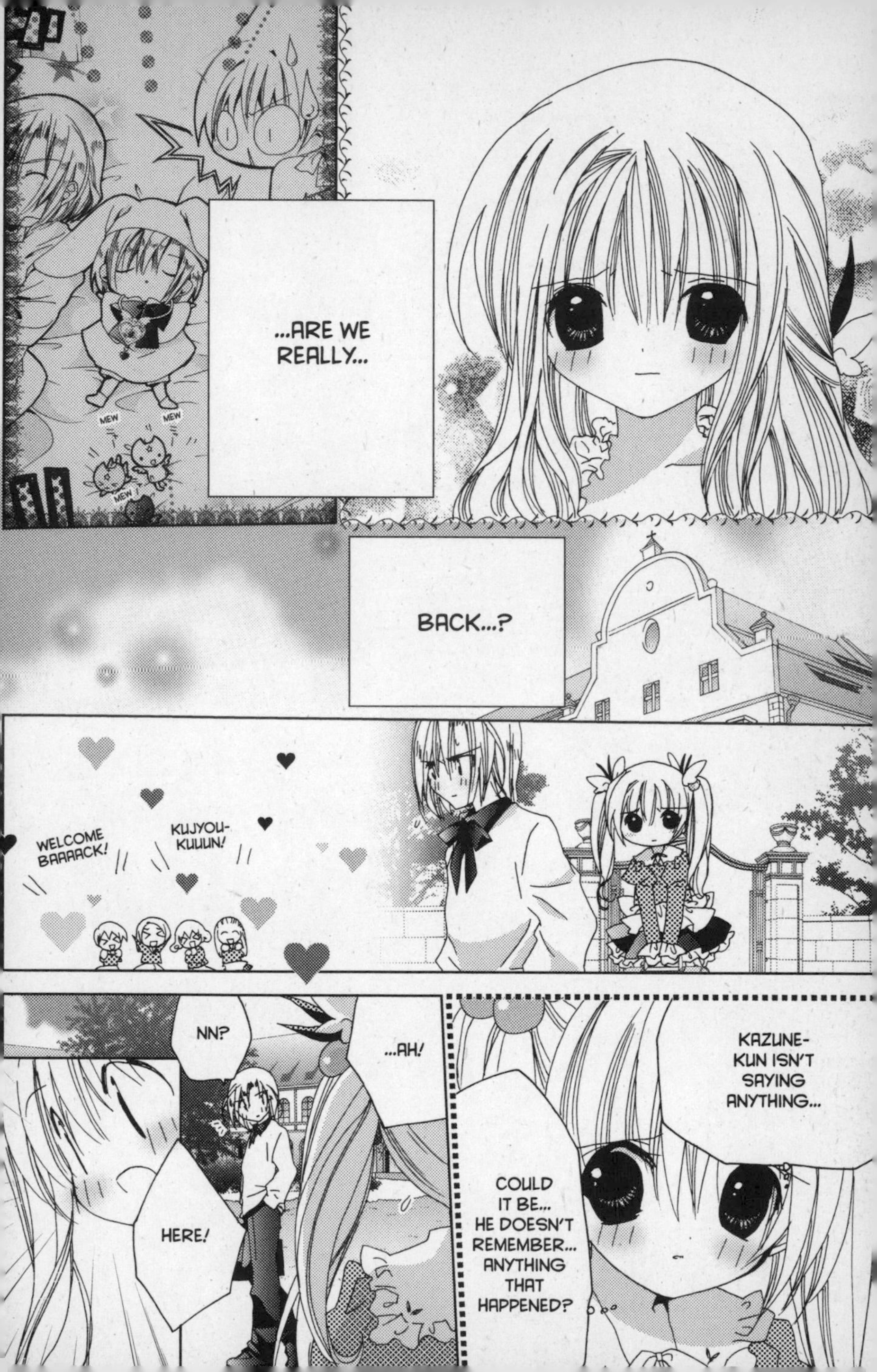
...ARE WE REALLY...
MEW
MEW
MEW
BACK...?
KUJYOU-KUUUN!
WELCOME BAAAACK!
KAZUNE-KUN ISN'T SAYING ANYTHING...
COULD IT BE... HE DOESN'T REMEMBER... ANYTHING THAT HAPPENED?
...AH!
NN?
HERE!

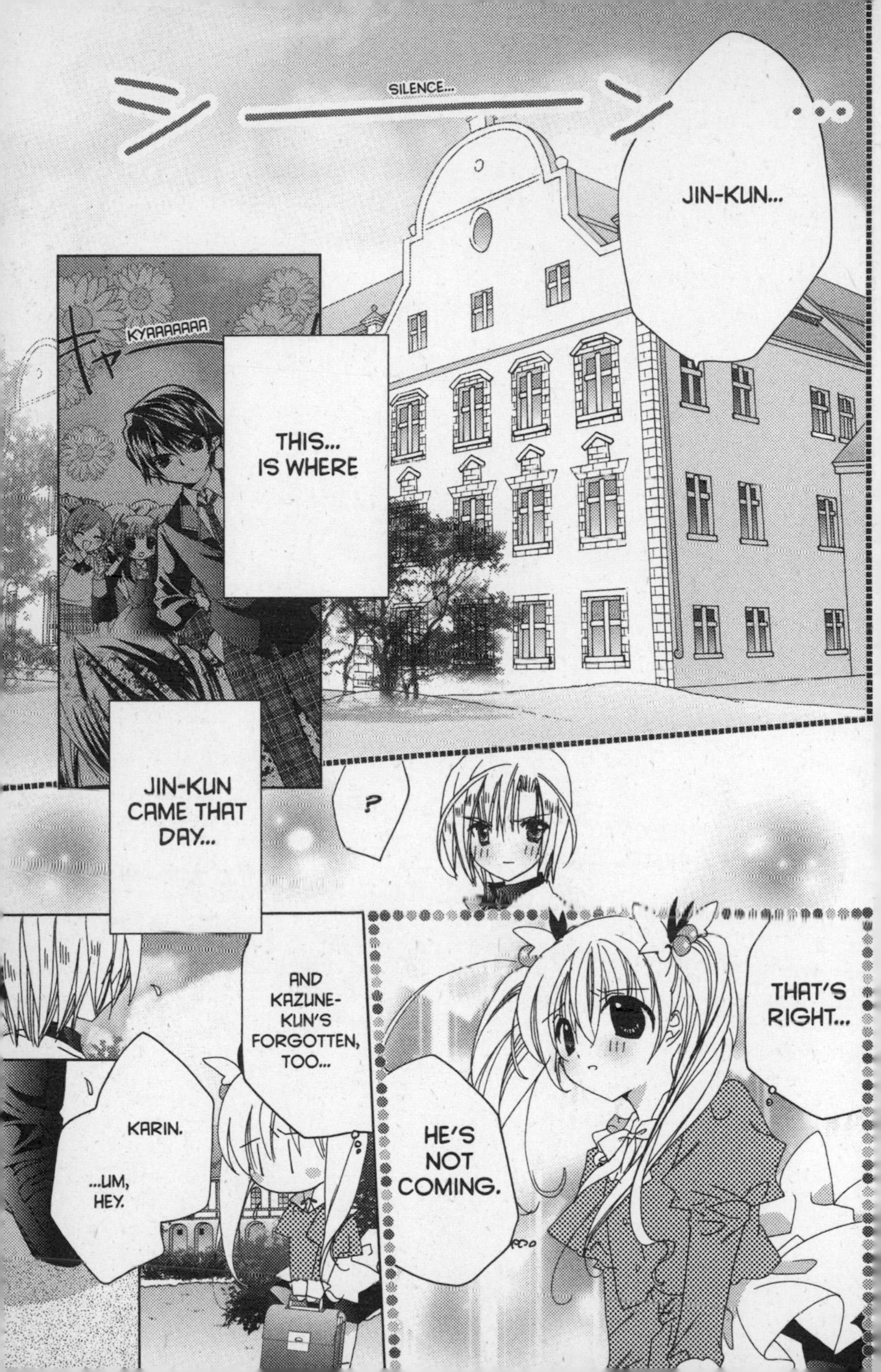
. . .
JIN-KUN...
SILENCE...
KYAAAAAAA
THIS... IS WHERE
JIN-KUN CAME THAT DAY...
?
THAT'S RIGHT...
HE'S NOT COMING.
AND KAZUNE-KUN'S FORGOTTEN, TOO...
KARIN.
...UM, HEY.

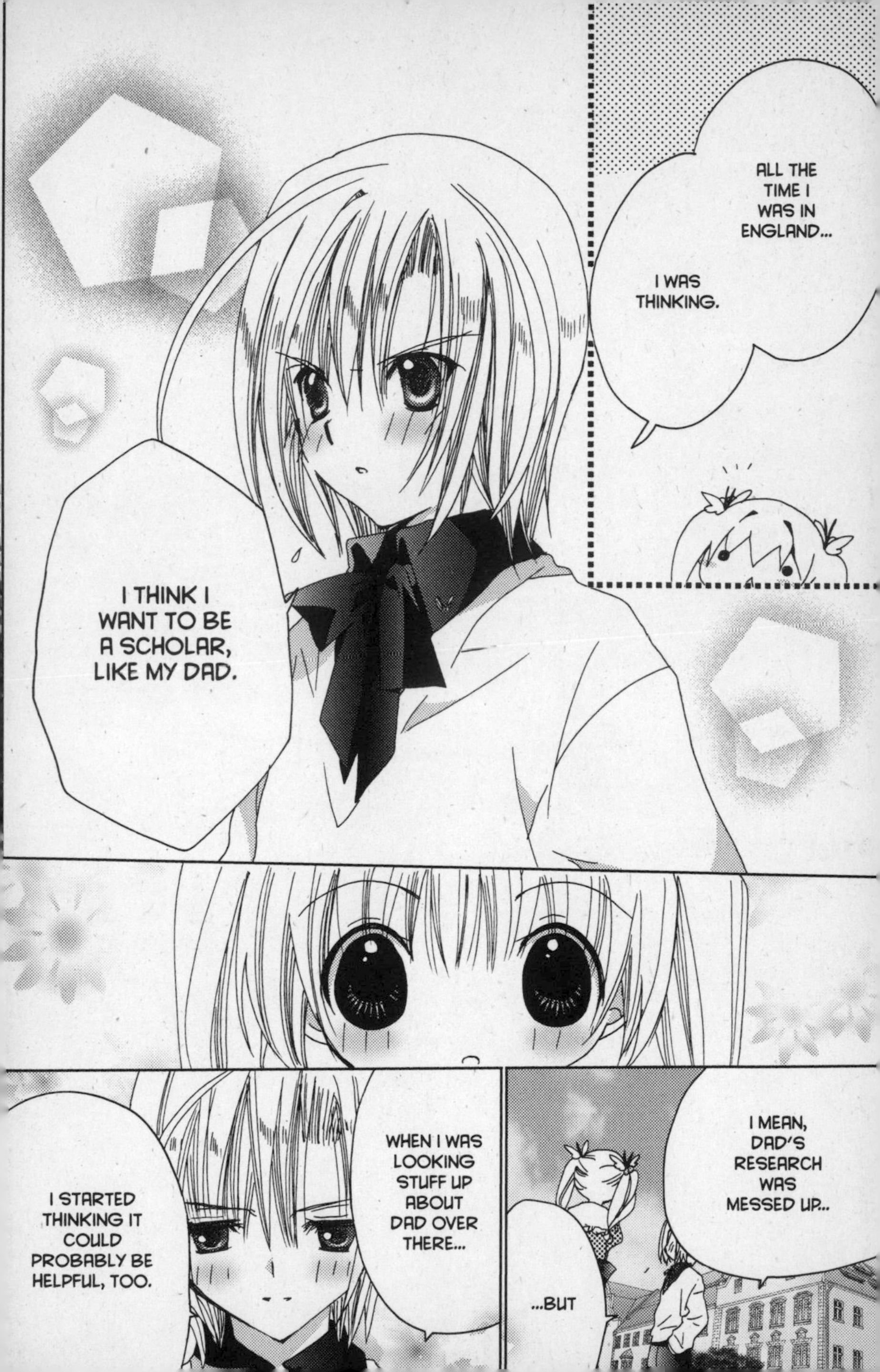
ALL THE TIME I WAS IN ENGLAND...
I WAS THINKING.
I THINK I WANT TO BE A SCHOLAR, LIKE MY DAD.
I MEAN, DAD'S RESEARCH WAS MESSED UP...
...BUT
WHEN I WAS LOOKING STUFF UP ABOUT DAD OVER THERE...
I STARTED THINKING IT COULD PROBABLY BE HELPFUL, TOO.

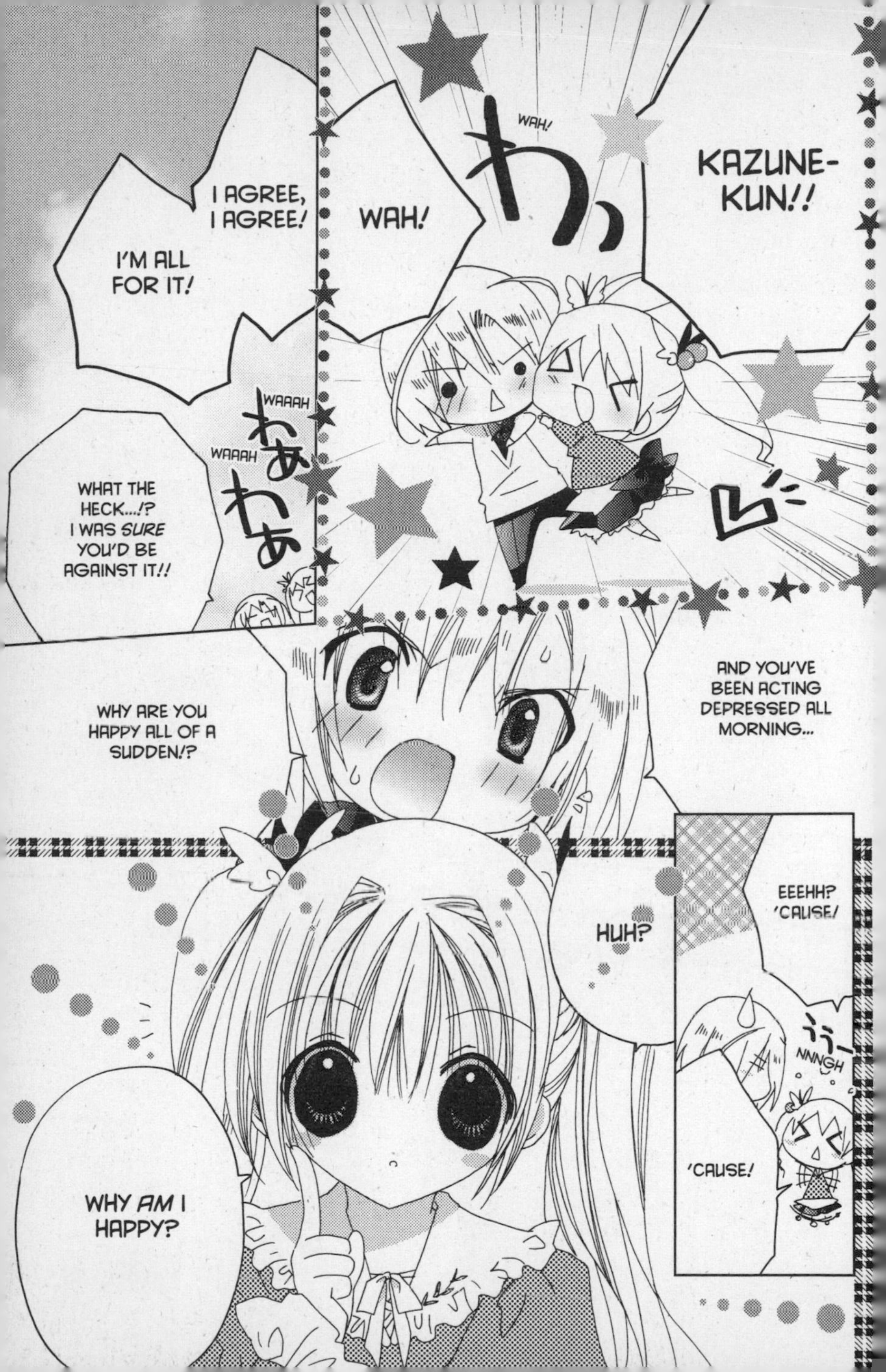
KAZUNE-KUN!!
WAH!
WAH!
I AGREE, I AGREE!
I'M ALL FOR IT!
WAAAH
WAAAH
WHAT THE HECK...!? I WAS *SURE* YOU'D BE AGAINST IT!!
AND YOU'VE BEEN ACTING DEPRESSED ALL MORNING...
WHY ARE YOU HAPPY ALL OF A SUDDEN!?
EEEHH? 'CAUSE!
NNNGH
'CAUSE!
HUH?
WHY *AM* I HAPPY?

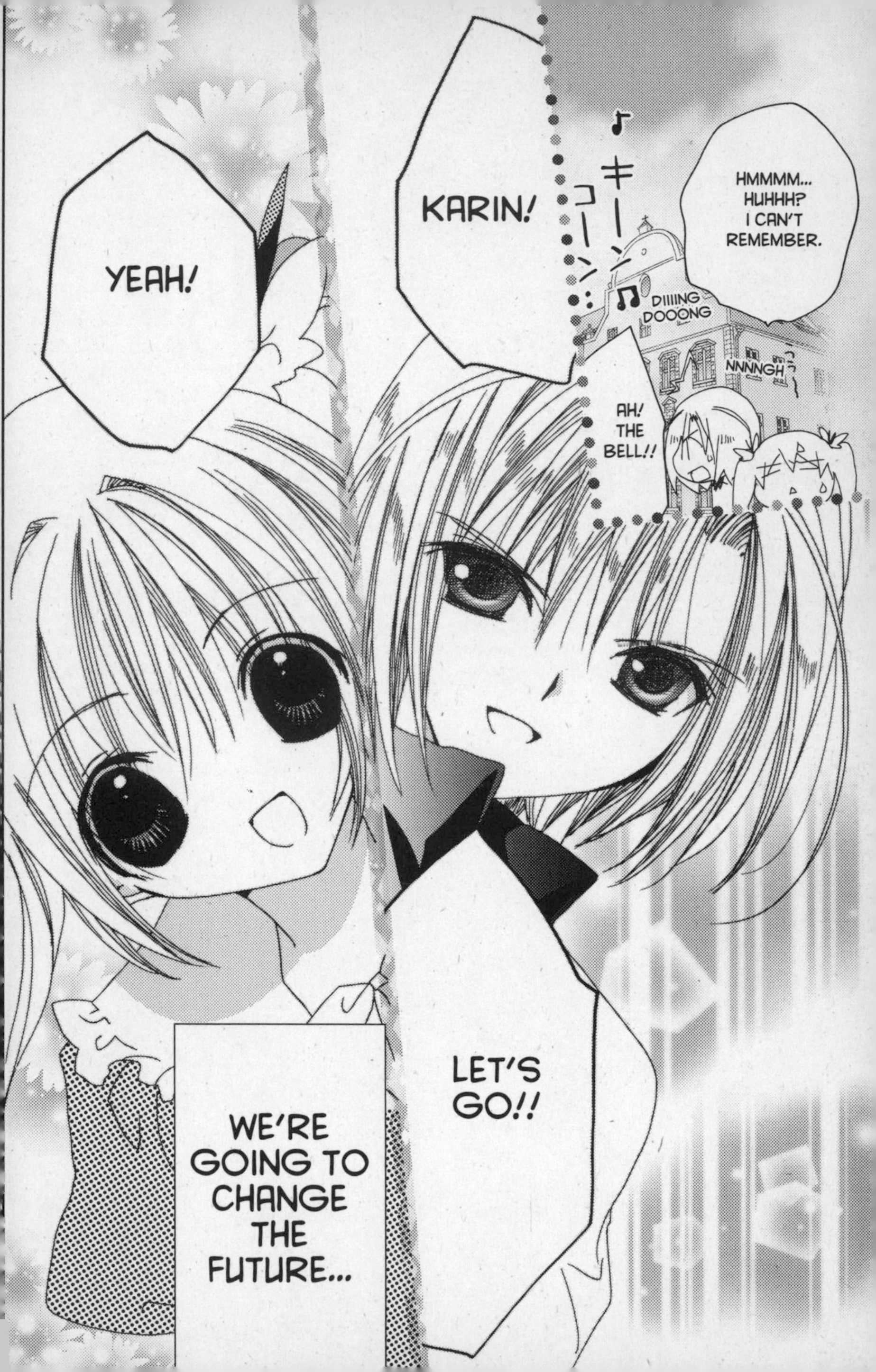

HMMMM... HUHHH? I CAN'T REMEMBER.
♪キーンコーン♪
DIIIING DOOONG
NNNNGH
AH! THE BELL!!
KARIN!
LET'S GO!!
YEAH!
WE'RE GOING TO CHANGE THE FUTURE...

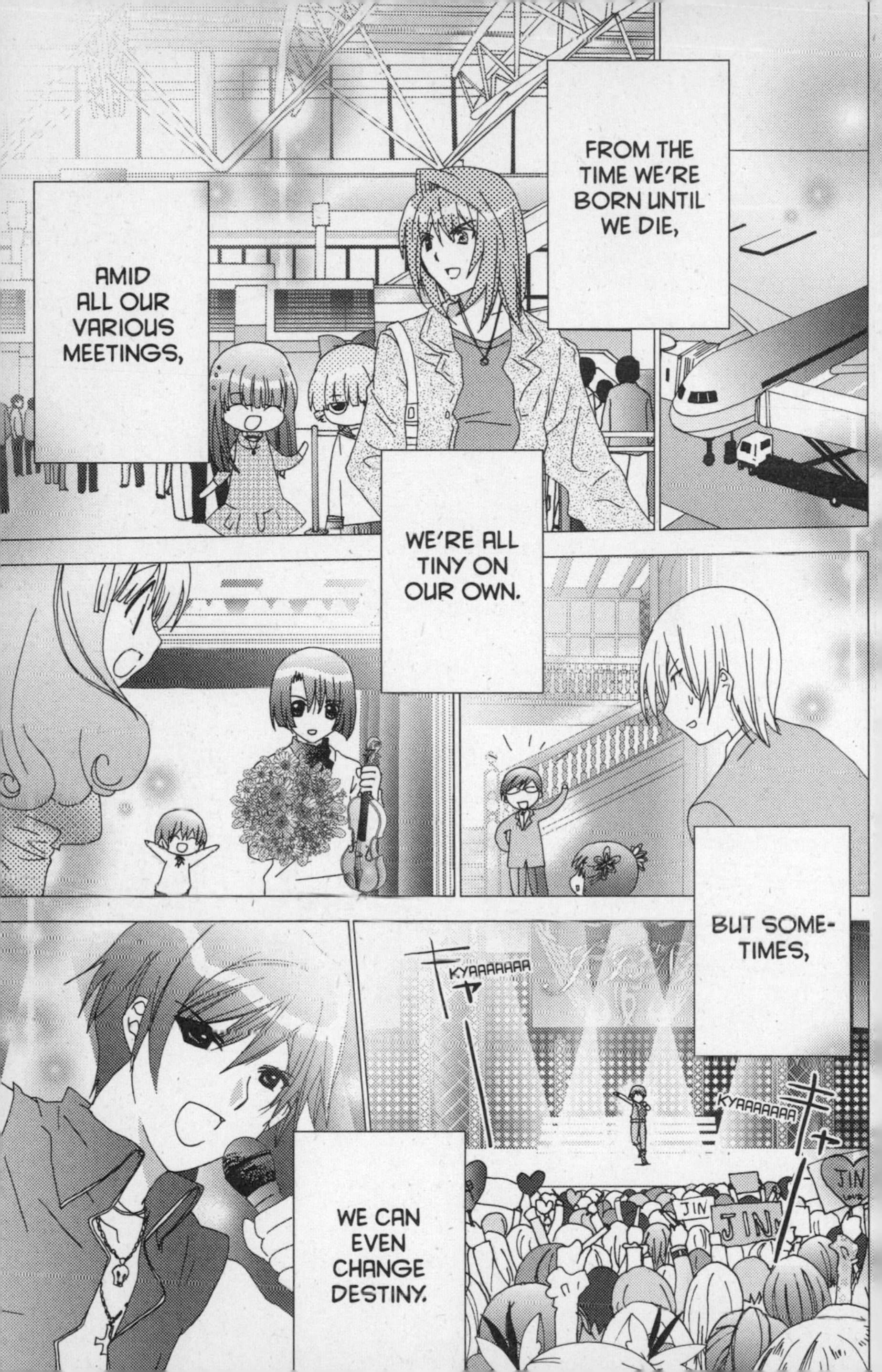
FROM THE TIME WE'RE BORN UNTIL WE DIE,
AMID ALL OUR VARIOUS MEETINGS,
WE'RE ALL TINY ON OUR OWN.
BUT SOME-TIMES,
KYAAAAAAAA
KYAAAAAAAA
JIN
JIN
JIN
WE CAN EVEN CHANGE DESTINY.

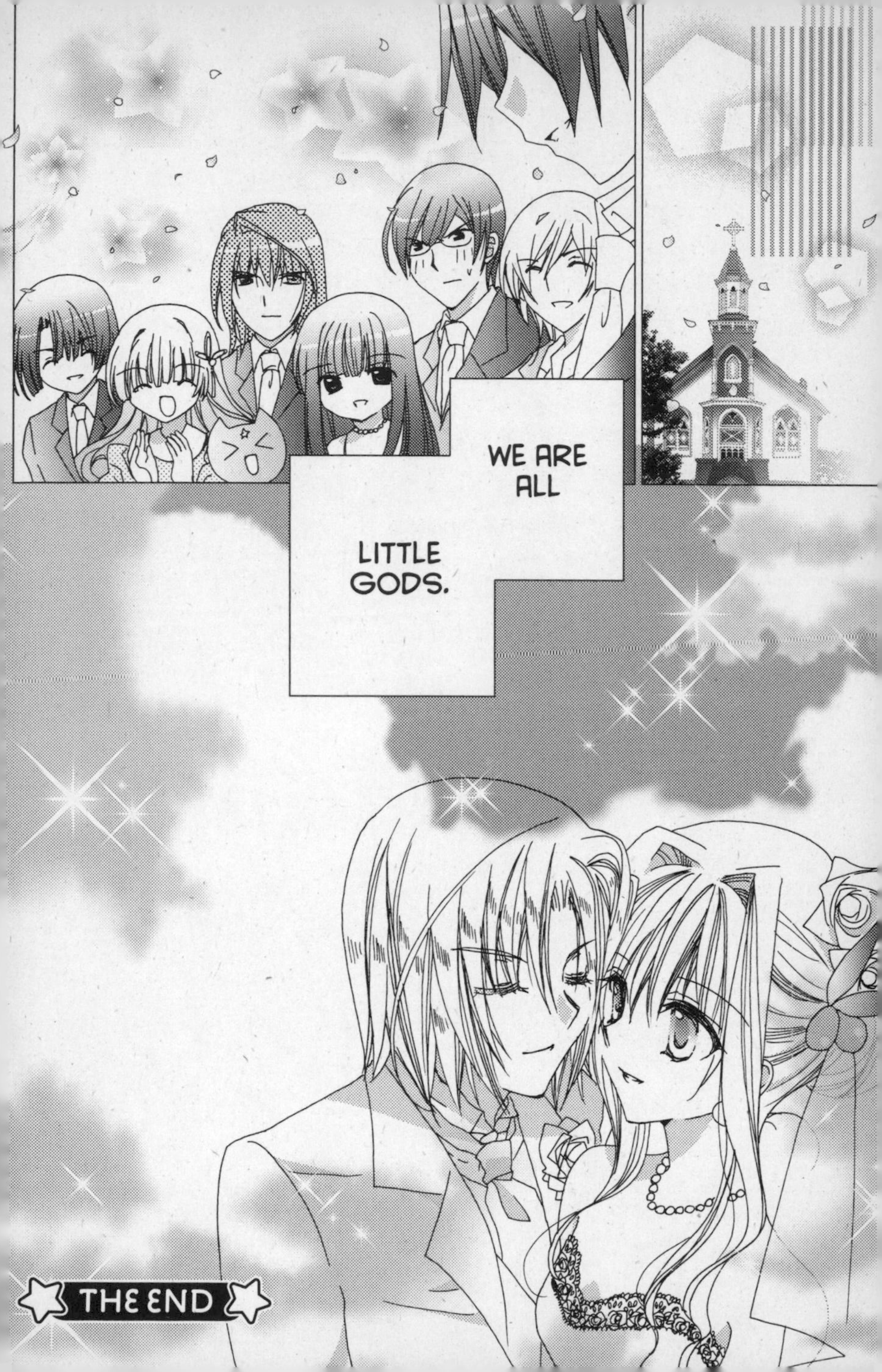
WE ARE ALL LITTLE GODS.
THE END

▨ HELLO! I'M KOGE-DONBO. THIS IS THE FINAL VOLUME OF *KAMICHAMA KARIN CHU.* THANK YOU FOR STICKING WITH ME FOR ALL THIS TIME!! AS FOR MYSELF, I HAD KIND OF PLANNED FROM THE BEGINNING TO HAVE *CHU* END A CERTAIN WAY, AND THIS TIME, I GOT PRETTY CLOSE TO ENDING IT THAT WAY, SO I'M HAPPY...OR RATHER, RELIEVED, I GUESS...IF ALL OF YOU ENJOYED IT, TOO, THEN I'M REALLY, REALLY HAPPY.

▨ AS FOR *CHU*, THE STORY IS OVER, BUT I HEAR THEY'RE GOING TO LET ME DRAW *KAMICHAMA KARIN* SOMETIMES IN THE SPECIAL EDITIONS OF *NAKAYOSHI*, SO I HOPE YOU'LL COME HANG OUT WITH KARIN-CHAN, KAZUNE-KUN, AND THE OTHERS.

▨ WELL THEN, I TRULY THANK YOU FOR READING *KAMICHAMA KARIN CHU* FOR SUCH A LONG TIME!! LET'S MEET AGAIN AT *KARIN* AND AT MY NEXT SERIES!

JUNE 2008,
KOGE-DONBO*

*I'M CHANGING
MY PEN NAME!

KOGE-DONBO'S
HOMEPAGE:
HTTP://KOGE.
KOKAGE.CC/

THANK YOU TO EVERYONE WHO HELPED
WITH *KARIN* AND ALL YOU FANS!!

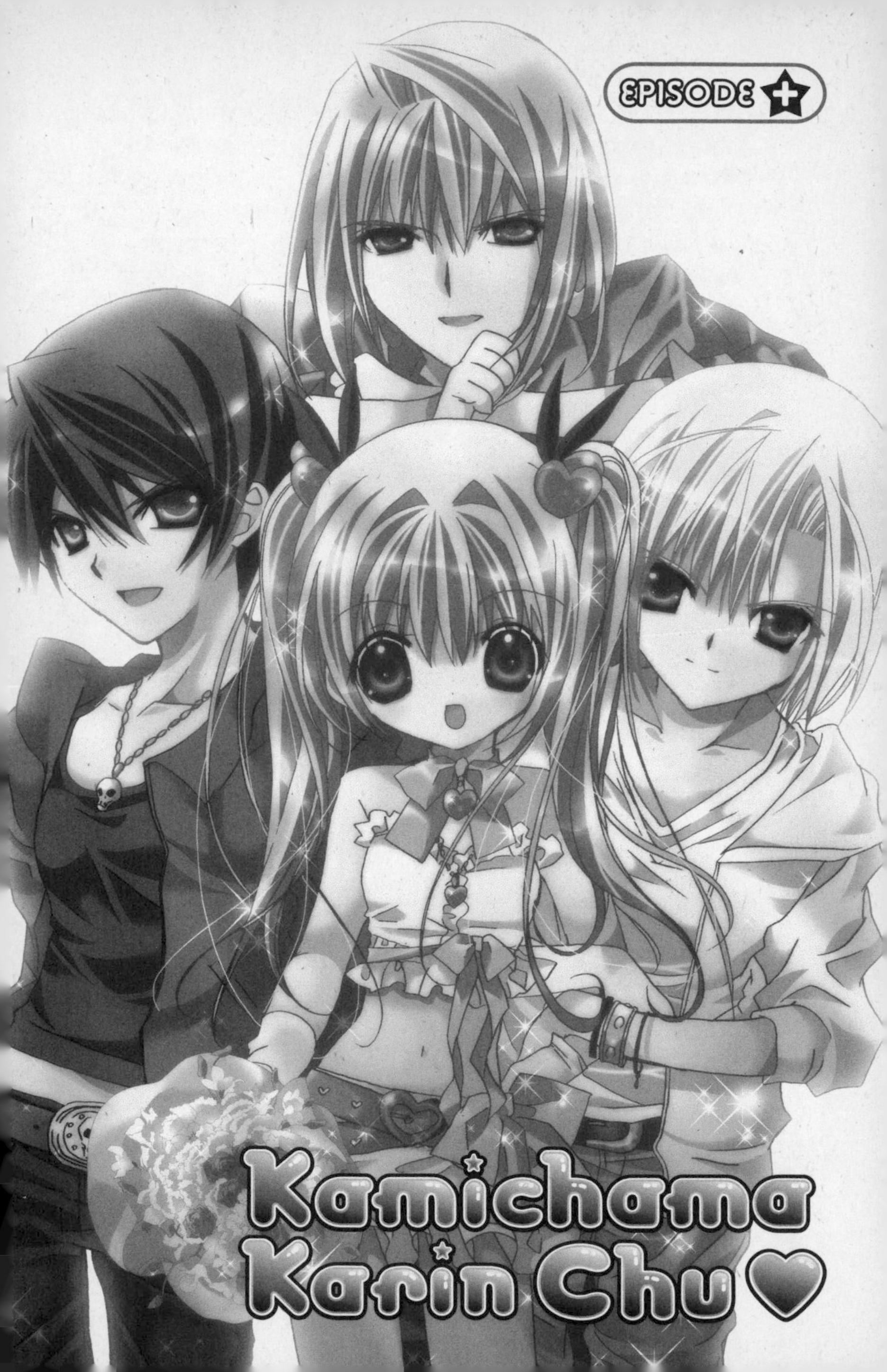
EPISODE +
Kamichama Karin Chu♥

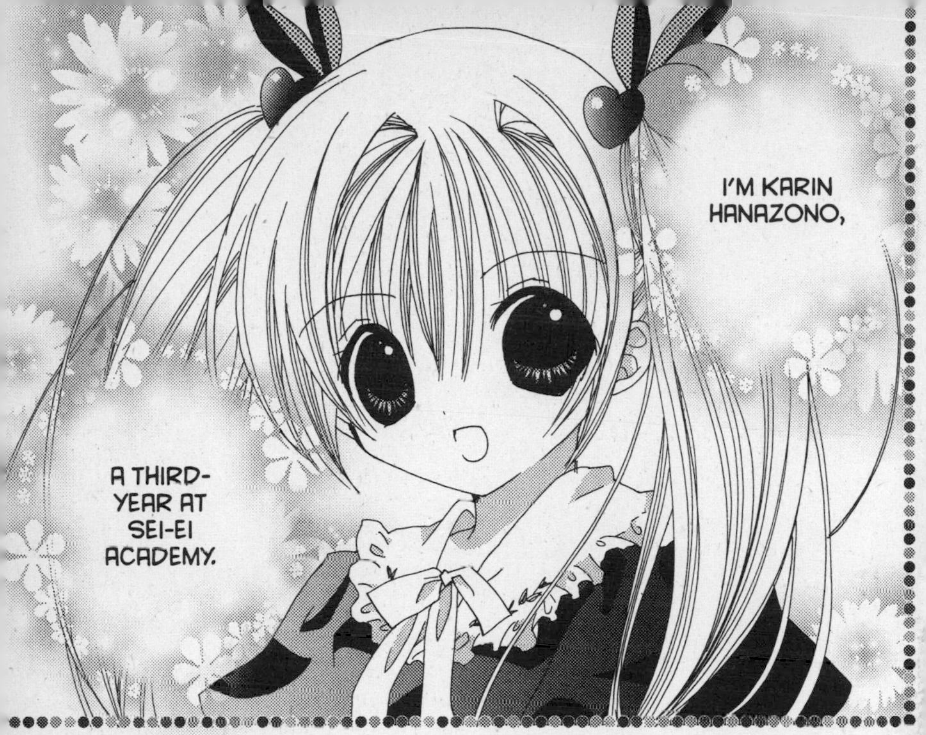
I'M KARIN HANAZONO,
A THIRD-YEAR AT SEI-EI ACADEMY.

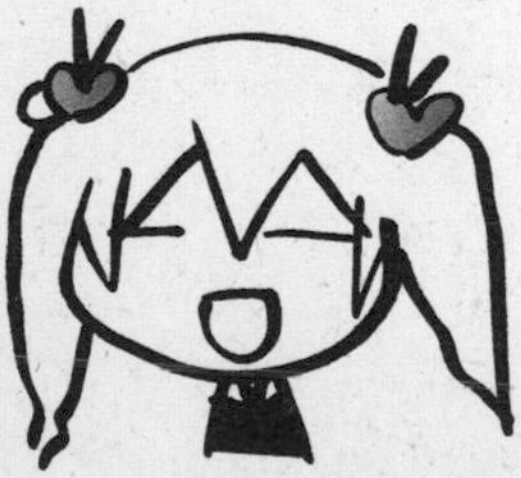
SUDDENLY I'M A THIRD-YEAR!?

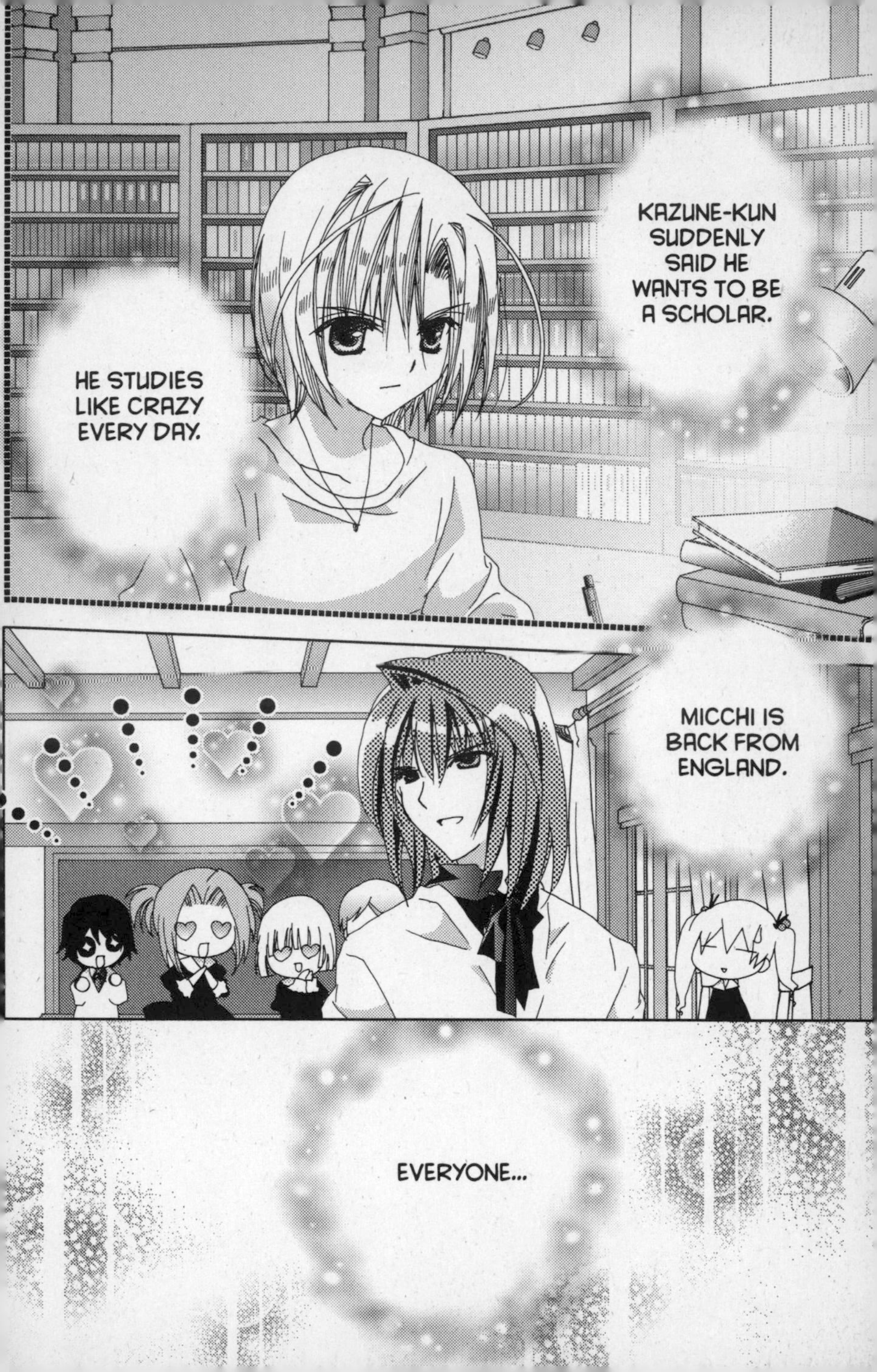
KAZUNE-KUN SUDDENLY SAID HE WANTS TO BE A SCHOLAR.
HE STUDIES LIKE CRAZY EVERY DAY.
MICCHI IS BACK FROM ENGLAND.
EVERYONE...

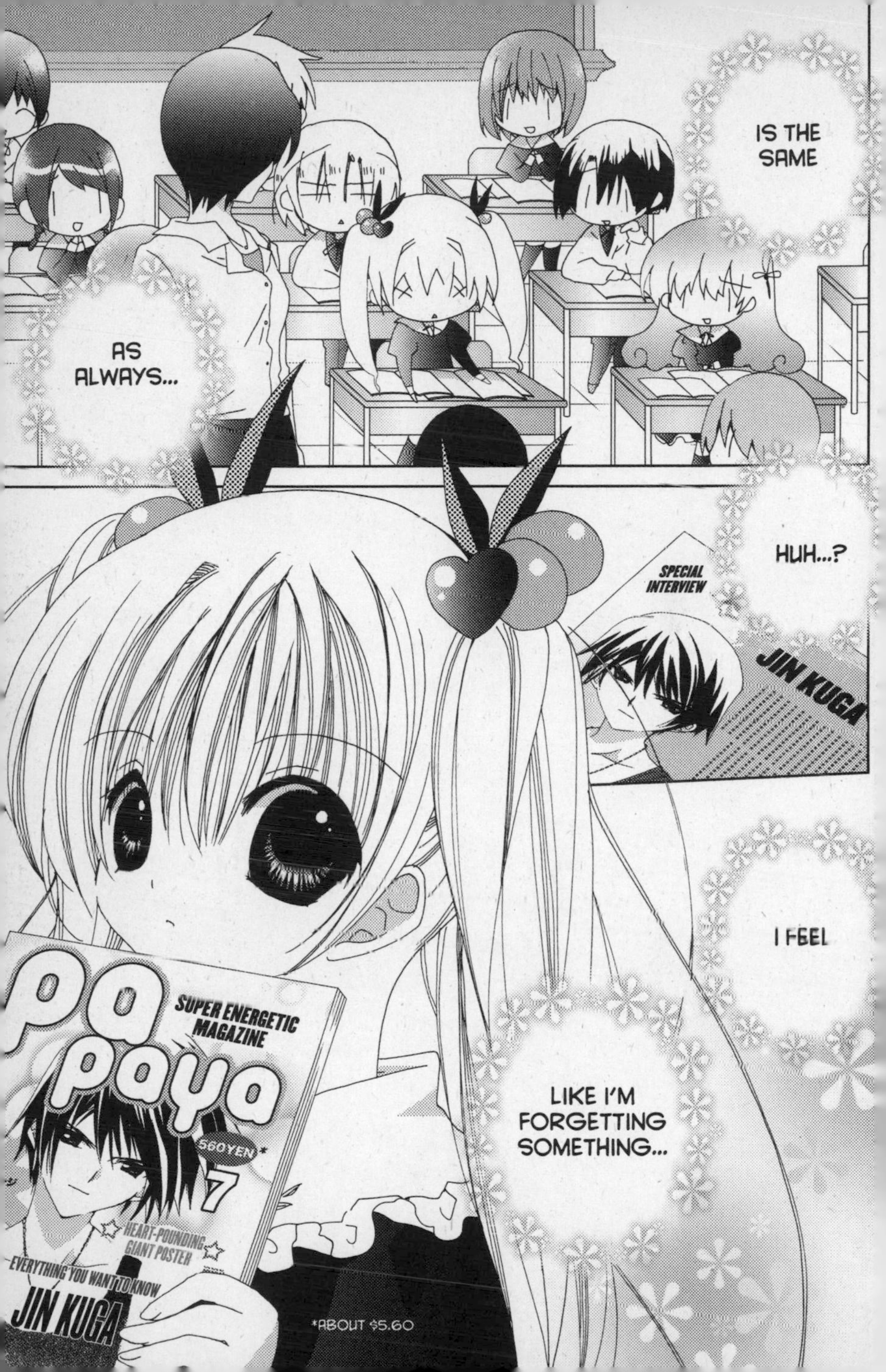
IS THE SAME
AS ALWAYS...
HUH...?
SPECIAL INTERVIEW
JIN KUGA
I FEEL
LIKE I'M FORGETTING SOMETHING...
papaya
SUPER ENERGETIC MAGAZINE
560YEN*
7
HEART-POUNDING GIANT POSTER
EVERYTHING YOU WANT TO KNOW
JIN KUGA
*ABOUT $5.60

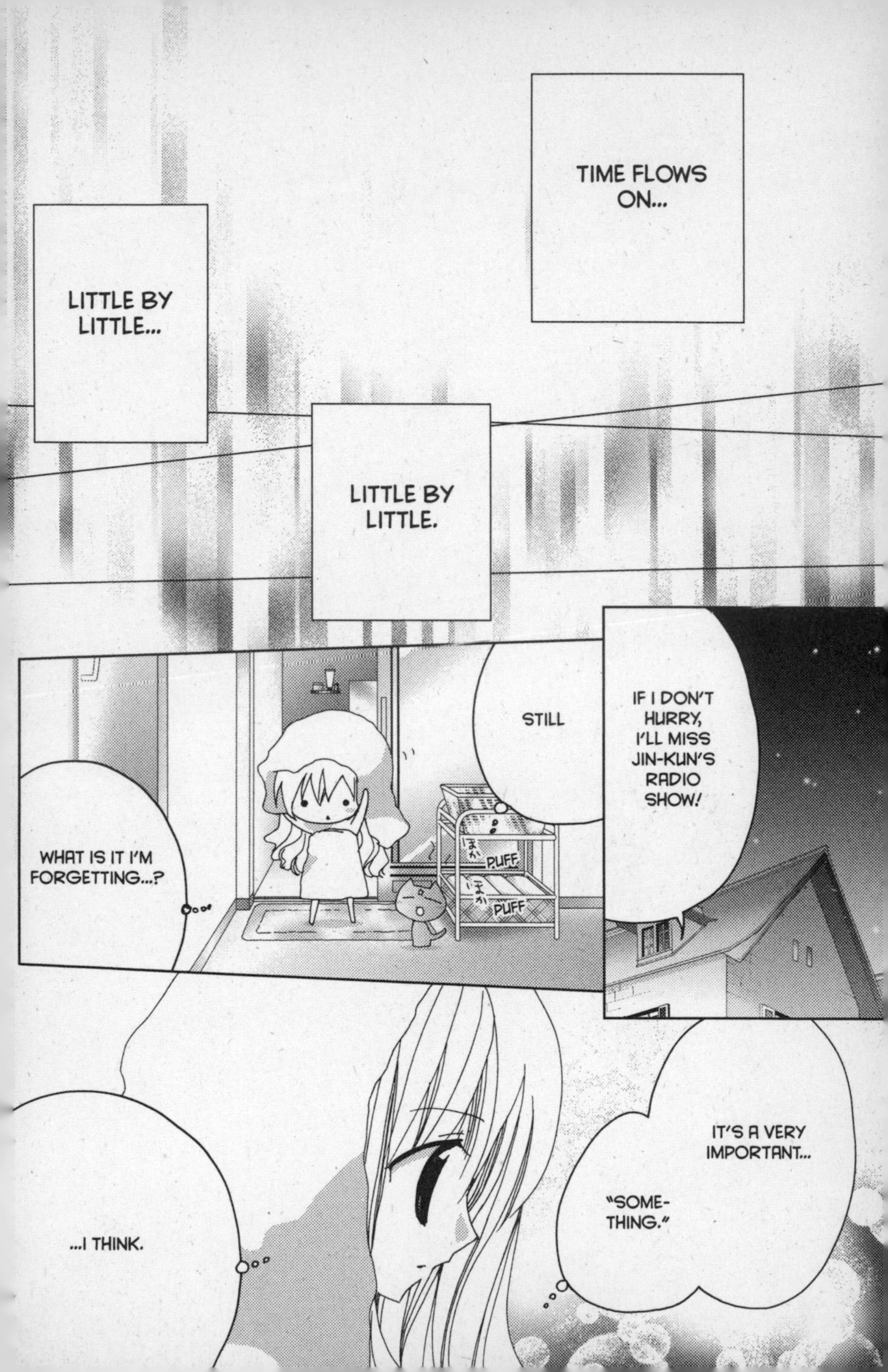
TIME FLOWS ON...
LITTLE BY LITTLE...
LITTLE BY LITTLE.
IF I DON'T HURRY, I'LL MISS JIN-KUN'S RADIO SHOW!
STILL
WHAT IS IT I'M FORGETTING...?
PUFF
PUFF
IT'S A VERY IMPORTANT...
"SOME-THING."
...I THINK.

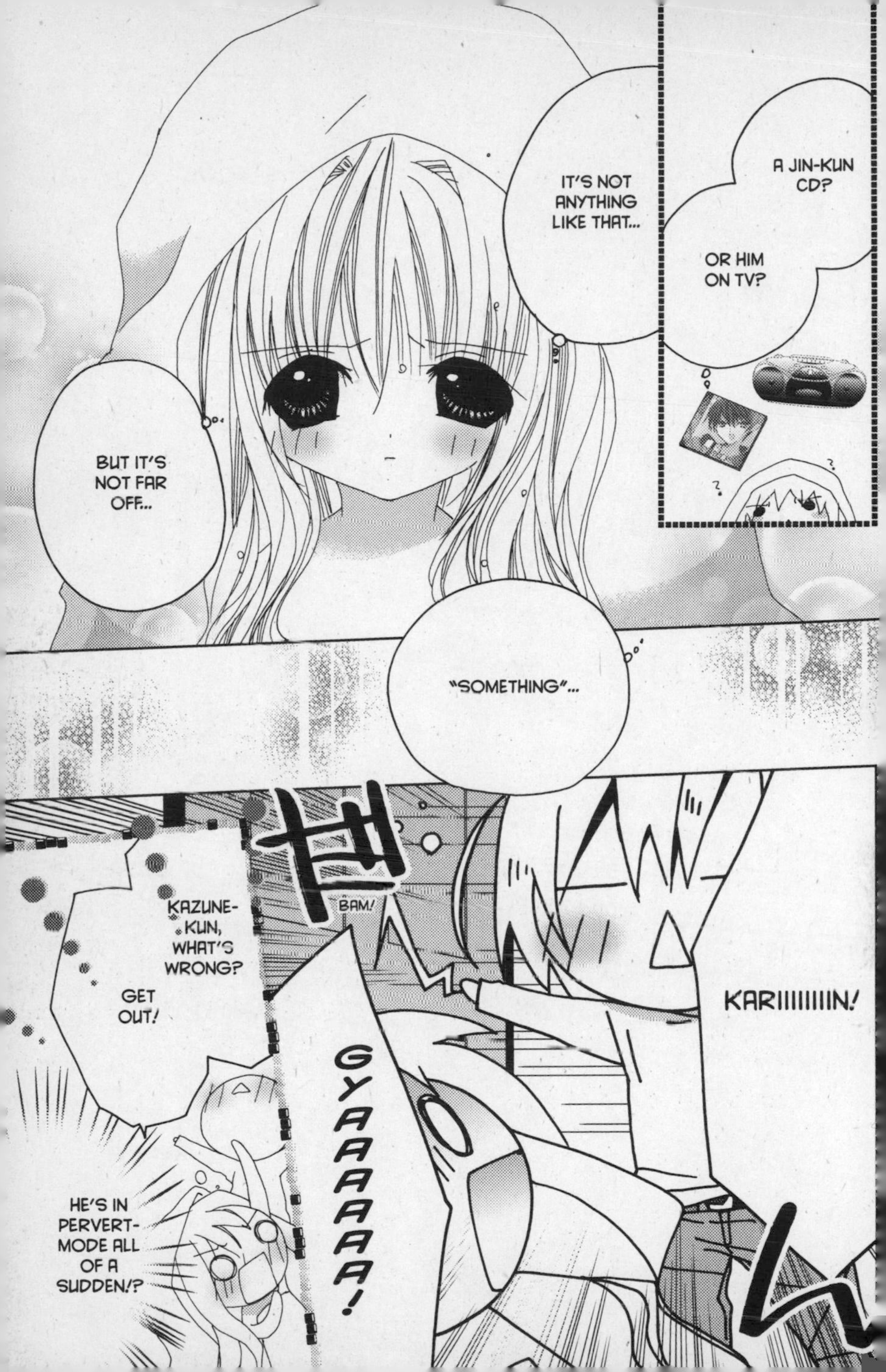
A JIN-KUN CD?
OR HIM ON TV?
IT'S NOT ANYTHING LIKE THAT...
BUT IT'S NOT FAR OFF...
"SOMETHING"...
KARIIIIIIIIN!
BAM!
KAZUNE-KUN, WHAT'S WRONG?
GET OUT!
GYAAAAAAA!
HE'S IN PERVERT-MODE ALL OF A SUDDEN!?

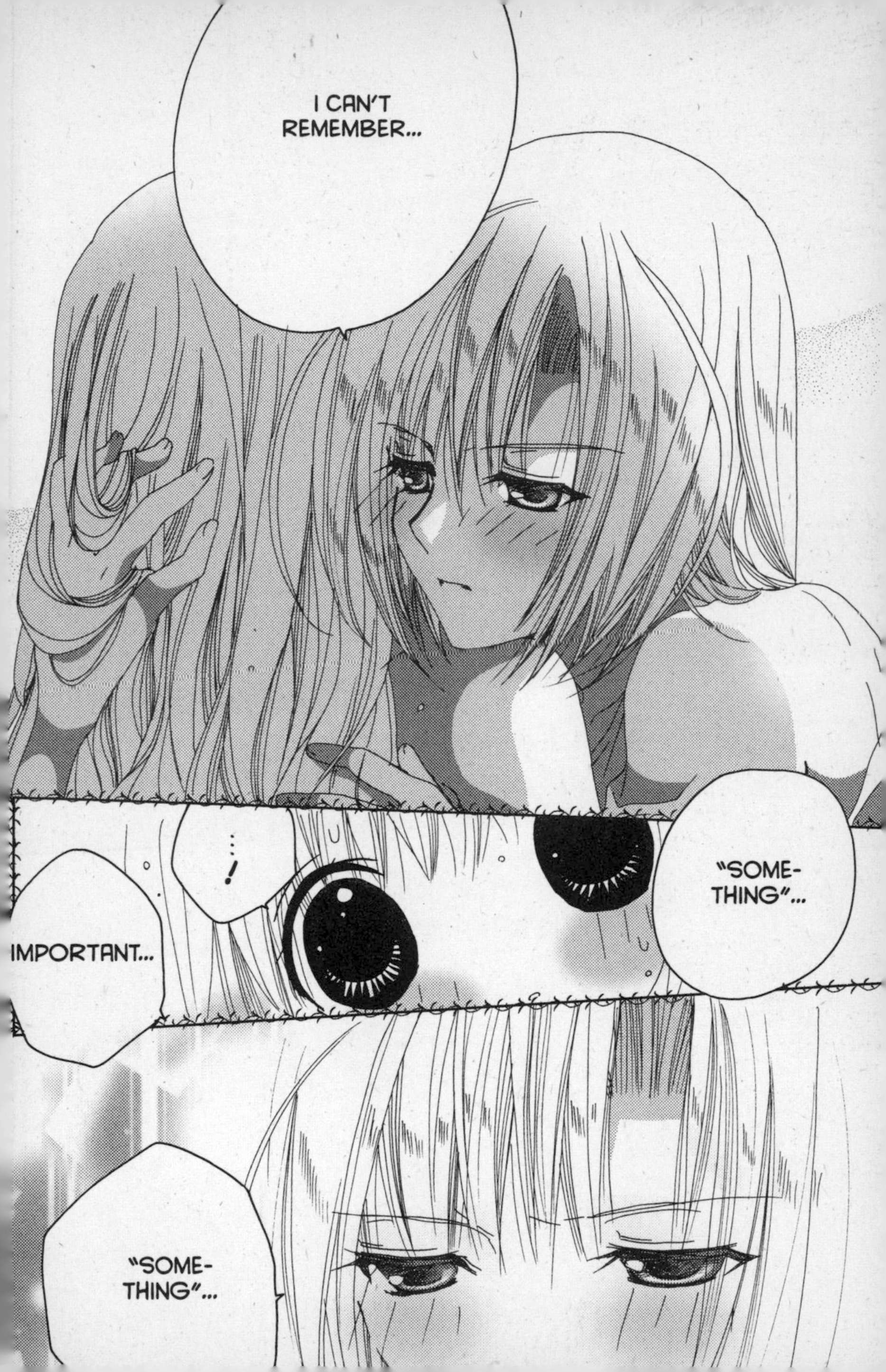
I CAN'T REMEMBER...
"SOME-THING"...
...!
IMPORTANT...
"SOME-THING"...

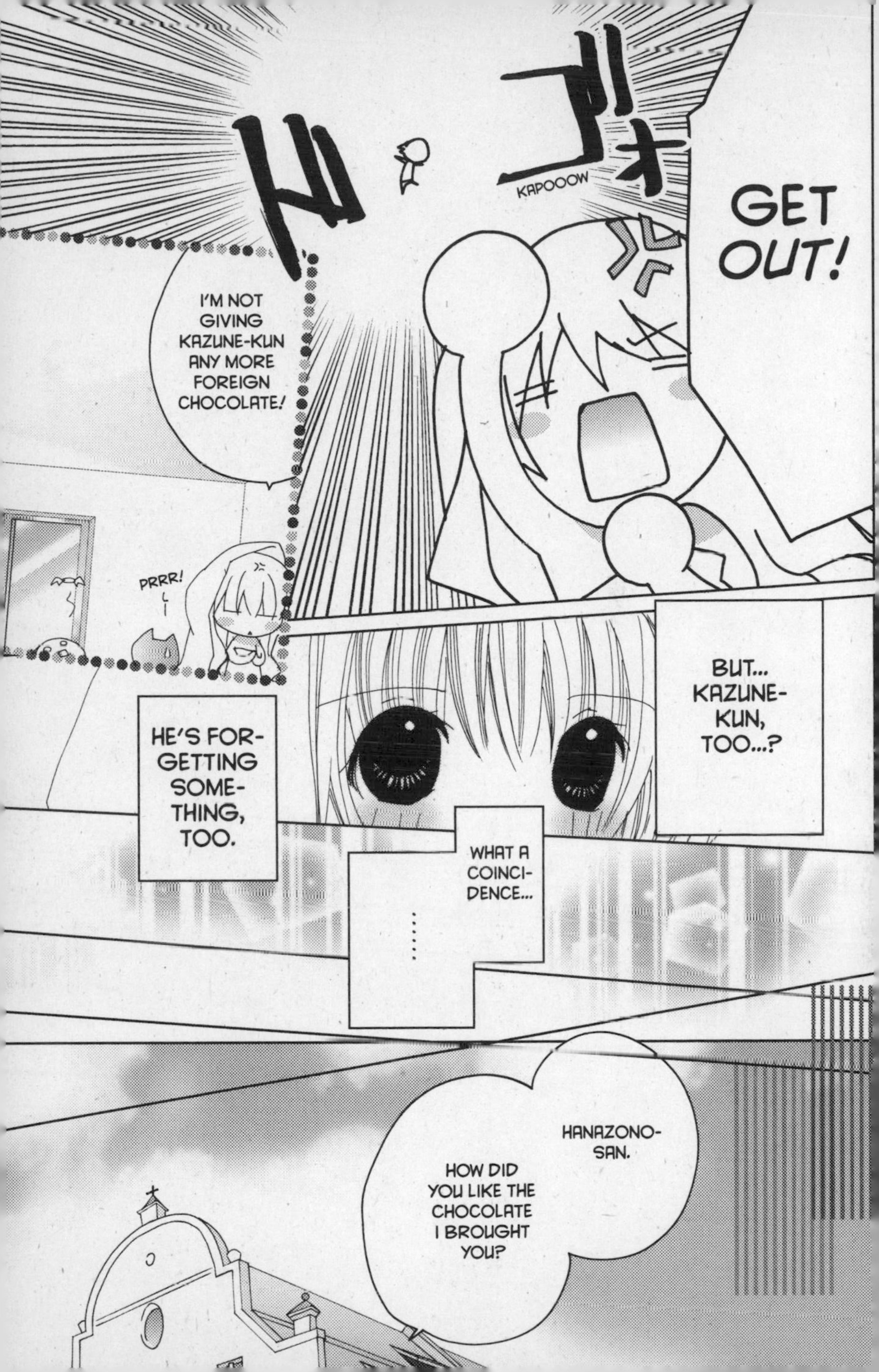
KAPOOOW
GET OUT!
I'M NOT GIVING KAZUNE-KUN ANY MORE FOREIGN CHOCOLATE!
PRRR!
BUT... KAZUNE-KUN, TOO...?
HE'S FOR-GETTING SOME-THING, TOO.
WHAT A COINCI-DENCE...
......
HANAZONO-SAN.
HOW DID YOU LIKE THE CHOCOLATE I BROUGHT YOU?

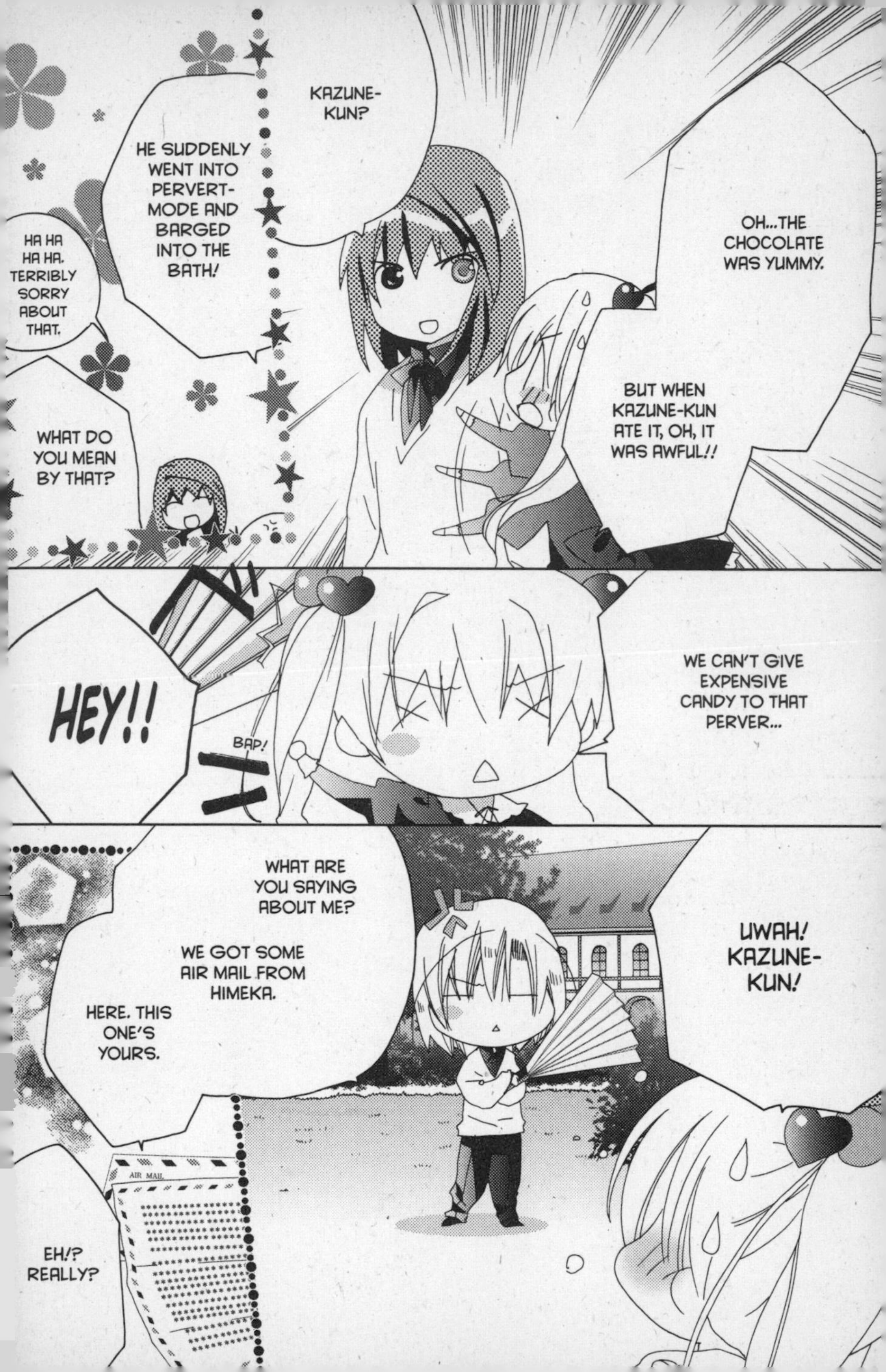
OH...THE CHOCOLATE WAS YUMMY.
BUT WHEN KAZUNE-KUN ATE IT, OH, IT WAS AWFUL!!
KAZUNE-KUN?
HE SUDDENLY WENT INTO PERVERT-MODE AND BARGED INTO THE BATH!
HA HA HA HA. TERRIBLY SORRY ABOUT THAT.
WHAT DO YOU MEAN BY THAT?
WE CAN'T GIVE EXPENSIVE CANDY TO THAT PERVER...
HEY!!
BAP!
UWAH! KAZUNE-KUN!
WHAT ARE YOU SAYING ABOUT ME?
WE GOT SOME AIR MAIL FROM HIMEKA.
HERE. THIS ONE'S YOURS.
EH!? REALLY?
AIR MAIL

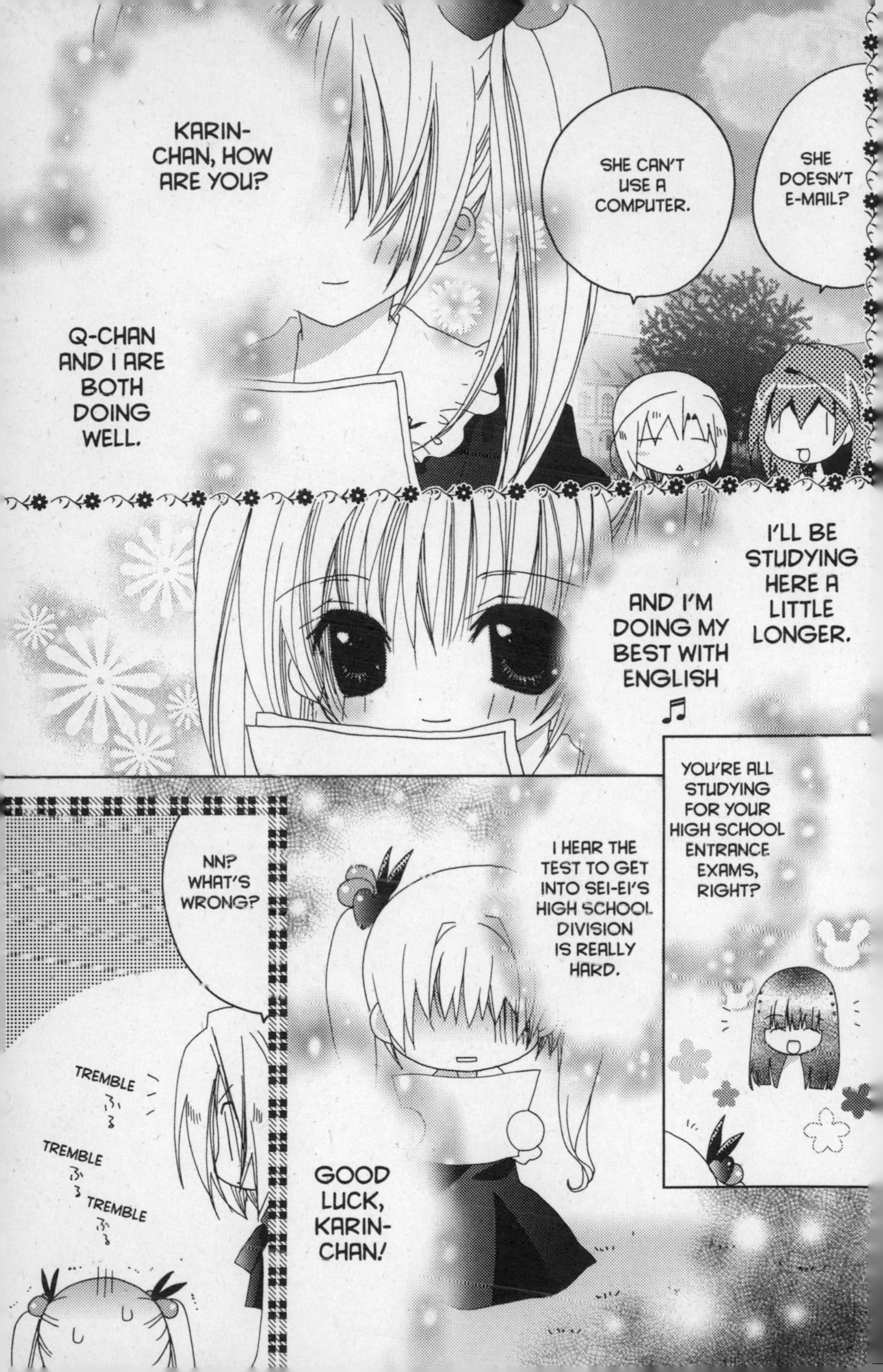
SHE DOESN'T E-MAIL?
SHE CAN'T USE A COMPUTER.
KARIN-CHAN, HOW ARE YOU?
Q-CHAN AND I ARE BOTH DOING WELL.
I'LL BE STUDYING HERE A LITTLE LONGER.
AND I'M DOING MY BEST WITH ENGLISH ♫
YOU'RE ALL STUDYING FOR YOUR HIGH SCHOOL ENTRANCE EXAMS, RIGHT?
I HEAR THE TEST TO GET INTO SEI-EI'S HIGH SCHOOL DIVISION IS REALLY HARD.
GOOD LUCK, KARIN-CHAN!
NN? WHAT'S WRONG?
TREMBLE ふる
TREMBLE ふる
TREMBLE ふる

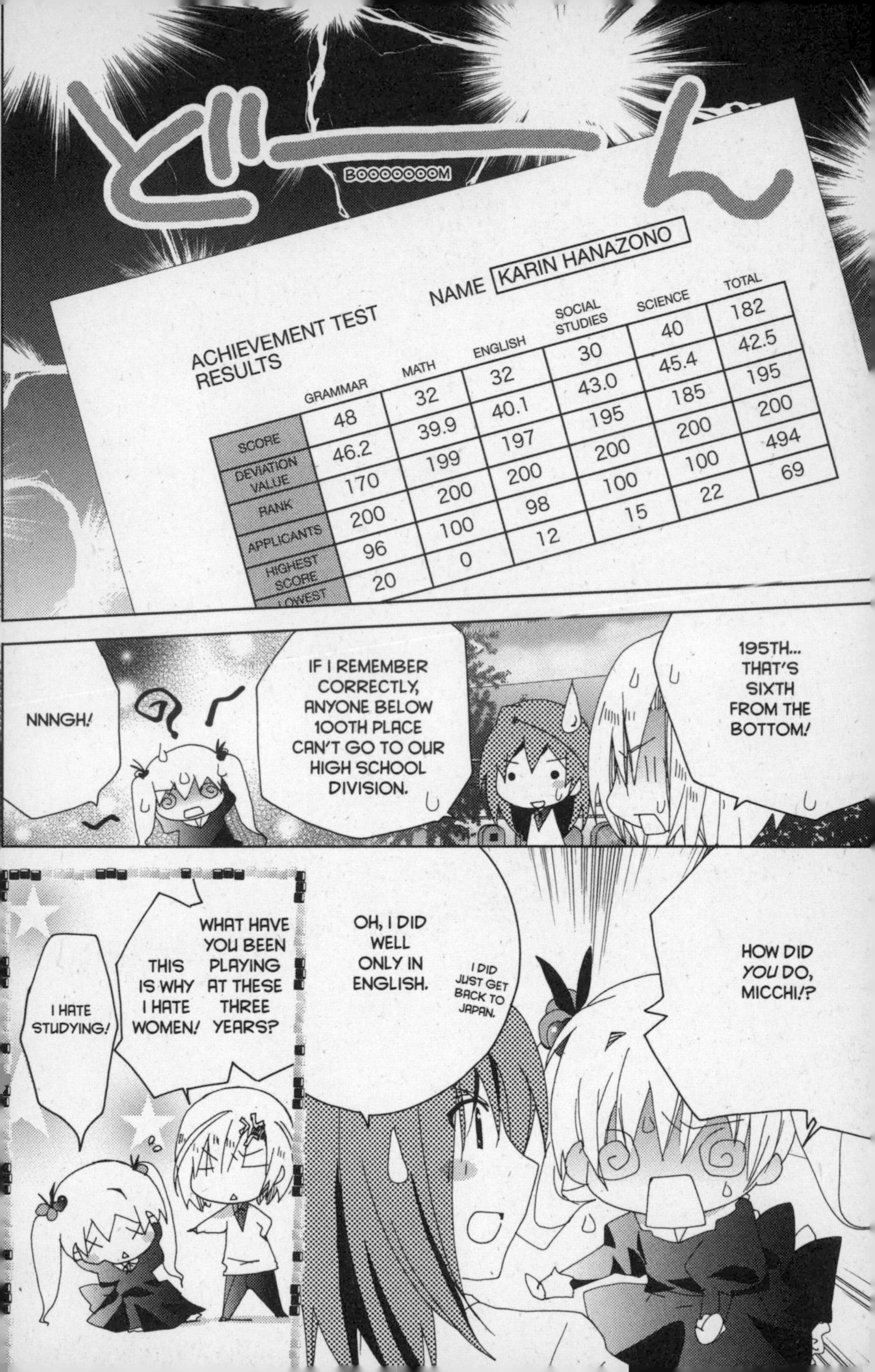
とーん
BOOOOOOOOM
ACHIEVEMENT TEST RESULTS
NAME KARIN HANAZONO
GRAMMAR MATH ENGLISH SOCIAL STUDIES SCIENCE TOTAL
SCORE 48 32 32 30 40 182
DEVIATION VALUE 46.2 39.9 40.1 43.0 45.4 42.5
RANK 170 199 197 195 185 195
APPLICANTS 200 200 200 200 200 200
HIGHEST SCORE 96 100 98 100 100 494
LOWEST 20 0 12 15 22 69
195TH... THAT'S SIXTH FROM THE BOTTOM!
IF I REMEMBER CORRECTLY, ANYONE BELOW 100TH PLACE CAN'T GO TO OUR HIGH SCHOOL DIVISION.
NNNGH!
HOW DID YOU DO, MICCHI!?
I DID JUST GET BACK TO JAPAN.
OH, I DID WELL ONLY IN ENGLISH.
WHAT HAVE YOU BEEN PLAYING AT THESE THREE YEARS?
THIS IS WHY I HATE WOMEN!
I HATE STUDYING!

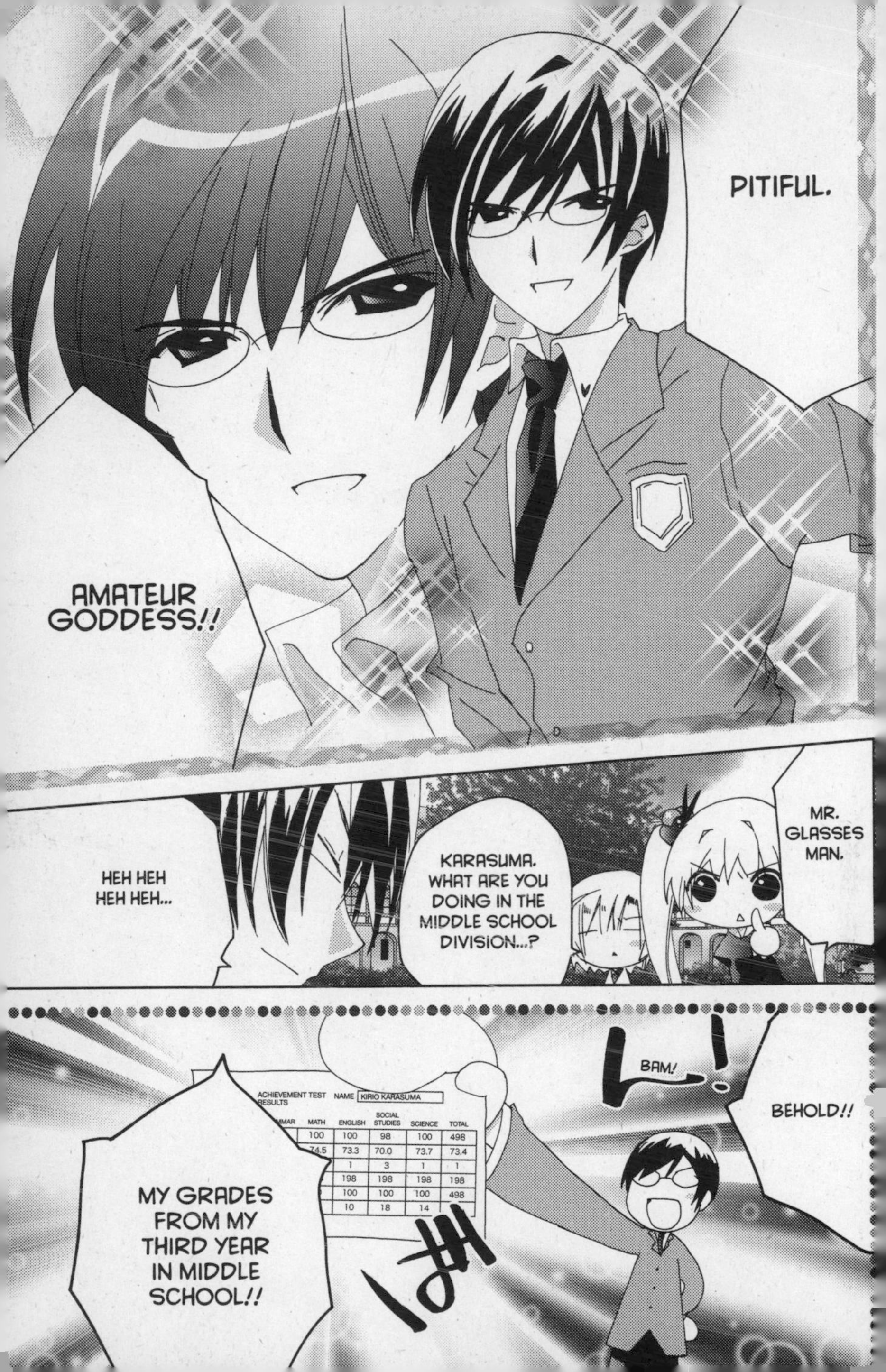
PITIFUL.
AMATEUR GODDESS!!
MR. GLASSES MAN.
KARASUMA. WHAT ARE YOU DOING IN THE MIDDLE SCHOOL DIVISION...?
HEH HEH HEH HEH...
BAM!
BEHOLD!!
ACHIEVEMENT TEST RESULTS NAME KIRIO KARASUMA
MATH ENGLISH SOCIAL STUDIES SCIENCE TOTAL
MY GRADES FROM MY THIRD YEAR IN MIDDLE SCHOOL!!

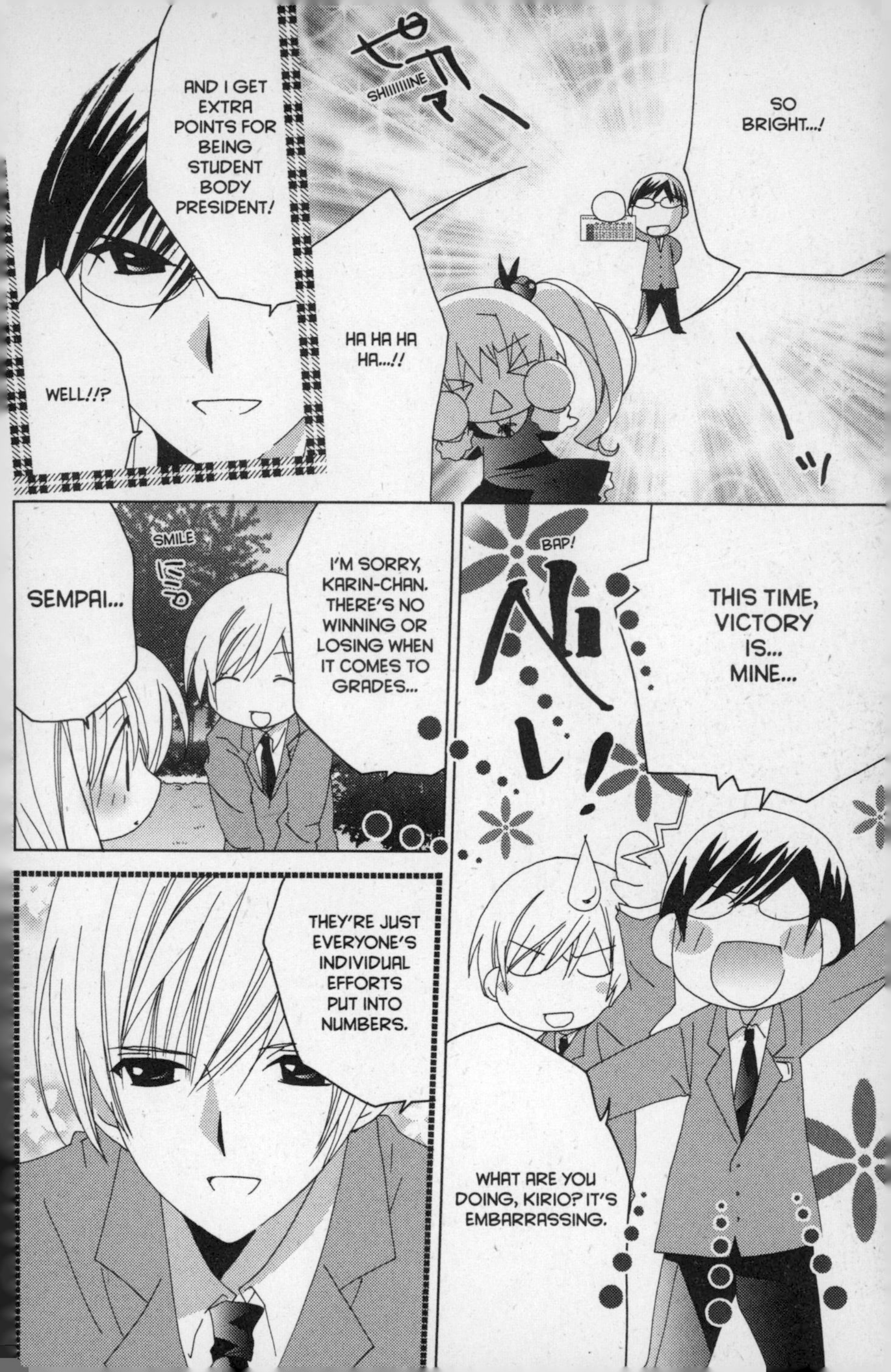
SHIIIIINE
SO BRIGHT...!
AND I GET EXTRA POINTS FOR BEING STUDENT BODY PRESIDENT!
HA HA HA HA...!!
WELL!!?
THIS TIME, VICTORY IS... MINE...
BAP!
WHAT ARE YOU DOING, KIRIO? IT'S EMBARRASSING.
I'M SORRY, KARIN-CHAN. THERE'S NO WINNING OR LOSING WHEN IT COMES TO GRADES...
SMILE
SEMPAI...
THEY'RE JUST EVERYONE'S INDIVIDUAL EFFORTS PUT INTO NUMBERS.

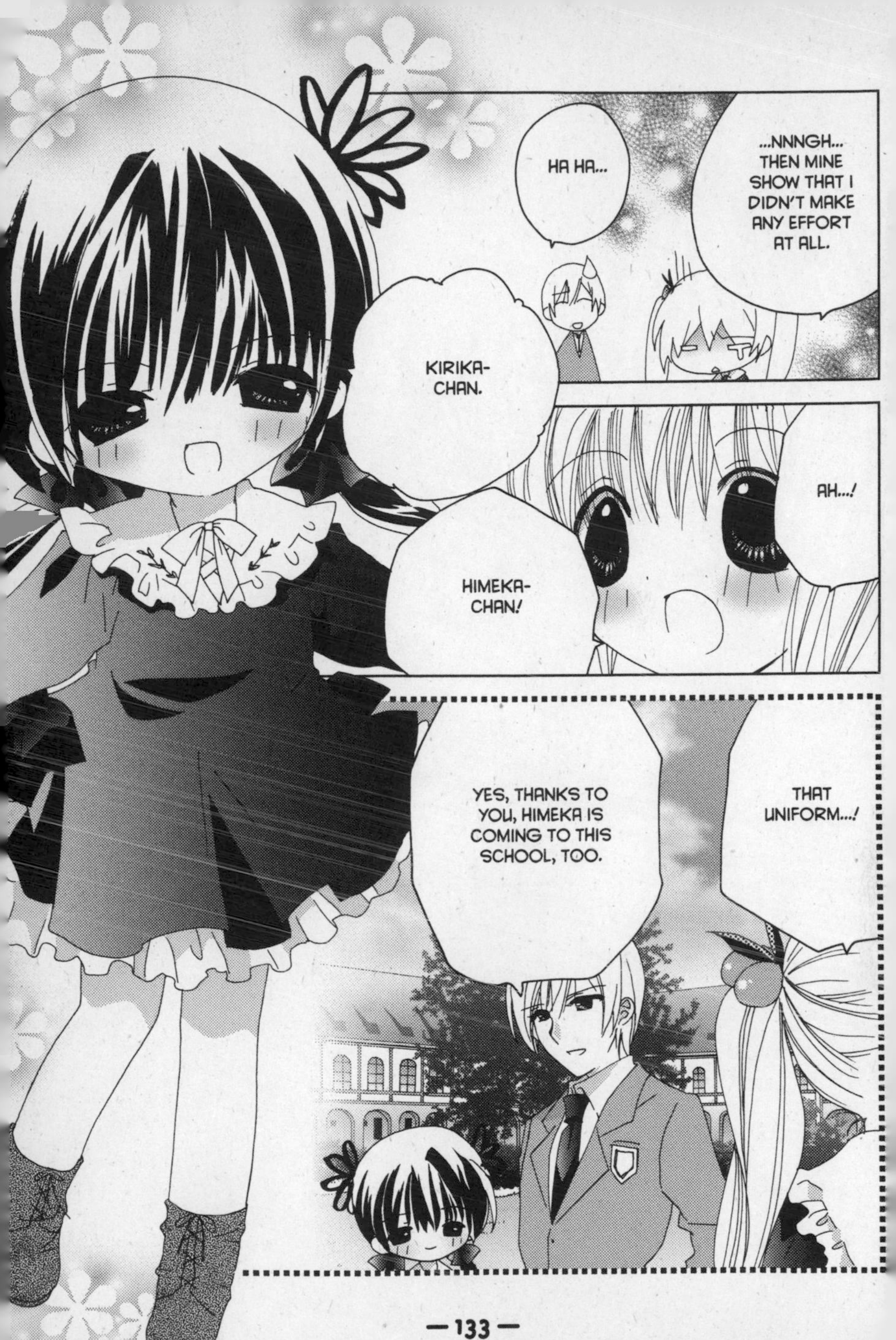
...NNNGH... THEN MINE SHOW THAT I DIDN'T MAKE ANY EFFORT AT ALL.
HA HA...
KIRIKA-CHAN.
AH...!
HIMEKA-CHAN!
THAT UNIFORM...!
YES, THANKS TO YOU, HIMEKA IS COMING TO THIS SCHOOL, TOO.

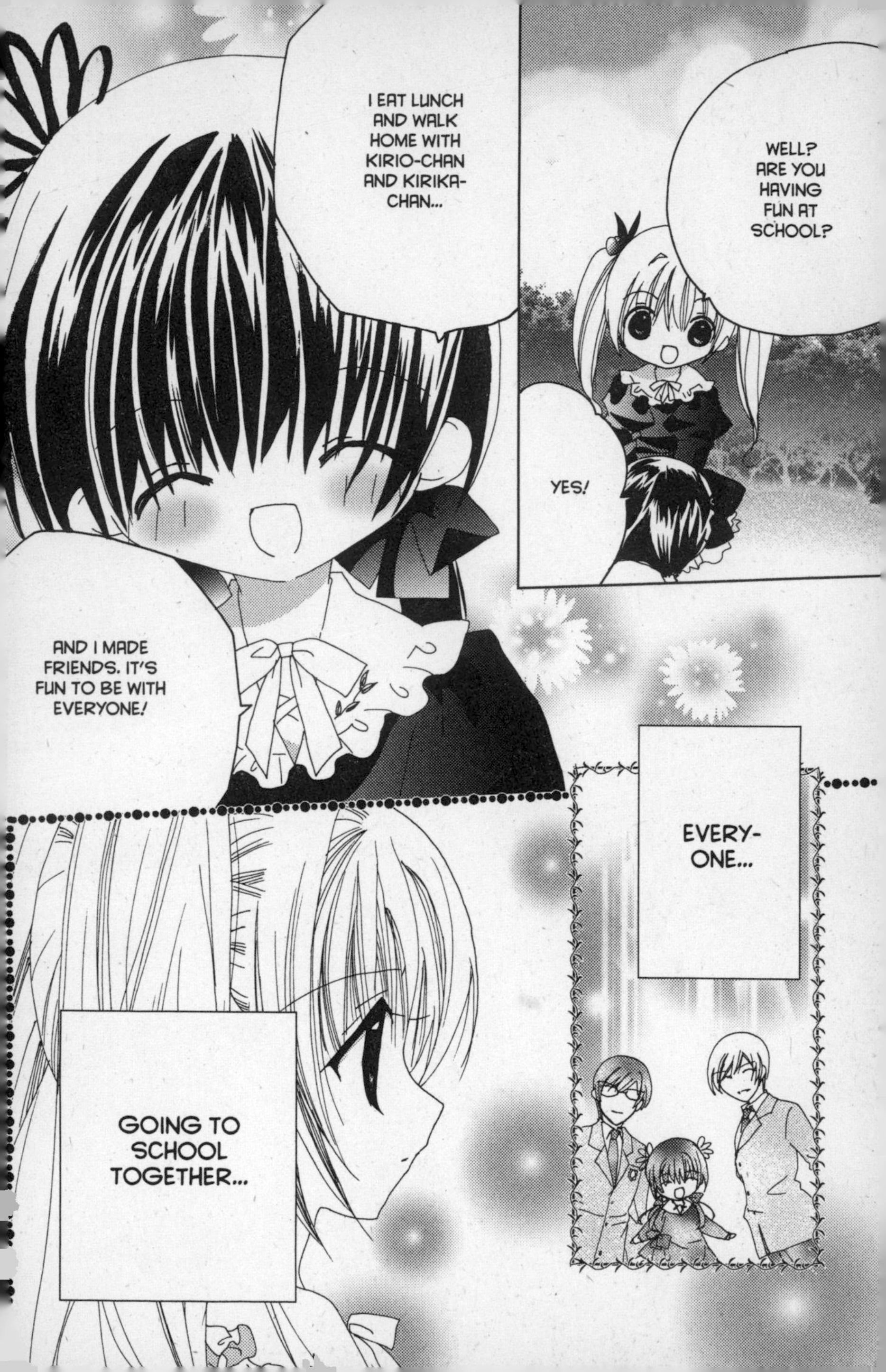
WELL? ARE YOU HAVING FUN AT SCHOOL?
YES!
I EAT LUNCH AND WALK HOME WITH KIRIO-CHAN AND KIRIKA-CHAN...
AND I MADE FRIENDS. IT'S FUN TO BE WITH EVERYONE!
EVERY-ONE...
GOING TO SCHOOL TOGETHER...

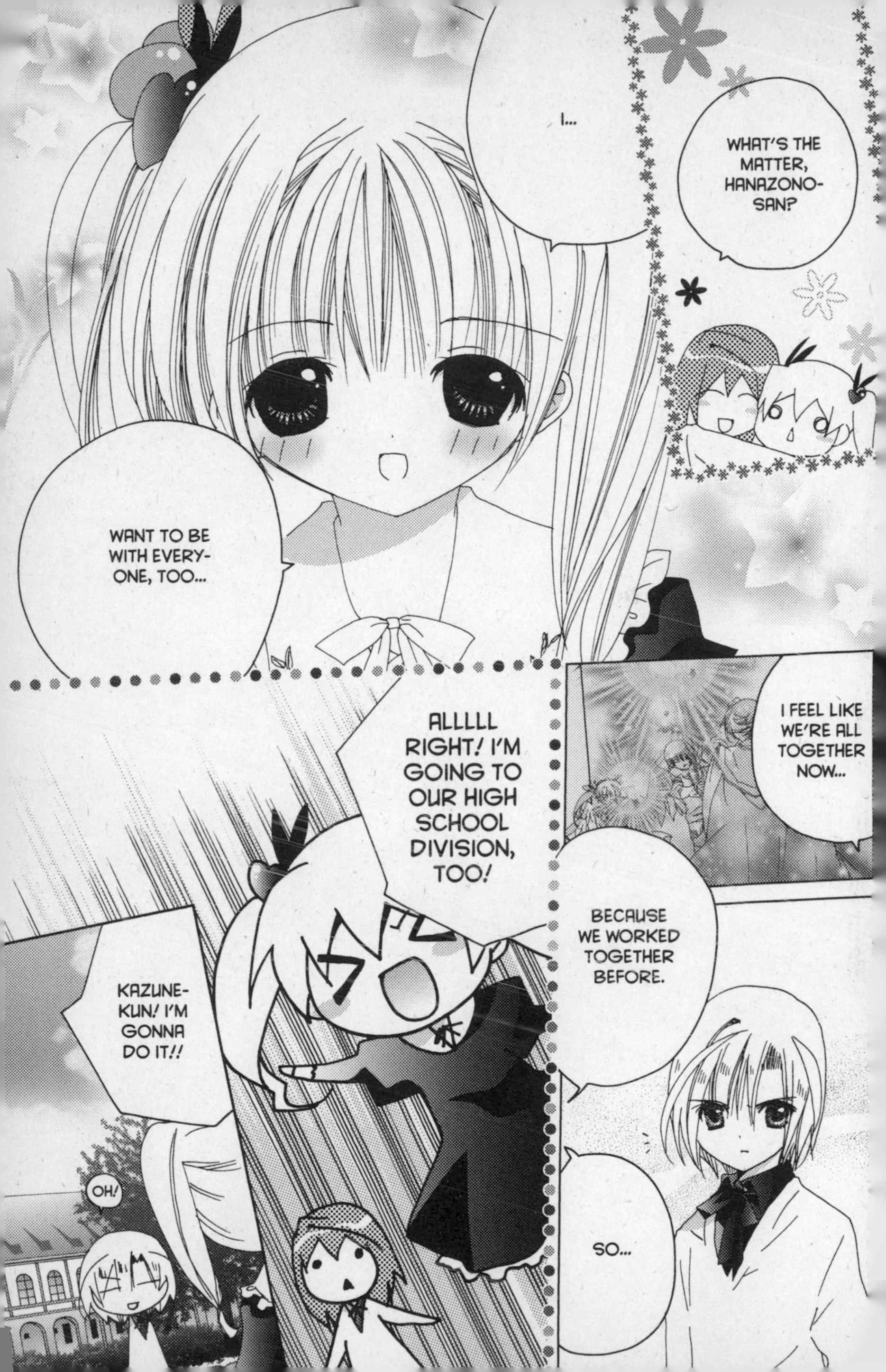
WHAT'S THE MATTER, HANAZONO-SAN?
I...
WANT TO BE WITH EVERY-ONE, TOO...
I FEEL LIKE WE'RE ALL TOGETHER NOW...
BECAUSE WE WORKED TOGETHER BEFORE.
SO...
ALLLLL RIGHT! I'M GOING TO OUR HIGH SCHOOL DIVISION, TOO!
KAZUNE-KUN! I'M GONNA DO IT!!
OH!

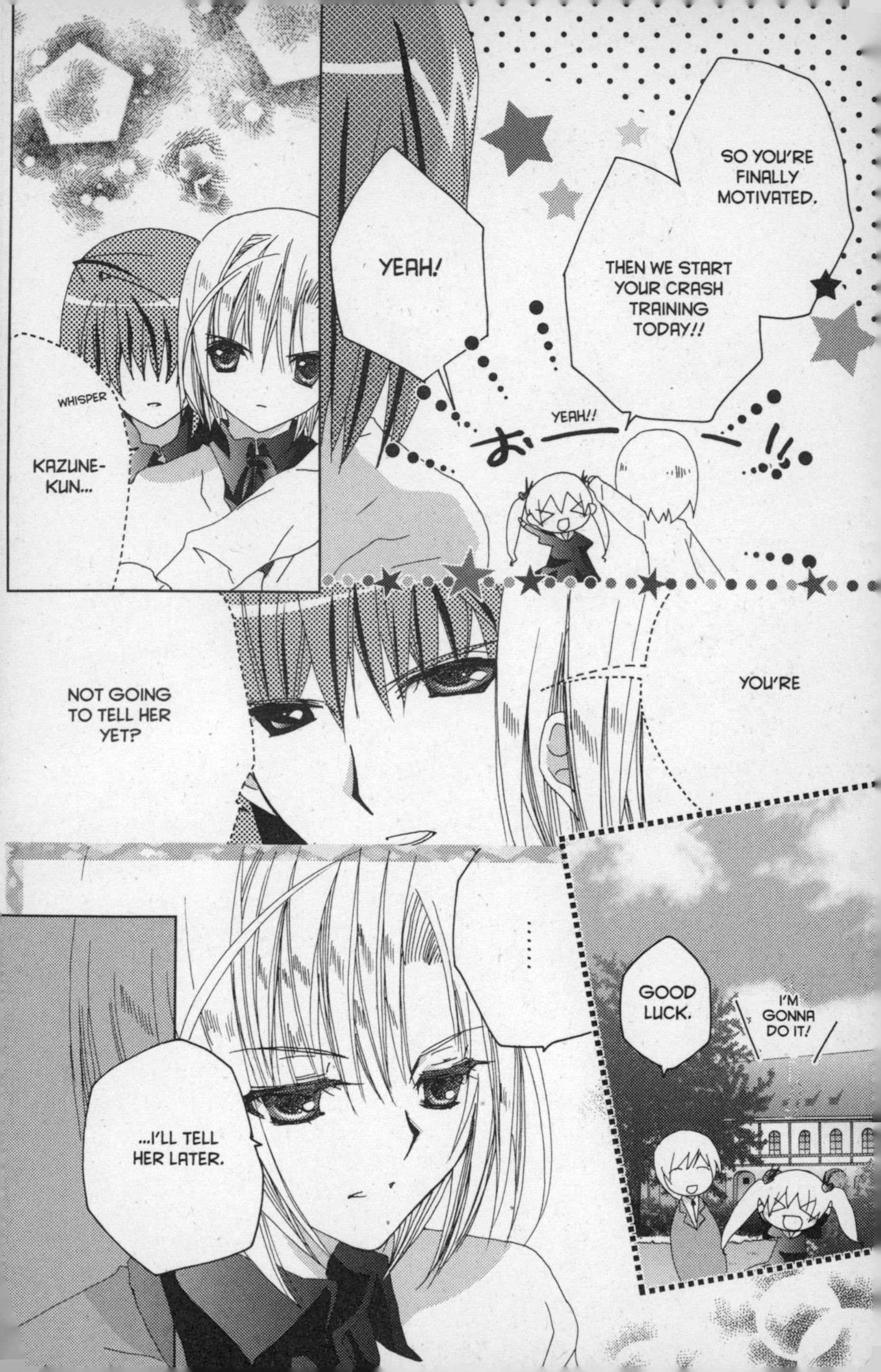
SO YOU'RE FINALLY MOTIVATED.
THEN WE START YOUR CRASH TRAINING TODAY!!
YEAH!!
おーー!!
YEAH!
WHISPER
KAZUNE-KUN...
YOU'RE
NOT GOING TO TELL HER YET?
I'M GONNA DO IT!
GOOD LUCK.
......
...I'LL TELL HER LATER.

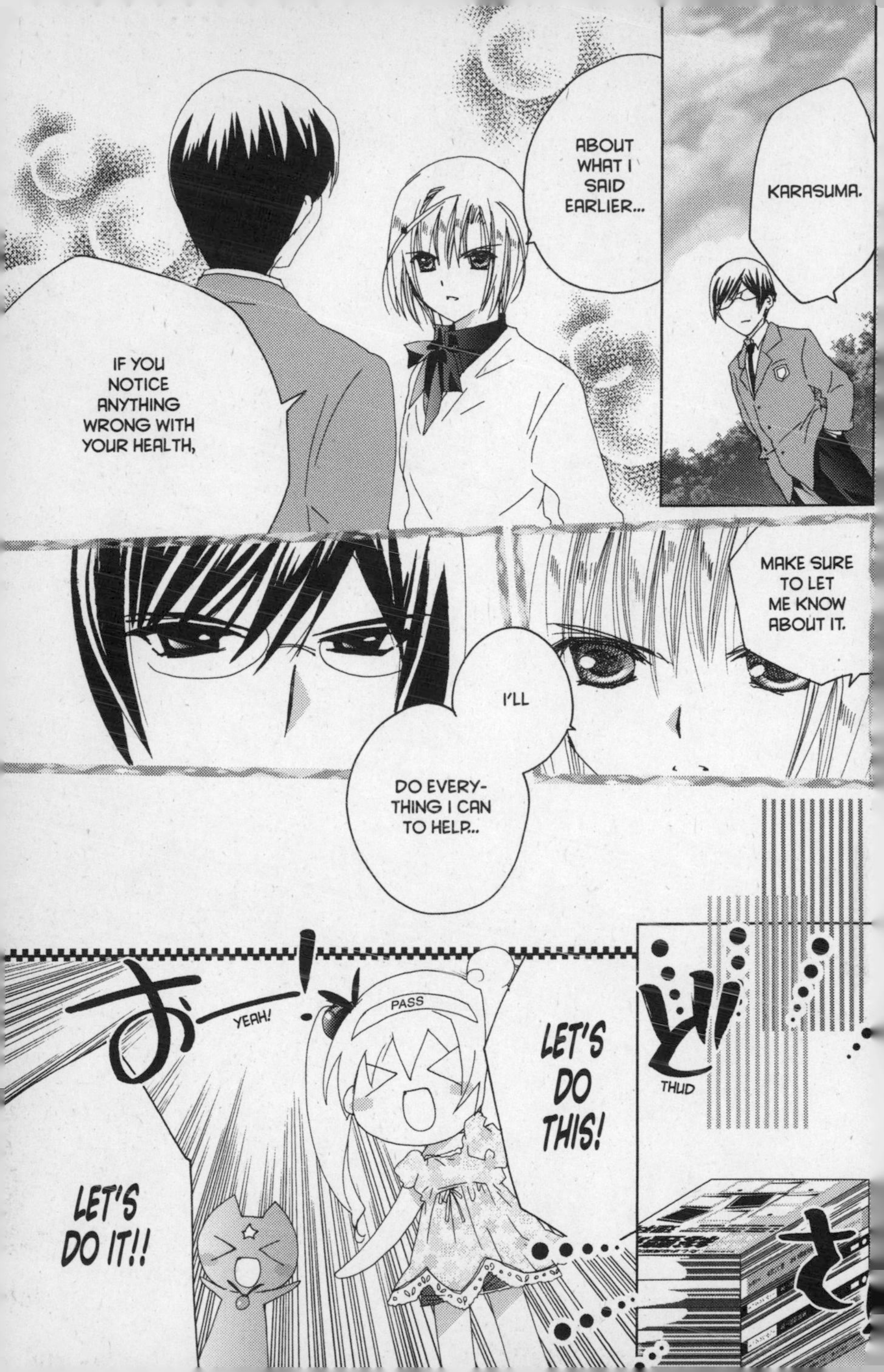
KARASUMA.
ABOUT WHAT I SAID EARLIER...
IF YOU NOTICE ANYTHING WRONG WITH YOUR HEALTH,
MAKE SURE TO LET ME KNOW ABOUT IT.
I'LL
DO EVERY-THING I CAN TO HELP...
THUD
お—!
YEAH!
PASS
LET'S DO THIS!
LET'S DO IT!!

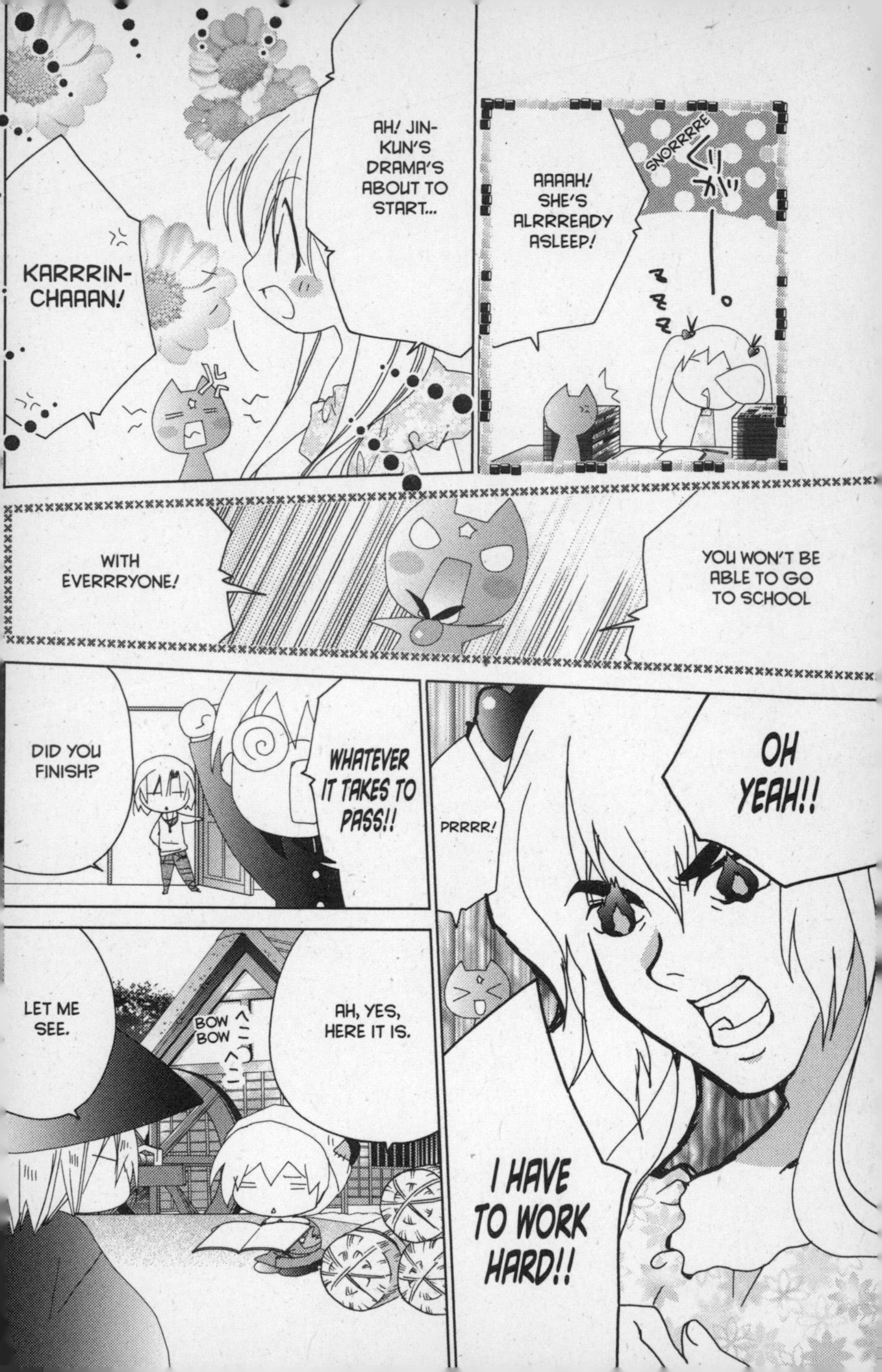
SNORRRRE
AAAAH! SHE'S ALRRREADY ASLEEP!
AH! JIN-KUN'S DRAMA'S ABOUT TO START...
KARRRIN-CHAAAN!
YOU WON'T BE ABLE TO GO TO SCHOOL
WITH EVERRYONE!
OH YEAH!!
PRRRR!
I HAVE TO WORK HARD!!
WHATEVER IT TAKES TO PASS!!
DID YOU FINISH?
AH, YES, HERE IT IS.
BOW BOW
LET ME SEE.

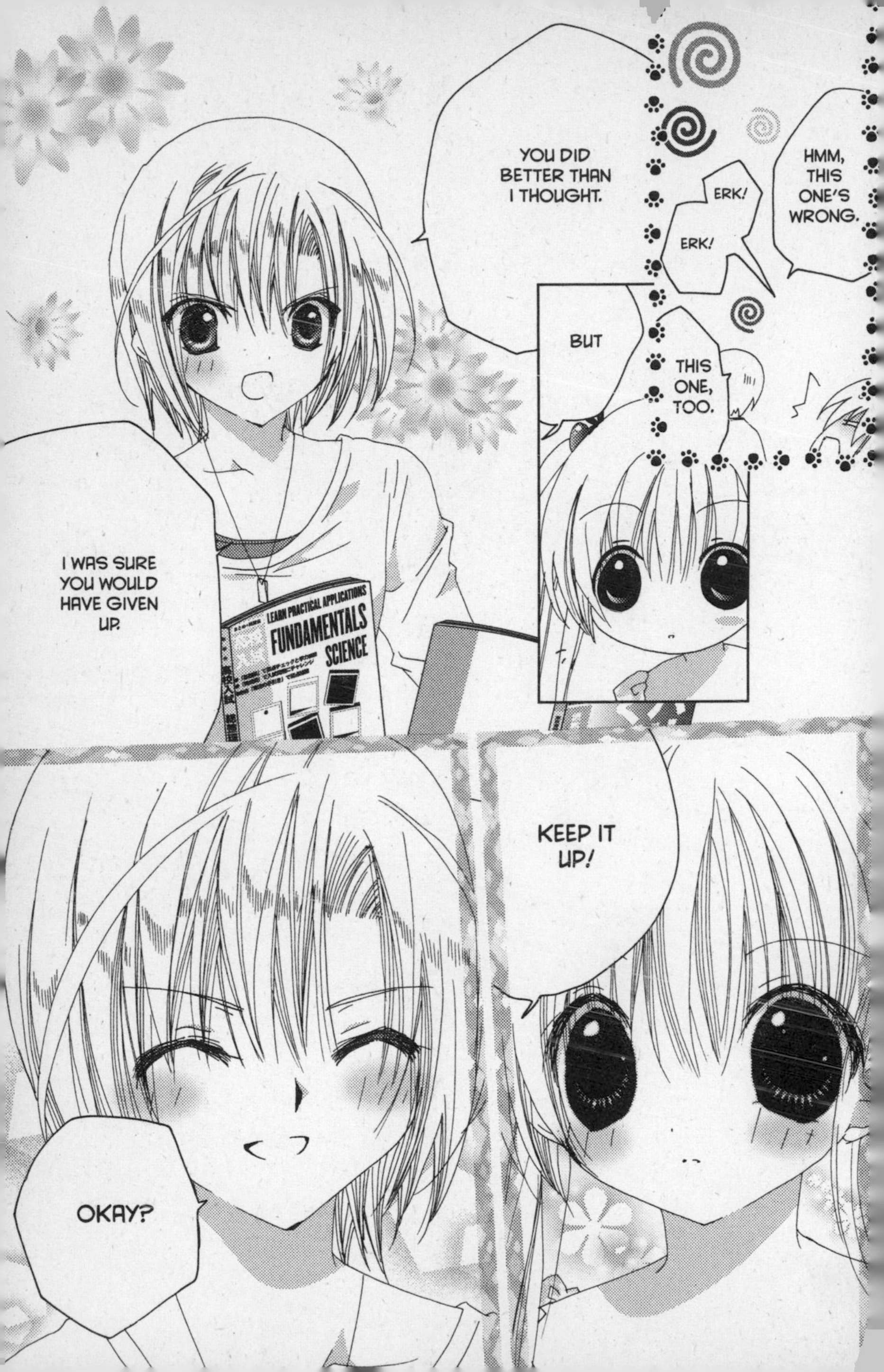
HMM, THIS ONE'S WRONG.
ERK!
ERK!
BUT
THIS ONE, TOO.
YOU DID BETTER THAN I THOUGHT.
I WAS SURE YOU WOULD HAVE GIVEN UP.
LEARN PRACTICAL APPLICATIONS
FUNDAMENTALS
SCIENCE
KEEP IT UP!
OKAY?

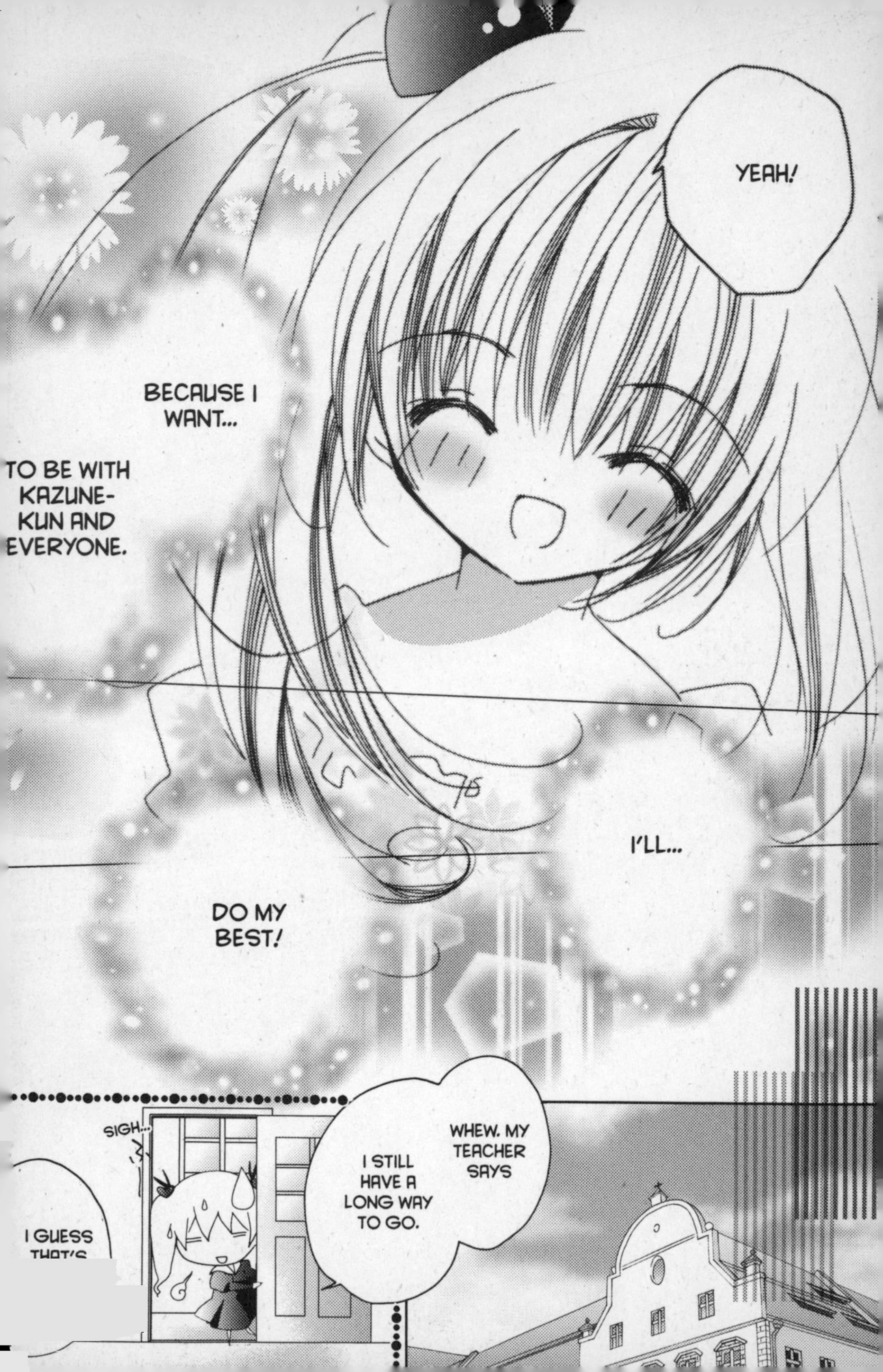
YEAH!
BECAUSE I WANT...
TO BE WITH KAZUNE-KUN AND EVERYONE.
I'LL...
DO MY BEST!
WHEW. MY TEACHER SAYS
I STILL HAVE A LONG WAY TO GO.
SIGH...
I GUESS THAT'S

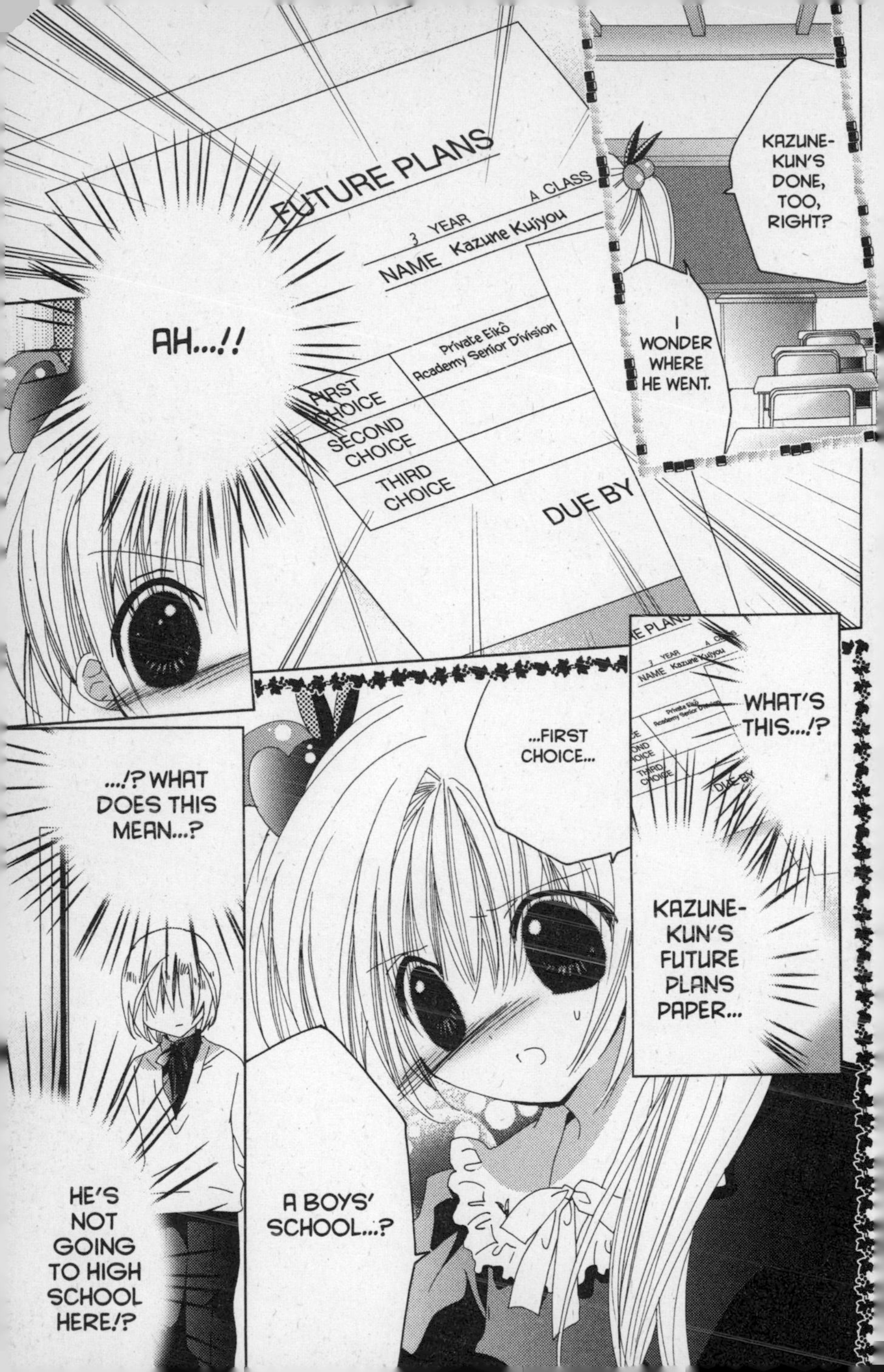

KAZUNE-KUN'S DONE, TOO, RIGHT?
I WONDER WHERE HE WENT.
FUTURE PLANS
3 YEAR A CLASS
NAME Kazune Kujyou
FIRST CHOICE
Private Eikô Academy Senior Division
SECOND CHOICE
THIRD CHOICE
DUE BY
AH...!!
WHAT'S THIS...!?
KAZUNE-KUN'S FUTURE PLANS PAPER...
...FIRST CHOICE...
A BOYS' SCHOOL...?
...!? WHAT DOES THIS MEAN...?
HE'S NOT GOING TO HIGH SCHOOL HERE!?

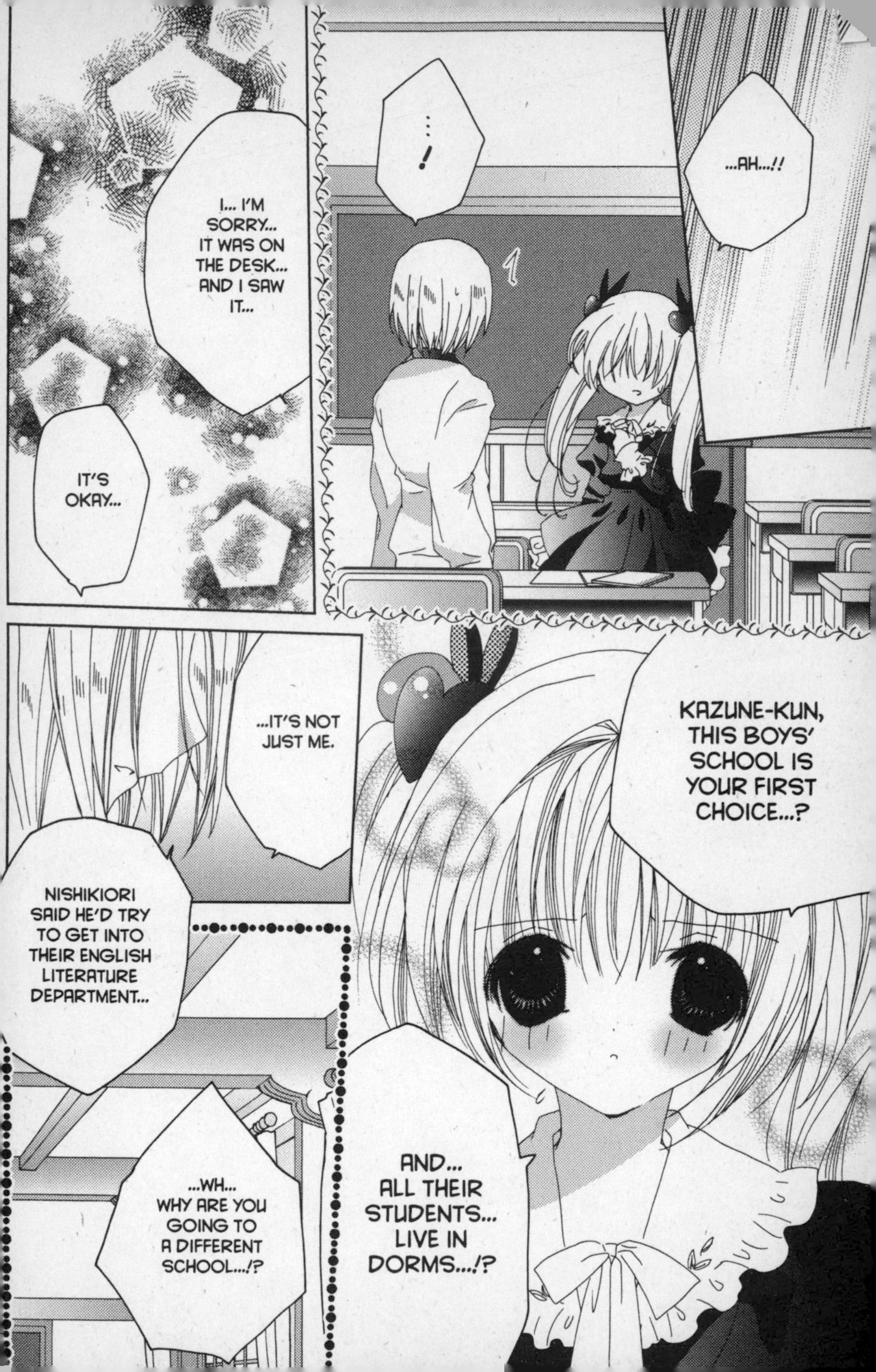
...AH...!!
...!
I... I'M SORRY... IT WAS ON THE DESK... AND I SAW IT...
IT'S OKAY...
KAZUNE-KUN, THIS BOYS' SCHOOL IS YOUR FIRST CHOICE...?
AND... ALL THEIR STUDENTS... LIVE IN DORMS...!?
...IT'S NOT JUST ME.
NISHIKIORI SAID HE'D TRY TO GET INTO THEIR ENGLISH LITERATURE DEPARTMENT...
...WH... WHY ARE YOU GOING TO A DIFFERENT SCHOOL...!?

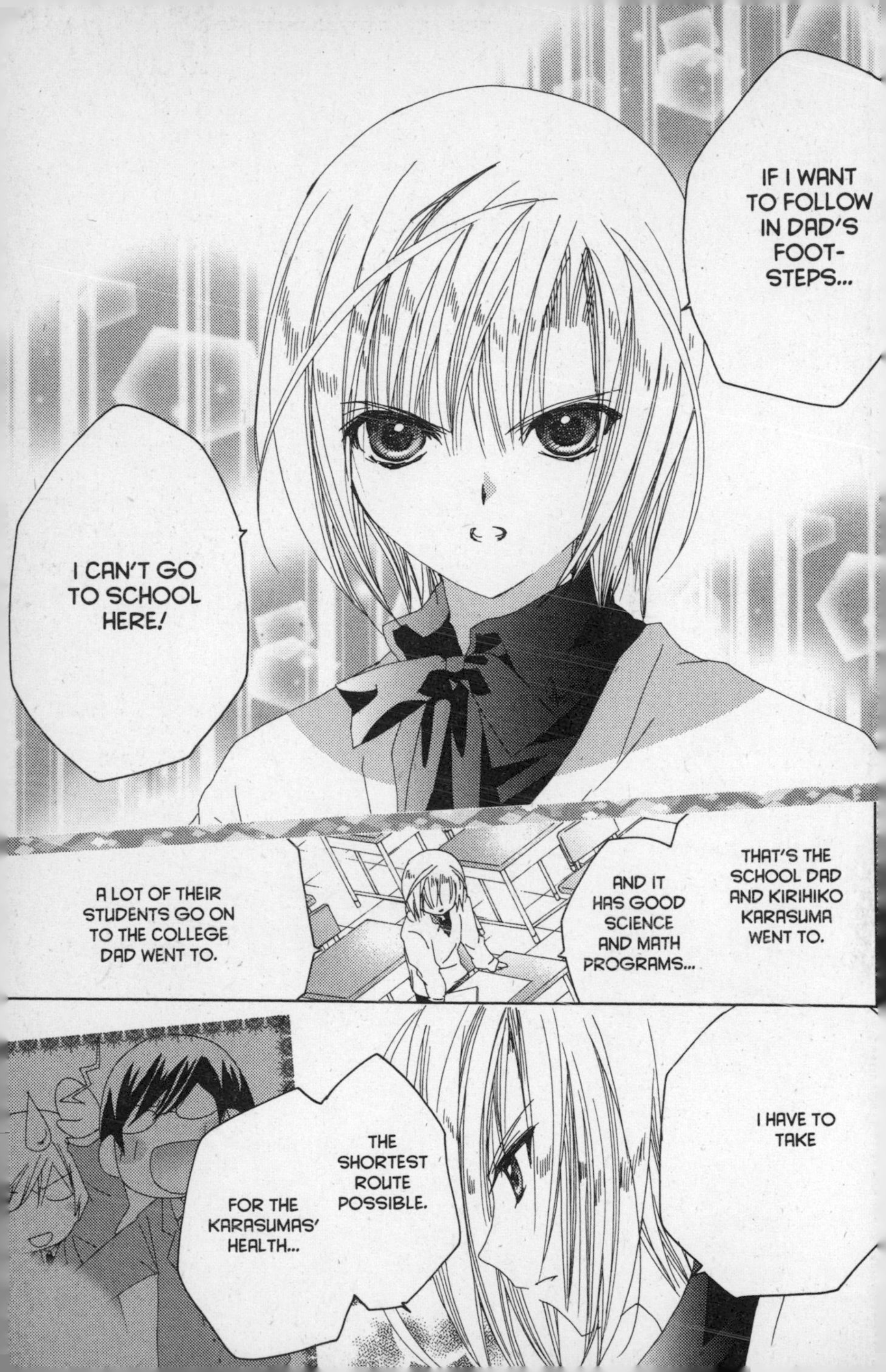
IF I WANT TO FOLLOW IN DAD'S FOOT-STEPS...
I CAN'T GO TO SCHOOL HERE!
THAT'S THE SCHOOL DAD AND KIRIHIKO KARASUMA WENT TO.
AND IT HAS GOOD SCIENCE AND MATH PROGRAMS...
A LOT OF THEIR STUDENTS GO ON TO THE COLLEGE DAD WENT TO.
I HAVE TO TAKE
THE SHORTEST ROUTE POSSIBLE.
FOR THE KARASUMAS' HEALTH...

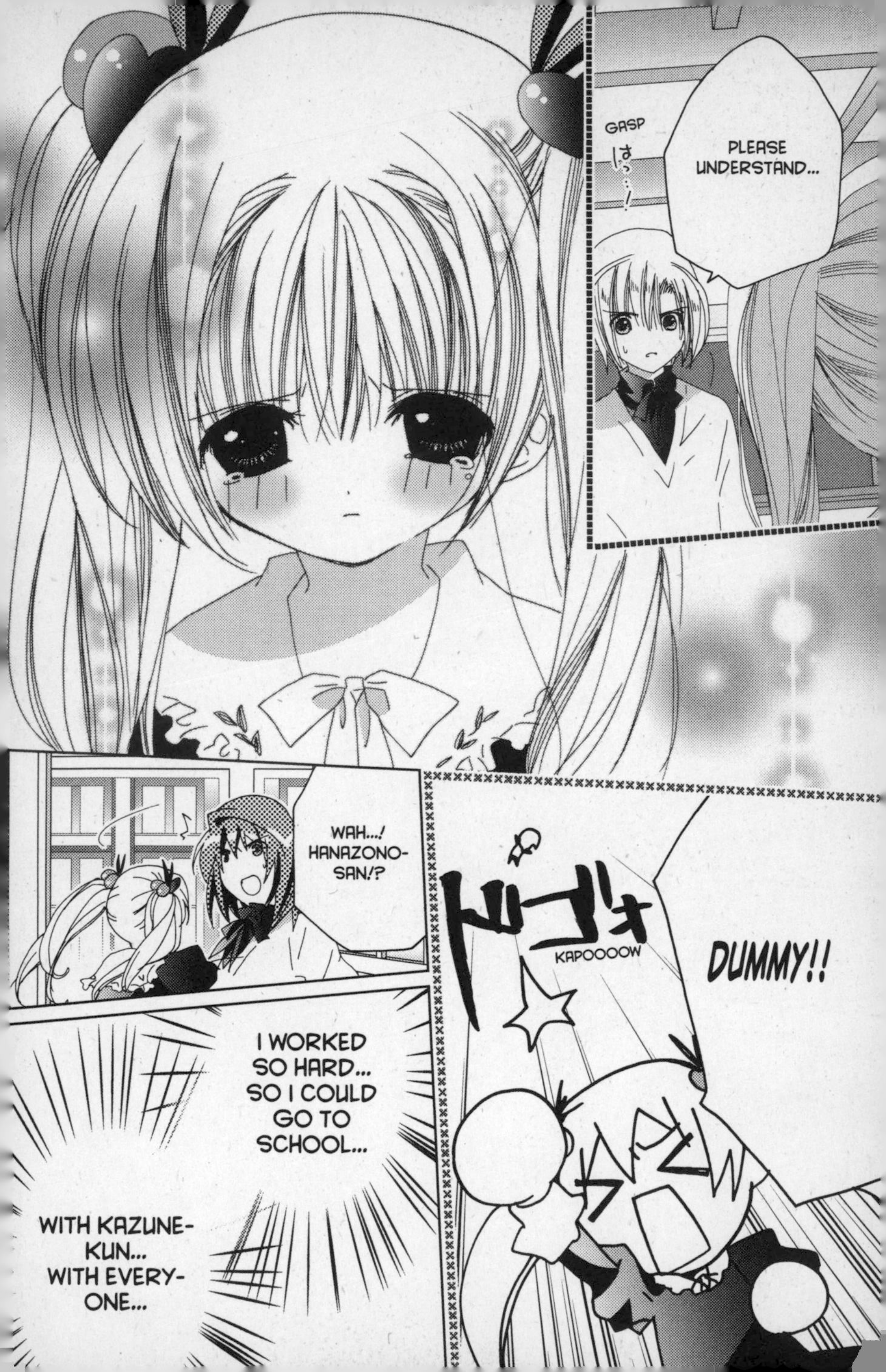
GASP
はっ…!
PLEASE UNDERSTAND...
ドゴォ
KAPOOOOW
DUMMY!!
WAH...! HANAZONO-SAN!?
I WORKED SO HARD... SO I COULD GO TO SCHOOL...
WITH KAZUNE-KUN... WITH EVERY-ONE...

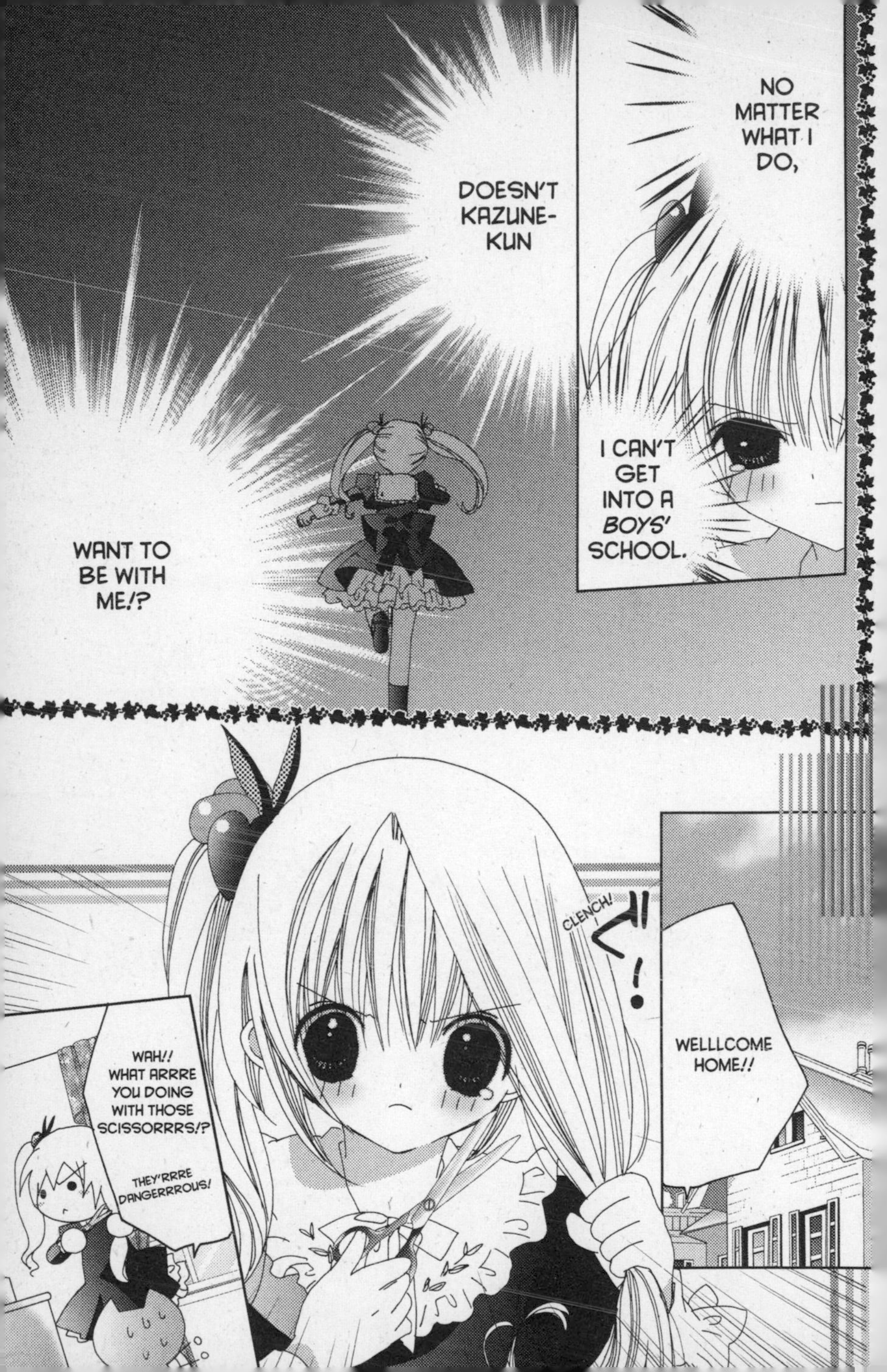
NO MATTER WHAT I DO,
I CAN'T GET INTO A *BOYS'* SCHOOL.
DOESN'T KAZUNE-KUN
WANT TO BE WITH ME!?
WELLLCOME HOME!!
CLENCH!
WAH!! WHAT ARRRE YOU DOING WITH THOSE SCISSORRRS!?
THEY'RRRE DANGERRROUS!

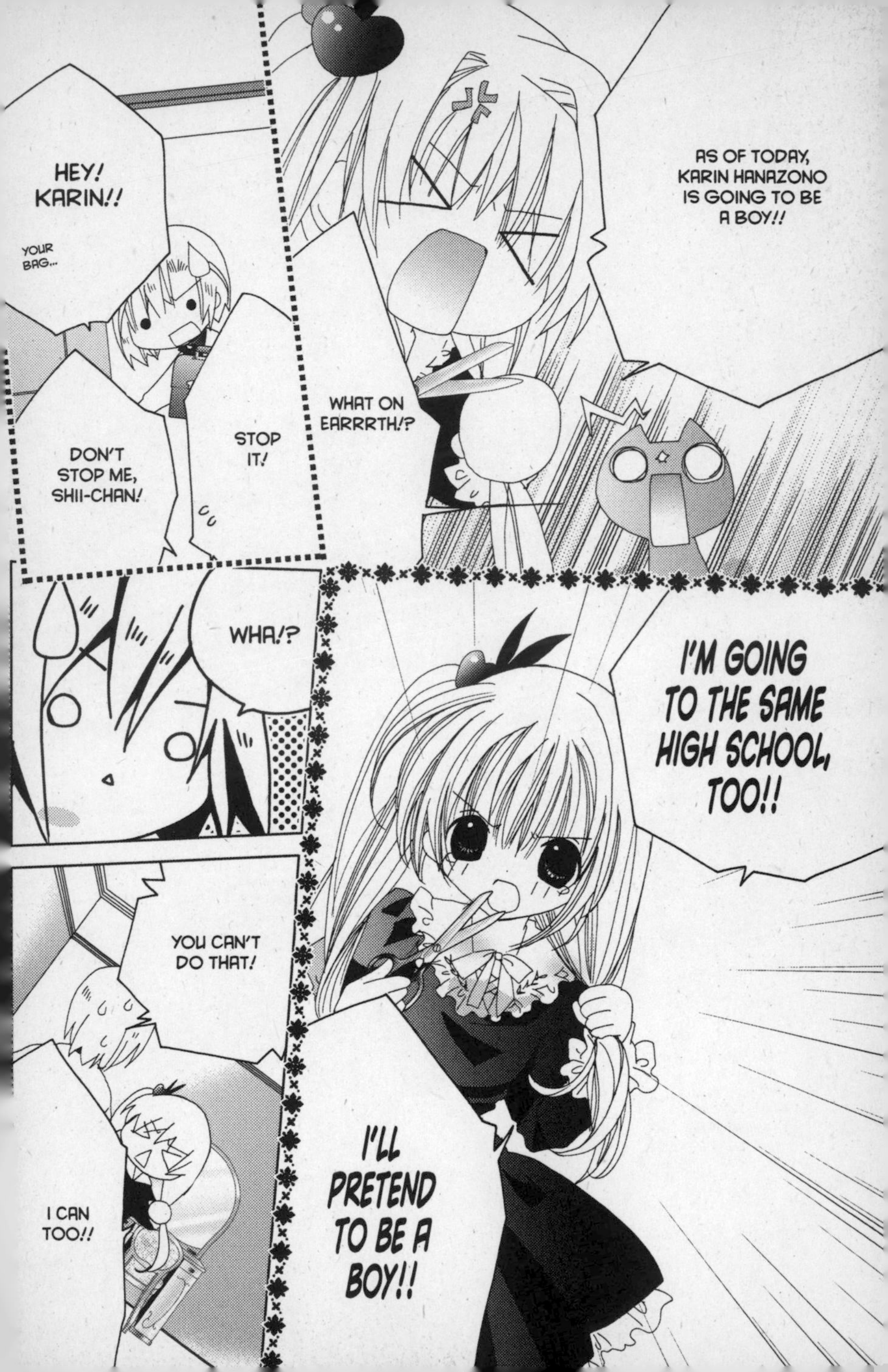
AS OF TODAY, KARIN HANAZONO IS GOING TO BE A BOY!!
WHAT ON EARRRTH!?
HEY! KARIN!!
YOUR BAG...
STOP IT!
DON'T STOP ME, SHII-CHAN!
I'M GOING TO THE SAME HIGH SCHOOL, TOO!!
I'LL PRETEND TO BE A BOY!!
WHA!?
YOU CAN'T DO THAT!
I CAN TOO!!

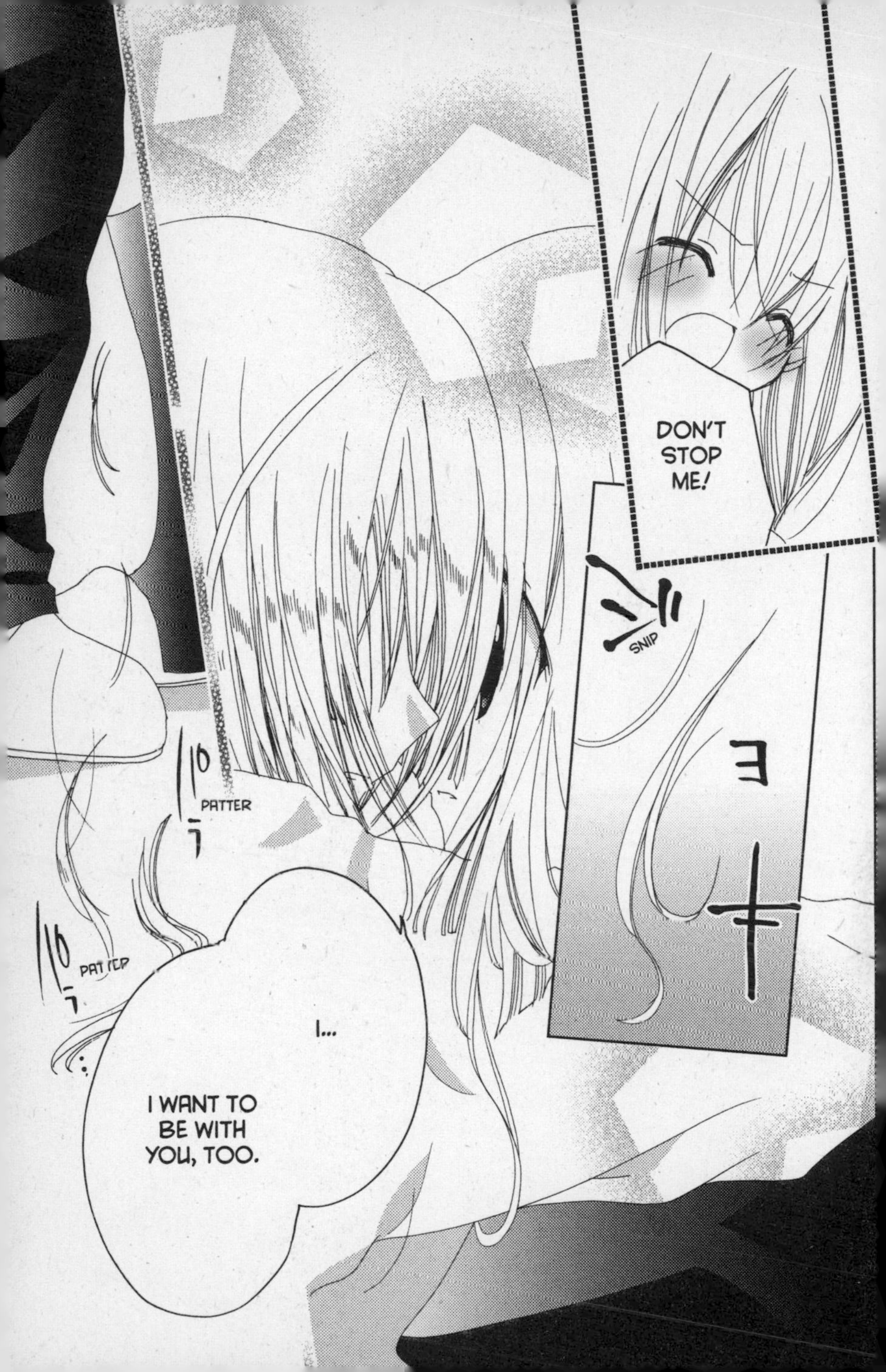
DON'T STOP ME!
SNIP
PATTER
PATTER
I...
I WANT TO BE WITH YOU, TOO.

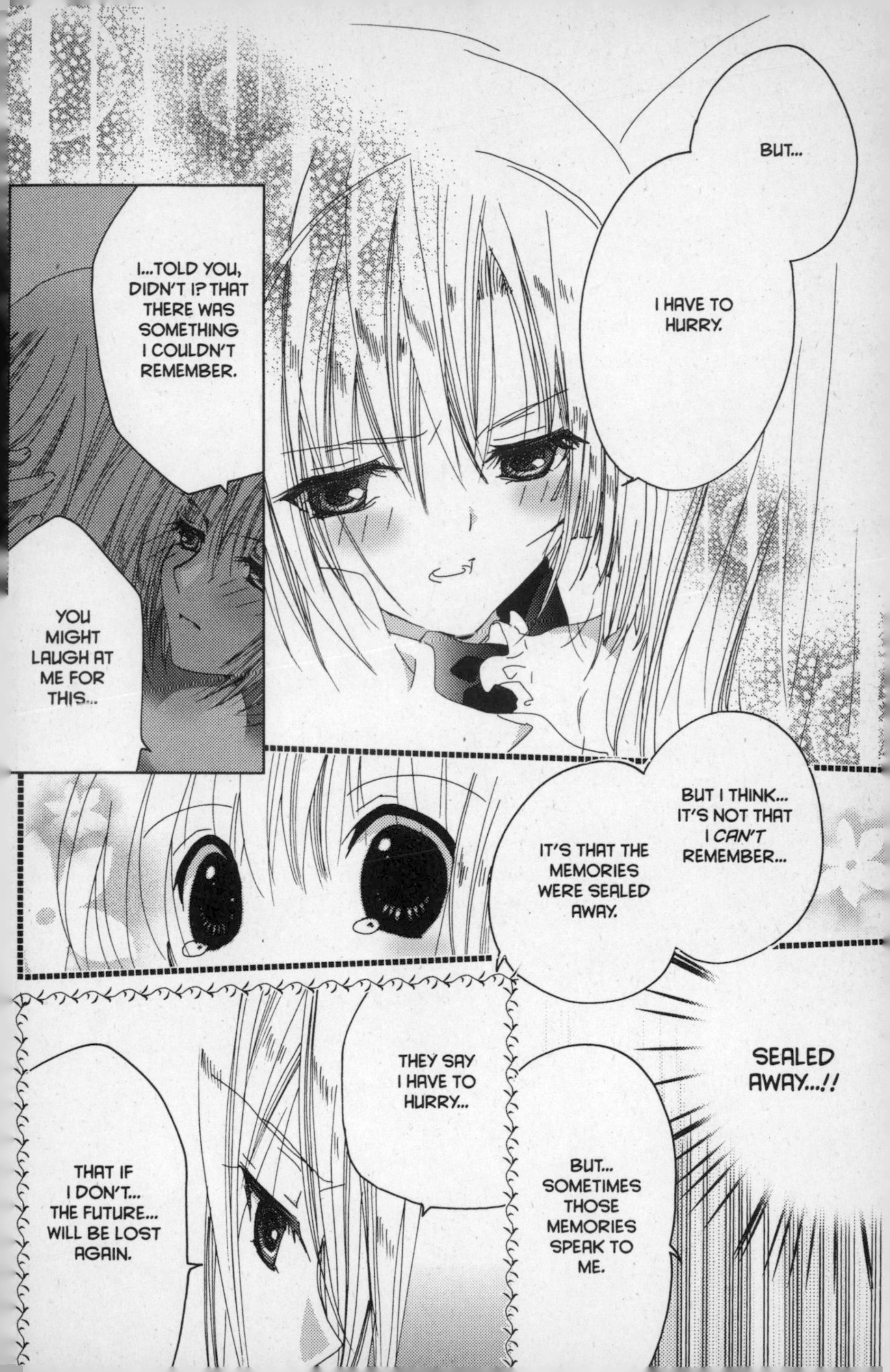
BUT...
I HAVE TO HURRY.
I...TOLD YOU, DIDN'T I? THAT THERE WAS SOMETHING I COULDN'T REMEMBER.
YOU MIGHT LAUGH AT ME FOR THIS...
BUT I THINK... IT'S NOT THAT I *CAN'T* REMEMBER...
IT'S THAT THE MEMORIES WERE SEALED AWAY.
SEALED AWAY...!!
BUT... SOMETIMES THOSE MEMORIES SPEAK TO ME.
THEY SAY I HAVE TO HURRY...
THAT IF I DON'T... THE FUTURE... WILL BE LOST AGAIN.

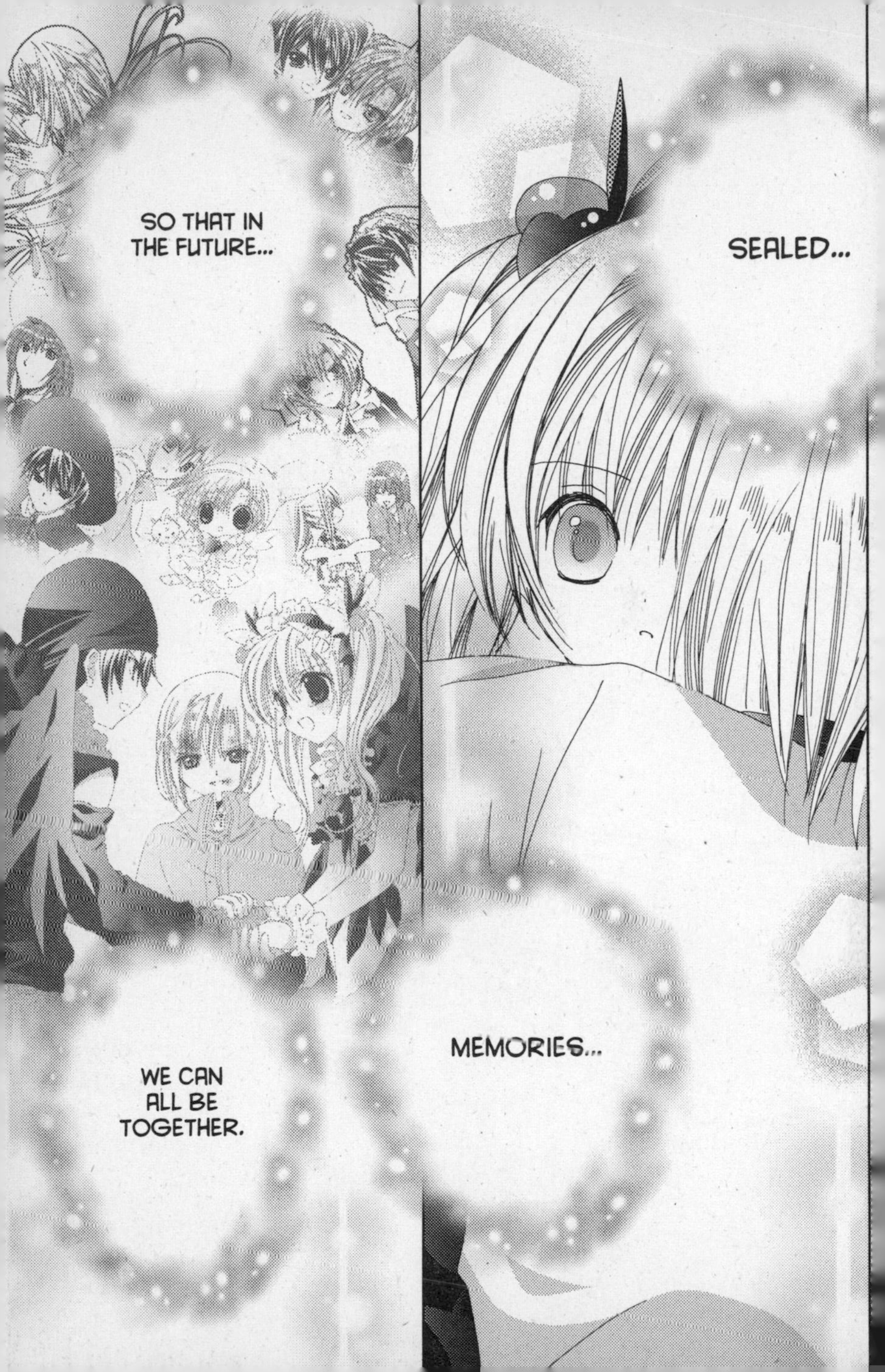
SEALED...
MEMORIES...
SO THAT IN THE FUTURE...
WE CAN ALL BE TOGETHER.

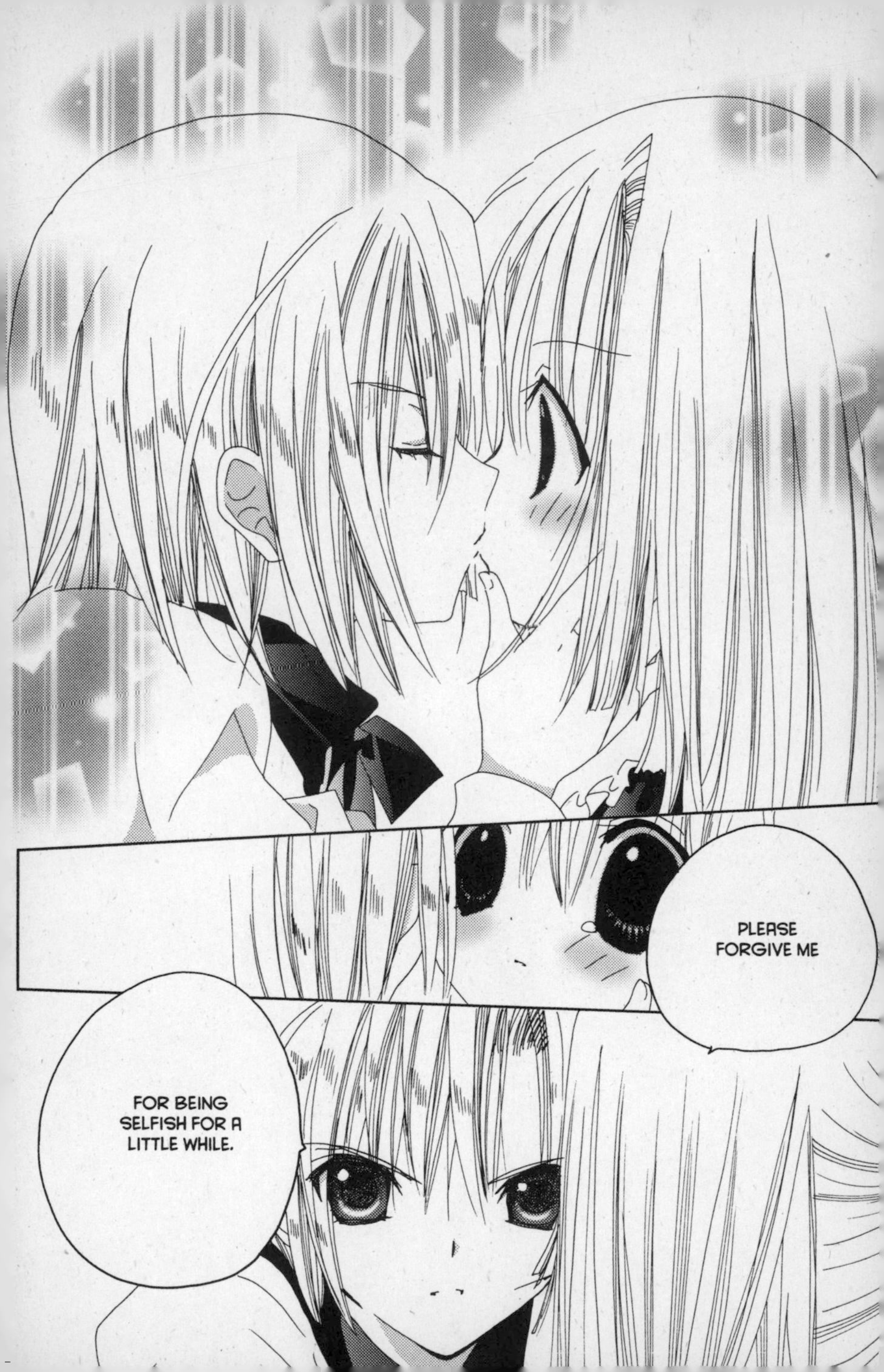
PLEASE FORGIVE ME
FOR BEING SELFISH FOR A LITTLE WHILE.

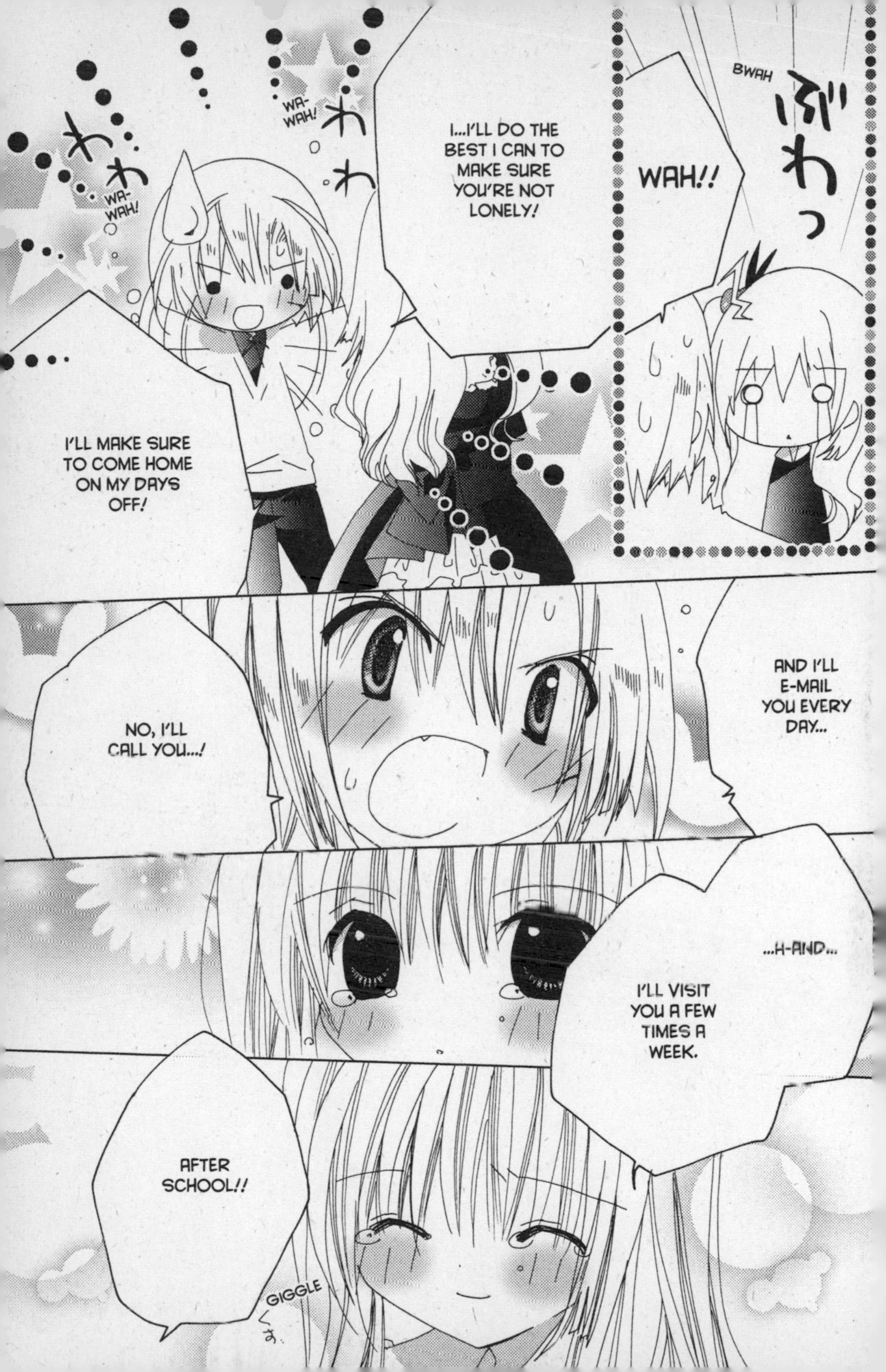
BWAH
ぶわっ
WAH!!
I...I'LL DO THE BEST I CAN TO MAKE SURE YOU'RE NOT LONELY!
WA-WAH!
わわ
WA-WAH!
わわ
I'LL MAKE SURE TO COME HOME ON MY DAYS OFF!
AND I'LL E-MAIL YOU EVERY DAY...
NO, I'LL CALL YOU...!
...H-AND...
I'LL VISIT YOU A FEW TIMES A WEEK.
AFTER SCHOOL!!
GIGGLE
くす

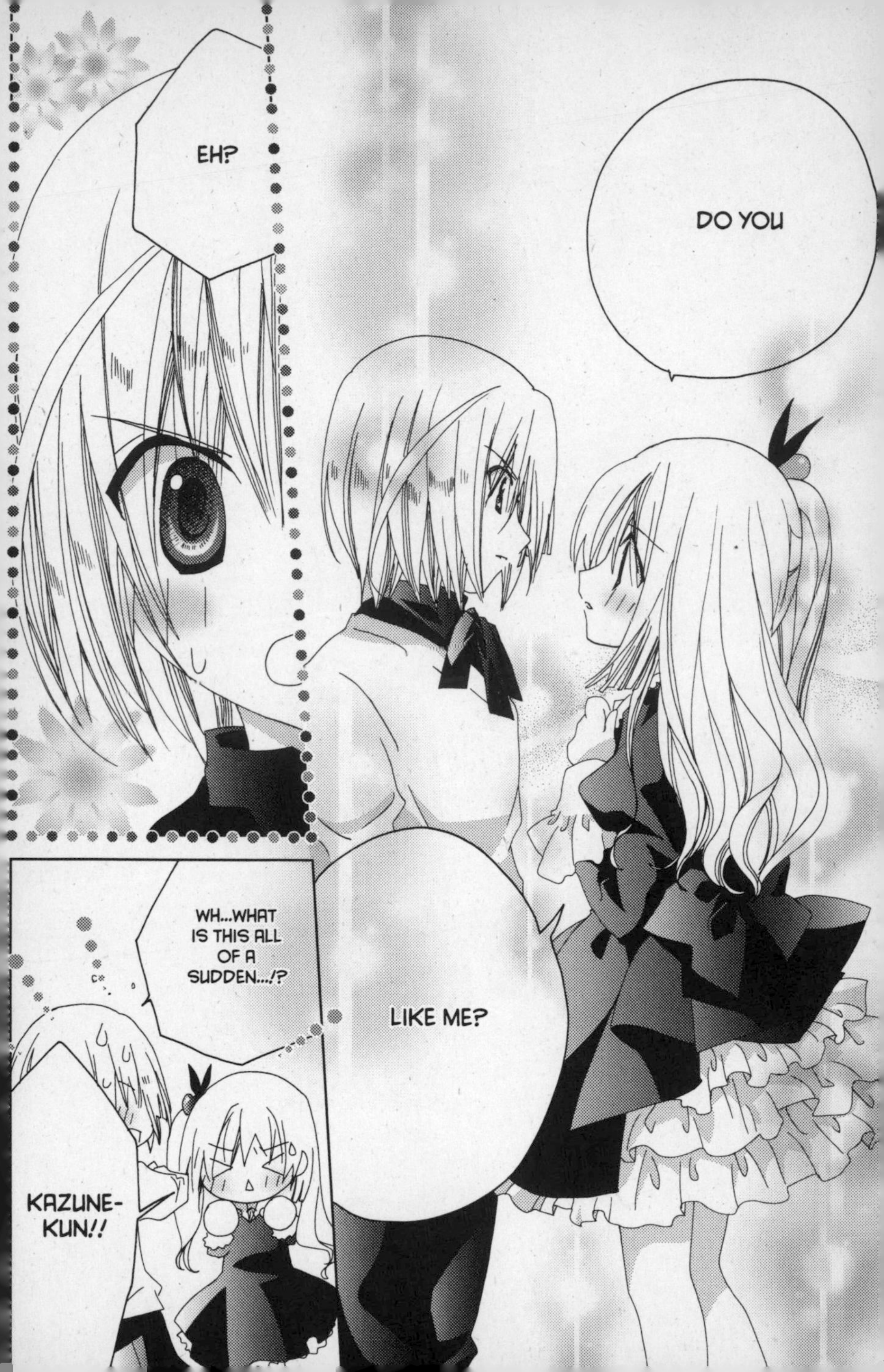
DO YOU
LIKE ME?
EH?
WH...WHAT IS THIS ALL OF A SUDDEN...!?
KAZUNE-KUN!!

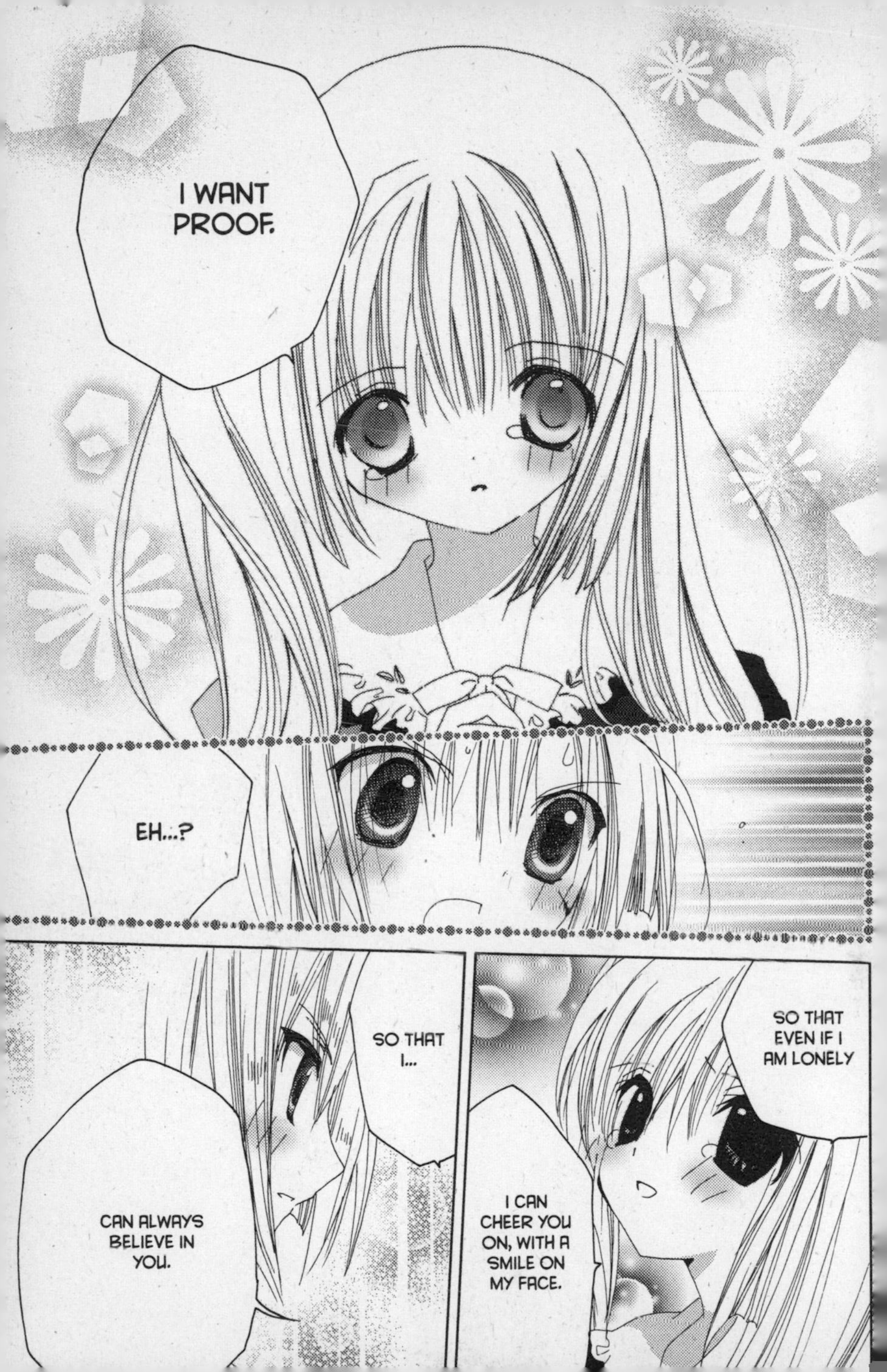
I WANT PROOF.
EH...?
SO THAT EVEN IF I AM LONELY
I CAN CHEER YOU ON, WITH A SMILE ON MY FACE.
SO THAT I...
CAN ALWAYS BELIEVE IN YOU.

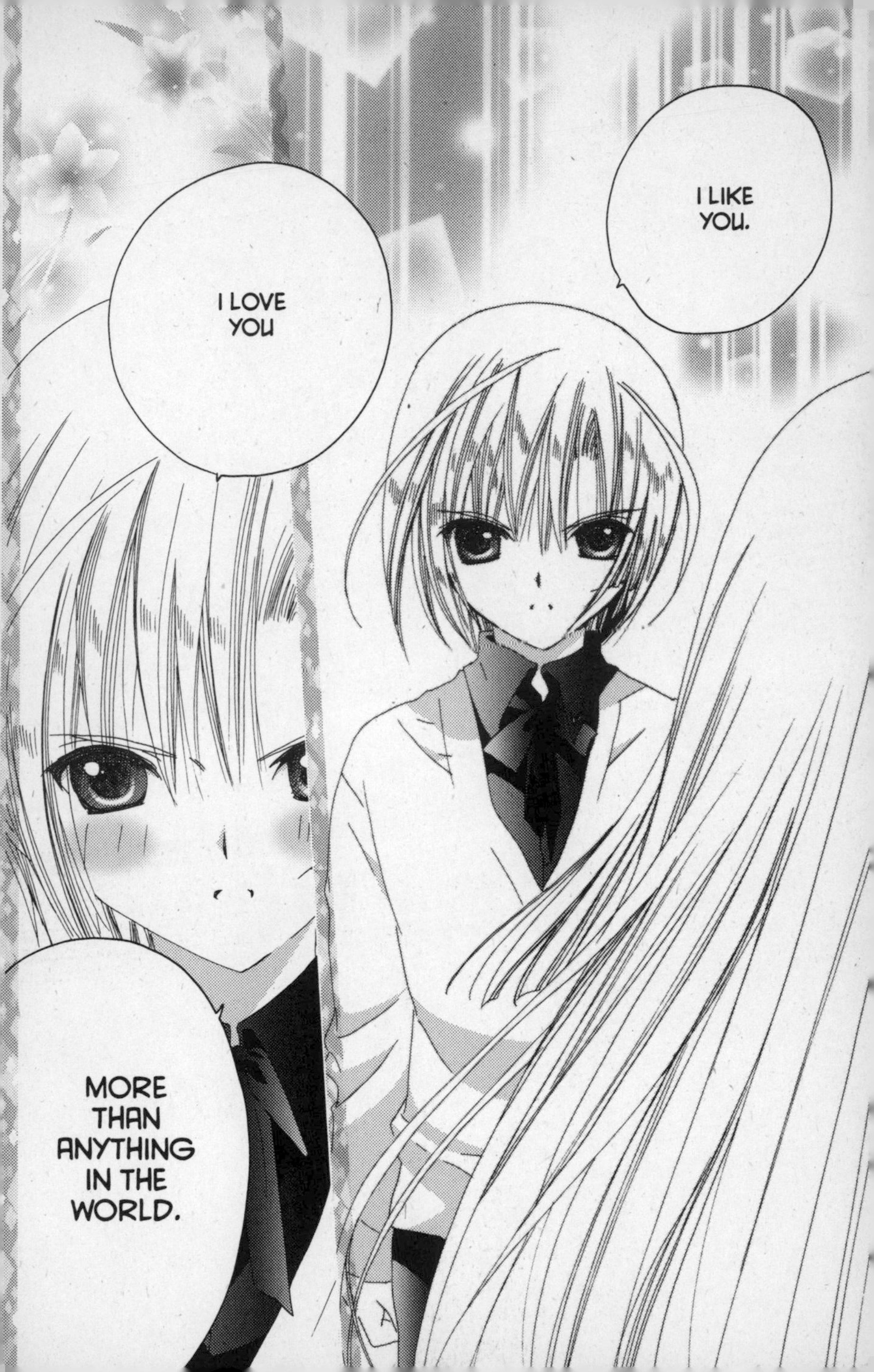
I LIKE YOU.
I LOVE YOU
MORE THAN ANYTHING IN THE WORLD.

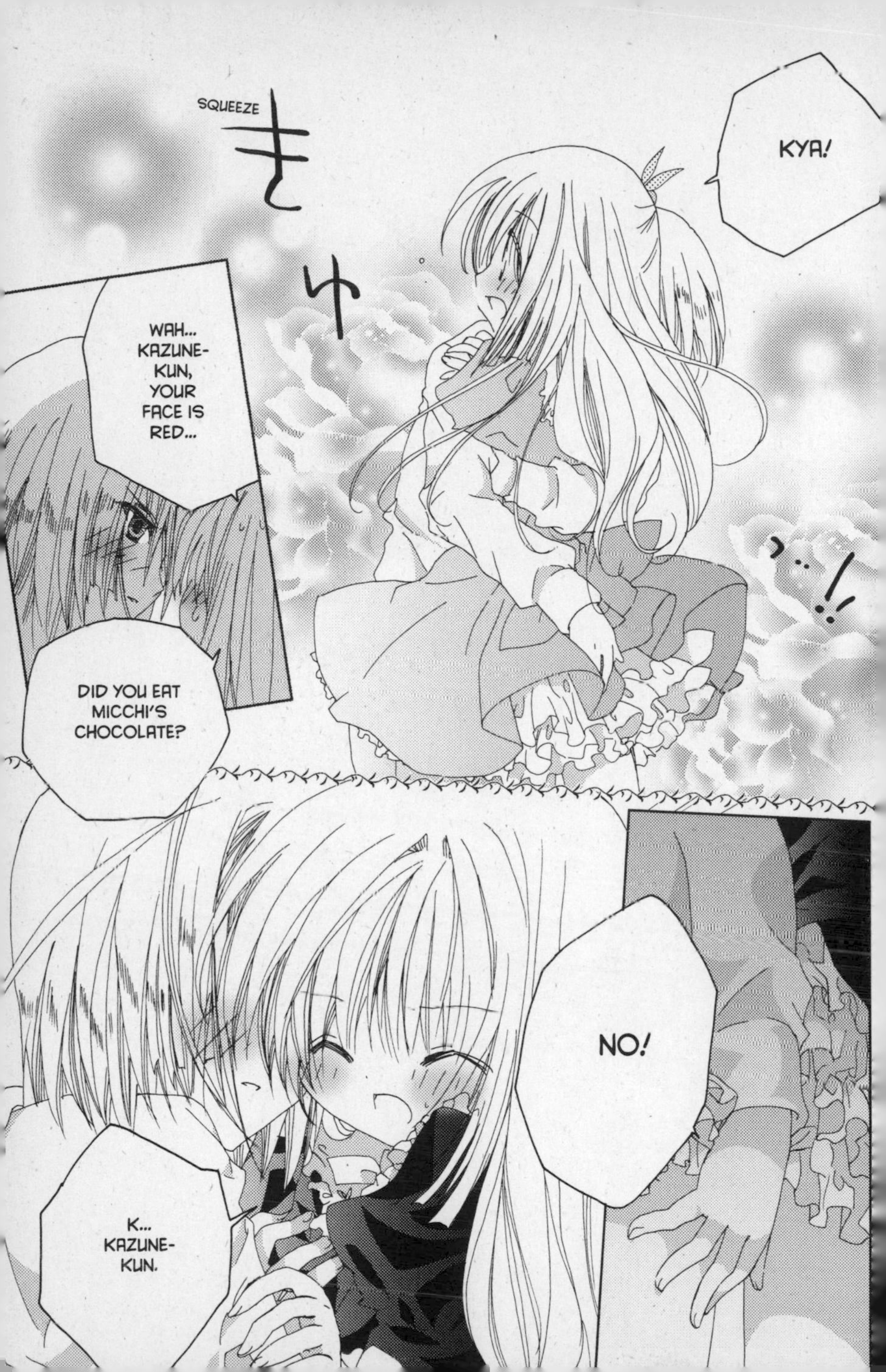
KYA!
SQUEEZE
きゅ
WAH... KAZUNE-KUN, YOUR FACE IS RED...
DID YOU EAT MICCHI'S CHOCOLATE?
NO!
K... KAZUNE-KUN.

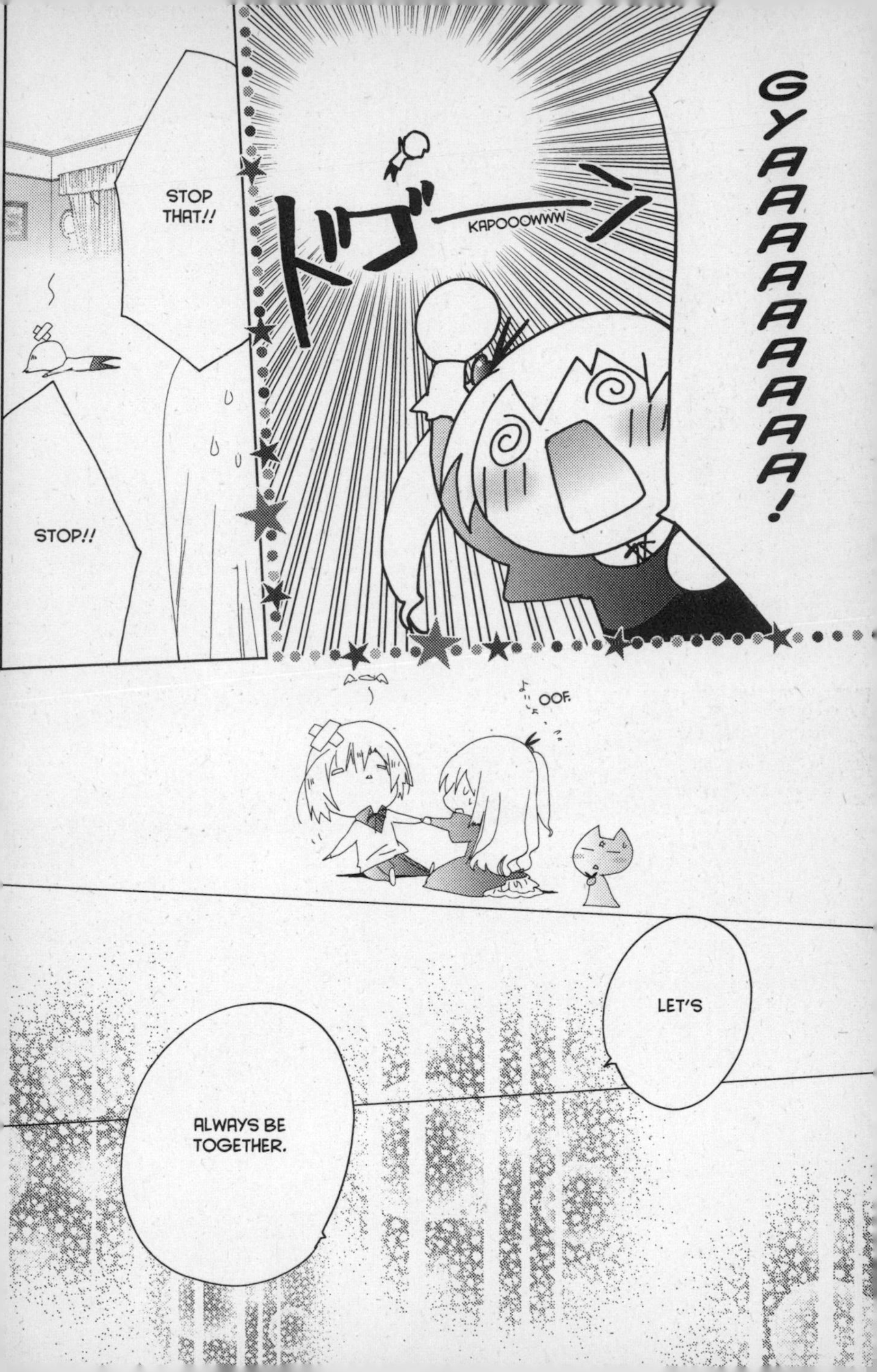
GYAAAAAAAAA!
トグーン
KAPOOOWWW
STOP THAT!!
STOP!!
OOF.
LET'S
ALWAYS BE TOGETHER.

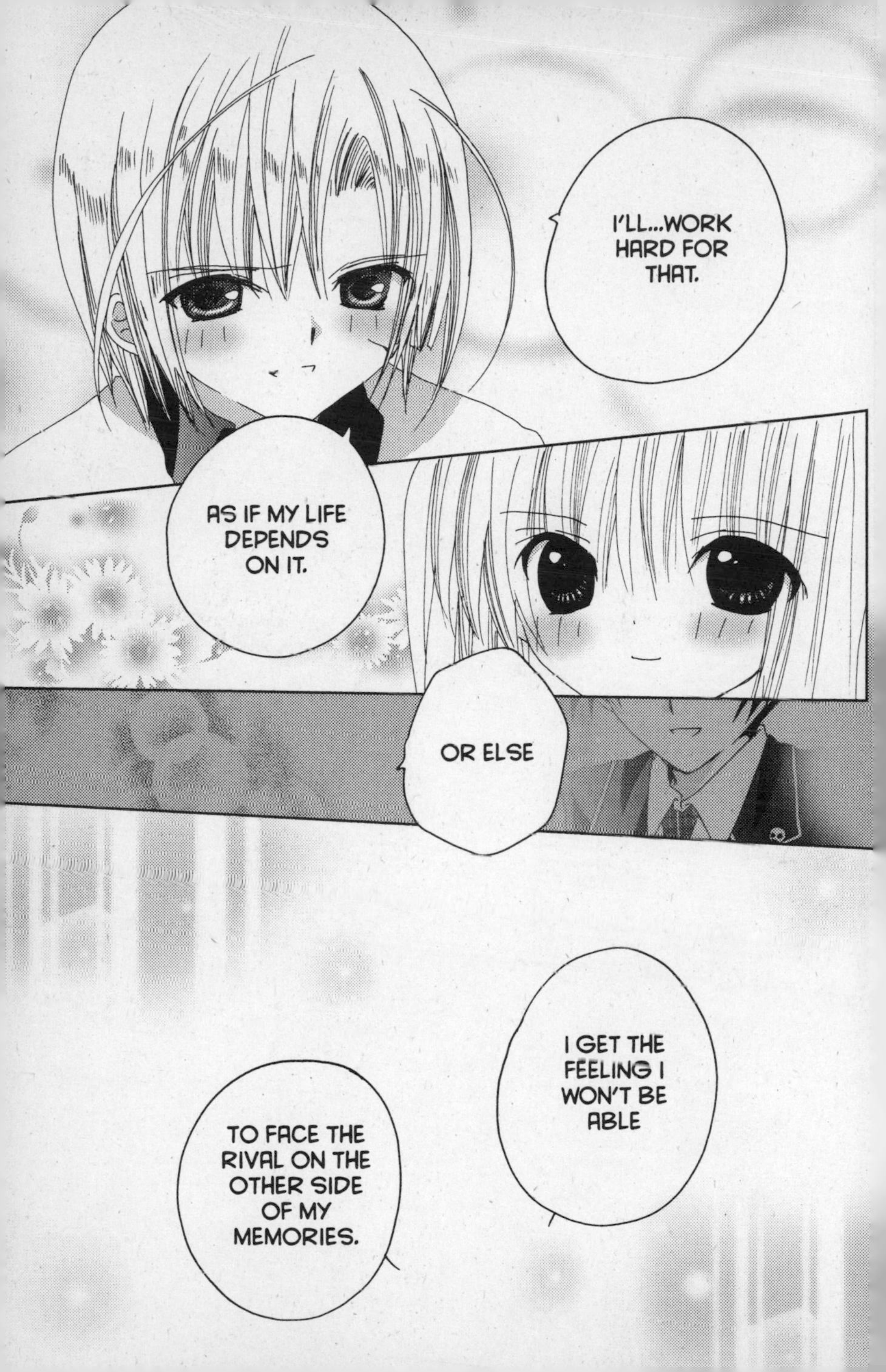
I'LL...WORK HARD FOR THAT.
AS IF MY LIFE DEPENDS ON IT.
OR ELSE
I GET THE FEELING I WON'T BE ABLE
TO FACE THE RIVAL ON THE OTHER SIDE OF MY MEMORIES.

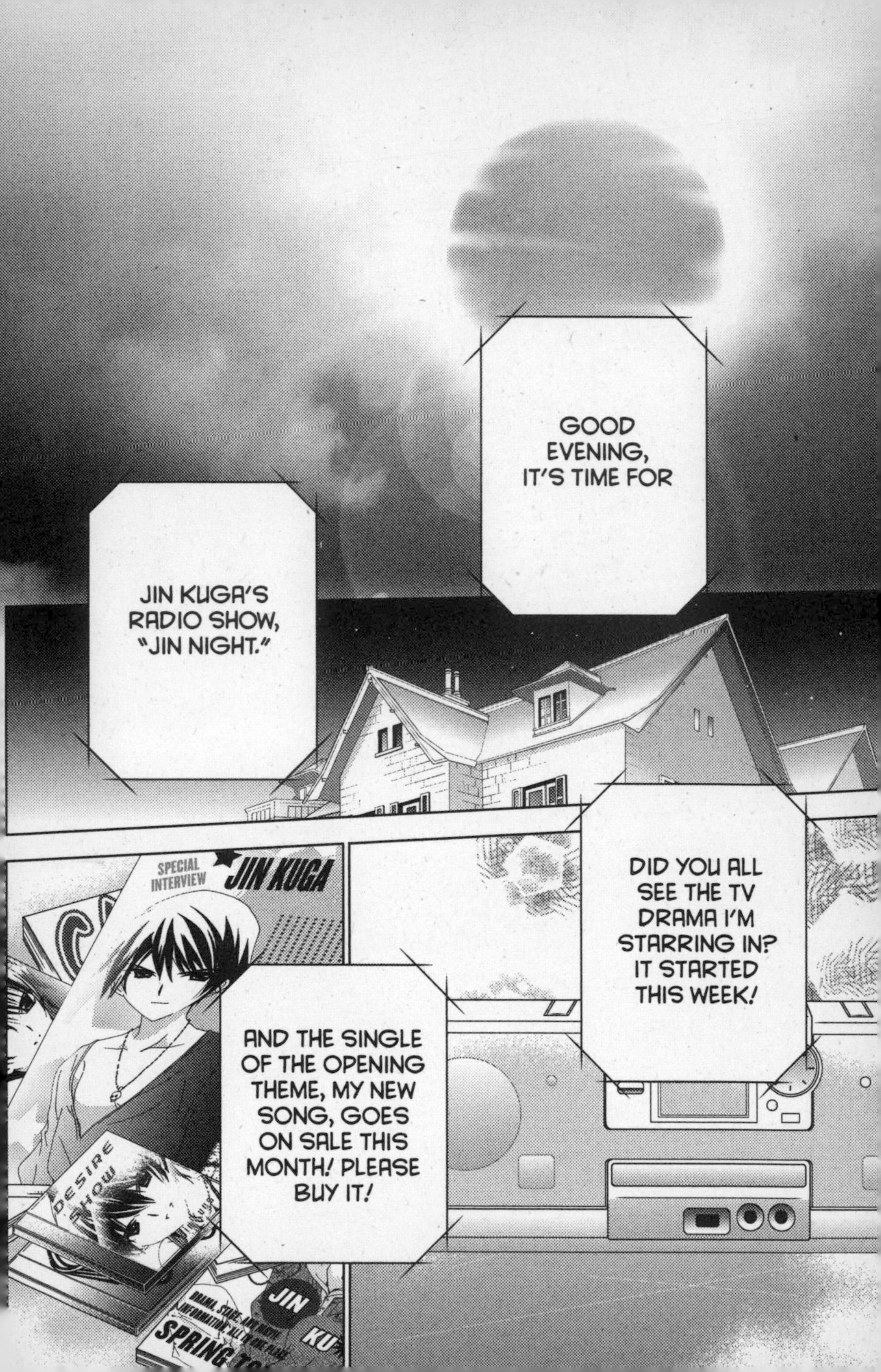
GOOD EVENING, IT'S TIME FOR
JIN KUGA'S RADIO SHOW, "JIN NIGHT."
DID YOU ALL SEE THE TV DRAMA I'M STARRING IN? IT STARTED THIS WEEK!
SPECIAL INTERVIEW
JIN KUGA
DESIRE SHOW
AND THE SINGLE OF THE OPENING THEME, MY NEW SONG, GOES ON SALE THIS MONTH! PLEASE BUY IT!
JIN

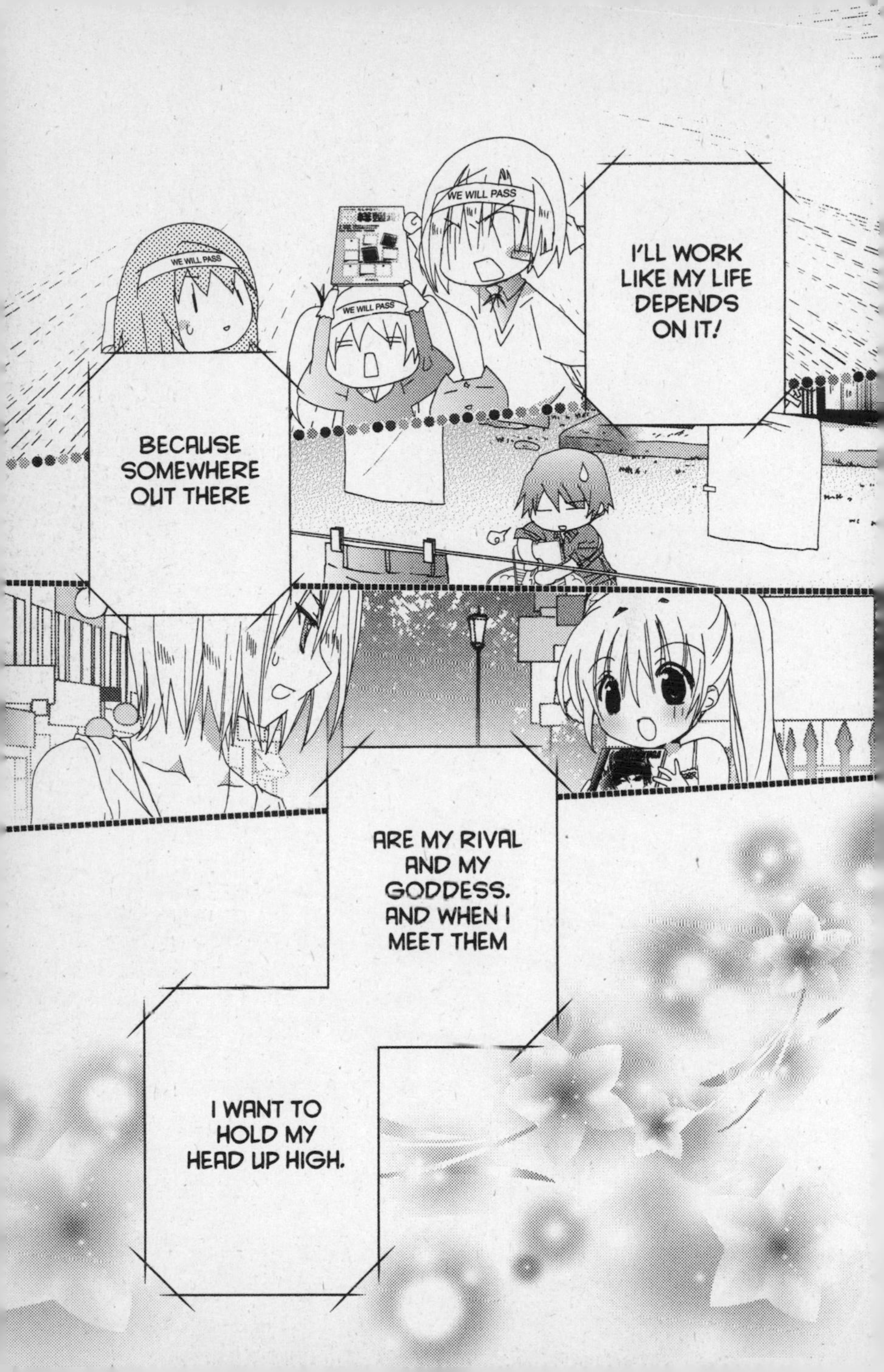
I'LL WORK LIKE MY LIFE DEPENDS ON IT!
WE WILL PASS
WE WILL PASS
WE WILL PASS
BECAUSE SOMEWHERE OUT THERE
ARE MY RIVAL AND MY GODDESS. AND WHEN I MEET THEM
I WANT TO HOLD MY HEAD UP HIGH.

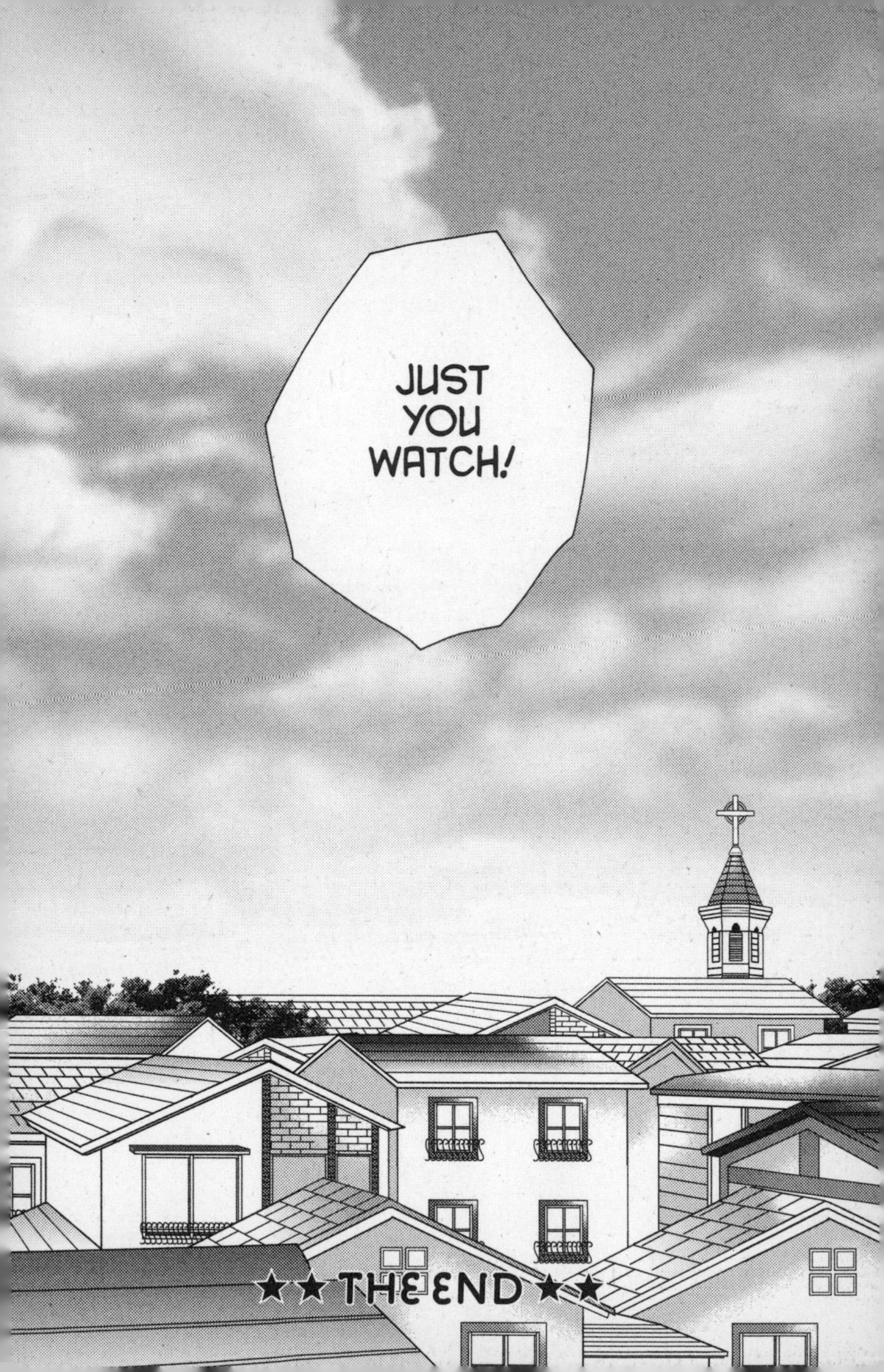
JUST YOU WATCH!
★★ THE END ★★

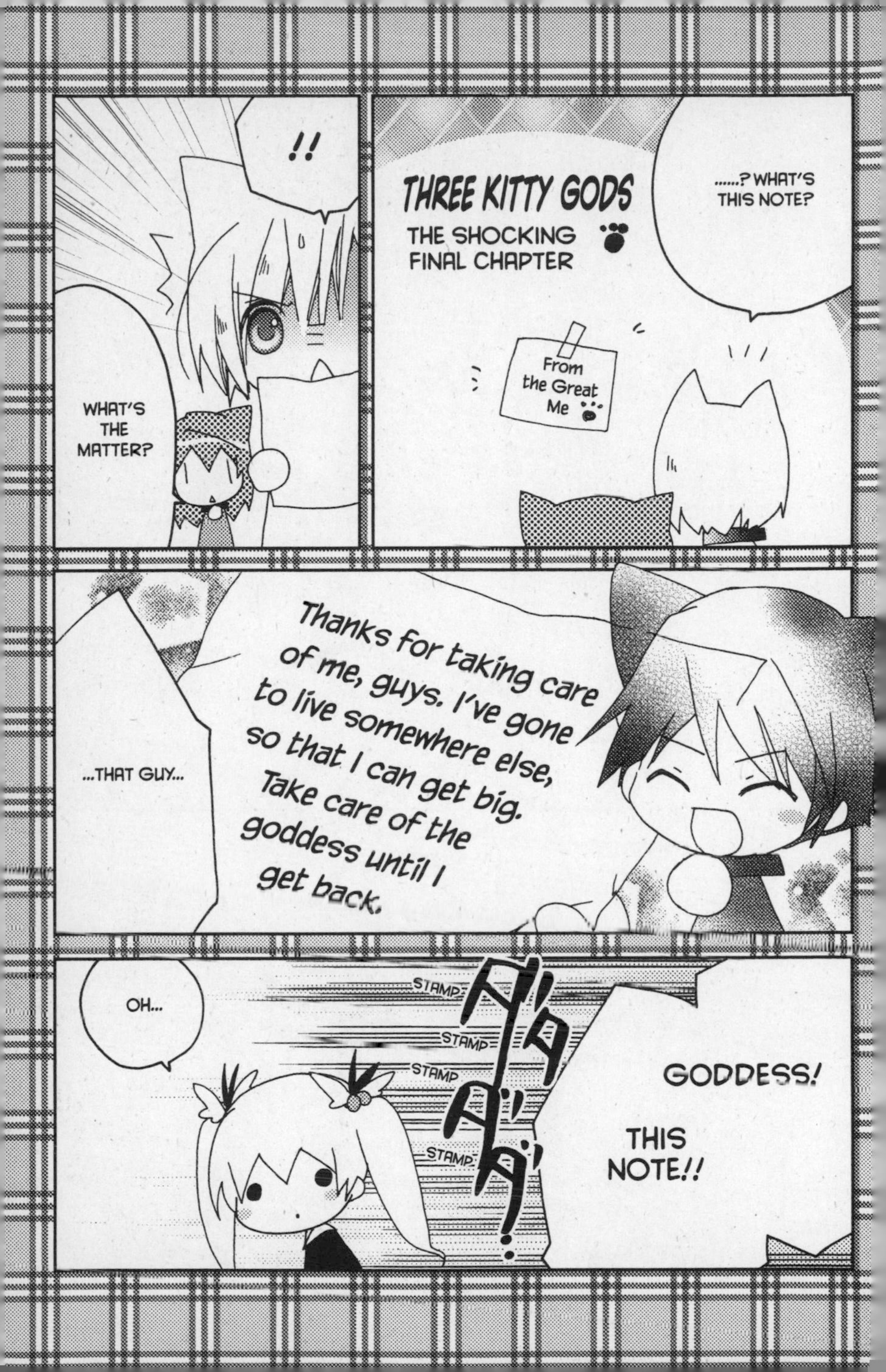

THREE KITTY GODS
THE SHOCKING FINAL CHAPTER
......? WHAT'S THIS NOTE?
From the Great Me
!!
WHAT'S THE MATTER?
Thanks for taking care of me, guys. I've gone to live somewhere else, so that I can get big. Take care of the goddess until I get back.
...THAT GUY...
GODDESS!
THIS NOTE!!
STAMP
STAMP
STAMP
STAMP
OH...

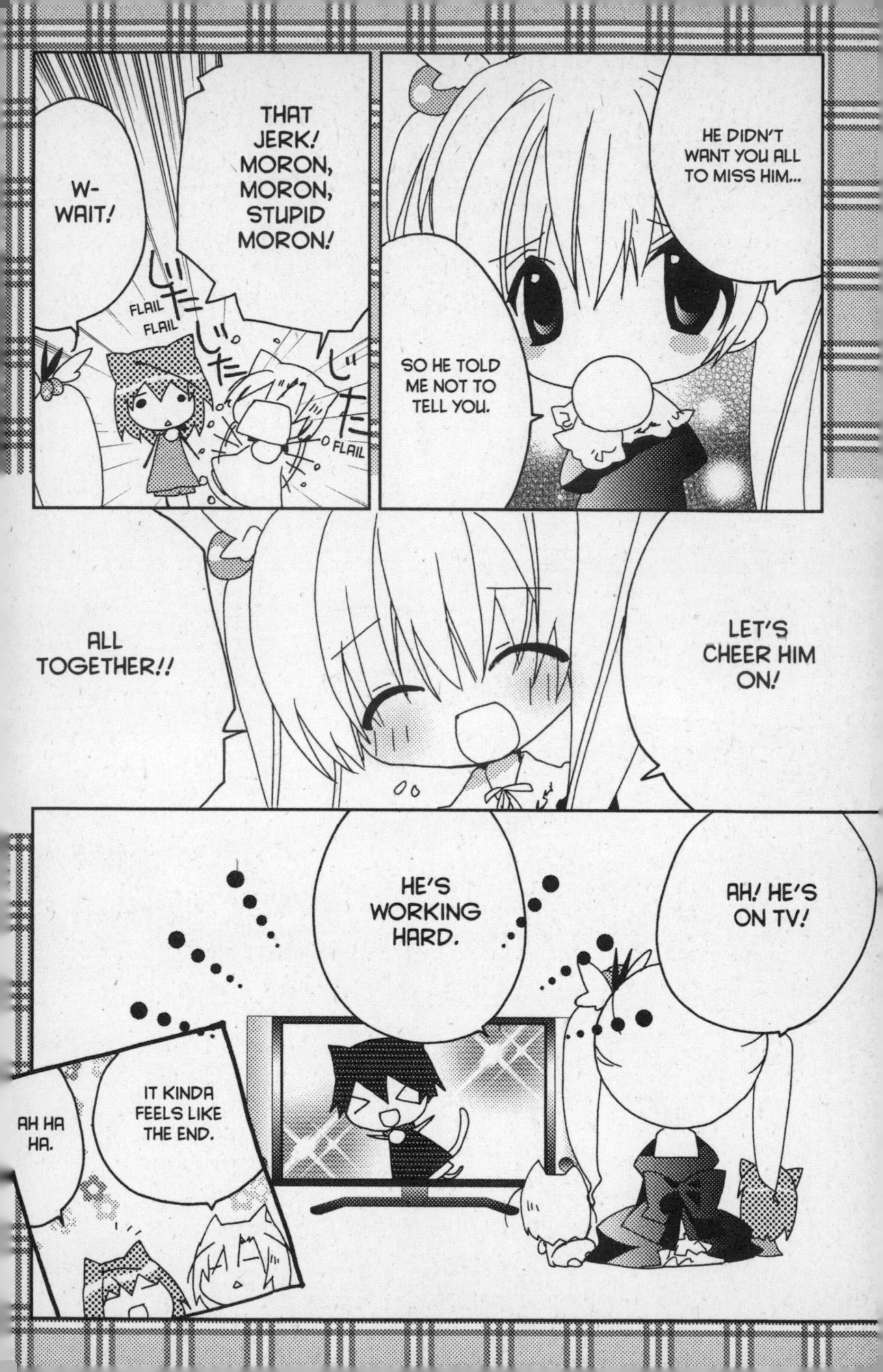
HE DIDN'T WANT YOU ALL TO MISS HIM...
SO HE TOLD ME NOT TO TELL YOU.
THAT JERK! MORON, MORON, STUPID MORON!
W-WAIT!
FLAIL FLAIL
FLAIL
LET'S CHEER HIM ON!
ALL TOGETHER!!
AH! HE'S ON TV!
HE'S WORKING HARD.
IT KINDA FEELS LIKE THE END.
AH HA HA.

COMIC KAMICHAMA KARIN CHU

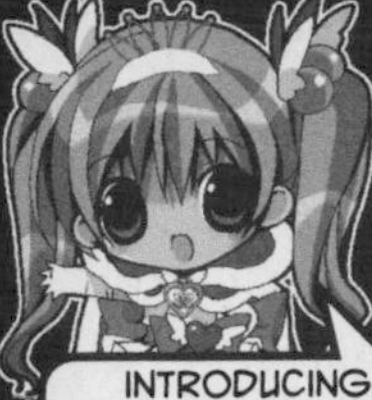

SPECIAL ILLUSTRATION GALLERY

INTRODUCING THE DRAWINGS YOU ALL SENT TO THE *KARIN CHU* ILLUSTRATION GALLERY...THEY ALL HAVE SO MUCH HEART PUT INTO THEM!

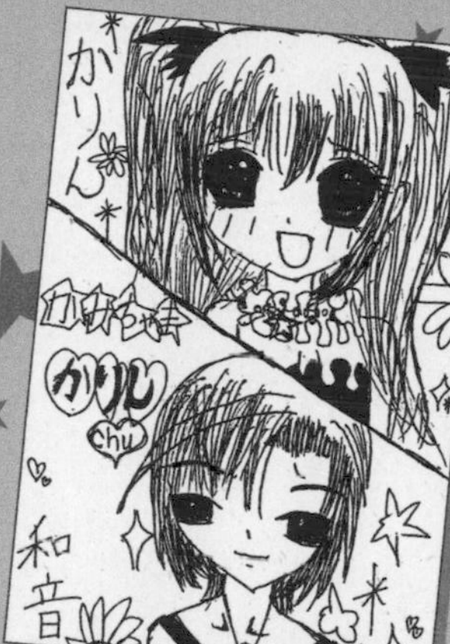
かりん
かみちゃま
かりん
chu
和音

RYÔKO HATTORI, AICHI PREFECTURE

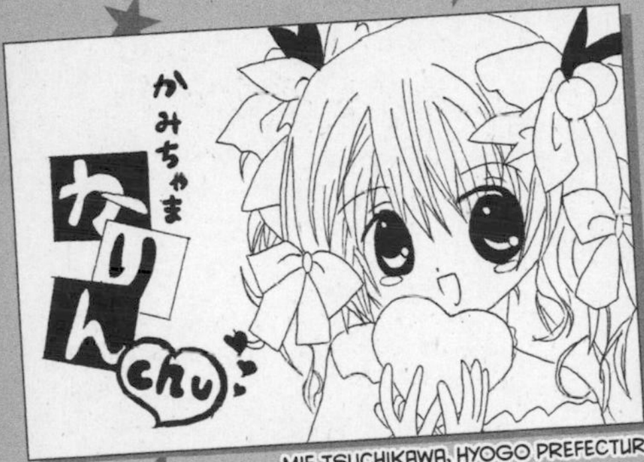
かみちゃま
かりん
chu

MIE TSUCHIKAWA, HYOGO PREFECTURE

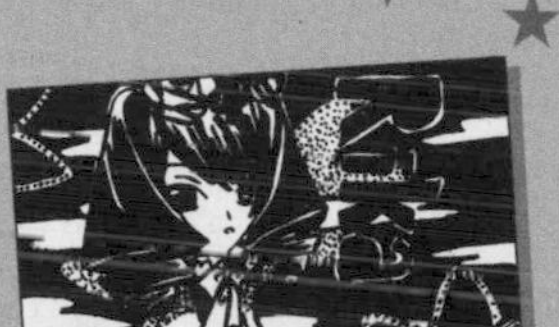

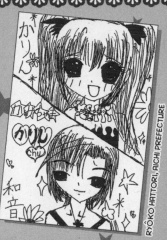

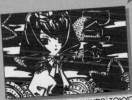

MOMOKA MATSU-URA, TOKYO

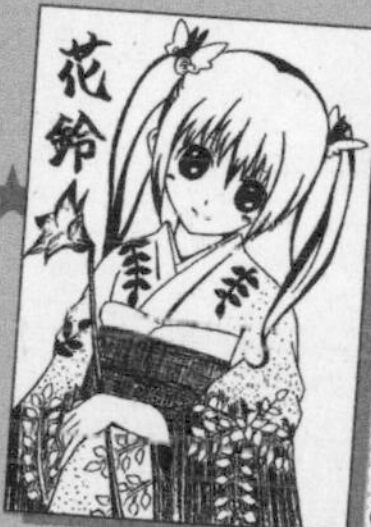
花鈴

HONCKA KANDA, YAMANASHI PREFECTURE

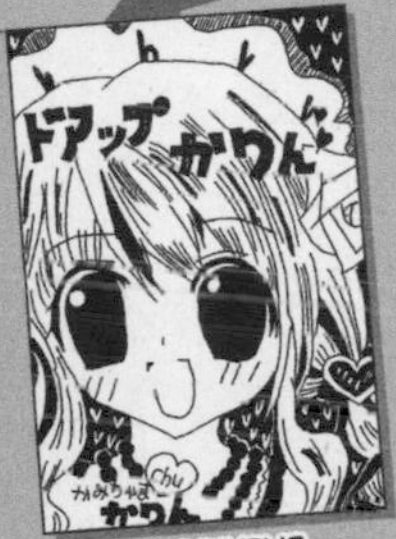

ARISA MORIYAMA, NIIGATA PREFECTURE

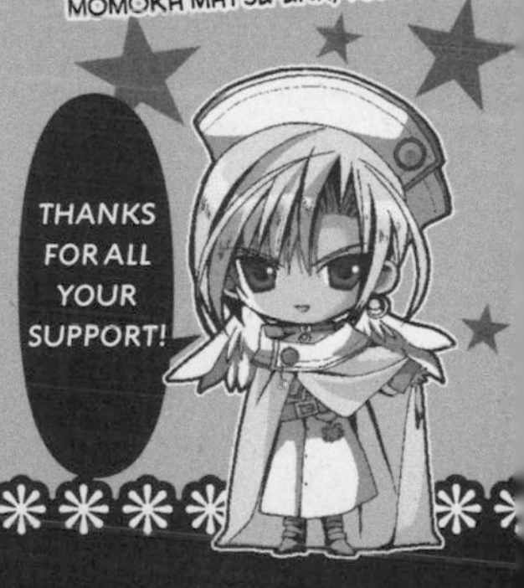
THANKS FOR ALL YOUR SUPPORT!

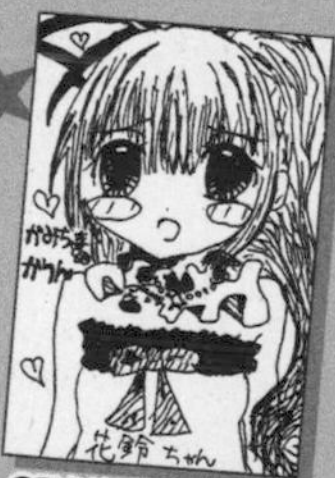
花鈴ちゃん

SAKI HASEGAWA, IBARAGI PREFECTURE

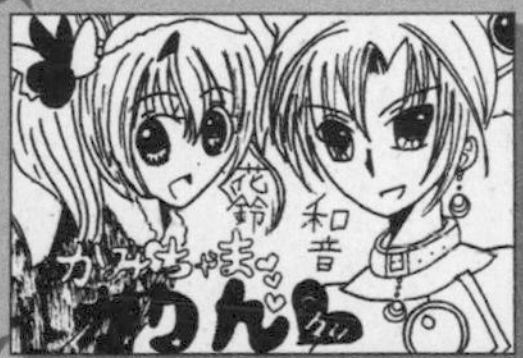
花鈴
和音

HIKARI KAJI, CHIBA PREFECTURE

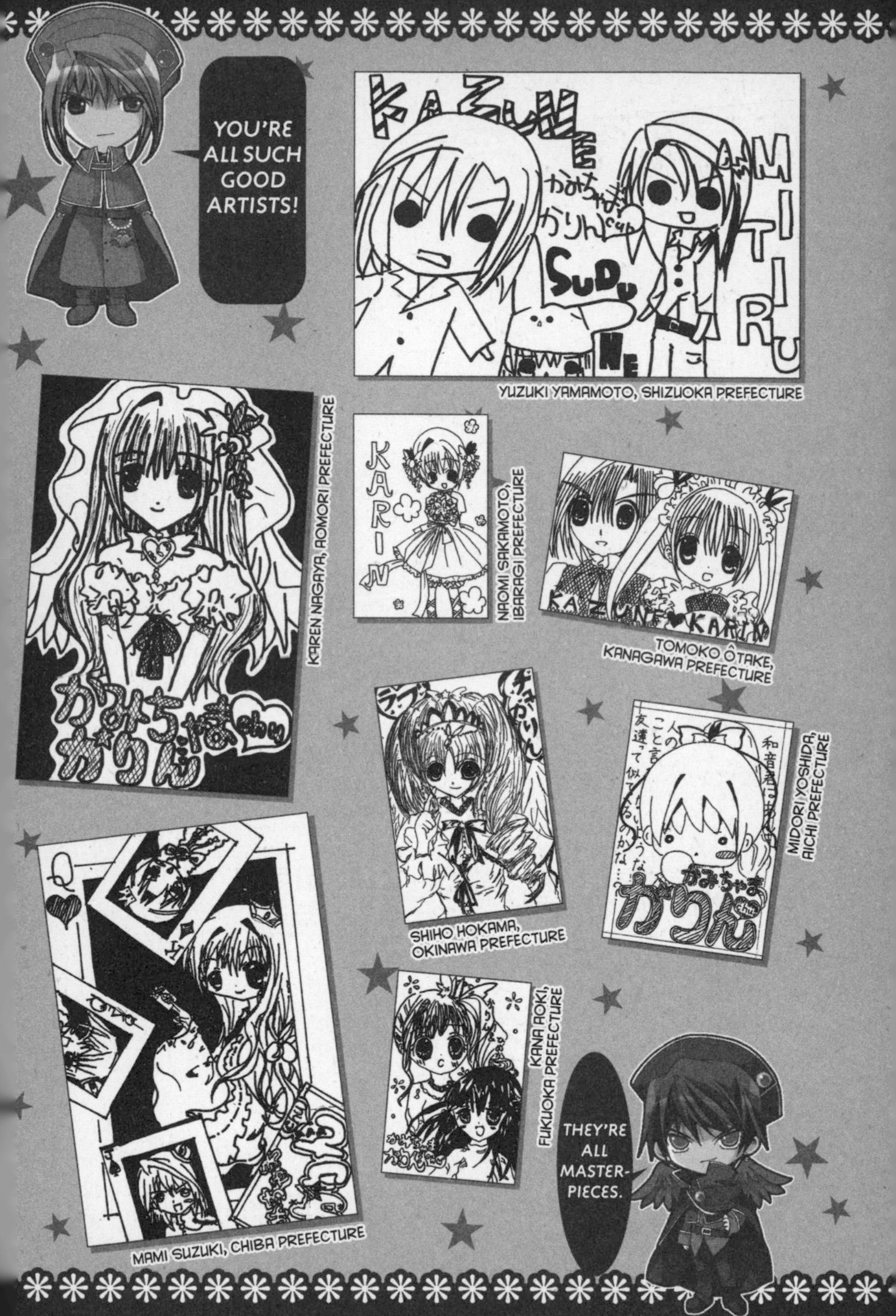
YOU'RE ALL SUCH GOOD ARTISTS!
YUZUKI YAMAMOTO, SHIZUOKA PREFECTURE
KAREN NAGAYA, AOMORI PREFECTURE
NAOMI SAKAMOTO, IBARAGI PREFECTURE
TOMOKO ÔTAKE, KANAGAWA PREFECTURE
MIDORI YOSHIDA, AICHI PREFECTURE
SHIHO HOKAMA, OKINAWA PREFECTURE
MAMI SUZUKI, CHIBA PREFECTURE
KANA AOKI, FUKUOKA PREFECTURE
THEY'RE ALL MASTER-PIECES.

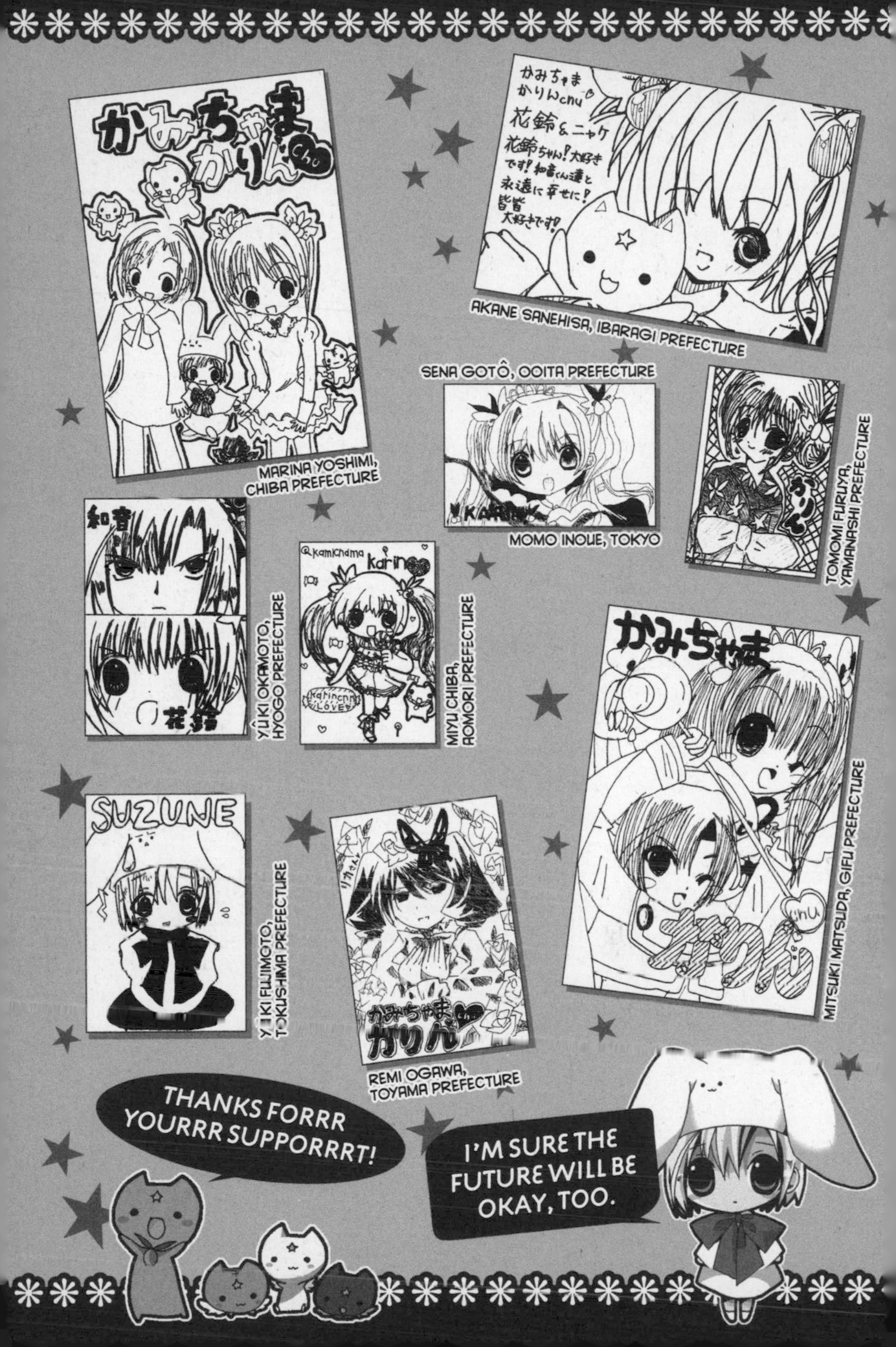
かみちゃまかりんchu♡
Akane Sanehisa, Ibaragi Prefecture
かみちゃまかりんchu
Marina Yoshimi, Chiba Prefecture
Sena Gotô, Ooita Prefecture
かりん
Tomomi Furuya, Yamanashi Prefecture
Momo Inoue, Tokyo
和音
花鈴
Yûki Okamoto, Hyogo Prefecture
Miyu Chiba, Aomori Prefecture
かみちゃま
Mitsuki Matsuda, Gifu Prefecture
SUZUNE
Yûki Fujimoto, Tokushima Prefecture
かみちゃまかりん
Remi Ogawa, Toyama Prefecture
THANKS FORRR YOURRR SUPPORRRT!
I'M SURE THE FUTURE WILL BE OKAY, TOO.

ABOUT THE CREATOR

Koge-Donbo, *Kamichama Karin Chu*

Koge-Donbo, who also creates under the pen name Kokoro Koharuno, chose this unusual pseudonym in honor of Akira Toriyama's cat! This popular and prolific creator is currently working on several manga series including *Di Gi Charat* and *Kamichama Karin Chu*.

Born on February 27, Koge-Donbo is a Pisces with blood type A. She loves traditional Japanese culture: She was a member of her college's aikido club and is now studying the art of Noh drama. Koge-Donbo is also fond of traveling and eating curry, ramen, and *okonomiyaki*.

WORKS

CURRENT

Di Gi Charat
Kon Kon Kokon
Kamichama Karin Chu
Sumo Ou
Princess Concerto
Aquarian Age

COMPLETED

Pita-Ten
Tiny Snow Fairy Sugar
Kamichama Karin
Koihime Soshi
Yoki Koto Kiku

I'M SO HAPPY

TRANSLATION NOTES

Japanese is a tricky language for most Westerners, and translation is often more an art than a science. For your edification and reading pleasure, here are notes on some of the places where we could have gone in a different direction, or where a Japanese cultural reference is used.

Kamichama Karin Chu, title

Kami is the Japanese word for a god. When talking about a great, powerful god, normally it would be referred to as *kami-sama* because *-sama* is used to confer great respect. In Kazune's opinion, however, Karin is not great enough to be called *kami-sama*, at least at first. So he says she's more like a *kami-chama* because *-chama* is like a baby-talk version of *-sama* and conveys her cute childishness as a goddess. *Chu* is a Japanese pronunciation of the English "two," and it's also the sound a kiss makes, very fitting for this sequel to *Kamichama Karin* ❤

Nakayoshi, page 119

Before *Kamichama Karin chu* became a series of graphic novels, each chapter was published in a manga magazine in Japan called *Nakayoshi*.

YOU'RE ALL
STUDYING
FOR YOUR
HIGH SCHOOL
ENTRANCE
EXAMS,
RIGHT?

High school entrance exams, page 129

In Japan, middle school students are allowed to choose what high school they want to go to, but to get in, they have to pass the school's entrance exam. It's kind of like how you have to get a high score on the SATs or ACTs to get into a good college here. Karin is going to the middle school division of Sei-ei Academy, but if she wants to get into the academy's high school division, she has to pass their test.

Okonomiyaki, page 166

Loosely translated as "fried to your liking," an *okonomiyaki* is a pizza-like pancake fried with various ingredients—whatever you like.

STOP

TOMARE!

u're going the wrong way!

MANGA IS A COMPLETELY DIFFERENT TYPE OF READING EXPERIENCE.

TO START AT THE *BEGINNING*, GO TO THE *END*!

THAT'S RIGHT!

Authentic manga is read the traditional Japanese way—from right to left, exactly the *opposite* of how American books are read. It's easy to follow: Just go to the other end of the book, and read each page—and each panel—from right side to left side, starting at the top right. Now you're experiencing manga as it was meant to be!